NOTE TO USERS

This reproduction is the best copy available.

UMI®

The Nazification of Vienna and the Response of the Viennese Jews

Ilana Fritz Offenberger

MAY 2010

A DISSERTATION

Submitted to the faculty of Clark University, Worcester,
Massachusetts, in partial fulfillment of the requirements for
The degree of Doctor of Philosophy in the Department of History

And accepted on the recommendation of

Debórah Dwork

Debórah Dwork, PhD
Chief Instructor

UMI Number: 3407632

Dissertation Publishing

ProQuest LLC
789 East Eisenhower Parkway
P.O. Box 1346
Ann Arbor, MI 48106-1346

ACADEMIC HISTORY

Name (in Full): Ilana Fritz Offenberger   **Date:** May 2010

Place of Birth: Brookline, Massachusetts   **Date:** January 5, 1979

Baccalaureate Degree: BA, German

Source: Skidmore College, Saratoga Springs, NY   **Date:** May 2000

DISSERTATION COMMITTEE

Debórah Dwork, PhD
Chief Instructor

Walter Schatzberg, PhD
Committee Member

Evan Burr Bukey, PhD
Committee Member

DEDICATION

For the Jews of Vienna

Those who got out

And those who were trapped behind

In memory of my grandfather, Dr. Fritz Offenberger

and his parents, Heinrich and Berta

ACKNOWLEDGEMENTS

When I discovered the "aryanization" papers of my great-grandfather Heinrich Offenberger's apartment house in Wien 3., Fasangasse 20, I did not know that one day I would have the great fortune to devote my life to researching and writing the history of Vienna's Jews under Nazi oppression. On receiving this archival material in 1998, I felt an overwhelming desire to reconstruct the history, but I did not yet know how. Many people guided and helped me to accomplish this feat. The completed dissertation is the best way to express my deep gratitude.

First and foremost, I gratefully recognize the opportunity to study under the direction of Debórah Dwork. Debórah, Rose professor of Holocaust history and director of the Strassler Center for Holocaust and Genocide Studies at Clark University, is an exceptional woman. As my dissertation advisor and mentor, she always led by example. She challenged me continually: encouraging me to work harder, dig deeper, "look to the left, look to the right -- widen the lens." Her unwavering belief in me and my scholarly pursuit, made this project possible.

The Strassler Center for Holocaust and Genocide Studies at Clark University is an unparalleled program for the advancement of research, scholarship and education. The staff, professors, visiting faculty, and my fellow graduate students all contributed to my success. Dr.Tatyana Macaulay, program director, took me under her wing from the first day I walked into the Center and will always hold a special place in my heart. The center could not run smoothly without the dedication of Margaret Hillard, Ghi Vaghn, and Mary Jane Rein. Over the years I had the privilege of learning from Professors Simon Payaslian, Robert Jan van Pelt, Bob Melson, Yehuda Bauer, Barbara Harff, and Thomas Kühne -- and each encouraged my work. To the graduate students before me and after me: Beth Cohen, Beth Lilach, Christine Schmidt, Rachel Iskov, Sarah Cushman, Dottie Stone, Tiberiu Galis, Naama Haviv, Jeff Koerber, Adara Goldberg, Stefan Ionescu, Jody Russel Manning, Raz Segal, Emily Dabney, Cristiana Andriani, Betsy Anthony, Alexis Herr, Natalya Lazar, Joanna Sliwa, Micheal Gehran, Khatchig Mouradian, Kimerly Partee, Michael Broknov and Jan Taubitz -- I extend my thanks and pledge my support. We will shape the future of this field!

The first program in the United States to offer a PhD in Holocaust and Genocide Studies could not exist without the generous support of benefactors, patrons, sponsors, friends, supporters, donors, and contributors. In particular, I would like to acknowledge David and Lorna Strassler, the Rose Family, Marc and Cathy Lasry, the Crown family, and the Conference on Jewish Material Claims Against Germany for sponsoring my five years of graduate study and dissertation research. I am forever grateful for the opportunities they ensured through their financial support.

An exceptional team of historians, researchers, educators, librarians, archivists, and fellows at the United States Holocaust Memorial Museum in Washington, D.C. has enriched my work over the years. I am honored to have received an invitation to spend nine months as a visiting scholar at the Center for Advanced Holocaust Studies. This fellowship made it possible for me to investigate the newly acquired archives of the Jewish Community of Vienna (IKG), upon which much of this work is based. I acknowledge and thank Anatol Steck, whose hard work helped to bring the IKG archive to the USHMM. I would also like to pay special tribute to the staff of the Benjamin and Vladka Meed Registry of Holocaust Survivors at the USHMM, in particular Steven Vitto. Megan Lewis, thank you for imparting your research expertise -- it guided me through the archives and made this project a reality.

To produce a complete and accurate depiction of Jewish life in Nazi Vienna, my study depended upon numerous archival collections. The first person accounts recorded by the Survivors of the Shoah Visual History Foundation in Los Angeles were invaluable to my research. I offer special thanks to Dan Yalovsky whose assistance made my research efficient and inclusive. In Vienna, I conducted research at the Wiener Bibliotek, the Documentationsarchiv des Österreichischen Widerstandes, and the Österreichisches Staatsarchiv. I was fortunate to receive assistance from Hubert Steiner and Christian Kucsera at the Archiv der Republic, and from Ingo Zechner, Lothar Hoebling, and Susanne Belovari in the Archives of the Jewish Community in Vienna. My exploration of the Dachau and Buchenwald concentration camps and their archives were no less important to my research and understanding. To Barbara Kinkaert and the other researchers behind the Servitengasse 8 project, I extend my thanks. Doron Rabinoivi, I thank for sharing valuable advice and knowledge. Roland Engel, your camaraderie during my early research pursuits in Vienna, brought this project to life.

The Jews of Vienna who escaped, the legacy they left behind, and their children who chose to carry it forward, also share in my accomplishment. The relationships I formed through letters, emails, telephone calls, coffee meetings, lunches, dinners, lectures, and conferences, provided reinforcement that this project needed to be done. For the archival materials, letters, documents, and photographs, I thank Jacques Hasten, Charles Stein, George Czuzcka, Ella Carroll, Erna Winter, Gertrude Silberstern, Alix Kowler, Lucie Benedict, Walter and Paul Schatzberg, Tom Weiss, Max Furst, and the late George Wellwarth and Eric Nash. I would also like to thank the second and third generation, Lisa Gruenberg, Joanna Saper, Larry Lencz, and Ted Shealy. It was an honor for me to learn about your families and to incorporate their stories into this manuscript.

Professor Reinhard Wagnleiter, at the University of Salzburg, started me on the path of historical research and writing in 1999, allowing me to create my own independent study under his tutelage. His incredible support was followed by Reinhard Mayer at

Skidmore College, who helped me intertwine my interest of the German language with the history of the Holocaust. Senior Historian Martin Dean from the USHMM took great interest in my first archival findings. Our first meeting in 2001 developed into a lasting intellectual relationship which has greatly assisted me over the course of my graduate study. To the careful readers of my dissertation, Tom Weiss from MIT, Evan Bukey from University of Arkansas, and Walter Schatzberg from Clark University, I owe great thanks. Each read the final manuscript word for word, offering invaluable insight and suggestions for improvement. George Czuzcka watched the project develop, reading and commenting, chapter by chapter.

A dissertation cannot be written without protected time and space. For this luxury, I would like to thank Linda McDavitt, whose attitude, spirit, and belief in me -- in addition to the perfect space -- made it possible for me to finish this dissertation. The staff at Ahearn Appraisal Associates, Howe, our special visitor Nell, and "awesome" Gina, put a smile on my face at least once a day. To my great friends near and far: Adam Pignatelli, Tim Herrick, Christine Brown, Heather Ahearn, Amy Craigen, Jack Tomaiolo, Emily Webbe, Nathan Marcus, Mary Hartnett, and Derek John, your belief in me kept my spirits high. Dmitry Matousov, thanks for teaching me about the fight. I am grateful to Youssef Moutawakil for always encouraging me to go ahead. My dear friend Ashley Guittarr demonstrated confidence in me from the very start. Kelly Cuddyer, my *Goumadi*, would have moved a mountain to help me accomplish this goal, and for that I am extremely grateful.

Over the course of my research, I connected with distant family members, whose kindness and understanding launched me forward on my journey: my cousins in Prague, Peter, Jidka, Miki and Zuzana Marek and the late Franzi Wintersteinová; in Vienna, Maximilliane Resch, Xandi and Käthe Ganser; and in Israel, Suzi and Fredi Weis and family. My synchronicitous meeting with Michlcan Amir at the USHMM confirmed that I was traveling the right path. Cheering me along is a great fan club in Rochester, NY, my aunts, uncles, cousins, and beloved grandparents Golde and Abe Hersch. My brothers Cam and Scott and the extended Neely family provided a support system in the Boston area. My older sister Dahlia has been there for me unconditionally. My sister's family, her husband Craig, and their two little ones, give me something to look forward to. Helen Riley and Henry Garvin, this history is also written for you.

My amazing parents, Max and Suzy, have always understood and stressed the value of education. I admire their individual personalities and achievements. My passion, dedication, perseverance, and honesty, comes from them both. I thank them for letting their nineteen-year-old daughter go to Austria for a year and begin this journey. At last, I honor the three persons without whom there would be no manuscript: My Omi, Ida, for introducing me to Vienna; my Helly, for inspiring me to think critically; and my grandfather Fritz, for choosing to carry on.

CONTENTS

List of Illustrations...ix

List of Tables xi

List of Maps..xii

Introduction..1

Chapter 1:
From the Opera to the Streets..14

Chapter 2:
The Anschluss Pogrom: Panic, Chaos, and Confusion in March 1938.............49

Chapter 3:
The IKG: Co-opted by the New Masters..85

Chapter 4:
Turning Point: Vienna to Dachau...120

Chapter 5:
Rescue and Destruction: Daily Life during a Mass Exodus.............................153

Chapter 6:
Escape! November Complications, but Emigration Continues.........................202

Chapter 7:
Transition to Deportation..242

Chapter 8:
Caught in the Vicious Cycle: From a Working Jewish Community to a Council of Jewish Elders...287

Epilogue:
Going Home: The Aftermath of the Holocaust for the Jewish Community.........334

Appendixes..349

Bibliography..356

LIST OF ILLUSTRATIONS

Illustration 1:"Gemütlichkeit, Dancing and Drinking in a Public Park, 1930s" 14

Illustration 2:"Vienna Opera Ball, 15 January 1938" 25

Illustration 3: "Austrian Nazis Celebrate Hitler's Coup: An enthusiastic crowd in
Vienna carrying a policeman who has donned the Nazi emblem"..........................41

Illustration 4: "Initial Humiliations: Jews forced to Scrub the Streets"....................49

Illustration 5:" Elka, Harry, Mia, Leo, & Uri Gruenberg -
Last Family Portrait, c. 1938" 51

Illustration 6: "IKG Logo" 86

Illustration 7: "Institutions of the Jewish Community of Vienna, October 1938" 92

Illustration 8: "IKG Flow Chart, Administration in 1938"..................................99

Illustration 9: "Sample Emigration Questionnaire, Harry Gruenberg"....................110

Illustration 10: "Original IKG Emigration Chart" 118

Illustration 11: "A Jewish Bookstore Locked Up and Defaced with the Message:
'Is in Dachau!!!'" 127

Illustration 12: " 'Organized Emigration': Article from the
Zionistische Rundschau, 3 June 1938" 160

Illustration13: "Lines Outside the Consulate" 165

Illustration14: "Assets Declaration Form"..191

Illustration15: "Inside the IKG Offices" 194

Illustration16: "Postcard: Erwin Lencz and his younger sister Erika
on the Ship to America, October 1938" 202

Illustration 17: "General Store and Home of Leopold and Mathilde Vulkan
(née Trepper), Gersthofferstrasse 166, Vienna 13"......................211

Illustration18: "Leopold Berl Informs the Assets Transfer Agency of the
Reduction of his Assets due to the Damage from the
November Pogrom (12 December 1938)." 216

Illustration 19: "Letters to the Assets Transfer Agency Explain Reveal
Inability to Pay First Installment of Jewish Tax" 218

Illustration 20: "Wilhelm Monias, Italian Front, WW1".................................. 219

Illustration21: "Recently-Released: Brothers Leo, Alexander, and Karl Deutsch
Pose with Parents Rosa and Geza, Sister Irene, and Niece Ingeborg,
for the Last Time Before Departing to Shanghai, April 1939"......... 229

Illustration 22:"Release Certificate from the Buchenwald Concentration
Camp, Authorized by the Gestapo in Berlin (20.12.38)".................231

Illustration 23: "Thirteen-year-old Mia Gruenberg Practices her English,
Seeking the Opportunity to Immigrate to England, July 1939".........237

Illustration 24: "Original IKG Diagram, Population Figures of the
Jewish Community of Vienna, 1934-1939" 242

Illustration 25: "Forced to Wear the Yellow Star of David" 262

Illustration 26: "Official Proclamation! *Jüdisches Nachrichtenblatt*,
12 September 1941" 266

Illustration 27: "Sample Written Statement as printed in the
JüdischesNachrichtenblatt" 268

Illustration 28: "Star Distribution at Grüne Torgasse 26,
Internal IKG Memo, 17 September 1941" 269

Illustration 29: "IKG Population Statistics: Deportations, Deaths, Births:
1 January 1942 - 31 December 1942" 320

LIST OF TABLES

Table 1: "Nationalities of Vienna's Jews as of September 1939"...........................28

Table 2: "Jewish Distribution in Vienna's City Districts" 30

Table 3: "Percentage of Jews in Trade and Professions, 1930s" 32

Table 4: "Who Filled out the Emigration Questionnaires?"...............................114

Table 5: "Original IKG Emigration Statistics, March 1938- December 1939"..........146

Table 6: "National Quotas for Vienna's Jews Waiting to Enter the USA,
        November 1938" 171

Table 7: "Original IKG Emigration Statistics, Countries of Destination,
        March 1938-December 1939" 180

Table 8: "Original IKG Map, Total Emigration to Various Countries,
        as of 31 October 1939" 181

Table 9: "Original IKG Emigration Statistics, 809 Jews with Permission
        to enter over 40 Countries, November 1939" 182

Table 10: "IKG Relief Work Supported by the JDC"..258

Table 11: "Distribution of Jewish Stars throughout the City"........................... 274

Table 12: "Transports from Vienna" 305-306

Table 13: "The Jewish Star is to appear on All Jewish Homes and Institutions,
        April 1942" 314

LIST OF MAPS

Map 1: Austria-Hungary 1878-1918..11

Map 2: Ethnic Groups in the Habsburg Empire, 1910..............................12

Map 3: Vienna 1910, Jewish Percentile in Population by District..........................13

Map 4: Deportations from Vienna, 1941-45..333

NOTE TO THE READER

All translations by the author unless otherwise specified.

Introduction

Edith Kurzweil fled Vienna on a *Kindertransport* in 1938. She was one of approximately 200,000 Austrian Jews targeted for destruction after Anschluss and 136,000 to escape from the Nazi web before the Judeocide began. Fortuitous circumstance spared Edith from murder but did not shield her from the scars of family division and permanent separation. Still looking to answer questions about her past some seven decades later, Kurzweil began to analyze correspondence between her mother and grandmother from April 1940 through November 1941.[1] Her work, "Nazi Laws and Jewish Lives: Letters from Vienna," unpacks the step by step destruction of her Viennese Jewish family while simultaneously indexing all German decrees imposed against them between 1938 and 1942.

In her opening remarks, Kurzweil noted that comprehensive detailed research on the Jewish community of Vienna during the Nazi period has not yet been done. "Upon translating and decoding some of these shriveled transparent pages," she wrote, " it struck me that in spite of all the letters and memoirs that have been published, of the histories and theses, the theoretical and scholarly debates, the transcripts or trials and testimonies, the confessions and denials by perpetrators, the thoughtful exhibitions in Holocaust museums… no one has documented the incremental effect of specific decrees aimed to dehumanize the Jews who remained in the Nazis' realm; and how their everyday lives were being transformed and traumatized…the increasingly throttling grip in which the Nazi authorities held every Viennese Jew who had not yet managed to escape."[2]

---

[1] Edith Kurzweil, *Nazi Laws and Jewish Lives: Letters from Vienna* (New Brunswick: Transaction Publishers, 2004), 2-3. Edith's mother Mimi Weisz escaped in April 1940 after catching the last boat out of Genoa; her grandmother Malvina Fischer was trapped and deported to Lodz in 1941.
[2] Kurzweil, *Nazi Laws and Jewish Lives:*2.

The Nazification of Vienna and the Response of the Viennese Jews is the work Kurzweil envisioned. A scholarly exploration and analysis of Viennese Jewry under Nazism, it is a study of daily life before, during, and after the Anschluss of March 1938. At once a comprehensive history that relates to all families, *The Nazification of Vienna and the Response of the Viennese Jews* values the individual while remembering to incorporate his/her experience into the larger history of the community as a whole. By examining the histories of numerous ordinary Viennese Jews (and their families) and placing them into a chronological narrative of life in Vienna under Nazi occupation, it describes the simultaneous rescue and destruction of this community.

The Nazification of Vienna and the Response of the Viennese Jews aims to contribute to Holocaust scholarship and the more recent study of genocide prevention. In Holocaust history literature, art, and memorials, the genocidal period -- the concentration camps, gas chambers, and mass murders -- holds the foreground, while the pre-genocidal period slips to the margins. The Holocaust Memorial located behind the Vienna State Opera stands as a significant exception. After reviewing many proposals, the Austrian government commissioned the artist Alfred Hrdlicka to erect his "dedication to the street washing Jew" on Albertinagasse in the first district in 1999.[3] A wise choice: the sculpture reminds viewers that the roots of this genocide took hold in the public squares and busy streets of Vienna in March 1938, when neighbors turned a blind eye to the suffering of their neighbors, and the social contract between Austria's Jews and their government shattered. Like Hrdlinka's composition, *The Nazification of Vienna and the Response of the Viennese Jews* focuses on the early stages of the genocide and emphasizes that the destruction of the Jews did not begin in the death camps; it ended there.

---

[3] The sculpture is part of Hrdlicka's larger design, "Against War and Fascisim." See James E. Young, *The Texture of Memory: Holocaust Memorials and Meaning* (New Haven: Yale University Press, 1993), 110.

Chapter One: "From the Opera to the Streets" introduces who the Jews of Vienna were and how they lived prior to March 1938. A diverse and multi-faceted group, Vienna's Jews came from regions all over the Austro-Hungarian empire, spoke different languages, held different political beliefs, and practiced different trades. Many tried to assimilate; others remained Orthodox, but all contributed to the dynamic atmosphere that defined Vienna at the turn of the century and in the three decades thereafter. Providing an overview of the "long road to Anschluss," Chapter One begins by explaining how Vienna's Jews perceived the lingering threat of Austrian/German union, and thus how they viewed the Nazi rise to power in Germany. Astute observers such as the contemporary British statesman Norman Bentwich suggested that more Jews should have left Austria before Anschluss. Reflecting upon the interwar period, Bentwich noted that Austrian Jews "lived in the shadow of Nazi violence…the writing was on the wall for all to see."[4] Yet did they understand the looming German threat, with its implications for their families and community? And if so, why did so few leave between the years 1933 and 1938? "From the Opera to the Streets" discusses the complexities of this frequently asked question and goes on to scrutinize the weekend of German annexation, the impact it had on the Jewish community, and the toll it took immediately. In a state of shock and denial, with an urgency to make life altering decisions, and few options, how did Vienna's Jews respond?

The second chapter lays bare the devastation that followed the German takeover. "The Anschluss Pogrom: Panic, Chaos, and Confusion for Vienna's Jews in March 1938" offers a new perspective on the Anschluss period, the violent eight weeks that followed the union,

---

[4] Norman Bentwich, historian and witness, scrutinized the situation facing Austrian Jewry in the 1930s. See Norman Bentwich, "The Destruction of the Jewish Community in Austria 1938-1942," in Josef Frankel ed., *The Jews of Austria: Essays on their Life, History and Destruction* (London: Valentine Mitchell,1967), 467.

reconstructed through the voices of Jews and gentiles, native Austrians and foreigners. Survivor testimonies, memoirs, and letters, together with contemporary diplomatic reports from members of the American legation in Vienna tell this gruesome chapter in history, redefining it as a pogrom. Chapter Two reveals this time period as significant in another way as well. It was at this point that a pattern was set: this was the first time that the German/Austrian perpetrators forced their Viennese Jewish victims to act as the agents of their own destruction, demanding that they implement and oversee the boycott of their own enterprises. Jews' lives fell apart during this period. Thoughts of hope and denial shifted to actions of extreme despair and helplessness, from unprepared flight to suicide. Still, no one faction of Vienna's Jews gravitated toward one response over another; the community remained a diverse and varied group of individuals. It was at this point, too, that warning bells sounded but went unheard. The high number of family suicides in the spring of 1938 among wealthy Jews who had the option to take flight, reflects the extremity of the situation and the danger that lay ahead.

The Anschluss pogrom unified Vienna's Jews behind a common quest to escape from Nazism. Chapter Three: "The IKG: Co-opted by the New Masters" describes the reopening of the Jewish Community of Vienna (IKG) in May 1938 under the Nazi administration, marking this development as the birth of institutionalized cooperation and collaboration between the victims and their oppressors. This chapter delineates the new "rescue" operation, how it was proposed and implemented from the top down, and the blind obedience from the bottom up required for success. Only 1,743 Jews emigrated from Austria before Anschluss, and Jews took varied actions during the Anschluss pogrom. After the reopening of the IKG, however, Jews unified to support a system of mass exodus from Austria. Twenty-five-thousand Jews applied for emigration on behalf of themselves (and their families) in the very first days of the community's reconfiguration. Desperately seeking assistance, these people were willing to go anywhere, pay any price, and leave everything behind to ensure their safety. "The IKG: Co-opted by the New Masters" describes how daily life changed for Vienna's Jews in May 1938, introducing the central role and work of the IKG including its structure, institutions, leaders, employees, volunteers, and members. Months before the opening of Eichmann's infamous *Zentrallstelle*, a fully operational system for mass emigration was underway that required the assistance of foreign aid committees and total cooperation from Vienna's Jews. The rescue had begun, but so too were the roots of genocide planted one foot deeper.

While the terror of the Anschluss pogrom persuaded Vienna's Jews that it was necessary to cooperate with the Germans and follow an organized emigration procedure, many believed they lived in a society where a basic rule of law still applied. This was a false construct. Hitler's order from 24 May 1938 called for the immediate capture of "criminal" and "asocial" Jews, igniting a wave of over 1800 arrests throughout the city in a matter of weeks. Chapter Four: "Turning Point: Vienna to Dachau" scrutinizes the arrest, questioning, holding, transfer, and deportation of Viennese Jewish men targeted for slave labor, exposing new details about this cruel and secretive process. In contrast to the public display of violence that exploded during the Anschluss pogrom, these arrests were acts of terror initially camouflaged by decency. "Turning Point: Vienna to Dachau" begins to speculate why resistance did not emerge as a more common Jewish response to Nazism already in the very early stages of the genocide. It identifies the moment at which the Germans removed these men from Viennese society, broke them down physically and spiritually, and assumed full power over them. It also describes the impact these arrests had on the families left behind and the Jewish community at large. At the outset of these random arrests, Eichmann had already attained his initial goal: Vienna's Jews were looking toward a future for their families outside of Austria. Cooperation and obedience had been established, retraining courses were overflowing, and the emigration system was well underway. The arrests made Vienna's Jews more vulnerable and even more willing to cooperate with their German oppressors for the chance to leave.

Emigration may have been the agreed solution to the misery of Vienna's Jews, but it was nevertheless an extremely difficult process. It required patience, diligence, and cooperation, as well as difficult decisions under unfamiliar circumstances. Having assumed its role as the central life-line for Viennese Jews, the IKG as an institution worked with great determination to promote emigration for all. Still, there were no guarantees, and often family members were forced to leave loved ones or realtives behind. Why some got out and others were caught in the Nazi web is a question that has burdened many Viennese Jewish refugees and their descendents to this day.[5] Ruth Kluger, for example, seven-years-old at the time of the Nazi takeover, remained trapped in Vienna in 1941. Her mother declined the opportunity to send her to England on a *Kindertransport,* believing that a mother and daughter should not be separated. Both Ruth and her mother survived incarceration in Theresienstadt and Auschwitz-Birkenau, and immigrated to the United States in 1947. In her memoir, Ruth, now a seventy-nine-year-old woman and a distinguished professor at the University of California, still questions why her family was unable to make it out of Vienna before they were deported.

Chapter Five: "Rescue and Destruction: Daily Life during a Mass Exodus" explores the question Kluger continues to ponder, as well as others concerning the emigration/immigration process. It credits the people who and institutions that helped to make the emigration operation run so successfully that it dispatched over two-thirds of the community to countries around the

---

[5]Ruth Kluger, *Still Alive, A Holocaust Girlhood Remembered* (New York: The Feminist Press at the City University of New York, 2001), 49.

world between 1938 and 1941. "Rescue and Destruction: Daily Life during a Mass Exodus" also identifies the many factors that could delay plans for flight, or hold applicants back for good: quotas, visas, affidavits, passports, tax-clearance certificates. It notes the important role played by the foreign aid committees, supporting the Jewish community's emigration endeavors and social welfare system. And still, despite recognizing the IKG's grand success enabling the flight of over 130,000 individuals, Chapter Five reveals the mass expulsion as a period marked by desperation, turmoil, and disappointment. Family separation is a theme that looms large. The IKG poured its energy into the emigration operation, offering total cooperation to the Germans, and became caught in a vicious cycle: while promoting the rescue of the community, the leaders unknowingly became agents of their own destruction. The price of rescue was all too often at the cost of permanent family separation.

Vienna's Jews never stood by passively during the reign of Nazi occupation. People resisted persecution and expropriation, people resisted dehumanization, and people resisted the destruction of their families. Sometimes they succeeded. Chapter Six: "Escape! November Complications, but Emigration Continues" demonstrates the struggle of Vienna's Jews to survive on a daily basis -- to preserve their dignity and to save their loved ones -- and illuminates previously unrecognized or unacknowledged acts of resistance, resilience, and persistence. At the same time, it identifies the trap from which many Jews were unable to emerge after the November Pogrom. Spanning the period from October 1938 to October 1941, Chapter Six focuses on the aftermath of the infamous "Night of Broken Glass," pointing to the challenges it posed to the organized emigration effort and the permanent destruction it left behind. Vienna's Jews may have been shocked by the terror of the pogrom (the physical destruction, the arrests and deportations) but they were more devastated by the results of this destruction. Looking at various Viennese Jewish families and how they experienced this period, "Escape! November Complications, but Emigration Continues" reveals how people's lives changed due to the terror of the pogrom and how their emigration plans fell apart. This chapter reviews the financial dimension of emigration. Addressing the plight of Vienna's wealthiest Jews, we see that in fact they were not so lucky to have assets at this time. Their losses, during and after the pogrom affected not only their immediate families, but the entire ailing community. And still, despite the November Pogrom wave of terror which destroyed some people's chances to escape and tore more families apart, Vienna's Jews continued to press emigration forward. Individuals' efforts together with the IKG enabled the escape of another 70,000 persons from Nazi Vienna after November 1938, including the remarkable release and emigration of five of every seven men deported from Vienna to Dachau and Buchenwald.

The IKG kept focused on the rescue operation until flight became virtually impossible, until the Germans prohibited emigration from the Reich and foreign aid committees cut off funding. The privilege to run this operation was never free, and over time the price to save just one life became more expensive. Ultimately, for a brief period, the price of one Jew's rescue was the cost of another's destruction. Chapter Seven: "Transition to Destruction" describes the first six months of 1941, when the Germans ordered the IKG to run both the emigration and deportation processes simultaneously. It explains how and why the IKG carried out the "resettlement" of Vienna's Jews to Poland, and did so with precision and efficiency. The IKG turned a blind eye to the unknown fate of some, because it was still enabling the rescue of others. Even one person's dispatch to safety was enough to keep the IKG offices open and running and keep up cooperation with the Nazi enemy. This problematic transition from rescue to destruction, from emigration to deportation, is explored in Chapter Seven, which scrutinizes how, when, where, and why, the deportation process -- of Jews by other Jews -- began in Vienna. Not knowing what the future held and continuing to hope for the best, the IKG deported over 8,000 persons to ghettos in the east in February and March 1941. Their ability to run this process was made possible by the routine of cooperation and collaboration, set in motion years prior. Elucidating the vicious cycle that had been established, "Transition to Destruction" unpacks the German decree of 1 September 1941, demanding that all Jews over the age of six wear the yellow Star of David on their clothing. Breaking down the process of distributing the Jewish star, scrutinizing and analyzing the role of both the community and individuals in following these new German orders, this chapter reveals this antisemitic legislation from a new and different angle. It was not the "hardest blow" by any means for this community, but another order Berlin demanded the IKG carry out. And they did, in the hope that emigration and rescue would carry on if they continued to cooperate. How the Jewish leadership and individual families interpreted these events as they unfolded, how they responded to these changes, and why, is laid bare in this chapter.

Destruction without rescue began in October 1941 when the Germans put an end to emigration. They informed the leaders of the IKG that no further emigration trains would roll. Instead, they ordered the IKG to organize deportation trains. Chapter Eight: "Caught in the Vicious Cycle: From a Working Jewish Community to a Council of Jewish Elders" elucidates daily life for Jews who remained in Vienna in 1941 and 1942. It explores how people experienced the steadily increasing impoverishment of their community, the restrictions and humiliations, and the severed communication with their relatives and loved ones abroad. And it looks closely at how people reacted and responded when they were summoned for "resettlement"? Unpacking the details, Chapter Eight analyzes who was deported from Vienna, when, and to where, as well as who was involved in the structuring of the deportation process and who carried it out. The IKG changed from an institution which promoted the emigration and rescue of 136,000 Viennese Jews to an entity that organized the deportation and destruction of over 55,000 others. How did Jews become woven into the fabric of their own destruction and how can we best identify, understand, and define their role in the history of the genocide?

When Austria was liberated in 1945 few of Vienna's Jews returned to reclaim their *heimat*. The vibrant Jewish community of pre-Anschluss Vienna vanished over the course of the Nazi occupation; the high hopes of those who escaped and survived perished with their relatives and loved ones who were murdered in the ghettos, camps, or annihilation sites of the "final solution." In the Conclusion: "Going Home: The Aftermath of the Holocaust for the Jewish Community" the importance of preserving the family unit looms large. Family division began in 1938 and continued through the war. The scars of permanent separation never healed, but sealed the complete destruction of the Jewish community of Vienna.

The Nazification of Vienna and the Response of the Viennese Jews thus depicts this community's experience under Nazism, dispelling the myth that Vienna's Jews were "the lucky ones," and revealing the active struggle in which they were engaged for years to overcome the extreme odds against them.

Map 1: Austria-Hungary 1878-1918

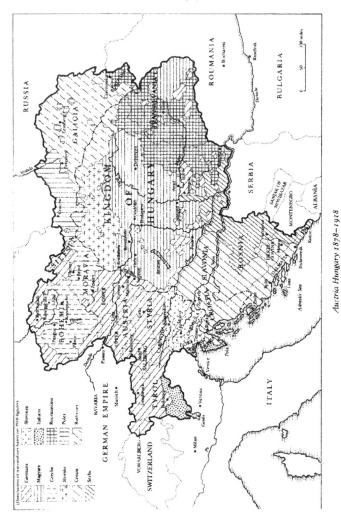

Source: Allan Palmer, *Twilight of the Habsburgs, The Life and Times of Emperor Francis Joseph.* (New York: Atlantic Monthly Press, 1994).

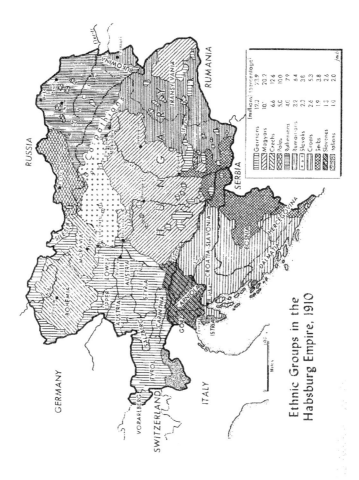

Source: William O McCagg Jr., *A History of Habsburg Jews 1690-1918.*
(Indianapolis: Indiana University Press, 1989).

Map 3: Vienna 1910, Jewish Percentile in Population by District

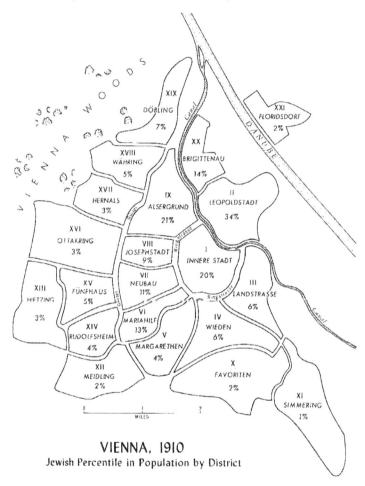

VIENNA, 1910
Jewish Percentile in Population by District

Source: William O McCagg Jr., *A History of Habsburg Jews 1690-1918.*
(Indianapolis: Indiana University Press, 1989).

Chapter One

From the Opera to the Streets

Illustration 1: *Gemütlichkeit, Dancing and Drinking in a Public Park, Vienna 1930s*

Sources: Paul Hoffmann, *The Viennese: Splendor, Twilight and Exile*
(New York: Anchor Books, Doubleday, 1988); Original source: Bettmann Archive, Inc.

During the late 19th century, in the capital of the fifty-million-strong Austro-Hungarian Empire,

a ditty was sung praising the tolerance among Franz Joseph's many subjects: "The Christians,

the Turks, the Heathen and Jew, have dwelt here in ages old and new. Harmoniously and

without any strife, for everyone's entitled to live his own life."[1] There, in Vienna, Jews had

settled for over a century. Discovering both a safe haven and a chance for new opportunity, they

planted their roots. The emperor offered them freedom and security, which they relished, and in

return they served proudly as his most loyal subjects. Even after the Emperor's death and the fall

---

[1] Hilde Spiel, *Vienna's Golden Autumn: 1866-1938* (New York: Weidenfeld and Nicolson, 1986), 27. Original
source is unknown.

of the monarchy, they felt protected. It was precisely this bond to their Austrian *Heimat* (homeland) that crippled Austrian Jews in the face of Nazism.

The Writing on the Wall: Austria's Jews and the Pre-Anschluss Atmosphere

Austria's Jewish population throughout the 1920s and 30s averaged approximately two hundred thousand in a country of close to seven million. Over 90 percent of the Jews lived in the capital city, Vienna, where they comprised nearly 10 percent of the total city population.[2] Austria's Jews witnessed the growth of Nazism in Germany, Hitler's invitation to power in 1933, and an attempted Nazi takeover of Austria in 1934. Still, none of these events inspired them to leave their homeland. As they watched the new Nazi dictatorship ostracize and persecute German Jews -- from the first boycott of Jewish stores in April 1933 to the declaration of the Nuremburg laws in 1935 -- they remained unwilling to leave their homes. According to historian Bruce Pauley, the Jewish *Stimmung*[3] in Vienna throughout the thirties was that the Nazi regime in Germany was little more than a passing phenomenon.[4] His research has shown that during these critical years, reports from Viennese-Jewish newspapers such as *Die Wahrheit* (The Truth) helped people to stay calm, reminding them that Jews had survived every historical crisis in the past. Accounts from Viennese Jewish émigrés and concentration camp survivors express a similar sentiment. Valerie A., who was in her early-twenties when the Nazis took over Germany, recalled: "We knew what was going on there [in Germany], but we were dumbfounded. We said

---

[2] Percentage and Population of Jews in Vienna: 1900: 8.77% (146,926 of 1,675,325); 1910: 8.63% (175,318 of 2,020,309); 1923: 10.7 percent (201,513 of 1,865,780); 1934: 8.54% (177,869 of 2,080,408). USHMM microfilm # 294, CAHJP- A/W 126, *Report of the Vienna Jewish Community. A description of the activity of the Israelistische Kultusgemeinde Wien in the period from May 2nd 1938- December 31st 1939*), 11.
[3] This commonly used German term translates to: atmosphere, mood, disposition.
[4] Bruce Pauley, *From Prejudice to Persecution: A History of Austrian Anti-Semitism* (Chapel Hill & London: The University of North Carolina Press, 1992), 326.

that could never happen in Austria! All those proud Austrians! Oh Austria, the country of love and music and fun. That could not happen to Austria!"[5]

Pauley has argued that Viennese Jews were filled with a false sense of security on the eve of the Anschluss because they had lived through "six decades of anti-Semitic agitation accompanied by next to nothing in the way of concrete anti-Semitic legislation."[6] Pauley's analysis is well-founded: a bond to the homeland, a desire for true belonging, and a sense of security which lingered from the days of the Emperor Franz Joseph, convinced Austria's Jews they were safe from the Nazi threat. "Jews felt protected by the crown, by Franz Josef -- he was larger than life," George Czuzcka explained.[7] Sandor Ultman agreed: "We thought in those days of the monarchy that it was the very best life -- a very happy life."[8] "'Not in Austria!'" Erika Spitzer's father Hugo said repeatedly, while addressing the situation in Nazi Germany. "He was very proud to be an Austrian," Erika reflected. "He loved the King Franz Joseph and said, 'Don't be silly. Austria will never come under Hitler. No Austrian will ever be a Nazi!'"[9] Although the days of Franz Josef and his grand empire had come to an end, Austria's Jews still felt protected -- particularly the men who had fought for the imperial army in World War I. These war veterans understood a Nazi threat as imminent, but they didn't think it would affect them. They were persuaded that the Austrian government, which they had served faithfully, would come to their aid. They encouraged their families and friends to remain calm. "My parents were not panicking

---

[5] Valerie, A., 1995. "Interview by Survivors of the Shoah Visual History Foundation," Santa Barbara, CA, USA, November 3. Interview Code 08291, Tapes 1-4.

[6] Pauley, *From Prejudice to Persecution:* 326.

[7] George Czuzcka was thirteen when his family and he fled from Nazi-Vienna to the United States in 1939. George Czuzcka, private interview with author, May 2007. Washington, D.C.

[8] Sandor Ultman was thirty-eight when his wife and he fled from Nazi-Vienna to Shanghai (1941). Sandor, U., 1997. "Interview by Survivors of the Shoah Visual History Foundation," Bondi, AU, July 20. Interview Code 04144, Tapes 1-4.

[9] Erica Spitzer was twenty-five when she fled to England in 1939. Her father Hugo Spitzer was sixty-one when the Germans deported his wife and him to Minsk, Maly Trostinces in 1942. See Erica, B., 1996. "Interview by Survivors of the Shoah Visual History Foundation," Upminster, Essex, UK, October 15. Interview Code 20825, Tapes 1-6.

about the situation," Max Weiss recalled, "primarily because Father and Grandfather had been in the Austrian army."[10]

When relatives phoned Karl Langer and warned him to leave Austria, he said, "'Why? I haven't done anything. I was an officer! I have medals!'"[11] His daughter Marion recalled him as "very optimistic, thinking: 'It will pass.'"[12] Curt Klein-Bernard shared a similar memory of his father Bela, who served four years of the war on the Russian front: "Father was hopeful, always said it couldn't get any worse."[13] Alix Grabkowicz expressed remorse while describing her father Dr. Joseph Grabkowicz as "an officer in the Austro-Hungarian Army [...] and a very devoted Austrian." She understood this false sense of security as her father's ultimate weakness and what eventually sealed the tragic fate of her family. "He was a great patriot," she recalled, "and that was very bad. If he had a different direction in life, my family would have left when... when it was necessary to leave."[14] Joseph did not leave. Neither did Karl or Bela, nor did they encourage their children or families to do so. These men were not the exception; they represent the majority. Only 1,739 Jews of a total 191,458 living in Austria in 1934[15] emigrated prior to the Nazi entry on 11 March 1938, "when it was *necessary* to leave."[16] This minute figure elucidates just how few Jews took seriously the threat of Nazism invading Austria and affecting their

---

[10] Max, W., 1996. "Interview by Survivors of the Shoah Visual History Foundation," Staten Island, NJ, USA, February 25. Interview Code 12544, Tapes 1-4.

[11] Marion, A., (date currently unavailable). "Interview by Survivors of the Shoah Visual History Foundation," (location currently unavailable). Interview Code 42176.

[12] Ibid.

[13] Curt, K.B., 1994. "Interview by Survivors of the Shoah Visual History Foundation," Los Angeles, CA, USA, December 15. Interview Code 00382, Tapes 1-6.

[14] Alix, K.., 1997. "Interview by Survivors of the Shoah Visual History Foundation," Lenox, MA, USA, October 16. Interview Code 34544, Tapes 1-5.

[15] These figures are derived from charts and graphs printed in the following report drawn up by the Jewish Community of Vienna in 1940. See USHMM microfilm # 294, CAHJP- A/W 126, *Report of the Vienna Jewish Community. A description of the activity of the Israelistische Kultusgemeinde Wien in the period from May 2nd 1938-December 31st 1939*: p.10, p.18.

[16] Alix, K., 1997. "Interview by Survivors of the Shoah Visual History Foundation," Lenox, MA, USA, October 16. Interview Code 34544, Tapes 1-5.

personal lives.[17] It was not just Austrian Jewish males who lived during the reign of Franz Josef;

practically everyone in this community refused to leave before Anschluss. Despite numerous

warning signs that Nazism was drawing near, Austria's Jews -- regardless of social class, age,

gender, degree of religious observance, education, or political affiliation -- kept hope for a

peaceful future in their country.

The Long Road to Anschluss

The *grossdeutch* ideal, the notion of achieving a greater Germany and of all German

blood belonging to one land, lay not only in the heart of the Austrian-born German leader Adolf

Hitler, but also at the heart of the Austro-German Anschluss philosophy, over a century old.[18]

The idea skyrocketed following World War I and the collapse of the Austro-Hungarian Empire,

which ended the approximately 650-year reign of the Habsburg monarchy. In 1918 the first

Republic of Austria formed in approximately one-eighth of the former empire's size. Made up

of seven million German-speaking Austrians, in comparison with the multi-ethnic empire of fifty

million inhabitants, Austria was left like a head without its body. Many citizens of the new

republic longed for unification with Germany due to this new precarious situation, but the

outside world would not permit such a merger. The League of Nations --the world's new peace-

keeping body-- feared a unification of the two defeated powers and strictly forbade it. At the

treaty of St. Germain in 1919, they forced Austria "to abandon its chosen name of 'German-

---

[17] Almost three times as many Jews (5,500) immigrated to Austria during this same four-year period (1934-1938). This shocking figure reveals how many Jews (both inside and outside of the country) still considered Austria a safe haven. See USHMM microfilm # 294, CAHJP- A/W 126, *Report of the Vienna Jewish Community. A description of the activity of the Israelistische Kultusgemeinde Wien in the period from May 2nd 1938- December 31st 1939*: p.10, 18.

[18] Robert H. Keyserlingk, *Austria in World War II: An Anglo-American Dilemma* (Kingston; Montreal: McGill-Queen's University Press, 1988).

Austria,' and call itself plain 'Austria.'"[19] Furthermore, they drew up articles in both the treaties

of Versailles[20] and St. Germain[21] to protect Austria's sovereignty and to govern Austro-German

political relations. Despite these restrictions, for almost two decades prior to the actual

Anschluss in March 1938, many German-speaking Austrians held onto the idea of a union with

Greater Germany, and factions of both the Austrian and German governments continued to press

for Anschluss. Austrians and Germans openly defied the peace treaties of Versailles and St.

Germain while pushing toward this union, and each time they violated international law, their

desire for strength through unity evidenced itself to the world -- Austria's Jews included. Still,

even after the Nazis came to power in Germany, these warnings did not motivate Austrian Jews

to leave.

Hitler's accession to power and the growing popularity of Nazism in Austria revived the

Austro-German desire for Anschluss in 1933.[22] Nazi propaganda trumpeted Hitler's aspiration to

expand his empire, starting with the incorporation of the German-speaking world. In Vienna,

enormous banners hung above the most famous sights with Nazi slogans that read: "Common

---

[19] Gordon Brook-Shepherd, *The Anschluss* (Philadelphia; New York: J.P. Lippencott Company, 1963), xvi.

[20] "Germany acknowledges and will respect strictly the independence of Austria within the frontiers which may be fixed in a treaty between that State and the principal allied and associated powers; she agrees that this independence shall be inalienable except with the consent of the Council of the League of Nations." [Treaty of Versailles. Signed June 28, 1919. SECTION VI, ARTICLE> 80.] See *New York Times*, 21 March 1931: 1. See also, Sir Frederick Pollack, *The League of Nations* (London: The Lawbook Exchange, Ltd., 2003).

[21] "The independence of Austria is inalienable otherwise than with the consent of the Council of the League of Nations. Consequently Austria undertakes in the absence of the consent of the said Council to abstain from any act which might directly or indirectly or by any means whatever compromise her independence, particularly, and until her admission to membership of the League of Nations by participation in the affairs of another power."[Treaty of St. Germain-en-Laye. Signed Sept. 10, 1919. SECTION VIII, ARTICLE >88.] See *New York Times*, 21 March 1931: 1. Also see Sir Frederick Pollack, *The League of Nations*. (London: The Lawbook Exchange, Ltd., 2003).

[22] Note: Austria and Germany drew near to Anschluss before the Nazi takeover of Germany. In 1931, the two countries joined in an economic partnership in the form of a customs union. When news of this union reached the United States, the headlines of the *New York Times* reported: "VIENNA SEES UNION WITH REICH BEGUN. VIENNA SEES 'ANSCHLUSS'. GERMANY AND AUSTRIA JOIN IN FULL CUSTOMS UNION; EVASION OF TREATIES SEEN. *Austro-German Union Barred By Terms of Two Peace Treaties*. The immediate problem, brought to a head by the dire economic situation, is the creation a single economic unit out of the two German-speaking peoples. A political union is forbidden by the treaties of Versailles and St. Germain." See *New York Times*, 22 March 1931: 1-2.

blood belongs in a common land!"[23] or "One People, One Land, One Leader!"[24] While Nazi-Germany tried to woo Austria into its arms, Austria's chancellor Engelbert Dolfuss opted to outlaw the Nazi party and set up a dictatorship of his own. But his efforts to suppress the growing influence of Nazism did not succeed. Instead, Nazi sympathizers in Austria grew in strength, making their way underground. Austrian Nazi supporters joined the army, police, and the civil service, and they tried to seize power. In February 1934 --after civil war erupted in Vienna between the government forces and left-wing militias ("Red Vienna" came to an end, and "Austro-fascism" prevailed) -- the world witnessed Austria's outlawed Nazi party step into the spotlight. The party had grown in size and intended to overthrow the new Austrian government led by the Christian Socialists. The *New York Times* reported:

> The Austrian Section of the German Nazi party said today in a manifesto that ... the Nazi party... will fight the Dollfuss government tooth and nail so that a new Austria may arise after the Dollfuss system has met its deserved downfall ... Leader of the Austrian Nazis in Germany ... said that Chancellor Dolfuss of Austria was 'caught in a trap.' 'The only way out ... is toward the German Reich. Unless he avails himself of this his doom is sealed.[25]

This dark scene of political unrest in 1934 made the country even more vulnerable to a Nazi threat.[26] It also demonstrated to the world the mounting Nazi pressure in Austria and that a longing for Austro-German unification had resurfaced.[27]

---

[23] Translated from the original German, "*Gleiches Blut gehoert in ein gemeinsames Reich!*"

[24] Translated from the original German, "*Ein Volk, Ein Reich, Ein Fuehrer!*"

[25] *New York Times*, 13 February 1934: 1-3.

[26] Paul Hofmann, *The Viennese: Splendor, Twilight and Exile* (New York: Doubleday Dell Publishing Group, Inc., 1988), 205-218.

[27] In 1934, as these warning signs erupted, the world powers came to action. The headline of the *New York Times* on 18 February 1934: "NAZI GERMANY IS CAUTIONED BY BRITAIN, FRANCE AND ITALY TO KEEP HANDS OFF AUSTRIA." The paper reprinted the texts of the peace treaties that guaranteed to protect Austria's independence. *New York Times*, 18 February 1934: headline, 1.

Six months after Austria's civil war, the illegal Nazi party in Austria launched its first serious attempt to unify the country with its blood-brothers in Germany. SS-Regiment 89 and other members of the underground Nazi party attempted a coup d'etat and assassinated the Austrian chancellor. The headlines of the *New York Times* on 26 July 1934 read: "Austrian Nazis Kill Dollfuss, Revolt Fails; 147 Plotters Held; Martial Law In Effect; Italian Army, Navy Planes Ready To Act."[28] The event became known as the unsuccessful putsch of 1934, as the illegal Nazi party was held back by the Austrian army and police force. Nevertheless, the intent of the underground Nazi party to take over Austria and to achieve Anschluss with Germany was clear.[29] Again, the Jews of Austria did not budge.

The chancellor's successor, Kurt von Schuschnigg, led Austria into an even deeper political crisis and eventually straight to Anschluss with Germany. His political strategies, specifically his willingness to negotiate with the outlawed Austrian Nazi party, proved his greatest weakness. On 11 July 1936, he attended a meeting with Hitler and von Papen (German ambassador to Austria since 1934), during which he made a dangerous deal that if Nazi Germany recognized Austria's sovereignty, Austria would conduct its domestic and foreign policy as a "German" state. To help improve Austro-German relations and avoid friction between the two countries, he committed to working closely with Austrian Nazi party members (although the party itself was still an illegal underground movement). He also agreed to offer Artur Seyss-Inquart, a leader of the Austrian Nazi party, the position of state counselor in the Austrian government.[30] This momentous turning point in the development of Austro-German Anschluss

---

[28] *New York Times.* 26 July 1934: 1.
[29] Evan Burr Bukey, *Hitler's Austria: Popular Sentiment in the Nazi Era 1938-1945* (Chapell Hill and London: The University of North Carolina Press, 2000); Radomir Luza, *Austro-German Relations in the Anschluss Era* (Princeton: Princeton University Press, 1975); Margaret Macmillan, *Paris 1919: Six Months That Changed The World* (New York: Random House, 2003).
[30] Kurt Schuschnigg, *Austrian Requiem: Chancellor of Austria and Prisoner of Hitler* (New York: G.P. Putnam's Sons, 1946), 9.

later became known as the 1936 Austro-German Pact or July Agreement. Historian Gordon Brook-Shepherd dubbed it the "half-way mark down the 'evolutionary' path to Anschluss," [31] but he understated the case. The new cooperation between the Austrian government and the outlawed Nazi party solidified the beginning of Austro-German unification and, ultimately, the beginning of the end for the Jews.

By the close of 1937, Schuschnigg had started to lose control of political affairs in Austria. "Nazi underground terror in Vienna was again in full swing," the by then former chancellor recalled in his postwar memoir, *Austrian Requiem.* "Telephone booths exploded, tear gas bombs were thrown, and mass demonstrations were arranged in order to induce the Austrian police to intervene. Once the police dispersed the crowds, Berlin protested that we did not keep our share of the bargain [1936 Agreement] and allowed the persecution of National Socialism."[32] The chancellor felt the Nazis trying to blackmail him and coax Austria into a full partnership with Germany. He recognized this initial blackmail, but was unable to contain it. On 12 February 1938, at Hitler's retreat in Berchtesgaden Schuschnigg was faced with a final ultimatum: give the Austrian Nazis a free voice in Austria, or face a German invasion. He opted for non-aggression and returned to Vienna.

George Czuzcka, a thirteen-year-old Jewish boy living in Vienna, read about the Chancellor's expected visit to Germany while sitting on the trolley car one late afternoon, headed to the thirteenth district for a weekend visit with his aunt and uncle. George found this news frightening. "Hitler was the boogey-man to me then," he reflected many years later. "I was afraid! Would they keep our guy Schuschnigg there? Would they kill him? What would happen to him?" When George arrived at his destination and explained his concern to the adults, his

---

[31] Brook-Shepherd, *The Anschluss,* xvi.
[32] Schuschnigg, *Austrian Requiem: Chancellor of Austria and Prisoner of Hitler,* 9.

uncle, who had lived for a couple of years in Germany under the Hitler regime, quickly tried to comfort him. "Don't worry. Hitler's not so bad," he told his nephew.[33] George was only thirteen, but he sensed danger and understood that the current situation and the future for Austria did not look good. The adults in his family -- like the majority of Austria's Jews -- witnessed Schuschnigg's gradual demise and Nazism infiltrate the Austrian government, but they still were not prompted to change their lives. Despite this very clear warning sign on 12 February 1938, they continued to believe in the future of independent Austria and that the threat of Nazism would pass.

The outside world, on the other hand, took notice of Hitler's ultimatum and Schuschnigg's submission of power immediately. Popular and well-read American newspapers, magazines, and journals reported that Nazism had sunk its teeth into Austria and that the Austro-German longing for Anschluss had finally been achieved. They reported that Vienna had capitulated to Berlin, Hitler was in control of Austrian affairs, and that the Nazis were celebrating their success. For example, on 16 February, the first page of the *New York Times* reported: "Austria Capitulates to Germany; Pro-Nazis Get Key Posts in Cabinet; Berlin Hails Unity of Two Nations… Comment was unanimous that Chancellor Hitler would now in effect dictate Austrian policy… Vienna yielded to a Berlin ultimatum and appointed pro-Nazi Ministers to control the police, foreign affairs and the administration."[34] G.E.R. Gedye,[35] Central European correspondent for the *New York Times,* reported by wireless one week later (21 February) on the growing popularity of Nazism and the deteriorating situation for Austria's Jews: "There was unrest in Vienna where the Nazis came out and demonstrated … Jews were persecuted coming

---

[33]George Czuzcka, private interview with author, May 2007. Washington, D.C.

[34] *New York Times,* 16 February 1938: 1.

[35] G.E.R. Gedye was expelled from Vienna by order of the Nazis immediately following the March invasion. See "Nazi Terror in Austria," *The New Republic,* 20 April 1938.

out of the opera, but were beaten off by a detachment of Schuschnigg's Storm Troopers. But, in the provinces there was no objection, just full on Nazi support, demonstrations, and swastikas and no violence."[36] That same day the headlines read: "Hitler Demands Right of Self-Determination for Germans in Austria... Nazis Celebrate in Austrian Fêtes."[37] The following week (28 February) the popular magazine *Life* reported that Austria and Germany achieved Anschluss on 12 February 1938 and that the impact of Nazism was detrimental to Austrian culture.[38] Set below a large glorified photograph of the Vienna Opera Ball, a dramatic caption read: "Vienna's Opera Ball ends an era. Vienna danced with a good heart for the last time January 15 ... History will look back on this scene as the last of the great Viennese Opera Balls, because the soul of Vienna cannot long survive in the violent asceticism of Nazism."[39] "Austria Succumbs to Hitler," the title of a *New Republic* article proclaimed on 2 March 1938. "Independent Austria is now a memory," the author lamented. "The Fuehrer is putting into action the words of 'Mein Kampf;' he is bringing about *Anschluss* (Austro-German union). Austria is to be the Eighth Gau (district) of the Third Reich."[40] And the *Nation* reported (5 March): "The probabilities are that Hitler will in the end have his victory in Austria."[41] The western world understood that Nazism had seized control of Austrian affairs and that Anschluss had arrived, but evidently recognizing this reality was a burden simply too heavy to bear for the Jews of Austria.

Twenty-four-year-old Erika Spitzer (whose mother Elsa was Jewish and whose father Hugo was Protestant) attended the opera ball on 15 January 1938. That evening, as she danced her last waltz in Vienna, gentile friends repeatedly told her, "Get out of Austria!" They advised

---

[36] *New York Times,* 21 February 1938:1-3.
[37] *New York Times,* 21 February 1938: 1.
[38] "The question was only whether Germany would take Austria with blood or with diplomacy. On Feb. 12 the issue was decided. Germany took Austria without blood, with diplomacy." See "Nazi Germany Woos and Wins Gay Little Austria," *LIFE,* 28 February 1938: 50.
[39] *LIFE,* 28 February 1938: 51.
[40] *New Republic,* General Articles, 2 March 1938: 94-96.
[41] *Nation,* Volume 146, 5 March 1938: 216- 293.

her to leave the country and to transfer her father's money to Switzerland immediately.[42] It was the second time that friends warned Erika and her family to leave Austria, but neither she nor her parents took action. The Spitzers, a well-educated and affluent family, enjoyed a comfortable life and they were not ready to leave it behind.

Illustration 2: *"Vienna Opera Ball, 15 January 1938"*

Source: *LIFE*, 28 February 1938: 50.

[42] The Spitzer family had circles of friends in Vienna which included well known actors and actresses; the Von Trapp Family Singers were the first people to warn them to leave Austria. The Spitzers waited too long. After Anschluss, German law marked Elsa as a Jew and Erika as a mischlinge child. Hugo converted to Judaism to keep the family together. Erica, B., 1996. "Interview by Survivors of the Shoah Visual History Foundation," Upminster, Essex, UK, October 15. Interview Code 20825, Tapes 1-6.

The prospect of Austro-German Anschluss was alive and visible long before its implementation, as were the dangers of Nazism. Most of Austria's Jews, however, did not believe a terrible threat lurked ahead. Between the Nazi rise to power in Germany and the Nazi takeover of Austria some five years later, numerous warning signs appeared that might have encouraged them to leave, or at least to take precautionary steps to prepare for departure. Jews had time to consider the situation of the Jews in Germany and to map out emergency courses of action, but they did not. The vast majority of Austria's Jews stayed put and hoped for a peaceful future. They held on to this hope until Nazism invaded their private lives and flight was no longer an option but a necessity -- a matter of life or death.

Austria's Jews: The Jews of Vienna

Throughout the twenties and thirties -- on the long road to Anschluss -- Austria's Jews witnessed political tension and rising antisemitism. Many were well aware of Hitler's aspirations. Yet, despite these critical developments, less than one percent of their community fled from Austria before the Nazi takeover in March 1938. There are key explanations for this, some unique to their community and history, and others more general. Diversity within their community, a history of survival through centuries of persecution, a general hope for the future, and denial of the present loom large. To understand why so few Jews left Austria before Anschluss, let us a look at how they lived, as individuals and as a community, and consider their history, success, and daily lives in Vienna.

Cultural, spiritual, and political diversity enriched the Viennese Jewish community but was an added challenge when it came to preparing for the Nazi threat. On the eve of Anschluss, they were not a homogenous body or even a unified group of individuals with different beliefs;

they were divided along many fault lines.[43] Throughout the second half of the nineteenth century and the beginning of the twentieth, Jews settled in Vienna from all over the enormous territory of the Austro-Hungarian Empire and were all considered Austrians, regardless of where they were born.[44] As historian William M. Johnston has noted, "In all of history few great cultural centers have drawn upon so rich and varied a hinterland or promoted the intermingling of so many and such diverse cultural and racial types.... Its composers fused music out of Hungarian, Czech, Austrian, and gypsy themes; its dialect incorporated words from the same variety of sources; its theater drew upon German, French, Italian, and Spanish forerunners; and architecture came to be modeled almost indiscriminately on modes from all centuries and styles."[45]

After the war and the collapse of the empire, the happy Vienna that Johnston had described as "the ultimate melting pot, the archetype of cultural blending" changed for the worse.[46] Only those citizens born within the small boundaries of the new Austrian republic were automatically granted Austrian citizenship; the rest became natives of the country in which they had been born, such as Czechoslovakia, Poland, Romania, Hungary, or Yugoslavia. Some individuals fell in a legal chasm and became stateless subjects -- unable to obtain Austrian citizenship because they were not born in the new territory of Austria, while their country of birth refused to grant them citizenship as they resided in Austria. These new citizenship laws posed a great problem for Jews when the Nazis invaded and forced their exodus. Immigration to

---

[43] 88 congregations and 356 secular associations existed in Vienna in March 1938. See Herbert Rozenkranz, "The Anschluss and the Tragedy of Austrian Jewry 1938-1945," in Josef Frankel ed., *The Jews of Austria: Essays on their Life, History and Destruction* (London: Valentine Mitchell,1967), 481. For more on diversity, see Harriet Pass Friedenreich, *Jewish Politics in Vienna, 1918-1938* (Bloomington, Indiana University Press, 1991). See also David Rechter, *The Jews of Vienna and the First World* (London, Littman Library of Jewish Civilization, 2001).

[44] All Jews living in the Austro-Hungarian Empire received equal rights, but the German-speaking Austrians had an advantage because the official language of the emperor and Parliament was German. All affairs were conducted in German.

[45] William M. Johnston, *Vienna, Vienna: The Golden Age 1815-1914* (Milan, Italy: Arnoldo Mondadori Editore, 1981), 6.

[46] Ibid.

the U.S., for example, depended upon set quota figures for each country, which meant that the Jews of Vienna fell into at least half a dozen different national categories. Two members of the community with similar backgrounds and the same resources at their disposal thus had completely different chances to manage immigration to America. Even families were torn apart due to these border and nationality changes: parents born in Bukovina, for instance, were considered Romanian; their children, born in Vienna, held Austrian nationality. Vienna's history and geographical background made its Jewish community far more diverse than their coreligionists in most other European cities and this had a significant impact on their future.

Table 1: "Nationalities of Vienna's Jews"

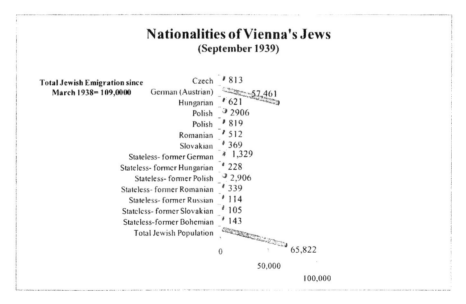

Nationalities of Vienna's Jews
(September 1939)

Total Jewish Emigration since
March 1938= 109,0000

Czech	813
German (Austrian)	57,461
Hungarian	621
Polish	2906
Polish	819
Romanian	512
Slovakian	369
Stateless- former German	1,329
Stateless- former Hungarian	228
Stateless- former Polish	2,906
Stateless- former Romanian	339
Stateless- former Russian	114
Stateless- former Slovakian	105
Stateless-former Bohemian	143
Total Jewish Population	65,822

0   50,000   100,000

Source: USHMM microfilm # 294, CAHJP- A/W 126:
Report of the Vienna Jewish Community, May 2nd 1938- December 31st 1939.

By the 1930s, Vienna's Jews lived dispersed throughout the city's twenty-six districts, fell into different socio-economic classes, and belonged to a range of political parties. Religion divided the community, too. While some were assimilated Jews, others were conservative or orthodox in their practice. Others renounced the Jewish faith and converted or became "without confession,"[47] and still others had strong Jewish-nationalist aspirations and identified as Zionists.[48] The community also suffered from a split between westernized Jews and *Ostjuden* (Jews from eastern Europe). Eastern European Jews swarmed into Vienna from Galicia, Bukovina, and other provinces in the dual-monarchy before, during, and after World War I. Mostly they fled persecution and economic strife, but some also looked for greater opportunity in the empire's capital city. When they reached Vienna, they settled primarily in the second district together with other Jews. This area, officially called *Leopoldstadt* (Leopold's City) after the Holy Roman Emperor Leopold I who reigned in the late seventeenth century, was located just outside of the inner city and north of the Danube canal. By the early twentieth century it carried the nickname *Mazzesinsel,* "Matzah Island," poking fun at the large percentage of eastern European Jews who lived there. In both their public and private lives, Ostjuden preferred to preserve many practices of shtetl life, speaking Yiddish and keeping a traditional Jewish household, and many scorned reform Jews who refused to do so.[49] Some could not accept emancipated Jews' decisions to shave their beards, work on Saturdays, and adapt to modern ways, denouncing them as heretics.

---

[47] Derived from the original German word, "Konfessionslos."

[48] Historian George Berkley defines these groups as Integrationists, Zionists, and Orthodox. According to his research there were five times as many Integrationists as Zionists, and the amount of Orthodox Jews was even smaller than the Zionists. See George E. Berkley, *Vienna and Its Jews: The Tragedy of Success: 1880s-1980s* (Cambridge: Abt Books, 1988), 119-125.

[49] Yehuda Bauer, *A History of the Holocaust: Revised Edition* (Danbury, Ct: Franklin Watts, 2001), 35-60.

Table 2: "Jewish Distribution in Vienna's City Districts"

DISTRICTS		Number of Jews 1934	1939
1.	INNERE STADT	9,621	4,241
2.	LEOPOLDSTADT	50,922	27,223
3.	LANDSTRASSE	12,947	3,347
4.	WIEDEN	5,126	1,045
5.	MARGARETEN	3,837	949
6.	MARIAHILF	7,520	2,430
7.	NEUBAU	8,679	2,741
8.	JOSEFSTADT	5,841	1,728
9.	ALSERGRUND	19,421	8,500
10.	FAVORITEN	3,642	796
11.	SIMMERING	515	166
12.	MEIDLING	2,489	586
13.	HIETZING	5,564	643
14.	RUDOLFSHEIM	3,000	620
15.	FÜNFHAUS	2,575	1,440
16.	OTTAKRING	4,112	1,215
17.	HERNALS	3,020	588
18.	WÄHRING	5,031	1,063
19.	DÖBLING	5,282	1,140
20.	BRIGITTENAU	15,014	4,364
21.	FLORIDSDORF	1,875	154
22.	GROSS-ENZERSDORF	253	5
23.	SCHWECHAT	152	239
24.	MÖDLING	489	37
25.	LIESING	649	74
26.	KLOSERTNEUBURG	292	73

Source: USHMM microfilm # 294, CAHJP- A/W 126:
Report of the Vienna Jewish Community, May 2nd 1938- December 31st 1939

Austria's emancipated Jews, on the other hand, saw Ostjuden as poor, primitive, and culturally isolated and backward. They believed that eastern European Jews came from, as historian Bryan Mark Rigg has put it, "anachronistic ghettos and only learned 'Polish Talmudic barbarism' in comparison to refined German *Bildung* (education)."[50] They worked to become a part of Austrian society and dispersed themselves throughout the city districts -- among Jews and non-Jews-- while the Ostjuden kept to themselves. As integrationist Jews pushed for equal

---

[50] Bryan Mark Rigg, *Hitler's Jewish Soldiers: The Untold Story of Nazi Racial Laws and Men of Jewish Descent in the German Military* (Kansas: University Press of Kansas, 2002).

rights, following in the footsteps of Moses Mendelsohn, Martin Buber, and Franz Rosenzweig, they tried to escape negative associations with the past.[51] The Ostjuden posed a direct challenge to this aim. The Ostjuden were the one faction of the community that failed to integrate into Austrian society and therefore, in the eyes of the assimilationist Jews, threatened the future of Viennese Jewry. Thus, each religious branch, as well as each individual Jew, had an idea of how to live, and how to prepare (or not prepare) for the oncoming Nazi threat. This "civil war"[52] (as Pauley has called it) within the Jewish community resulted as an organic product of modern times, but in the face of a Nazi attack, it made the Jews weak and vulnerable. National Socialist ideology did not consider Jews' different backgrounds or individual beliefs, nor did it distinguish between Ostjuden and Jeckes, rich and poor, young and old, or sick and healthy. Nazism defined all Jews as in racial terms belonging to a biological entity: *Der Jude*.

As historian Harriet Pass Friedenreich has argued, factionalism hurt the Viennese Jews, but also represented their vitality.[53] One trait they all shared -- despite their differences -- was a love and appreciation for the livelihoods they established and the progress they made in the growing cosmopolitan metropolis of Vienna. As individuals and as a community, they luxuriated in the opportunity to plant roots in a place where they were granted equal rights and allowed to live freely. In return, they flourished not only within their community, but enriched almost all spheres of Austrian society, contributing to the success of the capital. Although they comprised only a small minority of the total population (10%), their continued achievements in Vienna shone bright.

---

[51] Paul Mendes-Flohr, *German Jews: A Dual Identity* (New Haven: Yale University Press, 1999).

[52] Pauley, *From Prejudice to Persecution: A History of Austrian Anti-Semitism*, 326.

[53] See Harriet Pass Friedenreich, *Jewish Politics in Vienna, 1918-1938* (Bloomington, Indiana University Press, 1991).

Table 3: "Percentage of Jews in Trade and Professions, 1930s"

Percentage of Jews in Vienna's Trade and Professions, 1930s

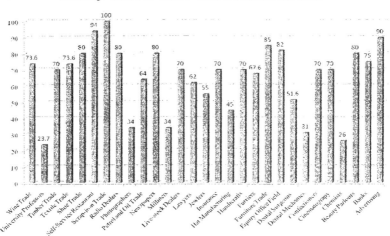

Source: Statistics are based on
Herbert Rozenkranz, "The Anschluss and the Tragedy of Austrian Jewry 1938-1945," in Josef Frankel ed.,
The Jews of Austria: Essays on their Life, History and Destruction (London: Valentine Mitchell,1967) 480.

By the 1930s, Jews owned some 33,000 of Vienna's 146,000 businesses. They participated in the social, political, and cultural activities of the city, and held an unusually high proportion of positions in the trades and professions, making up 51.6% of the dentists and physicians, 23.7% of university professors (45% of the medical faculty), and 62% of the lawyers. These types of successes encouraged Austrian Jews to see themselves as citizens like all others. Despite their diverse backgrounds, the majority considered themselves, as one survivor explained "Viennese first and Jewish second. One had nothing to do with the other."[54]

---

[54] Helen, H., 1995. "Interview by Survivors of the Shoah Visual History Foundation," Newbury Park, CA, USA, February 21. Interview Code 00903, Tapes 1-2. See Chart, "Percentage of Jews in Trade and Professions."

Jews continually reflected upon their achievements (past and present), assuring themselves they served as an asset to Austrian society and their government and countrymen would protect them if needed. They failed to recognize that the larger gentile population regarded them with fear and envy. They were correct that they were an asset, but the conclusion they drew -- protection if needed -- was erroneous. This misjudgment became particularly dangerous as the Nazis took over Germany in 1933 and permeated the Austrian underground. Jews did not feel as safe and secure as they had in the days of the monarchy, but they still believed that the Austrian government would uphold its end of the social contract and guarantee their basic civil rights. This mistake became their principal weakness in the face of Nazism. They did not accept that the perceived social contract collapsed overnight (11-12 March 1938), and they did not know any way to respond to government authority other than as law-abiding citizens. "What most Austrian Jews forgot was that they had survived popular outburst of anti-Semitism because they had enjoyed the protection of emperors, bishops, abbots, and aristocrats," Bruce Pauley has observed. "Under Hitler, however, legal authority changed from being the protector of the Jews to their persecutor."[55]   The Jews could not survive the brutality of Nazism by reacting and responding as civilized, law-abiding citizens, yet they knew no other way to engage with the government.

Exposed and vulnerable to the Nazis' every whim, and without protection from the state, the Jews needed to defend themselves. But instead of focusing their efforts on self-defense or resistance, most Jews responded to the new Nazi government as they would to any legitimate government: as civilized and obedient citizens. They tried to rationalize even the most irrational demands and to uphold their end of the social contract, even after its abandonment. This firm belief that the Austrian government would protect them crippled the Jewish community from the

---

[55] Pauley, *From Prejudice to Persecution: A History of Austrian Anti-Semitism*, 326-327.

outset of Anschluss. Karl Grunwald, a ten-year-old Jewish boy living in Vienna, witnessed the shock and intimidation Jews experienced with the Nazi takeover. He had learned about the persecution of Jews under the Czar and during pogroms but, like the majority of Austria's Jews, he felt sure that those barbaric times had passed. In the enlightened world of 1938, "Nobody ever dreamt that such a thing would happen—it was unthinkable," he reflected some fifty years later. "The more it happened, the deeper the shock… and in a way it is understandable that there was no resistance because nobody thought that something like this could ever happen. Even if you told them at the beginning -- nobody would have believed it."[56]

Many Jews did not believe Nazism would prevail because they were in denial; they did not *want* to accept this as reality, Grunwald explained. Other survivors of all ages and backgrounds concurred. "The atmosphere in Vienna was gray leading up to the Anschluss," Alois Gottfried recalled, thirty-one years old at the time. "We knew Hitler wanted Austria, it was on the menu a long time before, but -- the young people didn't pay attention, just like we didn't pay attention during World War I. We just went on with our lives. People realized there was a real cloud over the whole country … but we didn't believe it. Intellectually you knew it was wrong, but since you thought you belonged to this country, this is your home — you couldn't realize it."[57] Twenty-four-year-old Raoul Klugmann noted: "We expected it, but you always hoped… You don't like to divorce everything and just leave."[58] Trude Adler, then eighteen years old, also agreed. "I think we all lived in Never-Never Land," she recalled some sixty years later."My mother going to the coffee house in the afternoon… and I had lots of dates … we were aware of Hitler but we did not consider him as a personal threat. [We were in] complete denial --

[56] Karl, G., 1997. "Interview by Survivors of the Shoah Visual History Foundation," New York, NY, USA, March 16. Interview Code 27992, Tapes 1-8.
[57] Alois, G., 1996. "Interview by Survivors of the Shoah Visual History Foundation," Los Angeles, CA, USA, February 23. Interview Code 12444, Tapes 1-2.
[58] Raoul, K.,1996. "Interview by Survivors of the Shoah Visual History Foundation," Great Neck, NY, USA, April 23. Interview Code 14413, Tapes 1-3.

this was our country! You were just as much of an Austrian ... as everybody else."[59]   These

survivors' recollections represent the majority. Eager to preserve the lives they worked so hard

to achieve, they believed they could persevere no matter how terrible the threat. They had

inherited a history of enduring antisemitic attacks, and this history of persecution encouraged

them to think: "This too shall pass." Not realizing -- how could they? -- that they lived in a pre-

genocidal stage of a catastrophe, they could not bring themselves to act upon a possible danger

that lay ahead-- they waited for it to strike.   They were caught in the grip of hope, denial, and

personal history.

As ordinary human beings going about their daily lives, it would have been unnatural and

unprecedented for the Jews of Vienna (either as a community or as individuals) to uproot their

homes and families prior to Anschluss. They were involved in the activities of their day-to-day

lives -- consumed by family affairs and personal relationships; careers or financial transactions;

academic training or physical activity   and they were thinking in the present, not about the

future. Alois Gottfried's younger brother Walter, one of the few Austrian Jews to leave Vienna

before the Nazi occupation, was very fortunate. He fled to Palestine at the age of twenty-nine,

after he was graduated from his studies in medicine at the University of Vienna. He wrote to his

brother in early 1938 and begged him to get out of the Austria. But Alois was hesitant. "I realize

that the situation is tough and it could happen any moment, but, what shall I do? Go to

Switzerland and if it doesn't happen I am a jackass there, who ran away from nothing? Who will

support me? I will have to stay calm and cross those bridges as I go there." Alois, like George

Czuzcka, Erika Spitzer, and so many others, saw the public signs that Anschluss was drawing

near and received personal warnings to leave Austria. He considered the threat of Nazism but

---

[59] Trude, A., 1996. "Interview by Survivors of the Shoah Visual History Foundation," West Los Angeles, CA, USA, January 10. Interview Code 10786, Tapes 1-3.

could not move himself to leave the country in which he was born until it became a matter of life or death. Sixty years later, he reflected sadly upon his decision to stay calm. "We waited and waited... and it did happen... and our world broke down." [60]

"Anschluss"--The Storm Hits: 11 March 1938

> *Friday, March 11 brought forth a terrific series of incidents and decisions which took place with lightening-like speed, which sealed the fate of independent Austria and transformed this country in less than twenty-four hours from a menaced, but relatively free country to one controlled and completely dominated and directed by Germany and the National Socialists.*

> ~Major G.S.C. Lowell M. Riley, military attaché to the United States,
> Secret Report to the Department of State, 12 March 1938

> *There is something about the thought of German troops actually moving across German borders for the first time since 1918, and especially into a country whose people are so well loved around the world as those of Austria, that causes observers to shudder.*

> ~ "The Seizure of Austria: Hitler's Worst Blunder,"
> *New Republic*, 23 March 1938: 181.

Germany and Austria declared official Anschluss Law to the outside world on Sunday, 13 March 1938, but nazification of Austria did not wait until then. On "Black Friday," 11 March 1938, Chancellor Schuschnigg capitulated to Nazi Germany. [61]   Foreign newspapers reported the underground Austrian Nazi party and its avid supporters as "provoking disorders" that day. Awakened and empowered by the anticipation of Anschluss, crowds of Nazi-sympathizers on the streets of Vienna and other smaller Austrian cities chanted, "Rather dead than red-white-red!" In Vienna, they infiltrated the side streets of the first district, including the famous Kaertnerstrasse, "howling their slogans, jeering Chancellor Schuschnigg, demanding his resignation and

---

[60] Alois, G., 1996. "Interview by Survivors of the Shoah Visual History Foundation," Los Angeles, CA, USA, February 23. Interview Code 12444, Tapes 1-2.
[61] "Special *Cable to the New York Times from London*," *New York Times*, 13 March 1938: 34.

whistling at the police ... the inhabitants of the inner city never had five minutes from noon to midnight without such howling choruses." [62]

At five o'clock in the evening, the radio broadcast the chancellor's resignation. "And so I take leave of the Austrian people with a German word of farewell uttered from the depths of my heart: God Protect Austria."[63] George Czuczka, who listened to the speech with his family, remembered that moments later "a Nazi came to the microphone, spoke for a few minutes, and said that as of tomorrow, Austria would be a part of Greater Germany."[64] But the transition took effect immediately. The *New York Times* reported that after the speech, "as though nothing had happened, the radio brought to Austria Beethoven's First Symphony. Nazis thereupon rushed into the streets shouting 'Sieg Heil!' [Hail victory!]."[65] With his resignation, Schuschnigg cleared the path for the totalitarian regime. [66]

Major G.S.C. Lowell M. Riley, military attaché to the United States, witnessed the harrowing events of 11 March 1938 as neither victim nor perpetrator, but through the semi neutral eyes of a foreigner. He sent a classified report on "Political Issues and Problems: Latest Development in Austria," to the State Department in Washington, D.C. the next morning. He described the outright lawlessness that erupted, confirming that the first twenty-four hours of Austro-German Anschluss revealed a "crisis."

Schuschnigg had resigned [...] From this time on, a great rush of Nazi demonstration and display began which lasted throughout the entire night of the

[62] G.E.R. Geyde, "Nazis Provoke Disorders," *New York Times*, 11 March 1938.

[63] "Review of the Week," *New York Times*, 13 March 1938; NARA, US-State Dept. Records, RG 59/M1209/Reel 7, 863.00/1674, Report # V-4527, "Political Issues and Problems. Latest Developments in Austria," Vienna, 12 March 1938, Lowell M. Riley, US-military attaché.

[64] George Czuzcka, private interview with author, May 2007. Washington, D.C.

[65] *New York Times*, "Review of the Week," 13 March 1938.

[66] His successor was the Austrian Nazi, Seyss-Inquart who had been working on the inside of the Austrian government since Schuschnigg appointed him State councilor following the 1936 July Agreement. For more contemporary reports on Seyss Inquart, see *New York Times*, 12 March 1938.

11th-12th. Great crowds, giving and demanding the Nazi salute and shouting "Heil Hitler!" assembled in various parts of Vienna. Swastika armbands were put on by the people including even a number of the police, the Nazi flag flown and displayed, and this was done on government buildings as well. Platoons and companies of young National Socialists began forming everywhere in the streets, marching to designated posts, controlling traffic and generally taking over the control of the town.[67]

The *New York Times* confirmed this radical transformation of power. Saturday's headlines read: "Nazis Seize Austria After Hitler Ultimatum," and Gedye's commentary stated, "The Nazis, with Dr. Arthur Seyss-Inquart, Interior Minister in the Schuschnigg Cabinet, as Chancellor, are in power." The intensity of Anschluss and the lightning-like speed with which it occurred, struck the Jews exceptionally hard. For years they witnessed the warning signs, but had always suppressed the dark possibility of a Nazi takeover. Suddenly a nightmare arrived and proved worse than they ever imagined.

Austria's Response and its Effect on the Jews

I made a close study of the crowd. It was composed of all classes. For one, workers and bourgeois stood side by side with undivided enthusiasm. My predominant impression was of young faces and rather shabby clothes. This was no host of reactionaries assembled to greet a reactionary triumph. Whatever their motive, it was the people of Vienna who lined the streets.
~R.H. Bruce Lockhart, eyewitness, Vienna: 15 March 1938[68]

The jubilant response of the Austrian population, and the participation of the government and police forces, left Austria's two hundred thousand-strong Jewish population facing uncertain and unprecedented circumstances on the evening of 11 March. Major G.S. Truman Smith, a

---

[67] NARA, US-State Dept. Records, RG 59/M1209/Reel 7, 863.00/1674, Report # V-4527, "Political Issues and Problems. Latest Developments in Austria," Vienna, 12 March 1938, Lowell M. Riley, US-military attaché.
[68] R.H. Bruce Lockhart, *Guns or Butter. War Countries and Peace Countries of Europe Revisited* (London: Putnam, 1938), 251.

second military attaché to the United States, confirmed that a large portion of the population openly supported the Nazi German takeover and that they had long anticipated its arrival. He reported to the State Department on Monday, 14 March: "the entire lack of resistance within Austria to the National Socialist Party and to the German Army, indicates the extent to which secret Nazi penetration within Austria has proceeded within the past few years."[69] Mass celebrations and demonstrations occurred throughout the streets of Vienna, revealing that Anschluss had not come simply as a result of Hitler's ultimatum and the Chancellor's resignation, but as the will of the nation. Immediately, people changed the pins on their lapels from the red/white national sign of Austria to the Nazi German swastika and tied swastika armbands onto their clothing, hung swastika flags from their homes, and replaced all patriotic Austrian symbols with Nazi insignia.

As the Jews watched friends and neighbors, colleagues and classmates, patients and business partners, teachers and caretakers rejoice in the news of Anschluss, they felt shocked, frightened, and devastated. Suddenly, they were isolated and appeared as outsiders in their own country. Nazis and ordinary Austrian citizens could identify them on the streets or in a crowd, not because they may have "looked Jewish," but because they failed to support the Nazi cause.[70] On the Saturday after Anschluss, Kurt Klein Bernard, a seven-year-old Jewish boy, walked with his father to the Prater and the atmosphere frightened him. "There were Hitler Youth on every corner and they collected money for the war effort and gave people lapels to wear after donating. It was dangerous therefore … to go in these areas because people could see that you hadn't

---

[69] NARA, US-State Dept. Records: RG 59/M1209/Reel 7: 863.00/1672. Report No. 15 -798, 14 March 1938. In this report he also recapped Major Riley's top points and described the political-military events that transpired over the weekend: the exact number of troops engaged in the occupation, what divisions were deployed and where they were from, and the bleak future of the Austrian army.

[70] This conclusion is drawn from the testimonies of Jewish survivors who recorded their testimonies at the SOSVHF. Most of the survivors mention in their testimonies about whether they looked Jewish or did not look Jewish, comparing themselves to the stereotypical representations of Jews which the Nazis determined and publicized.

contributed. [We were] the only ones who hadn't contributed."[71] Overnight, normal daily activities -- like taking a walk in the park -- became dangerous outings. The Austrians proved to support the German invasion and some had prepared for it long in advance. By doing so, they increased the Jews' vulnerability to Nazi violence. The Jews never anticipated such a response from the Austrian population, and they felt betrayed. For Freddy Schreiber and his family, "the real fear invaded ... after they saw the thousands of people cheering for Hitler."[72] The response of the Austrian public had prompted a turning point in their lives: they began to consider escape. They also wondered painfully why they had waited so long.

Austria's new political situation continued to darken the future for the Jews as police and civil authorities refused to aid them. All official laws protecting Austria's Jewish minority turned null and void instantly. Jews could no longer expect protection from anywhere; they were completely defenseless. Joseph Brod described his community as "free booty," [73] explaining that if a Nazi sympathizer harassed, beat, or robbed a Jewish person on the street, the victim could no longer turn to the police for help, as s/he would normally do. George Clare was one of these Jewish victims. He was in danger and tried to get help from a police officer he knew for many years, but the constable showed him no mercy. George was only a young teenage boy at the time but, as he walked home frightened that day, his life changed. He had witnessed the collapse of the social contract: "yesterday's protector ... transformed into tomorrow's persecutor

---

[71] Curt, K.B., 1994. "Interview by Survivors of the Shoah Visual History Foundation," Los Angeles, CA, USA, December 15. Interview Code 00382, Tapes 1-6.
[72] Fred, S., 1994. "Interview by Survivors of the Shoah Visual History Foundation," Los Angeles, CA, USA, December 15. Interview Code 00383, Tapes 1-5.
[73] Joseph, B., 1996. "Interview by Survivors of the Shoah Visual History Foundation," Encinitas, CA, USA, March 15. Interview Code 13315, Tapes 1-4.

and tormentor."[74] Support for Nazism had pervaded the entire atmosphere, beginning with the public and extending to the police force.

Source: *New York Times*, 13 March 1938: 37

A reporter for the *New York Times* photographed this radical transformation of power on Saturday 12 March and the newspaper published it the next day. The caption read, "Austrian Nazis celebrate Hitler's coup: An enthusiastic crowd in Vienna carrying a policeman who has donned the Nazi emblem."[75] The *Times* also reported that in Washington DC, "The German swastika was raised over the Austrian Legation at 2343 Massachusetts Avenue … in celebration

---

[74] See George Clare, *Last Waltz in Vienna: The Rise and Destruction of a Family: 1842-1942* (New York: Holt Rinehart and Winston, 1982), 178.
[75] *New York Times*, 13 March 1938: 37.

of the coup executed by Chancellor Adolf Hitler."[76] Germany violated the Versailles treaty openly, nevertheless around the world its unification with Austria was recognized and accepted. Mexico was the only country in the League of Nations to oppose the union.

Vienna's Jews Experience the Takeover

The Jews' reaction to the Anschluss varied from person to person, depending on age; gender; residence; political, religious, and economic background; and location at the time, but everyone except some children was afraid. Trepidation set in shortly after Chancellor Schuschnigg's farewell. "That night and the next everyone huddled around their radios,"[77] survivor Helen Herz recalled. Religious Jews gathered with family and prepared for the Sabbath, while non-observant Jews went about their typical Friday night activities. At home, at work, away on business, [78] or on vacation, Vienna's Jews heard the chancellor's speech and experienced a turning point in their lives. Martha Donath, a twenty-seven-year-old married woman from an assimilated, middle class, non-observant Jewish family, was in Vienna with her husband on the evening of the Anschluss. They had never spoken of leaving Austria, but all of that changed overnight because "the Anschluss was the end of our settled life."[79]

Old and young, rich and poor, religious and non-observant, after hearing the news of Anschluss,"[Jews] tried to keep a low profile and out of the way," survivor Kurt Klein noted.[80] Those out of town cut their trips short and returned to Vienna to make preparations for the future.

---

[76] "Minister to US Raises a Swastika," *New York Times*, 13 March 1938: 33.
[77] Helen, H., 1995. "Interview by Survivors of the Shoah Visual History Foundation," Newbury Park, CA, USA, February 21. Interview Code 00903, Tapes 1-2.
[78] Frank, D., 1995. "Interview by Survivors of the Shoah Visual History Foundation," Los Angeles, CA, USA, April 27. Interview Code 02123, Tapes 1-4.
[79] Martha, D., 1997. "Interview by Survivors of the Shoah Visual History Foundation," Hawthorn, CA, USA, August 6. Interview Code 34975, Tapes 1-4.
[80] Curt, K.B., 1994. "Interview by Survivors of the Shoah Visual History Foundation," Los Angeles, CA, USA, December 15. Interview Code 00382, Tapes 1-6.

Children on school trips went home early.[81]   People cancelled all plans because they didn't know what would happen from one moment to the next.[82]   While the Nazis demonstrated in the streets with crowds of Austrian civilian and police supporters at their sides, Jews no longer felt safe in their homes or on the streets. Joseph Brod was among those who "drew into a shell"[83]and stayed inside their homes, but others were afraid to endanger their families and refused to go home. Charles Stein, a twenty-two-year-old medical student at the University of Vienna, knew the Gestapo would come looking for him, so he avoided his home that Friday and for many nights thereafter. He found safety on the streets -- alone, out of sight, and on the run --[84] but it was only temporary. Life as he knew it had come to an abrupt end.

Children's Experiences

Jewish children experienced the Nazi takeover differently from the rest of their community. Some were frightened, while youth and naïveté sheltered others. Anschluss changed their lives permanently but, unlike their parents, children only understood this to varying degrees. Some children witnessed the convoy of military might enter Vienna from a closer perspective than most adults but were not frightened by it; they were simply awed. Ignorant of the Nazis' ambitions, they were swept away by the general jubilation. "It all seemed very exciting to me at the time, and I have often looked back at that day and my enjoyment of it

---

[81] Trude Kutner was a sixteen-year-old girl from a middle class family of assimilated, non-practicing Jews. At the time of the Anschluss, she was in dressmaking academy and they were away on a school trip, skiing in Mariazell. This was where she heard the news on the radio. Her class planned to return to Vienna on Saturday, but the trip was called off early and they all went home that night. Before she got home she watched her teacher sow a swastika on the Austrian flag. See Trude K., 1995. "Interview by Survivors of the Shoah Visual History Foundation," Denver, CO, USA (day/month currently unavailable). Interview Code 06321, Tape 1.

[82] Joseph, B., 1996. "Interview by Survivors of the Shoah Visual History Foundation," Encinitas, CA, USA, March 15. Interview Code 13315, Tapes 1-4.

[83] Joseph, B., 1996. "Interview by Survivors of the Shoah Visual History Foundation," Encinitas, CA, USA, March 15. Interview Code 13315, Tapes 1-4.

[84] Charles Stein, private interview conducted by Ilana Offenberger, USHMM, Washington, D.C., May 2005.

as an exercise in irony," George Wellwarth recalled, six years old at the time. George lived in the ninth district, very close to the city center where the vast majority of Nazi-demonstrations took place. His gentile nanny took him outside to view the crowd and the image remained ever-present. "The event that remains so vivid was, of course, the euphemistically named Anschluss. Naturally I had no idea what it meant at the time and was thrilled by the seemingly endless pageantry of the marchers strutting uniformly as if the little lead soldiers in my toy box at home had come to life ...and the endless hysterical cheering as if the whole world as I knew it had become populated exclusively with people who had their mouths stuck open in a rectus of ecstasy and their right arms paralyzed at a 45-degree angle."[85] Alix Grabkowicz, a fourteen-year-old girl, also living near the city center, had a similar experience when she walked home from swim practice on Tuesday, 15 March 1938, the day Hitler delivered his infamous speech to a wildly cheering crowd of over 200,000 people gathered on the historic Heldenplatz. "I was walking through Rotenturmstrasse -- Kaertnerstrasse, to Wiednerhauptstrsse -- when I had to push my way through masses of people in the streets screaming 'Heil Hitler.'"

> The atmosphere was catching and something I had never experienced. There were thousands of people screaming and preparing for Hitler's arrival. I felt like screaming too because it was just a general outcry—it was unbelievable! ... People were just screaming their heads off! When I finally got home, I told my father about it and that's the very first time I was told about the situation and how things were bad for Jews.[86]

---

[85] George E. Wellwarth, *Leben mit oesterreichischer Literatur: Begegnung mit aus Oesterreich stammenden amerikanishen Germanisten 1938/1988: Elf Erinnerungen,* (Wien: Dokumentationsstelle fuer neue oesterreichische Literatur,1990), 43-52. Note: this text was originally composed in English and translated to German by GabriellePisarz for this collection in 1990. The quote above is taken from the original English text, part of a personal collection made available to the author by George Wellwarth. George Wellwarth was professor of Theater and Comparative Literature at the State University of New York at Binghamton and was the author of numerous works including: *The Theater of Protest and Paradox* (1964), *Spanish Underground Drama* (1972), and *Modern Drama and the Death of God* (1986).
[86] Letter from Alix G. Kowler to the author, 1 August 2003. See also, Alix , K., 1997. "Interview by Survivors of the Shoah Visual History Foundation," Lenox, MA, USA, October 16. Interview Code 34544, Tapes 1-5.

George's and Alix's experiences demonstrate how childhood naïveté protected some youngsters during the Anschluss. Other children were not naïve to the implications of Anschluss at all -- they understood the danger as their parents did, and felt fear. Twelve-year-old Siegfried Buchwalter, like George and Alix, also lived near enough to the city center to witness the Nazi takeover, but he was not impressed by the events, only frightened. As he walked with his father to synagogue on Saturday morning, 12 March, he saw a sea of swastika flags and thought to himself, *"Eine neue Zeit hat angefangen* (a new time has begun). The message of this time was: 'You people will leave, you will go to Palestine—we don't have a place here for you anymore.'"[87] Lisbeth Steiner, a thirteen year old, lived with her family in a nice apartment on the outskirts of Vienna. She too, was frightened. She watched the Germans march into the city from her window and her first thought was: "We have to get out of here... we have to leave." When she addressed her father, he put his arm around her and said, "'Well, we can't just pick up and go like that....'" Her father, a manufacturer of awnings and windows, had already been thrown out of his job by his non-Jewish partner months prior to the Nazi takeover, but still was not convinced it was time to leave Austria.[88]

While some children remember listening to the chancellor's speech, watching the crowds outside their windows, or being caught in Nazi demonstrations, others missed these impressive moments altogether. For six-and-a-half-year-old Gabriele Mintz, her first memory of Anschluss was waking up on Saturday morning to the surprise of seeing suitcases packed and hearing her mother say: "We are no longer Austrians. Hitler has taken Austria."[89] Gabriele cried when she realized this meant she had to leave her home. Her next memory of Anschluss was the delicious

[87] Siegfried, B., 1996. "Interview by Survivors of the Shoah Visual History Foundation," Baltimore, MD, USA, October 18. Interview Code 21190, Tapes 1-7.

[88] Lisbeth, M., 1995. "Interview by Survivors of the Shoah Visual History Foundation," Tenafly, NJ, USA, December 6. Interview Code 09668, Tapes 1-4.

[89] Marjorie Perloff, *The Vienna Paradox: A Memoir* (New York: New Directions Publishing Co., 2004), 34.

ham sandwiches she ate while waiting in the train station to cross the border.[90] Years later Gabriele reflected upon her mother's ability to make "what must have been a nightmare ... so relatively benign."[91]

Anschluss affected all children differently, depending upon what each was exposed to, but all Jewish children living in Vienna at the time witnessed the nightmare their parents had dreaded for so long. If they didn't understand then how Anschluss would change their lives permanently, they would in time.

Conclusions

Life changed for all Austrian Jews on Friday evening (11 March 1938) and, regardless of how divided they had been and how different they were from each other, they all faced the same catastrophe. They had held on to a false sense of security for years. Suddenly, it came to an end. They had to reconsider the future seriously, and there was no time to waste. Under extreme duress, in this new atmosphere of fear, anxiety, and confusion, they needed to make life-altering decisions. The largest looming question was how and where to find long-term safety? Would the Nazi threat blow over? Could they remain calm? Should they stay put? Or, was it time to give up hope of a future in Austria? Was it time to pick up everything and leave?

A minority understood the need to flee immediately. Ilse Schueller Mintz, a thirty-year-old woman with two young children, was one of these few. She packed her bags after hearing the chancellor's resignation speech. "When on Friday afternoon we heard the terrible news, our first thought was: 'away!'" she wrote in a letter to her sister a few days after Anschluss. "I packed

---

[90] Ibid.
[91] Perloff, *The Vienna Paradox: A Memoir*, 37.

half the night, then lay awake in bed for a few miserable hours."[92] Ilse managed to leave Vienna that first weekend of the Anschluss. Her two children and she, with a few members of their extended family, boarded a train bound for Switzerland on Sunday, 13 March at ten o'clock at night. At the train station she said a quick goodbye to those family members who could not come too. She never saw them again. Ilse was from an assimilated, upper-middle class family, and she left everything behind except for a few suitcases. Somehow, she understood that it was time to leave, no matter what the sacrifice -- she had waited long enough.

Ilse experienced the nightmare that all of Austria's Jews dreaded: uprooting their lives and starting over. Fortunately, she faced this dilemma and made the decision to leave everything and run. Fortuitous circumstance further enabled her family and her to get out of Austria intact -- preserving some possessions and some positive memories. For the majority of Austria's Jews, this was not the case. Some, like Helen Herz, planned to leave -- if and when the Germans invaded -- but encountered unexpected difficulties after the takeover that left them unprepared to do so. Others did not consider flight an option, either before or after Anschluss, for a variety of reasons unique to each individual, and for reasons many shared. A persistent belief in the basic social contract between the state and its citizens coupled with a sense of themselves as citizens in good standing weighed heavily in this decision. Men like Hugo Spitzer and Joseph Grabkowicz had an opportunity to leave, but self-delusion and hope -- the sense of security that lingered from the days of Franz Joseph -- encouraged them to wait for the storm to blow over.

---

[92] Perloff, *The Vienna Paradox: A Memoir*, 35.

Chapter Two

The Anschluss Pogrom: Panic, Chaos, and Confusion for Vienna's Jews in March 1938

It is not your fault that you cannot believe me, because it is impossible for you to conceive of the diseased and degenerate mentality which lies behind the pathological antisemitism of the Nazis.... [I]t is impossible for you to imagine what it means for one-sixth[1] of the population of Vienna to be made pariahs over-night, deprived of all civil rights...
~G.E.R. Geyde, NYT Central European Correspondent, Vienna, March 1938[2]

It appears in short that while the Germans have stopped short of an actual bloody pogrom, the Jews have left to them only the liberty to starve at leisure.
~ John C. Wiley, American Consul General, Vienna, April 1938[3]

Illustration 4: "Initial Humiliations: Jews forced to Scrub the Streets"

Sources: Paul Hoffmann, *The Viennese: Splendor, Twilight and Exile*
(New York: Anchor Books, Doubleday, 1988); Original source: UPI/ Bettmann Newsphotos.

---

[1] This figure is incorrect. The Jews comprised approximately one-tenth of the population of Vienna in 1938.
[2] See G.E.R. Gedye, *Fallen Bastions: The Central European Tragedy*. (London: Victor Gollancz Ltd, 1939): 304.
[3] See NARA, US-State Dept. Records, RG 59/M1209/Reel 7: 863.4016/174, Dispatch No.202, "Situation of Jews in Austria," Vienna, 15 April 1938: 12.

Introduction, The Sexualization of Violence

Vienna's Jews did not consider the decision to leave Austria lightly, no matter how intense the German threat became. They had terrible difficulty parting from the place they loved and considered home -- many never recovered from this forced separation. At age eighty-six, the Viennese émigré Harry Gruenberg reflected upon his youth and famous lyrics came to his mind: "*Wien, Wien, nur Du allein wirst stets die Stadt meiner Träume sein* (Vienna, Vienna, only you will always be the city of my dreams)." In his memoirs, he went on to describe how this popular song from the 1930s matched his spirit when he was young and handsome. "In spite of the hardships my family experienced and the times when there was not enough money for food," he wrote, "I feel I had a very happy childhood. And most of all -- I was in love with Vienna!"[4] Harry, like many of Vienna's Jews, remained nostalgic about Vienna throughout his entire lifetime -- even after the inhumanity the Nazis forced him to witness and endure.[5] It had been his home.

Harry Gruenberg was born in Vienna on 5 February 1921, to Leib (Leo) and Elcia (Elka) Gruenberg, both originally from Kolomea, a small town or *shtetl* in Galicia. Elka came to Vienna before World War I and Leo after; they had an informal Jewish wedding in Vienna in 1920 and were only moderately religious. Leo had volunteered for the German army, was wounded on the Russian front in 1915 and taken prisoner. After the war, he found it difficult to get work in Vienna and was for the most part unemployed. Elka, like many women, took care of the household, but did not have an income. Thus, the Gruenbergs belonged to the lowest

---

[4] Harry Gruenberg Archival Collection, Harry Gruenberg, Chapter 1: Early Childhood Years (unpublished memoirs: 2000), 9-10. Gruenberg Family Archive, Weston, Massachusetts.
[5] See Leo Spitzer, *Hotel Bolivia: The Culture of Memory in a Refuge from Nazism.* (New York: Hill and Wang, 1998) 143.

economic bracket and struggled to get along.[6] Nevertheless, they wanted to have children, and thanks to the financial support of family members, they managed to do so. They rented a two-bedroom flat in a large apartment house in the ninth district (Alserstrasse 12) and there they raised their family.

Illustration 6: "Elka, Harry, Mia, Leo, & Uri Gruenberg - Last Family Portrait, c.1938"

Source: Harry Gruenberg Archival Collection, courtesy of Dr. Lisa Gruenberg

Harry had two younger siblings, Uri (b. 1923) and Mia (b. 1926), and for a while his paternal grandmother lived with the family as well. He also had a large extended family in Vienna and visited frequently with many aunts, uncles, and cousins, and every week with his maternal grandmother, Sabine Helwing. Sabine lived in a nice sized apartment in the second district, overlooking the Donau Canal and there the family gathered together regularly. Harry enjoyed his close-knit family for the first seventeen years of his life and recalled, "My social life revolved

[6] For more information on Leo and Elka Gruenberg, see Harry Gruenberg Archival Collection, Harry Gruenberg, [MRIN 5] Notes for Leo and Elka Gruenberg-15, 19 August 1995: 1. Gruenberg Family Archive, Weston, Massachusetts.

mostly around the family."[7] In his memoir he wrote longingly of the time when his family lived together in free Austria: "My parents took us to many of the charming parks in Vienna ... on hikes into the Vienna Woods... to the palace, the gardens and the zoo of Schönbrunn... to the Prater amusement park in the second district not far from grandmother's place... to the swimming areas on the Alte Donau."[8]

When the Germans took over Austria in March 1938, Harry witnessed the sudden disintegration of the home he loved. From the window of the fourth floor apartment on Alserstrasse, he watched the German military move in -- the tanks lined the streets bumper to bumper outside his front door.[9] He heard the German airforce flying overhead, "just skimming the roof tops," and thought it was "a frightening sight!"[10] Although it may have been only a few planes, to Harry and other ordinary civilians it looked and sounded like hundreds.[11] Fear and confusion kept Harry inside the house throughout the weekend. On Monday, he did not go to school as usual because the state closed all schools in honor of Hitler's arrival and in celebration of Austria's union with Germany.[12] After a few more days, he felt that he needed to go outside to see what had transpired, so he went to the second district to check on his grandmother Sabine

---

[7] See Harry Gruenberg Archival Collection, Harry Gruenberg, [MRIN 1] Notes on Harry Gruenberg (unpublished notes), 12 June 1994: 2. Gruenberg Family Archive, Weston, Massachusetts.

[8] See Harry Gruenberg Archival Collection, Harry Gruenberg, Chapter 1: Early Childhood Years (unpublished memoirs: 2000), 10. Gruenberg Family Archive, Weston, Massachusetts.

[9] See Harry Gruenberg, *Oral Testimony recorded by Dr. Lisa Gruenberg*, 15 May 2004, Syracuse, NY, Tape 2, 1:28:00. Gruenberg Family Archive, Weston, Massachusetts.

[10] See Harry Gruenberg, *Oral Testimony recorded by Dr. Lisa Gruenberg*, 16 May 2004, Syracuse, NY, Tape 3, 5:45. Gruenberg Family Archive, Weston, Massachusetts.

[11] On 12 March 1938, Major Lowell M. Riley, US-military attaché reported: "As I write this report in Vienna some 20 large three-moter Junker passenger planes from Germany fly to and fro over the city. This, of course, amounts to German Reich, possibly German Army demonstration over Vienna." See NARA, US-State Dept. Records, RG 59/M1209/Reel 7, 863.00/1674, Report # V-4527, "Political Issues and Problems. Latest Developments in Austria," Vienna, 12 March 1938, Lowell M. Riley, US-military attaché: 2-3.

[12] When school reopened one week later, all Jewish students were separated from gentiles. Harry sat with the other Jewish students in the back row of the classroom, suddenly ostracized from his former classmates. When the semester came to an end a few months later, he was given a report card stamped "non-Aryan" that stated he had failed all courses and would never again be able to attend a school in the Greater German Reich. See Harry Gruenberg, *Oral Testimony recorded by Dr. Lisa Gruenberg*, 15 May 2004, Syracuse, NY, Tape 2, 1:03:21. Gruenberg Family Archive, Weston, Massachusetts.

and his aunt Josephine. On the way, he witnessed a scene of Nazi brutality unlike anything he had seen before in his life. From that moment forward, the days of his care-free youth and close-knit family life came to a startling end. Harry recalled that it was a beautiful sunny day.

> ....people were out walking and smiling. I came onto the square near our home, and a crowd had gathered around something, and they were laughing and talking.... I walked to the edge of the crowd and then pushed my way to the inside of their circle. They were watching what appeared to be a pile of rags moving in the dirt ...[I]t was a man, an orthodox Jew with a long beard and forelocks, his dark clothes covered with dust, his face bloody from a beating. The man moaned and struggled to stand up. The Jew began to beg for help. A young woman, dressed in a blue suit, moved into the center of the circle. Her wavy blond hair framed her lovely face. She grinned and winked at the crowd. She smiled down on the man with an expression of pity, and made as if to offer her hand to help him up. Turning again to the crowd, she slowly began to move her hips. She raised her skirt up over the tops of her stockings as she continued to gyrate, and then straddled the man who had slumped back to the ground. She relieved herself onto the man's upturned face.[13] The crowd applauded and whistled. ... The crowd broke into applause. She threw her head back and laughed, and the crowd roared with her. Some of the men clapped each other on the back. The Jew coughed and then lay still, staring at a small puddle of his blood mixing with her urine and seeping into the spaces between the cobblestones.[14]

Harry wanted to help the man, but felt helpless. "I saw this scene which really just disgusted me, but I couldn't do anything about it," Harry reflected decades later. [15] Confused and not knowing what to do, Harry ran as quickly as possible to his original destination. When he arrived, he

---

[13] For more on the subject of urination/defecation and dehumanization, see James Waller, *Becoming Evil: How Ordinary People Commit Genocide and Mass Killing* (USA, Oxford University Press: 2002); and James A. Tyner, *War, Violence, and Population: Making the Body Count* (New York, Guilford Press: 2009).

[14] See Dr. Lisa Gruenberg, *Searching for Mia*, (Unpublished Work for MFA, Lesley University, Graduate School of Arts and social Sciences: 2007) 124-126. Note: Dr. Gruenberg recorded this story in her father's words (Syracuse, NY: May, 2004). Harry Gruenberg recounted this memory to his wife and daughter shortly after the US news released photographs of the atrocities committed in Abu Ghraib prison. Also see Harry Gruenberg, *Oral Testimony recorded by Dr. Lisa Gruenberg*, 16 May 2004, Syracuse, NY, Tape 3, 10:42. Gruenberg Family Archive, Weston, Massachusetts.

[15] See Harry Gruenberg, *Oral Testimony recorded by Dr. Lisa Gruenberg*, 16 May 2004, Syracuse, NY, Tape 3, 12:38. Gruenberg Family Archive, Weston, Massachusetts.

carried on with the regularly scheduled activities of his day, trying to suppress the cruelty he had just witnessed. He didn't mention a word of what he had seen to his grandmother or to anyone else for many years thereafter. That scene, however, left a lasting impression and marked a significant turning point in his life. In March 1938, Harry -- like many of Vienna's Jews -- witnessed a spectacle of unrecognizable human behavior and the collapse of the social contract between the community in which he lived and the Jews, including him. Harry no longer recognized the place he had called home and suddenly realized he needed to get away. Nazi Germany imposed new societal norms and this was merely the first of many unjust actions to occur in broad daylight -- unquestioned -- in the days, weeks, and months to come. Such events marked the pre-genocidal period, signifying the end of Jewish life in Austria and the intensification of Hitler's larger war against European Jewry.

The Anschluss Pogrom

Daily life took a drastic turn for the worse for people like Harry Gruenberg after Anschluss. Carrying out a normal activity such as going to work, school, shopping, or visiting a relative became a great challenge. On the other hand, previously abnormal activities and uncivilized behavior became commonplace and accepted. Persecution, forced labor, disenfranchisement, random plundering, and arrests instantly became part of ordinary daily life and went publicly unchallenged. The police and government forces refused to help the victims. Worse, few Austrian citizens offered sympathy or aid. Indeed most condoned the perpetrators actions, either cheering loudly or looking on in silence.[16] If the victims looked to their leadership at the IKG for support, they found a weak and divided force unable to offer them the immediate unification

---

[16] For more information on public response, see Evan B. Bukey, *Hitler's Austria: Popular Sentiment in the Nazi Era 1938-1945* (Chapel Hill: The University of North Carolina Press, 2000); G.E.R. Gedye, *Fallen Bastions: The Central European Tragedy*. (London: Victor Gollancz Ltd, 1939).

and assistance they needed.[17] The leaders had not anticipated or prepared for Anschluss and Nazi Germany gave them little time to respond. On Friday, 18 March, the Germans closed the main offices of the Jewish community and arrested the president, two vice-presidents, and director. They intended to quell the voices of the IKG leaders, together with the rest of Austria's non-Jewish opposition, to prevent any unified resistance to Nazism. They were successful. The approximately 200,000 members of Vienna's Jewish community made their decisions at the grass roots level, with their families, friends, classmates, clubs, and societies. Some figure heads within the IKG, whom the Germans chose to harass and humiliate publicly but to spare arrest, tried individually to uplift their community. For example, Dr. Taglicht, the head rabbi of the community, obeyed when Nazi thugs insisted that he scrub the sidewalk, but he resisted dehumanization. He kept his faith in God and humanity and quietly proclaimed: "I am cleaning God's earth."[18] His response, a powerful act of spiritual resistance, offered hope and moral support to other Jewish victims around him, but did not help his despairing community as a whole. Anschluss turned the victims' lives upside down; suddenly they were in dire need of guidance and unity, but left on their own to confront the future.

In Austria, unlike in Germany, daily life for the victims changed overnight. The Nuremburg Laws, enacted over the course of five years in Germany, went into effect in May, stripping Jews of all civil rights. Contemporary American newspapers and journals recognized the rapid transition of power and reported on the condition of Austrian Jewry in comparison to their German neighbors. They concluded that Austrian Jews were in grave danger: "In a fortnight the Jews have been brought under an infinitely severer regime than was reached in

---

[17] At the time of Anschluss the IKG had 88 congregations and 356 secular associations. See Herbert Rozenkranz, "The Anschluss and the Tragedy of Austrian Jewry 1938-1945," in Josef Frankel ed., *The Jews of Austria: Essays on their Life, History and Destruction* (London: Valentine Mitchell,1967), 481.

[18] See Herbert Rozenkranz, "The Anschluss and the Tragedy of Austrian Jewry 1938-1945," in Josef Frankel ed., *The Jews of Austria: Essays on their Life, History and Destruction* (London: Valentine Mitchell,1967), 485.

Germany after a year," the *New York Times* wrote (23 March 1938).[19] The *New Republic* agreed: "worst of all is the treatment of the Austrian Jews.... Their fate is even worse than that of the Jews in Germany, where the persecutions were spread over a period of several years; in Austria, the full force of the sadistic Nazi attack has come overnight."[20] Historians of the Holocaust have emphasized the speed of the takeover and its effect on the Jews. George E. Berkley dubbed the aftermath of Anschluss as the period of *Blitzverfolgung* (lightning persecution) and Israeli scholar Hannah Weiner has argued that "panic took hold of the Jews of Austria [because] suddenly, they were prey to violent attacks, and their sense of security, which involved faith in a certain culture, as well as material security, disappeared overnight."[21] These conclusions stress that the speed of the takeover exacerbated the predicament of Austrian Jewry, and that the victims may have responded differently had Nazism been implemented over a longer stretch of time.

While it is true that Anschluss legalized Nazism in Austria overnight, it did not create violence overnight. The Austrian Nazi party was alive and empowered long before March 1938, waiting for this transfer to occur. Thus, the speed of the takeover alone did not drive Austria's Jews to a state of panic. What crippled them was the scale of the planned violence, the shocking number of ordinary Austrian citizens who turned against them-- including the government and police. Christian antisemitism, a history of Jewish persecution, and the growth of National Socialism in neighboring Germany, could not have prepared them for the atmosphere that governed the streets. Anschluss marked the beginning of government endorsed mass violence. Legalized Nazism unveiled a new and unanticipated (even by the Germans) level of hatred

---

[19]*New York Times*, 23 March 1938, p. 8.
[20] *New Republic*, "Nazi Terror in Austria," 20 April 1938: 317.
[21] Dalia Ofer and Hannah Weiner, *Dead-End Journey: The Tragic Story of the Kladovo-Sabac Group* (Lanham, New York and London: University Press of America, Inc., 1996) : 2.

harbored by ordinary citizens, changing the social norms of a previously coexistent population. Paul Schatzberg, born in Vienna and recently an instructor of Holocaust history at Baltimore Hebrew University, fled from Nazi Vienna with his parents and younger brother in March 1939. In his article, "Plunder in 1938," he has described how Austrian citizens unleashed a rush of brutality against Jews and turned into unrecognizable human beings. Drawing upon archival research and personal memory (he was twelve at the time), Schatzberg has explained:

> Within hours after the *Anschluss* of Austria, it was as if a medieval monster had been released from the sewers beneath Vienna. This monster consisted of thousands of Viennese ... and thousands more of bystanders and watchers who raised no objections. Suddenly these disaffected, angry people, whether Nazi party members or not, donned Swastika arm bands and, drunk with their sudden power, felt not only free, but justified, in entering Jewish apartments and homes ... threatening frightened occupants, brutalizing them, and robbing them of cash, jewelry, fur coats, and other valuables.[22]

Schatzberg's description paints an accurate picture of the new relationship between gentiles and Jews in Austria directly after Anschluss. The perpetrators and bystanders were free to treat Jews as they wished, and the victims -- immediately banned from employment, stripped of all aid, and denied protection from the police -- were defenseless against their attacks. Mr. Wallenfells, US treasury representative at the American consulate in Vienna, compared their situation to "a hounded beast breathing its last in a trap."[23] He explained that anti-Jewish legislation made it unbearable for Jews to carry on with their daily lives, and almost impossible for them to escape from Greater Germany. "They pursue us like wild animals (*Man hetzt uns*

---

[22] See Paul Schatzberg, "Plunder in 1938: Aryanization of Jewish Assets in Vienna, Austria and Causal Connections," (Philadelphia, St. Joseph's University: The 33rd Annual Scholars' Conference on the Holocaust and the Churches, 2003): 2.

[23] NARA, US-State Dept. Records, RG 59/M1209/Reel 7: 863.4016/177. See Enclosure No. 4 to dispatch No.217, "Statement by Treasury Representative Wallenfells," Vienna, 4 May 1938:2.

wie die wilden Tiere),"[24] an elderly Jewish female exclaimed to Mr. Gardner Richardson, the United States commercial attaché in Vienna, after describing the experiences her family and she endured after Anschluss. Another Jewish victim reported to him, "Nothing like this has happened since the days of Nero."[25] Members of the American legation in Austria made notes of these witness reports and sent them to the White House, along with their own eyewitness testimonies.

Reports of persecution of Jews after Anschluss, although shocking to the United States and the rest of the outside world, could not be disputed. Both in and outside of Germany, Nazi hatred of Jews was well-known. Hitler's regime believed it led a righteous mission to rid the world of Jews and therefore boasted of many of its achievements. Foreign newspapers and radio programs had little trouble reporting the Nazi violence perpetrated against Austrian Jewry: it was a public spectacle. But behavior outside civil bounds with no negative repercussion and indeed applause only led to ever more violent behavior. From the moment the Nazis seized Austria, they demonstrated their intent to dehumanize, disenfranchise, and expel Austrian Jewry from the Greater German Reich. When no political power stepped in to stop them, genocide was in the making.

Context

> *It was something horrible that happened those days in Vienna. And it was just the beginning of that whole thing.*
> ~Freddy Schreiber, Viennese Holocaust Survivor[26]

---

[24] See NARA, US-State Dept. Records, RG 59/M1209/Reel 7, 863.4016/172, "Seizure of Jewish Property and Persecution of Jews in Austria," in dispatch No.166, "Action Taken Against Jews in Austria, " Vienna, 25 March 1938, Gardner Richardson, Commercial Attache: 2.
[25] Ibid.
[26] Fred, S.,1994. "Interview by Survivors of the Shoah Visual History Foundation," Los Angeles, CA, USA, December 15. Interview Code 00383, Tape 2, 3:00.

There was a pandemonium; it was absolutely dreadful, right from the beginning.

~Natalie Kammerman, Viennese Émigré[27]

When does genocide begin? Who is responsible? What are the boundaries of responsibility? Historians have concluded that Nazi terror in Austria after Anschluss exceeded violence by the National Socialist regime in Germany from 1933 to 1938. Few, however, have drawn our attention to how the immediate post-Anschluss period paved the groundwork for genocide.[28] Paul Schatzberg has labeled this period "The Vienna Pogrom of Spring 1938." He has argued that the crimes perpetrated against Jews constituted a pogrom, but historiography of the Holocaust has failed to recognize the post-Anschluss actions as such.[29] Puzzling, when in fact, post-Anschluss terror was part of an ongoing series of pogroms, stretched out over a two-month span. As we now know, what occurred on the streets of Vienna at that time, that series of violent eruptions, was a prelude to genocide. The new relationships which developed between perpetrators, victims, and bystanders set a deadly precedent for how Nazi-Jewish affairs would proceed throughout the Holocaust. The victims suffered, the perpetrators danced, and the western democracies stood silent. The victims learned how to cooperate with Nazi demands so that they could survive for one more day; the Germans learned they were unstoppable and were empowered by their success. Eighteen months before World War II, during the pre-genocidal phase of the Holocaust, long before mass murder began was when intervention was needed and could have changed the course of history.

---

[27] Natalie, P., 1997. "Interview by Survivors of the Shoah Visual History Foundation," Kew, VIC, AU, June 20. Interview Code 32803, Tapes 1-3.

[28] See Gerhard Botz and Karl R Stadler. *Wien, Vom "anschluss" Zum Krieg: Nationalsozialistische Machtübernahme U. Polit.-soziale Umgestaltung Am Beispiel D. Stadt Wien 1938/39.* (Wien: Jugend & Volk, 1978).

[29] Schatzberg has suggested that the Anschluss pogrom has been overshadowed by the 1938 November Pogrom, which gained far greater international attention. This is likely. Our aim here is to scrutinize, perhaps for the first time, Vienna in March 1938 to look for early warning signs of genocide.

Changes in Daily Life during the Pre-Genocidal Period

Historian Evan Burr Bukey documented the pre-genocidal atmosphere in Vienna after Anschluss

in his work, *Hitler's Austria: Popular Sentiment in the Nazi Era 1938-1945.* He elaborated upon

the harsh but also bizarre character of Nazi viciousness:

> Humiliations and horrors visited on the Jews also had symbolic and ritualistic
> overtones: the rebellious masses attacked rich and poor alike, they stole cash,
> jewelry, furs, clothing and furniture; they tore Torah rolls from synagogues and
> prayer halls; and severed the beards of rabbis with scissors and rusty knives. On
> weekends storm troopers dragged hundreds of Jews to the Prater, the woodland
> preserve to the east of Leopoldstadt on the Danubian Canal. In the shadow of
> Vienna's enormous Ferris wheel they forced elderly men to submit to beatings, to
> do endless calisthenics, even to eat grass.[30]

Contemporary reports (newspapers, letters, and U.S. State Department records) document the

strange and barbaric acts Nazis forced Jews to perform in public venues like the Prater (Vienna's

largest park), the streets, and cafes. These reports lay bare the sadistic environment Nazism

forced Jews to live in and suggest how the roots of mass murder could flourish in such an

atmosphere of demonization.

John C. Wiley, American Consul General stationed in Vienna, reported regularly to

American Secretary of State Hull on the public display of violence after Anschluss. His reports

were descriptive and powerful and they were distributed by George Messersmith, Assistant

Secretary of State, to the office of international economic affairs, the division of European

affairs, and various legal advisors. In one report, Wiley explained how several hundred

uniformed S.A. men invaded the Prater, and conducted "a systematic drive against the Jews,"

---

[30] Bukey, *Hitler's Austria*: 134.

which reminded him of "beaters driving rabbits through a cornfield."[31] Appalled, he watched as

the Nazis drove the Jews to the entrance square, Prater Stern, and forced them -- approximately

seven hundred people of all ages and both sexes -- to gather together and perform physically and

spiritually degrading exercises. For one of these exercises, the S.A. forced the Jewish victim to

lift one leg and extend it forward. Then, they would pass by and seize the extended foot,

throwing the victim backward off balance onto the cobblestones. This sadistic act made a strong

impact on Wiley and he noted that the S.A. took particular pleasure in conducting this activity.

Later, a local physician informed him that many of the victims used for this sport needed

treatment for severe head wounds.[32]

Wallenfells, a treasury representative at the American consulate in Vienna, also

witnessed the madness that followed the German takeover. He watched Nazis publicly humiliate

Jews in parks, cafes, and on the streets of Vienna. Both frightened and astonished by this uncivil

behavior, he reported these outbursts to the state department in Washington and asked the

American government to pay attention to the Nazi rise to power in Austria. After describing the

inhumanity that transpired on one particular Sunday afternoon in the Prater, he commented in

disbelief: "All this was done in broad daylight in a public park."[33] On that Sunday, 24 April

1938, while walking through the Prater, Wallenfells had witnessed an intolerable situation in

which he was unable to intervene: the Nazis had forced a young Jewish girl whom he knew

personally to join a large group of Jews and march up and down the park singing derisive songs,

chanting 'Perish, Jew,' and then perform a military drill which left her and the others thoroughly

[31] NARA, US-State Dept. Records, RG 59/M1209/Reel 7: 863.4016/177. See Report No.217, "Intensified Persecution of the Jews in Austria," Vienna, 4 May 1938: 3.
[32] Ibid.
[33] NARA, US-State Dept. Records, RG 59/M1209/Reel 7: 863.4016/177. See Enclosure No. 4 to dispatch No.217, "Statement by Treasury Representative Wallenfells," Vienna, 4 May 1938:1.

exhausted.[34] Wallenfells was mortified, but as a single man felt there was nothing he could do other than appeal to the American government. The next day, 25 April 1938, his wife and he visited with friends in the fourth district and witnessed an equally frightening affair. Again he could not fathom how such behavior could be tolerated in the twentieth century. His wife and he saw a group of S.A. men, mere boys, enter a Jewish café opposite Favoritenstrasse 18 and force all the Jews inside to clean the café -- with all the curtains drawn back so the crowd outside could watch. The S.A. ordered the Jews to move furniture, pile up chairs, wash the floors, and clean the silver. Moreover, they instructed the victims to chant insulting and humiliating words and demanded middle-aged un-athletic men to do knee-bending exercises and jump over tables and chairs. Wallenfells emphasized in his report that all this was done before a jeering crowd -- "much to the delight of the onlookers" -- and not only in this café, but in cafés and restaurants throughout the city, even those located on the famous Ringstrasse.[35] If the violence did not occur inside a public venue, it took place on the streets in and outside of the city. Out in the seventeenth district (Hernals), Wallenfells reported: "Jews are being dragged out daily to have their heads shaved and the Nazi sign then painted thereon in black. The women in this locality are made to wash clothes for the brown shirts and to work hard at scrubbing all the floors and toilets for many hours at a stretch and in their best holiday garb."[36]

The public display of cruelty and injustice which Wiley encountered in the Prater, and Wallenfells witnessed in parks, cafes, and on the streets of Vienna, reflected a collapse of the social contract and, as we now know, reveal the roots of the genocide that was enacted later. These events occurred in the middle of the day and raised no objection from public spectators, only applause. And, no one was immune from such violence. John Wiley himself was

---

[34] Ibid.
[35] Ibid.
[36] Ibid.

endangered by Nazi thugs, the S.A., and the S.S. "I, myself, was accosted while on the Prater golf course by S.A. men who demanded in a threatening tone of voice to know whether I was a Jew or not," he explained in an official report to the White House on 4 May 1938. "On my replying that I was the American Chargé d' Affaires, they shouted that they wanted no foreign Jews in Vienna either and repeated the question as to whether I was a Jew.... I was actually detained for about ten minutes."[37] The American government took no action against Nazi brutality in Austria, despite knowledge party policies put their own citizens at risk. They were unaware of how Austria's regime change would eventually affect America.

Forced Labor --"Scrub Squads" (Putzschar) [38]

Eight-year-old Edith Berju-Kohn recalled walking to her father's store on Taborstrasse in the second district after the Anschluss. She saw a small crowd standing around laughing and having a good time. Not knowing what the laughter was about, her curiosity drew her into the crowd. Years later she described seeing elderly Jews scrubbing the sidewalk and scraping off the sides of a wall with their bare hands. Edith never forgot that image.[39]

A common way Nazis dehumanized and persecuted Jews in the early days of March was by forcing them to perform physical labor such as cleaning the city streets or the German soldiers' barracks.[40] This was another immense change in the daily life of Jews. All were

---

[37] NARA, US-State Dept. Records, RG 59/M1209/Reel 7: 863.4016/177. See Report No.217, "Intensified Persecution of the Jews in Austria," Vienna, 4 May 1938: 4.

[38] See NARA, US-State Dept. Records, RG 59/M1209/Reel 7: 863.4016/174, Dispatch No.202, "Situation of Jews in Austria," Vienna, 15 April 1938: 2.

[39] Edith, B., 1997. "Interview by Survivors of the Shoah Visual History Foundation," Vineland, NJ, USA, July 22. Interview Code 43759, Tapes 1-4.

[40] This is confirmed by the US consular reports and testimonies from the SOSVHF. For example, John C.Wiley reported: "[T]he indignities and persecution against the Jews continues unabated. ... Jewish men and women continue to be taken from their homes or on the streets and brought to Nazi barracks where they are compelled to scrub floors and toilets or are given physical exercises until they are exhausted." See NARA, US-State Dept. Records, RG 59/M1209/Reel 7: 863.4016/174, Dispatch No.202, "Situation of Jews in Austria," Vienna, 15 April

equally subject to this harassment. The labor details were humiliating and unjust, and spontaneous and unavoidable. Members of the S.A. stopped Jews on the streets while on their way to work or school, or they appeared at their doorsteps without warning and dragged them out on the streets. They forced their victims to clean up the city on their hands and knees -- to remove pro-Schuschnigg slogans and symbols, scrub away the *Kruckenkreuze* (Austrian crutch cross) from the cobblestone and pavement, and rub out signs of the *Vaterlandische Front* (Fatherland Front) from walls.[41] Gardner Richardson, U.S. commercial attaché, witnessed this unpleasant sight and reported it to the White House. He explained that the cleaning assignments seemed to be more about persecuting Jews than marking the regime change -- and noted that Jews scrubbed crosses off the street that were not there before Anschluss, but "placed there for a purpose by the Nazis."[42] According to historian George E. Berkley, the persecutors "added several features to make the work more in keeping with their purposes," such as adding acid to the water they forced the Jews to scrub with so their fingers burned; providing the victims with inadequate instruments to clean (i.e. toothbrushes); and forcing them to wear inappropriate clothing like lingerie or a fine fur coat while cleaning; or standing over them and urinating while they were performing this work.[43]

1938:1. Also see, Trude, A., 1996. "Interview by Survivors of the Shoah Visual History Foundation," West Los Angeles, CA, USA, January 10. Interview Code 10786, Tapes 1-3.

[41] *Vaterlandische Front*, VF, Fatherland Front, Patriotic Front , was a rightwing austrofascist political party started by Chancellor Engelbert Dolfuss in 1933 and led by Kurt Schuschnigg from 1934 until the German takeover in 1938. Dolfuss designed the VF as a single political party to join all loyal Austrians under one flag and control Austria's internal political turmoil. Simulteously he aimed to suppress any opposition and outlawed all other political parties, including the Social Democrats and the National Socialists. The patriotic symbol of the regime was a *Kruckenkreuz*, a crutch cross.

[42] See NARA, US-State Dept. Records, RG 59/M1209/Reel 7, 863.4016/172, "Seizure of Jewish Property and Persecution of Jews in Austria," in dispatch No.166, "Action Taken Against Jews in Austria, " Vienna, 25 March 1938, Gardner Richardson, Commercial Attache: 13.

[43] On this same issue Berkley continues, "Street-cleaning activities by no means exhausted the persecutors' repertoire." He then listed a number of alternative sights that a visitor walking around Vienna in those early days of the *Anschluss* could see. For a complete listing, see Berkley, *Vienna and Its Jews,* 260. For more details on the "Scrub Squads," see NARA, US-State Dept. Records, RG 59/M1209/Reel 7, 863.4016/172, "Seizure of Jewish Property and Persecution of Jews in Austria" 25 March 1938 by Gardner Richardson, Commercial Attaché to the

The Nazis' campaign of brutality on the streets of Vienna imposed a system of labor expectations. If the victim completed his work successfully, he received a certificate showing that he had performed all that could be required of him that day. According to Wiley the certificate protected the victim for twenty-four hours, preventing a second seizure the same day, but offered no protection against further forced labor on following days.[44] If, on the other hand, the S.A. were dissatisfied with the victim's work, they further dehumanized their victim as s/he labored (by urinating on him or shouting insults at him), and physically beat him. The American General Consul described a case of a young girl who after being "forced to work three hours, ... received such a buffet on the face for her slowness that her jaw and mouth were swollen all out of shape."[45]

German and Austrian Nazis ordered Jews of all ages and socio-economic backgrounds, both religious and nonreligious, to fulfill these forced labor details. They selected people randomly, elevating fear and anxiety among the Jewish community. Karl Gruenwald, a ten-year-old boy at the time of Anschluss, recalled that these random arrests created "a very strange environment ... you unknowingly walked as prey. ...You felt like a rat. You were afraid wherever you were, on the street, or in your home."[46] As Wiley explained, "The selection of Jews for this Nazi sport seems entirely a matter of chance. Many Jews have escaped entirely, while some few whose luck was bad, have been picked up three and four times." At the same time, he documented that some Nazis enjoyed forcing wealthy Jews to labor the most intensively -- they aimed to "give a dose of physical labor to those Jews who seemed unused to it -- such

---

American Consulate General in Vienna, in dispatch No.166, "Action Taken Against Jews in Austria, "Vienna, 25 March 1938, John C. Wiley

[44] See NARA, US-State Dept. Records, RG 59/M1209/Reel 7: 863.4016/174, Dispatch No.202, "Situation of Jews in Austria," Vienna, 15 April 1938: 2.

[45] Ibid.

[46] Karl, G., 1997. "Interview by Survivors of the Shoah Visual History Foundation," New York, NY, USA, March 16. Interview Code 27992, Tapes 1-8.

Jews, presumptive 'oppressors of the poor,' were given particularly unpleasant work." On the other hand, he explained, Jews who "appeared to belong to the laboring class and to be used to rough work were usually released after a few minutes."[47]

The artist Alfred Hrdlicka explained it best when he noted, "One can not always refer to Auschwitz, for it [genocide] started with the washing of the streets."[48] While a number of historians have described what happened in Vienna after Anschluss, few have drawn the critical correlation between these events and the genocide that lay ahead.[49] The destruction of the Jews did not begin in the death camps; it ended there. The new order that governed the streets of Vienna in 1938 revealed a breakdown in the rule of law, opening the door to increased violence and terror. Twenty-year-old Leopold Deutsch, who belonged to the lowest socio-economic bracket, reflected upon the day when the Nazis forced his sister and him to scrub paint off the sidewalk. Some fifty years later, Leopold revealed the lasting pain it caused. "It was so [long pause] unbelievable," he recalled. "So much hurt was in me. I could have killed every single one of them. Because, Why? What did we even do?"[50] No one came to their aid. Those who witnessed these acts of barbarity -- the bystanders -- cheered on the perpetrators, sanctioning and encouraging their actions. Karl Gruenwald remembered this new and unfamiliar atmosphere in which "people were taken off the street and used as a spectacle... and it was like the [Austrian] people were having a party, children and women laughing while the Jews were scrubbing the

[47] See NARA, US-State Dept. Records, RG 59/M1209/Reel 7: 863.4016/174, Dispatch No.202, "Situation of Jews in Austria," Vienna, 15 April 1938:2.
[48] Alfred Hrdlincka is the designer of Vienna's memorial "Against War and Fascism." See James E. Young, *The Texture of Memory* (New Haven: Yale University Press, 1993), 110.
[49] See Saul Friedlander, *Nazi Germany and the Jews: Volume 1: The Years of Persecution 1933-1939.* (New York: Harper Collins, 1997).
[50] Leo, D., 1997. "Interview by Survivors of the Shoah Visual History Foundation," San Francisco, CA, USA, May 17. Interview Code 29174, Tapes 1-5.

streets with their hands burning."[51] These events were an alarm bell that no one heard or knew

how to interpret. They called for action and intervention but fell upon deaf ears. In this new

social structure, the new masters forced Jews to perform degrading work, the victims -- taken

off-guard and without defense -- had no choice but to comply with their demands. The

perpetrators were emboldened by their success and free reign of power; the Jews were

progressively more intimidated.

Segregation, Marking, Disenfranchisement

Verbal and physical harassment were one form of ostracism. The Germans and their Austrian

allies strategically adopted other mechanisms to segregate Jews from Greater German society

directly following Anschluss. Aside from marking public areas with such slogans as: "Only for

Aryans!" or "No Dogs or Jews!", they discharged all Jews from their professions and educational

positions. Removing people from work or school meant stripping them of their core purpose in

life, and this took a great toll on the community. Many Jews went to work immediately after

Anschluss and were fired on the spot: sent home with no explanation, no final pay, and no idea

of how or when they might find work again. When thirty-three-year-old Lena Rosenblatt, an

educator at the Montessori School on Albertgasse 35 arrived at work on Monday (14 March) she

learned that the school had been shut down permanently.[52] Moritz Hirschbein, sixty years old,

arrived to work that same day and his partner told him to go home. "'I cannot work with a Jew,'"

he said in a matter-of-fact tone, "'Those are the rules.'" Moritz's eleven-year-old daughter,

Johanna, saw an unrecognizable expression on her father's face that day. He came home and

[51] Karl, G., 1997. "Interview by Survivors of the Shoah Visual History Foundation," New York, NY, USA, March
16. Interview Code 27992, Tapes 1-8.
[52] Lena, G., 1997. "Interview by Survivors of the Shoah Visual History Foundation," Washington, D.C., USA,
January 29. Interview Code 25357, Tapes 1-5.

said: "'So -- it all amounts to nothing. I have no money, I have no job.'" "My father was just broken at that point," Johanna recalled. "This was his business, but he couldn't get anything out of it. He had nothing. The guy just told him to leave." From that point forward, Moritz never went to work again. Johanna explained, "Father was at home all the time and I am sure that wasn't very good; he was not well."[53]

For Johanna and other children, the situation was similarly agonizing. Just as sixty-year-old Moritz's life reached a drastic turning point at this time, so did life for his daughter. The new law required all Jewish children to relocate to an all-Jewish school in the second district. This new school was far from Johanna's home, and the atmosphere both within and without was practically unbearable. Hitler Youth and other gentile children waited outside the building and hurled objects at the Jewish students on their way in and out. Inside the school the new forced arrangement of Jewish students and teachers who had recently been dismissed from other schools all over Vienna created a terribly chaotic atmosphere. Johanna soon stopped her public schooling and was tutored privately at home. Attending school in the second district marked the first time Johanna was afraid and it was at this point that her parents and she began to question the future of Vienna's Jews under the Nazis.[54] Life in Austria quickly became unmanageable for this Jewish family, as it did for so many others. Thus, the Nazis had begun to fulfill their aims, stripping both her father and her of their core existence in the public domain.

If fear and humiliation accompanied these life upheavals; so too did violence follow the Germans mission to designate all businesses owned by Jews. Sometimes Viennese Nazis, members of the S.A., or Hitler Youth took charge of labeling these premises and painted Jewish

[53] Johanna, S., 1996. "Interview by Survivors of the Shoah Visual History Foundation," Miami, FL, USA, February 21. Interview Code 12280, Tapes 1-7.
[54] Johanna, S., 1996. "Interview by Survivors of the Shoah Visual History Foundation," Miami, FL, USA, February 21. Interview Code 12280, Tapes 1-7.

stars on the store windows, or sarcastic phrases such as, "On vacation in Dachau!" Most often, however, they forced this on the Jewish victim, demanding that either that the Jewish owner, the owner's child, or another Jew, paint the word "Jew," the notice "Don't buy from Jews," or the Star of David on their store windows. Or, they forced them to carry such signs outside the stores. Trade commissioner Richardson witnessed this segregation marker as he drove through the Praterstrasse on a Saturday afternoon in late April 1938. He saw pickets in front of numerous stores and noted that while the picket usually was a member of the S.A, sometimes it was a person in civilian clothes with a Nazi armband, and often the Jewish storekeepers themselves.[55] Shocked by the cruelty of these events, Richardson reported the scene to the White House:

> The whole incident struck me as being absolutely brutal with no fair play.... In connection with the picketing of stores in the second district, that group of S.A. men walked along in front of the shops and frequently, without any provocation, slapped the faces of Jewish persons who were forced to hold up placards, in some cases they beat these people over the head.[56]

Similar to Wiley's and Wallenfell's reports, Richardson's account described the inhumanity that seized Austria: the violence that went uncontested, in public and in broad daylight. He documented the brutal method of the perpetrators forcing their victims to act as agents of their own destruction. What he observed was a breakdown of the rule of law that would follow a crooked path to genocide. But, like the others, he had no way of foretelling the future. He could not know that the relationship between the Nazis and the Jews was developing into a synergy that would sustain Hitler's program of mass murder. Not even the Germans understood this then.

---

[55] NARA, US-State Dept. Records, RG 59/M1209/Reel 7: 863.4016/177. See Enclosure No. 2 to dispatch No.217, "Statement by Trade Commissioner Richardson," Vienna, 27 April 1938.
[56] NARA, US-State Dept. Records, RG 59/M1209/Reel 7: 863.4016/177. See Enclosure No. 2 to dispatch No.217, "Statement by Trade Commissioner Richardson," Vienna, 27 April 1938.

Leopold Deutsch and Alix Grabkowicz, who witnessed these same events from a more personal perspective, were also not privy to such information. Nor was there anything that they, as victims, could have done. When Leopold, twenty years old, reported to work on Saturday March 12, he learned that as a Jew he had no future in Austria. He did not work that day, nor was he dismissed. Rather, the S.A. and S.S. harassed and humiliated him, making him the subject of their entertainment. First, they forced him to demonstrate that the business was being aryanized by painting a swastika on the window and writing "Don't buy from us." Then, to further discourage "Aryan" customers from entering, these men marked and exhibited Leo as if he were an item in the store window for sale: "I had to stand outside the store with a sign *Saujude*: I am a pig -- I am a Jewish pig. I had to hold [the sign] in front of the store," Leo recalled.[57] Some fifty years later, Leo reflected upon that particular moment in his long history, and its memory still brought him to tears. It is hard to know exactly how he felt that day -- a strong, healthy, twenty-year-old man, held on the street as a public spectacle, laughed at, and for the first time in his life, totally defenseless. He could not run, he could not hide, and he could not protest without risk to his life. What thoughts ran through his mind? Did he think about who might see him -- a girlfriend, a classmate, or a former enemy? Did he wonder how his mother and father would react if they saw him? Did he question what he had done to deserve this? Did he contemplate his future? Or, was he too scared and shocked to think of anything beyond how long he would have to stand there?

Different questions flew through Alix Grabkowicz's mind when her daily life fell apart at age thirteen. Alix reflected years later that she was uninvolved in and naïve about politics at the time, but politics involved her. As the Germans set out to segregate and mark her from the rest

---

[57] Leo, D., 1997. "Interview by Survivors of the Shoah Visual History Foundation," San Francisco, CA, USA, May 17. Interview Code 29174, Tapes 1-5.

of society, they scarred her life permanently. A few weeks after the annexation she encountered

the cruelty and hypocrisy of the new political order. Looking back she explained, "Things did

get worse rapidly-- one late afternoon my mother sent me to the close delicatessen to buy things

for supper. Two young Hitler Jugend were standing by the door. As I was entering I felt

somebody hitting me on the back. I kept walking- did my shopping and went home. Those two

boys stuck a paper sign on my back that read: *Arisches Schwein kauft beim Juden ein* (Aryan pig

shops at a Jewish store) -- they had taken me as an Aryan." Although the boys believed Alix was

a gentile and persecuted her as such, she did not feel protected or priviledged. Even if she did

not appear to "look" Jewish, she suffered all the consequences of being a Jew in Nazi Vienna.

Like Johanna Hirschbein, and all other Jewish children her age, she was kicked out of her school

and required to relocate to the Chajes Gymnasium in the second district. This new all-Jewish

school proved not only too far away from Alix's home in the fourth district, but too different

from her former school in the city center. At age thirteen, she stopped going to school. She

watched friends and relatives leave Vienna one after the next, and her opportunities to grow

inside Vienna narrowed: "All parks, swimming pools, movies, and even public benches were

forbidden to Jews and so it was a sad and lonely time," she recalled.[58] Alix started thinking

about getting out of Vienna and wrote letters to a friend in Antwerp asking if she could come for

a visit. Meanwhile she tried to persuade her parents to let her go.

External Responses

The western democracies were well informed about events in Vienna, but still they could not

foresee their significance for the Jews of Europe - and the world. The American journal *New*

---

[58] "I can assure you that the events of March 13, '38 have changed my life forever." Letter from Alix G. Kowler to the author, 1 August 2003:1,3,4.

Republic reported upon some of the life changes Vienna's Jews faced in the early March days. "Jewish shops in Vienna are being labeled and in many cases confiscated; employment is being denied to Jews; a non-Jewish woman was driven down the street as a public spectacle because she had bought something in a Jewish store; thousands of Jews have been arrested and sent to jail or concentration camps." [59] The *New York Times* offered some further details, particularly on the unrestrained violence: "Beating of Jews and plundering of Jewish-owned stores increased today. Jews were disappearing from Vienna life. ... One man was beaten and left wounded on the street. Another, leaving a cafe, was beaten while his wife looked on helplessly. A Jewish woman who withdrew 40,000 schillings from a bank was arrested without charge."[60] On 6 April 1938, less than a month after annexation, the United States consulate in Vienna received and forwarded to the White House a letter from an anonymous victim. The report, "S.O.S. Appeal to the World" described the new atmosphere with chilling intimacy:

> It is revolting and beneath human dignity what the S.S. people are doing with the Jews in Vienna....Defenseless women have been fetched every day...compelled to wash the streets...even if it is pouring rain. The women have wounds on their hands and many have fallen ill.
>
> Jewish men have been maltreated by these gangs for several weeks...they must perform the most...dirty work ten hours a day, without getting anything to eat. If one of them faints...he is beaten until he gets up again...the exhausted and starved men were then stood against a wall and shots were fired just over their heads.... These people come home half crazy, physically and mentally broken and ruined for their whole life. And this happens day after day. But not only young men are fetched, even sixty to seventy year old Jews (men of high education and culture)....Many older Jews have suffered apoplectic strokes as a result of overexcitement....Hundred and thousands of suicides occur which are not published in the papers.
>
> I could fill many pages, but I have not the strength. Sleeplessness and excitement have ruined my nerves. You will certainly understand that I cannot give you my name, but I swear to you that everything I write is true. When one of these tormented people complains to the police...the people merely shrug their shoulders and say..."we cannot do anything." Please help us. The only help

---

[59] *The New Republic,* 30 March 1938, *The Week: Hitler v. Freud: p.205.*
[60] *New York Times,* 14 March 1938, p. 8.

which we can expect is from abroad. Give ear to the cry for help of the hundreds
of thousands of honest Jews whose only fault is that they are Jews.
(Signed) One of the unhappy people who went through it personally.[61]

The consulate in Vienna translated this letter and sent it to the state department in Washington

with a number of other eyewitness reports on the situation (written mostly by official members

of the legation). The reports documented the chaos that had erupted in Vienna, but did not raise

much sympathy from the American government on behalf of Austria's Jews. America's

isolationist mentality prevented the country from intervening with such 'trivial' internal matters

overseas. Few realized that the situation in Austria represented far more than a tumultuous state

of affairs; that it was a transgression which threatened key concepts of civilization.

People who and organizations that *did* detect the enormity of the threat, and tried to jolt

the American government into action, were unsuccessful. One group, The Joint American

Committee for Protection of Minorities, sent a petition demanding official objection to

Anschluss to President Roosevelt on 30 March 1938: "WE APPEAL to the family of nations still

believing in Democracy to unite in this cooperative endeavor; to ask the Dictatorships to let the

people go; to welcome these minorities; to respect their integrity and grant liberty to all…. When

a dictator and a government openly, by statutes, and - in absence of statutes - by fiat and force of

arms, adopts and upholds an enormous wrong of oppression, persecution and violence, then good

men through the earth are bound to unite against it in a solemn and stern, though peaceful,

remonstrance."[62] The *New York Times* publicized the message of Dr. Hans Kohn, a professor of

[61] NARA, US-State Dept. Records, RG 59/M1209/Reel 7: 863.4016/174. See Enclosure No. 1 to dispatch No.202,
"Translation of Anonymous Letter received by the Consulate General," Vienna, 6 April 1938:1-2.
[62] NARA, US-State Dept. Records, RG 59/M1209/Reel 7: 863.00/1654, "A Petition to the President of the United
States: For Affirmative Announcement of the Application of the Diplomatic Policy of Non-Recognition with
Respect to the Forced Annexation of Austria by Germany, from Joint American Committee for Protection of
Minorities," 30 March 1938: 1-6. For further information see Christian Raitz von Frentz, *A Lesson Forgotten:
Minority Protection under the League of Nations The Case of the German Minority in Poland, 1920-1934*
(Hamburg: Arbeiten zur Geschichte Osteuropas, 1999), 87; 27; Margaret Macmillan, *Paris 1919: Six Months that*

history at Smith College, after he declared in a meeting of the New York Society for Ethical Culture on 10 April 1938: "Austria's fate and destiny is linked up with that of the whole world.... The end of Austria today is to have a startling effect on the world.... [Anschluss] is a violation of the nature of history."[63] These early efforts to warn of the dangers of Nazism were rare and made no impact. While the Nazis exercised their power in Vienna in the spring of 1938 and publicly displayed the force of Hitler's totalitarian regime, the free powers stood silent -- with the exception of these few individual voices. Bullied and without defense, the victims tried to remain calm and waited for aid to come from the outside world.

Jewish Responses

Not all Jews could cope with the new challenges of daily life. Everyone in Vienna's diverse and divided Jewish community -- regardless of occupation, income, place of residence or degree of religious observance -- faced the same crisis on Friday 11 March, but nobody knew what to do. People's livelihoods shattered suddenly and the country they trusted turned its back on them; years of assimilation into Austrian society proved to be only skin-deep, a "one-sided symbiosis," as Gershon Saloman called it.[64] Everyone needed to adapt to the new environment, but for some it proved spiritually and physically unmanageable. Persecution, forced labor, and disenfranchisement were simply too much for some people to bear, pushing them to loss of hope. Less than two weeks after Anschluss, Wiley reported to the White House that "practically all of the Jewish population is in a state of acute anxiety and depression...living in a state of legalized

---

Changed the World (New York: Random House, 2002); and MikolasTeich and Roy Porter, eds., *The National Question in Europe in Historical Context* (Cambridge: Cambridge University Press, 1993).
[63] *New York Times*, "Dr. Hans Kohn Warns of Fate of Austria,"11 April 1938:11.
[64] See Gershon Scholem, *Major Trends in Jewish Mysticism*. (Jerusalem: Schoken Publishing House, Ltd., 1941). After the Holocaust he wrote that Jewish assimilation into German society was never fully achieved, it was only a "one-sided symbiosis."

lawlessness without rights."[65] A little over a month later he reiterated the situation to the state

department in Washington, explaining that the condition of the community had worsened due to

"persistent attacks on the Jews from every angle." He explained that these attacks "had a most

unfortunate effect on the mental outlook of the Austrian Jews... some few are able to maintain

their balance in the face of what seems to be a hopeless impasse." "On the other hand," he

explained "is a state of hysterical depression which seems contagious."[66] While some Jews tried

to remain calm and keep faith in their Austrian heimat, they could not prevent hysterical

depression from spreading. Many people saw no future -- in or outside of Austria-- and turned to

suicide.

The atmosphere in the spring of 1938 drove an unprecedented number of Viennese Jews

at an abnormally fast pace to end their lives by suicide.[67] Over five hundred people killed

themselves within the first two months.[68] This was no secret at the time. Wiley reported to the

White House on 25 March that suicides were numerous, as did treasury representative

Wallenfells.[69] And American newspapers and journals also commented upon the high number of

suicides. While each of these reports documented the peak suicide rate, other reports claimed

that the official number of suicides was censored. An eyewitness, who remained anonymous for

safety purposes, stressed in a letter to Wiley on April 6: "hundreds and thousands of suicides

---

[65] See NARA, US-State Dept. Records, RG 59/M1209/Reel 7, 863.4016/172, Dispatch No.166, "Action Taken Against Jews in Austria," Vienna, 25 March 1938, John C. Wiley, American General Consul: 2, 14.
[66] Ibid: 14.
[67] NARA, US-State Dept. Records, RG 59/M1209/Reel 7, 863.4016/177, Dispatch No.217, "Intensified Persecution of the Jews in Austria," Vienna, 4 May 1938, John C. Wiley, American General Consul: 14.
[68] This number is the author's estimation. Rosenkranz claimed that there were 311 Jewish deaths in March and 367 in April 1938, and that the majority of these deaths were by suicide, but not all. See Herbert Rosenkranz, *Verfolgung und Selbstbehauptung. Die Juden in Österreich 1938-1945* (Wien, Munich: Herold, 1978), 485. Jonny Moser puts forward a lower figure of 482 persons. See Jonny Moser. *Demographie der jüdischen Bevölkerung Österreichs 1938-1945* (Vienna: DÖW, 1999), 22.
[69] NARA, US-State Dept. Records, RG 59/M1209/Reel 7, 863.4016/177, Dispatch No.217, "Intensified Persecution of the Jews in Austria," Vienna, 4 May 1938, John C. Wiley, American General Consul: 2.

occur which are not published in the papers."[70] Similarly, commercial attaché, Gardner

Richardson told the White House that the new regime forbad newspapers to publish accounts of

suicides.[71] Many deaths by suicide went unaccounted due to the nature of the act. Thus, in

addition to the hundreds of suicides that were recorded and gained attention overseas, many

more occurred that the outside world never gained knowledge of, and that the Jewish community

did not manage to record.

If little attention has been dedicated to the accuracy of the figures, even less has been

devoted to the significance of who committed suicide in those first days and the impact this had

on the community. Suicide was not limited to the weak, elderly, financially unstable, ill, or

physically impaired, as may be expected in this context. Rather, it was an option chosen by Jews

across the social spectrum. Jews of all ages, socio-economic backgrounds and professions, as

well as couples and entire families committed suicide rather than live under Nazi occupation.[72]

The figures reflect the impossibility of Jewish life under Nazism.[73] The *New Republic* described

the situation in Vienna as "the most sickening spectacle of Nazi barbarity in one of the most

highly civilized cities in the world," and prodded its readers to consider the Jewish despair in

Austria: "Is it any wonder that prominent men and women -- including skilled doctors and

writers -- have killed themselves rather than endure this senseless persecution?"[74] Members of

the American consulate shared similar sentiments in their reports to Washington, relaying how

---

[70] NARA, US-State Dept. Records, RG 59/M1209/Reel 7: 863.4016/174. See Enclosure No. 1 to dispatch No.202, "Translation of Anonymous Letter received by the Consulate General," Vienna, 6 April 1938:1-2.
[71] NARA, US-State Dept. Records, RG 59/M1209/Reel 7, 863.4016/172, "Seizure of Jewish Property and Persecution of Jews in Austria," in dispatch No.166, "Action Taken Against Jews in Austria, " Vienna. 25 March 1938, Gardner Richardson, commercial attaché: 2.
[72] See also Emil Mayer and Emil Rosser, *Viennese Types [Wiener Typen]: Photographs c.1910 by Dr. Emil Mayer* (Blind River Editions, 1st Edition, 2000).
[73] This conclusion has been adduced from contemporary--consular reports, newspapers, and letters -- and from survivor memoirs and testimonies.
[74] *The New Republic*, "The Week: Hitler v. Freud," 30 March 1938: 205.

the new environment had created an explosion of suicide led by mostly wealthy persons[75] and skilled professionals.[76] "There has been a campaign of indignity inflicted upon the Jews,"[77] the American consul explained. Others corroborated his description, explaining that the Nazis used "ruthless, spirit-breaking gangster tactics calculated to bring them to terms or to commit suicide."[78] Wiley noted that "even persons not yet directly affected by the Jewish persecution" had turned to suicide.[79]

Beyond the suicide of prominent community members, another type of suicide lowered the morale of Vienna's Jews. Less than two weeks after Anschluss, Gardner Richardson sent a note to the White House that *family* suicide was prevalent in the Jewish community.[80] Wiley followed up on this report one month later, identifying two specific cases. One family had been directly affected by the violence of Anschluss, the other had suffered indirectly. Still, both chose suicide. These families were financially secure and well-established in Vienna, and they still had a chance to flee the country -- if not all together, possibly individually. In the case of the first family, Wiley wrote:" [O]ut of desperation resulting from the savage mistreatment of Jews, a certain Herr Bergmann, proprietor of a large furniture store in the Praterstrasse (which had been plundered and taken over) killed himself, his wife, son, daughter in law, and grandchild Sunday

---

[75] Wallenfells reported: "This Jewess, and all other Jewish property owners, is exposed to ruthless, spirit-breaking gangster tactics calculated to bring them to terms or to commit suicide." See NARA, US-State Dept. Records, RG 59/M1209/Reel 7: 863.4016/177. See Enclosure No. 4 to dispatch No.217, "Statement by Treasury Representative Wallenfells," Vienna, 4 May 1938:1.

[76] Gardner Richardson, Commercial Attache wrote, "I know personally of a Jewish doctor and his wife who both committed suicide." See NARA, US-State Dept. Records, RG 59/M1209/Reel 7, 863.4016/172, "Seizure of Jewish Property and Persecution of Jews in Austria," in dispatch No.166, "Action Taken Against Jews in Austria, " Vienna, 25 March 1938, Gardner Richardson, Commercial Attache: 2.

[77] See NARA, US-State Dept. Records, RG 59/M1209/Reel 7, 863.4016/172, Dispatch No.166, "Action Taken Against Jews in Austria," Vienna, 25 March 1938, John C. Wiley, American General Consul: 2.

[78] NARA, US-State Dept. Records, RG 59/M1209/Reel 7: 863.4016/177. See Enclosure No. 4 to dispatch No.217, "Statement by Treasury Representative Wallenfells," Vienna, 4 May 1938:1.

[79] NARA, US-State Dept. Records, RG 59/M1209/Reel 7, 863.4016/177, Dispatch No.217, "Intensified Persecution of the Jews in Austria," Vienna, 4 May 1938, John C. Wiley, American General Consul: 14.

[80] See NARA, US-State Dept. Records, RG 59/M1209/Reel 7, 863.4016/172, "Seizure of Jewish Property and Persecution of Jews in Austria," in dispatch No.166, "Action Taken Against Jews in Austria, " Vienna, 25 March 1938, Gardner Richardson, Commercial Attache: 2.

evening."[81] In the second case (known to the consul general personally) he reported, "[N]o member of the family had been arrested, the family was still living in its own home, and still had adequate financial means. Nevertheless the general atmosphere so worked upon the father that in a fit of temporary insanity he killed himself, his wife, and child."[82] Family suicide revealed an extreme hopelessness that existed within Vienna's Jewish community. Those who committed suicide were already convinced in spring 1938 that there was no way back and no way out -- Jewish Vienna had come to an end. The fact that *so many* resorted to suicide so quickly -- at this time when they still had other options -- reveals the devastation created by Anschluss. And indeed, these suicides reflect what we now know constituted a pre-genocidal period in history.[83]

Suicide was the most extreme response to Nazi oppression; others chose the risk of taking immediate flight. Jacques Hasten was eight years old at the time of the Anschluss. He was born in Vienna in 1930 to Ephraim and Betty Hasten. He was one of three brothers. His family lived in Vienna's second district, in a large flat on the Vorgartenstrasse. They were upper-middle class and Jacques and his brothers were pampered by their maids and nannies. Jacques's father, Ephraim was a wealthy businessman in the timber industry and the Hastens spent their summers vacationing on Italy's Adriatic coast. His mother was a housewife and he recalls, a wonderful cook. After the Nazis assumed control of Austria, none of these luxuries mattered. "Wealth

---

[81] NARA, US-State Dept. Records, RG 59/M1209/Reel 7, 863.4016/177, Dispatch No.217, "Intensified Persecution of the Jews in Austria," Vienna, 4 May 1938, John C. Wiley, American General Consul: 4.
[82] Ibid: 14.
[83] Jewish suicides occurred throughout the entire reign of the Nazi occupation. The IKG recorded all suicides bfrom 15 October 1941 to 8 October 1943 and sent regular reports to the Gestapo, including the name, dates of birth, country of birth, last address, date of suicide, and type of death. For further details see: USHMM film # 742, IKG-A/W 169, *Uebermittlung der seitens der Spitalsdirektion periodisch erstellten Verzeichnisse der Selbstmoerder unde der nach Selbstmordversuchen ins Spital eingelieferten Personen, sowie der seitens des Friedhofsamtes erstellten Verzeichnisse der zur Bestattung freigegebenen Selbstmoerderleichen an die Gestapo, 10.1941- 03.1945.*

offered no protection if you were Jewish," Jacques explained in an interview some sixty years later.[84]

Determined to get his family out of the country, Efraim Hasten made quick decisions and uncomfortable arrangements. He came home one night, shut the blinds, and declared that the family would leave immediately: "'Pack one bag, we are leaving tonight!'" When Jacques's mother Betty resisted the idea, Efraim threatened to take the children and go without her. "'Fine,'" he said, "'but I am taking the kids and we are leaving tonight!'"[85] On that late evening in May 1938 -- barely two months after Anschluss -- the Hastens fled south across "the green border." Jacques recalls how one of his father's "Aryan" employees drove the family with their few suitcases in his father's Mercedes Benz to the Italian border. This man then turned around and drove home, keeping the car, the money he was paid for the favor, and whatever else he could seize.[86]

Efraim Hasten's actions speak for the many individuals who did not lose hope for a future life after Anschluss, although they understood their lives *in Austria* had come to an end. For these people, life under Hitler revolved around one primary concern: "How do we get out, because we have to get out," as thirty-four-year-old Karl Deutsch, a businessman, husband and father, remembered it.[87] This however was not so simple. It was not easy to get official permission to go, nor was it easy on a personal level to leave everything behind for an uncertain future. Flight was a risky pursuit that offered no guarantees, and demanded great sacrifice.

[84] *Boston Herald*, "Why Newton man fled Austria,"17 February 2000: 35.

[85] Jacques Hasten, private interview with author, May 2004. Newton, Massachusetts.

[86] Efraim Hasten did not have authorized papers for his family to exit Austria, nor did he have permanent entry visas to Italy. He had temporary travel visas to Palestine that proved sufficient for transit stay in Italy, but he took a serious risk of being turned back at the border with his family. Jacques Hasten, private interview with author, May 2004. Newton, Massachusetts. For further information on flight across "the green border," entrance and exit papers, and immigration to Palestine, see Chapter 5.

[87] Karl, D., 1997. "Interview by Survivors of the Shoah Visual History Foundation," Hasting-on-Hudson, NY, USA, February 5. Interview Code 25520, Tapes 1-4.

Nevertheless, ordinary persons -- rich and poor, old and young, male and female -- made this decision. Mothers chose to leave their children behind, children to leave their parents, sibling to leave siblings, and husbands to leave their wives. For the chance to reach a safe haven, extremely wealthy persons left behind their life's work, their property, and all their possessions.[88] Knowing that they could no longer practice in Austria, doctors, lawyers, and other professionals also chose flight. Students, too, banned from school, fled in the hope of an education elsewhere.[89] Historians have argued that wealthy people left -- they had the means to do so. Close scrutiny of a wide range of sources reveals that this is not the sole or even dominant pattern; the famous were merely the most visible. The events of Anschluss influenced individuals of all ages, financial status, faith, and professions to pack their bags overnight. The urgency was so great that people fled Vienna, often on impulse, in hope of preserving, maintaining, or rebuilding their lives. Some were successful; others were not. The initial decision to leave always bore a great burden of separation, but those who fled were convinced that they needed take this risk, regardless of the sacrifice. Maria Altmann, Valerie Abrahams, and Natalie Kammermann all fled Vienna at the cost of leaving their mothers behind. Twenty-two-year-old Maria Altmann, from a very wealthy family, fled with her husband to England and lied to her mother to try to protect her from the Gestapo. Valerie Abrahams and her husband decided to attempt flight after the Nazis forced her husband to scrub the streets; both reluctantly left their

---

[88] The financial records of Lilli and Karl Fuchs explain how one Czech couple left their home shortly after Anschluss in a "hurried escape," while claiming to go on a short vacation to Prague. For a detailed contemporary description of what this wealthy couple left behind, see OstA/AdR/06/VVst/VA, 998, Lilli Fuchs.

[89] Eighteen-year-old Rudi Pick was an only child from a family of middle class Czech Jews living in the 9th district. He was in his first year of study at Vienna's Technical University when the Germans took over in March 1938. That Sunday, 13 March, after less than two days of Nazi occupation, Rudi decided to board a train from Vienna to Bratislava, "to await further developments." He planned his departure with his parents and intended to meet them in Prague where his father could continue to work and he could resume his schooling. Years later, Harry credited his escape to his father's decision in 1919 to remain a Czech citizen (rather than acquire Austrian citizenship from the first Republic). In his memoirs he wrote, "I automatically also acquired Czechoslovak citizenship... a blessing in 1938 when the Nazis occupied Vienna... [and I] could go unhindered to Prague... to continue my technical studies." See Ella Pick, *My Mother's Diary*, Ed. Rudi Pick (Pompano Beach, FL, 1989):16, 3.

widowed mothers behind.[90] Seventeen-year-old Natalie Kammerman, from a middle-class family of Orthodox Jews, also fled from Vienna at the risk of permanent separation with her mother. Before Natalie left, she remembered her mother kept saying to her, "'you don't have to go, you can still get off the train.'"[91] But she went anyway.

What influenced these women and others to make this difficult decision is unique to each individual case, but the most significant catalyst was fear. The case of eighteen-year-old Trude Adler illuminates fear as fuel. Fear moved her to flee Vienna in spring 1938; she left friends and family for the chance to work as a parlor maid in England. She tried to withstand daily life in Vienna, but it became too much. Fear first set in when she witnessed Hitler and his supporting masses outside the Hotel Imperial. It intensified when the Gestapo knocked on the door at two o'clock in the morning and took her father away to the police station. And it reached a new level when Nazi men selected her for a forced labor assignment and she was dragged to the German barracks to clean pots and pans. When one SS officer in the barracks ordered her to get on her hands and knees and clean his boots, her life reached a turning point. Sixty years later she remembered that experience clearly: "The next run in with the SS -- that was a very powerful one because it changed my whole attitude and I decided to leave Vienna as fast as I could.... After this I said to my parents, 'I'm sorry, but I have to leave.'" Trude made the decision to leave, hoping that her parents would follow, but not knowing how or when.[92]

---

[90] See, Maria, A. 1996. "Interview by Survivors of the Shoah Visual History Foundation," Los Angeles, CA, USA, March 31. Interview Code 13821, Tapes 1-3; Valerie, A., 1995. "Interview by Survivors of the Shoah Visual History Foundation," Santa Barbara, CA, USA, November 3. Interview Code 08291, Tapes 1-4.

[91] Natalie, P. 1997. "Interview by Survivors of the Shoah Visual History Foundation," Kew, Victoria, AUS, 20 June. Interview Code 32803, Tapes 1-3.

[92] Trude, A., 1996. "Interview by Survivors of the Shoah Visual History Foundation," West Los Angeles, CA, USA, January 10. Interview Code 10786, Tapes 1-3. Similar was the case for Irene Goldrei, also eighteen years old when she fled in May 1938. Irene was from an extremely rich family of Czech Jews living in Vienna on the Argentinerstrasse in the 4th district, quite close to the Rothschilds. Although Irene did not endure physical abuse or humiliation on the same scale as Trude, the events following Anschluss made daily life unmanageable for her as well. She was afraid to carry on with normal activities and the only time she dared to leave the house was to go food

The same fear that drove many to commit suicide, or to risk the permanent separation that came with flight, encouraged others to stay. Fear gripped individuals without reference to class, age, gender, or religious observance. Some remained because they were too afraid to leave, so they tried to persuade themselves and others that Nazism was a passing phenomenon through which they would manage. [93] These people compared their situation to the one in Germany and, as they had done for so many years prior to Anschluss, to their long history of Jewish suffering. [94] Previous scholarship has suggested that those persons who chose to stay on in Nazi Vienna were mostly elderly men who had fought in WWI, but not all veterans took this route -- some turned to flight and others chose suicide. And not *only* veterans took this route -- Jews of different ages, classes, and professions, made the decision to stay. For example, the Hirschbein family was a middle-class family of five living in Vienna's seventh district, directly across the street from Nazi headquarters in an abandoned post office. Eleven-year-old Johanna Hirchbein, the youngest child in the family, recalled the nights of watching people go in and out of this building and how the fear intensified in her home. She also recalled how her forty-five-year-old mother Charlotte stood at the center of the family unit, encouraging everyone to remain calm. Johanna recalled her as practical -- assured that in time, things would be fine. After her father's sudden dismissal

---

shopping. Otherwise, Irene preferred not to go out, but even inside her home she was burdened with endless phone calls, Nazi threats stating that her sister would be arrested for associating with non-Jews, (what the Germans called, "Rassenschande"). Irene understood that life as she knew it in Vienna had come to an end. She needed to get out, no matter what the cost. The cost was great: leaving her mother, father and sister behind. But when Irene made this decision, the fear was so great, she was not focused on leaving her family: "I was too scared to be sad about leaving," she recalled some sixty years later. "I just wanted to get out of there." Irene, G., 1997. "Interview by Survivors of the Shoah Visual History Foundation," London, England, UK, July 10. Interview Code 31296, Tapes 1-5.

[93] The Mandelstams. Lucy Mandelstam, *Unpublished Memoirs*,1998:6.

[94] Hirschbein family. Johanna, S.,1996. "Interview by Survivors of the Shoah Visual History Foundation," Miami, FL, USA, February 21. Interview Code 12280, Tapes 1-7. Jassem family Gerta J., (date currently unavailable). "Interview by Survivors of the Shoah Visual History Foundation," (location currently unavailable). Interview Code 12715.

from work turned him into a broken man, it was her mother Charlotte who kept hope alive within the family and encouraged them to stay in Vienna.[95]

Ironically, the same factors that encouraged families like the Hirschbeins to stay drove others to flee. For example, while many persons from wealthy families fled Austria because they had the financial resources to do so, others rejected the thought of flight precisely because they were rich. They felt protected by their financial resources and could not bear the thought of starting over with nothing.[96] And, while some mothers and fathers sent their children abroad or went ahead of them, others would not consider separating from their children at such a dangerous time.[97] Then too, while some young adults felt they could only bring their parents to safety if they reached a safe haven first, others believed they could not leave their parents in Vienna alone and unprotected. Twenty-year-old Wilhelm Korn -- a strong and healthy young man, recently discharged from the Austrian army -- remained in Vienna because he could not bear the thought of leaving his mother Helen. He reflected upon the difficult decision many years later: "All the other children left Austria to save themselves; I wouldn't leave for nothing-- to leave my mother alone. I was a bit crazy about her because I watched how she cared for all of us with hardly anything."[98] During this time of crisis and disorder, thousands of individuals like Charlotte Hirschbein and Wilhelm Korn were forced to make extremely difficult decisions, all of which demanded great sacrifice. There were no correct answers and there was no solution to the

---

[95] Johanna, S.,1996. "Interview by Survivors of the Shoah Visual History Foundation," Miami, FL, USA, February 21. Interview Code 12280, Tapes 1-7.
[96] Wealth prompted the following persons (for example) to flee: Schueller-Mintz, Hasten, and Goldrei. Wealth prompted the following persons (for example) to remain: Grabkowicz, Spitzer, Bloch-Bauer, Adler.
[97] For more on parents who sent their children ahead see: Pick, Vulkan, Hirschbein. For more on parents who would not leave without their children, or allow their children to leave ahead of them, see: Kluger, Grabkowicz, Altmann-Bloch-Bauer.
[98] Wilhem was from a very poor family of four children, whom his mother had raised single-handedly when his father died following the Great War. They lived together in a small flat in the second district. After Anschluss, Wilhelm's siblings fled immediately. Wilhelm.K., 1996. "Interview by Survivors of the Shoah Visual History Foundation," East St.Kilda, VIC, AUS, August 28. Interview Code 19014, Tapes 1-8. .

dilemmas people faced. There were no guarantees. Nevertheless, the vast majority carried on, making the sacrifices necessary to try to save themselves and their loved-ones.

Conclusions

The spontaneous, unconstrained violence and chaos of Anschluss did not continue for long. On 23 April, Hitler appointed Josef Bürckel Reich Commissioner for the Reunification of Austrian with the German Reich and ordered him to take control over affairs in Austria and put an end to the public violence. The Nazi dictatorship was eager to implement a process of systematic expulsion and expropriation of Austrian Jewry. With this change, open persecution and plundering petered out, the terror of the pogrom dissipated, and suicide numbers decreased. Some Jewish victims, praying for a restoration of stability and order, felt reassured by Bürckel's appointment.[99] But for most the damage had been done: Hitler's Anschluss had convinced a majority that Austria was no longer their home.

Anschluss and the weeks directly following should be recognized as the Vienna Pogrom of spring 1938.[100] During those months, the Nazis and their friends humiliated and dehumanized Austrian Jews and created such an atmosphere of anxiety, fear, and distrust that Jews were willing to do anything "just to get out!" Even suicide surfaced as a reasonable option. G.E.R. Geyde, the Vienna correspondent for the *Times* (London) in March 1938, observed in his memoirs, *Fallen Bastions,* that after Anschluss every Jewish household started to accept suicide as "a perfectly normal and natural incident." In his memory, Austrian Jews spoke "about their

---

[99] Wiley documents this response of the Jews in his report to the State Department from 4 May 1938. With regard to the new aryanization decree (26 April 1938) he wrote, "the order of the Reichs Government requiring all Jews to declare their total fortune at home and abroad ... [has been] accepted with comparative equanimity. Indeed, they [the Jews] feel that there is a degree of safety in the ordinance, since it would tend to give official recognition to Jewish ownership." See NARA, US-State Dept. Records, RG 59/M1209/Reel 7: 863.4016/177. See Report No.217, "Intensified Persecution of the Jews in Austria" Vienna, 4 May 1938: 8.

[100] David Cesarani refers to the Anschluss as a "week-long pogrom." See David Cesarani, *Becoming Eichmann: Rethinking the Life, Crimes, and Trial of a "Desk Murderer"* (Cambridge: Da Capo Press, 2004), 62.

decision to commit suicide in the same tone of voice as they once would have told you that they might go on a short train ride."[101] While Gedye suggested that Jews grew to accept the act of suicide, eyewitness reports from Jews and members of the American legation reveal that these peak waves of suicide undoubtedly weakened Jewish morale, making the community more vulnerable to the Nazi threat. One Jewish woman from a prominent Czech-Jewish family recalled: "Quite a few people killed themselves in the first night -- our family doctor and his wife." She remembered how frightened her family and community became: "It was so dreadful; one can't even describe what one felt."[102]

Not all pogroms lead to genocide. Not all violence leads to genocide. Even Hitler's seizure of Austria did not automatically set in motion the Final Solution. But in retrospect the savage acts unleashed against the Jews of Vienna in 1938, may be considered harbingers of the genocide to come. They represented steps along the road to genocide. These events called for action and intervention, but were an alarm bell that no one heard or knew how to interpret. We now know the Anschluss pogrom was the Germans' first step to genocide, that its success emboldened their developing ideologies and practices, while simultaneously intimidating the Jews, squelching thoughts of resistance and encouraging blind obedience. Days after Eichmann arrived in Vienna to take control over the Jewish situation he boasted: "I have them completely in my hands. They dare not take one step without first consulting me....As it should be."[103] The Anschluss pogrom had set the stage for Eichmann's immediate success, laying the foundation for the future of Jewish cooperation and collaboration -- a desperate measure Jews took in order to preserve their lives.

---

[101] Gedye, *Fallen Bastions:* 304.
[102] Irene, G., 1997. "Interview by Survivors of the Shoah Visual History Foundation," London, England, UK, July 10. Interview Code 31296, Tapes 1-5. Also see, Wilhelm.K., 1996. "Interview by Survivors of the Shoah Visual History Foundation," East St.Kilda, VIC, AUS, August 28. Interview Code 19014, Tapes 1-8.
[103] Cesarani, *Becoming Eichmann,* 65-66.

Chapter Three

The IKG: Co-opted by the New Masters

Illustration 6: "IKG Logo"

Source: USHMM film # 294, IKG-A/W 126, IKG *Report May 2nd 1938- December 31st 1939.*

The terror of the Anschluss Pogrom brought the overwhelming majority of Vienna's Jewish

population to its knees. Most adults had been dismissed from their employment and did not know

how or where they could find new jobs, thus how they could provide their family's next meal.

Children were caught in a terrible new school environment where they were ostracized and

subject to random humiliations and harassment. The elderly watched their families and former

livelihoods unravel. The Nazis had made it clear that Jewish-Austria had come to an end.

Some individuals remained in denial, continuing to compare their situation to that in

Germany, now known as the Old Reich. Some fathers, like Dr. Joseph Grabkowicz (Alix's

father), Hugo Spitzer (Erika's father), and Heinrich Ultmann (Sandor's father) held on to the

same hope they had prior to Anschluss: a hope that Nazism would blow over, that foreign governments would contain German aggression. They did not push their families to take flight, but tried to keep them calm. Likewise, some mothers assumed this role. Lotte Jassem and Charlotte Hirschbein continued to tell themselves and their families they would be able to withstand Nazi persecution. "It will settle down. The Jews in Germany have survived for five years," Lotte told her thirteen-year-old daughter Gerta.[1] "Well, it's not going to be good for the Jews, but there are Jews living in Germany... we will survive," Charlotte explained to her three children and despairing husband who had recently been dismissed from his employment.[2] Years later, Gerta reflected how things would have been different if her parents had chosen flight: "Maybe if my parents had immediately sold everything and went to France....?"[3] Looking back on her father's position after Anschluss, Lucy M. noted with deep sorrow and regret: "Many people committed suicide out of despair, others managed to flee, but our family belonged to that optimistic and naïve majority who believed that it wouldn't last and that everything would be back to normal again."[4] These individuals who tried to remain optimistic about the future of Jewish-Austria in the face of such great adversity were quickly slipping to the margins.

For the rest of the community, such optimism offered little solace for their present condition. The events of the Anschluss Pogrom made it evident that they were not welcome to stay in Austria, but left them unsure of their alternatives. What should they do? Where should they go? How should they escape from the clutches of Nazism? Some individuals made radical

---

[1] Gerta J., (date currently unavailable). "Interview by Survivors of the Shoah Visual History Foundation," (location currently unavailable). Interview Code 12715.
[2] Johanna, S.,1996. "Interview by Survivors of the Shoah Visual History Foundation," Miami, FL, USA, February 21. Interview Code 12280, Tapes 1-7.
[3] Gerta J., (date currently unavailable). "Interview by Survivors of the Shoah Visual History Foundation," (location currently unavailable). Interview Code 12715.
[4] Lucy Mandelstam, *Unpublished Memoirs*, 1998: 6.

and impulsive decisions, packing up their bags and attempting to flee over the border illegally.[5] This decision, however, was not popular. People who left without proper documents could be captured on either side of the border and sent back to Vienna, only to face worse troubles than they had before they left. Rumors of such unsuccessful flight circulated through the community, discouraging others from attempting the act.[6] Others, who tried to flee legally, often met equally disappointing results. Most assumed that the first step was to go to the foreign embassy of the country to which they desired to immigrate. But this visit was not a simple task, nor was it necessarily the most logical first step in the process.[7] The queues outside the buildings sometimes stretched the full length of a city block, and the wait could be anywhere from hours to days. Many individuals were not physically fit to wait in these lines; all who waited were subject to random beatings and attacks from Nazi thugs. If they finally made it into an office, another set of problems awaited them: quota numbers, visas, passport requirements.[8] These people exited the government offices tired and discouraged. To resume a daily existence without fear, they were willing to pay any price. Quickly, the wide divisions between Vienna's Jews began to dissipate; they found themselves with a common goal to escape and an inability do so fast enough. They were desperately seeking aid, organization, and direction.

---

[5] Valerie Abrahams and her husband decided to escape illegally in April 1938. They left their widowed mothers behind.

[6] For example: Twenty-nine-year-old Franz Jung was working as professional opera singer in Prague when the Germans occupied his native Austria. He immediately sent money for his wife Franziska and the rest of his family in Vienna to join him in Prague. His wife came first, and as a Czech citizen had no trouble crossing the border. The situation was not as fortunate for his Hungarian-born mother and his sister, who also held Hungarian citizenship. Although Franz had paid someone to smuggle them over the border, both were refused entry to Czechoslovakia, turned over to the Nazis, humiliated, and then forced to make their way back to Vienna by foot. From Vienna they devised a new plan to escape through Hungary and eventually made it to Switzerland where they reunited with Franz and his wife before leaving for Cuba. See Frank. D., 1996. "Interview by Survivors of the Shoah Visual History Foundation," Los Angeles, CA, USA, April 27. Interview Code 02123, Tapes 1-4.

[7] Charles Stein, private interview with author, May 2005. Washington, D.C.

[8] The complications of the emigration process are detailed in Chapter Five, *Rescue and Destruction: Daily Life During a Mass Exodus*.

Reestablishment of the IKG

It was with complete knowledge of the Viennese Jews' vulnerable position that thirty-two-year-old Adolf Eichmann waltzed his way into Austria and set out to increase his rank and status in the Nazi hierarchy by making the region "Judenrein," free of Jews.[9] In the six weeks since Anschluss, 4,710 Jews had managed to emigrate from Austria despite numerous difficulties (almost five times as many as in the entire previous year), but it was not nearly enough.[10] Reinhard Heydrich, chief of the RSHA, sent Eichmann to Austria with the mission of restoring order and discipline and solving "the Jewish question." Eichmann's solution: to create and enforce a mass expulsion of Austrian Jewry via "emigration." Eichmann understood that such a vast undertaking could be accomplished only with the help of Jewish leaders and the cooperation of the Jewish people. He also understood that the Jews were terrified and desperate to get out of Austria and recognized emigration as the solution to their increasing misery. In this situation they would be forced to bow to cooperation and collaboration.

Eichmann made it his personal mission to reopen the offices of the IKG, closed since 18 March 1938, and restructure the Jewish community of Vienna according to his own specifications. His first step was to meet Dr. Josef Loewenherz, a lawyer and former vice-president of the community, who had been arrested and imprisoned with the other former leaders some weeks earlier. Loewenherz still sat behind bars faced with an unknown fate when Eichmann approached him and gave him his first assignment: to come up with a plan to facilitate

---

[9] In 1938 Adolf Eichmann was still only a second lieutenant SS-Untersturmfuehrer.
[10] See USHMM film # 295, IKG- A/W 123, *Report of the Vienna Jewish Community, January-February 1939* and A/W 125, *Report of the Vienna Jewish Community, May-June 1939.*

the emigration of 20,000 poor Jews from Vienna within one year.[11] It was not long before

Eichmann received consent from the heads of the security service in Berlin and Vienna (Franz

Six and Walter Stahlecker) to have Loewenherz released from prison (20 April 1938). He then

appointed him executive director of the IKG and began to mold him into his personal

messenger.[12] From that moment forward, Loewenherz served as the intermediary between the

German authorities and the Jewish people of Austria. Although he was completely powerless

before Eichmann, he was very powerful in the Jewish community; his word was the only one

that some 180,000 desperate Viennese Jews thought they could trust at this time.

Eichmann held a first meeting with Loewenherz and other future leaders of the IKG on

22 April 1938 at the Gestapo offices on Morzinplatz, a short distance from IKG headquarters.

He ordered Loewenherz and Alois Rothenburg, head of the Palestine Office, to create lists of

Jews who were fit to work for the new IKG and the *zionistishe Zentralverband* (Central Zionist

Union). Their task was to help sustain the community and operate the mass "emigration"

project. He urged them to select Zionist supporters because he knew that Zionists -- who already

wished to immigrate to Palestine -- would be most apt to cooperate with his plan for the future of

---

[11] He was escorted from his cell for his meeting with Eichmann and brought to the Hotel Metropol. See David Cesarani, *Becoming Eichmann: Rethinking the Life, Crimes, and Trial of a "Desk Murderer"* (Cambridge: Da Capo Press, 2004), 64.

[12] Eichmann forced Loewenherz to work under his close supervision and made it a point to continuously remind him of his subordinate and powerless position. During their very first meeting he slapped Loewenherz across the face, and throughout future encounters he continued to degrade, insult, and frighten him. During one particularly long meeting, he made Loewenherz stand for the duration, while he offered chairs to the other, younger Jewish representatives. Rabinovici explained that Eichmann took particular pleasure in exercising his power over Loewenherz. Scholar Hannah Arendt agreed that he was completely powerless under Eichmann's authority, writing of the latter's trial: "[T]he only Jews Eichmann remembered were those who had been completely in his power," (58) including Loewenherz. For further details see Doron Rabinovici, *Instanzen der Ohnmacht: Wien 1938-1945, Der Weg zum Judenrat* (Frankfurt am Main: Judischer Verlag, 2000), 85; Hannah Arendt, *Eichmann in Jerusalem: A Report on the Banality of Evil* (New York: Viking Press, 1963), 42, 58; Peter Z. Malkin and Harry Stein, *Eichmann in My Hands* (New York: Warner Books, 1990), 32.

the Jewish people.[13] On the other hand, he forbade the inclusion of any politically affiliated

assimilated Jews or members of the liberalist faction, the Union of Austrian Jews.[14] He knew

that the former members of these parties were the strongest opponents of the Jewish nationalists

and for the most part Austrian patriots, who believed that Austria was their only home.[15]

Loewenherz and Rothenburg submitted detailed lists of potential IKG workers five days later.

Loewenherz's report was thirty pages and Rothenburg's list was even longer. These were the first

of many lists that the Jewish leaders would be forced to draw up for the Nazi authorities.

Eichmann, however, did not accept either report (and this, too, would become a pattern) but

selected his own personnel for the new leadership of the IKG. He then informed the men that

the offices would reopen four days later, on 2 May 1938. At this moment, when the perpetrators

and victims began to discuss the reconfiguration of the IKG and future of Austria's Jews, the

victims unknowingly became agents in their own destruction.

One of the first meetings between the newly appointed leaders of the IKG and

representatives of community institutions took place in the conference room of the main

Community headquarters on Seitenstettengasse at 5 o'clock in the evening on 11 May 1938. The

meeting lasted exactly half an hour.[16] Loewenherz directed the meeting as chairman, with Emil

Engel, at his side. Eighty-two other individuals representing over eighty different Jewish

institutions throughout Vienna were summoned, and seventy-one persons representing seventy

---

[13] For more on the relationship between Eichmann and the Zionists, see Arendt, *Eichmann in Jerusalem*, 32-62. According to Arendt, Eichmann always despised the assimilationists and he was bored by the Orthodox. He identified with the Zionists, whom he saw as "idealists," like himself, individuals who were willing to put their cause ahead of themselves and their people. He studied the Zionist movement, learned basic Hebrew, and gained a knowledge of the Jewish nationalists that later helped him appease them.

[14] Rabinovici, *Instanzen der Ohnmacht*, 83.

[15] For more information on the political parties of the IKG prior to Anschluss, see Harriet Pass Friedenreich, *Jewish Politics in Vienna, 1918-1938* (Bloomington: Indiana University Press, 1991).

[16] According to the minutes of the meeting kept by M. Kasztan. See USHMM film #742, IKG- A/W 300, *Besprechung des Amtsdirektors mit Vereinsvertretern betreffend die Aufloesung bzw. die weiteren Aktivitaeten von Vereinen. 11.05.1938.*

institutions attended. Among them sat directors and managers from orphanages, kindergartens, homes for the blind, homes for widows, clothing shelters, soup kitchens, charities, various religious organizations, health organizations, women's unions and health organizations, small trade unions, and veterans clubs.

Illustration 7: "Institutions of the Jewish Community of Vienna, October 1938"

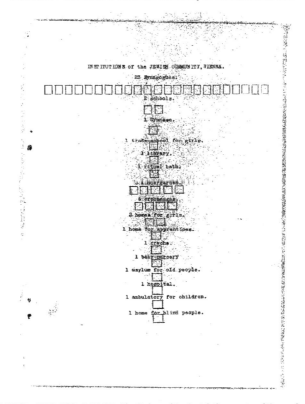

Source: USHMM film # 295, IKG- A/W 121, *The Budget of the Jewish Community of Vienna for the months of November and December 1938.*

After a brief greeting, Dr. Loewenherz addressed the issue at hand: the new financial structure of the IKG institutions, as per German demands. "Under order from the Gestapo ... all Jewish organizations that have not yet been closed are to come under the supervision of the IKG and no move will be made without consent of the community," Loewenherz began. He went on to explain that all Jewish organizations, needed to report all credits and reserves to the authorities. Most institutions receiving money from the community were to be shut down or carry on at a minimal level. Poorly funded organizations were to close and liquidate voluntarily, rather than have the German authorities undertake the task. On the other hand, those organizations receiving money from outside the community could continue to operate and levy membership fees at unlimited rates. Any additional money left at their disposal was to go to the general capital of the community.[17] After relaying these guidelines, Loewenherz reminded his audience that cooperating was in their favor: "This will make the situation easier for the authorities," he remarked, "as it will for the community."[18] He emphasized that the attendees must adhere closely to all orders, and noted that there was to be no discussion or debate of any points covered. Before the meeting was adjourned, he had all attendees sign their names on a sheet of paper next to the printed title of the organization they represented. Chairman Loewenherz, in short, had received his orders from Eichmann and held this meeting to pass along the directives.

A new power structure thus emerged. Loewenherz, serving as Eichmann's messenger, relayed to the rest of the community leadership what the Germans requested and he asked for

---

[17] According to the minutes of the meeting kept by M. Kasztan. See USHMM film #742, IKG- A/W 300, *Besprechung des Amtsdirektors mit Vereinsvertretern betreffend die Aufloesung bzw. die weiteren Aktivitaeten von Vereinen. 11.05.1938.*

[18] USHMM film #742, IKG- A/W 300, *Besprechung des Amtsdirektors mit Vereinsvertretern betreffend die Aufloesung bzw. die weiteren Aktivitaeten von Vereinen. 11.05.1938.*

their cooperation: "The authorities wish the IKG to become and remain the central point of Jewish existence and expect that the IKG will carry out this duty."[19] Eichmann had forced Loewenherz to cooperate, and now Loewenherz asked the leaders of the community institutions to cooperate. Objection to these orders was not an option, for anyone who defied the new German rules risked being imprisoned and sent to a concentration camp. But as there was no alternative, no one had reason to object. In their desperation, they set out to help rebuild the IKG and facilitate the mass emigration process. Forced, they agreed to carry out their duty henceforth under Nazi administration.

Eager to preserve the future for the Jewish people of Austria, no matter what the sacrifice, the IKG leaders and employees began to work together to seek an accommodation with the Nazi enemy. They accepted the position forced upon them, and a dangerous new level of cooperation developed between the perpetrators and victims. Shortly after Loewenherz's meeting with the administrative directors, the IKG directorate drew up a report for the Germans on what the IKG needed to rebuild their community and facilitate the mass emigration project.[20] They began by assuring the Nazi authorities that Austria's Jewish population strongly desired to leave the country and that the IKG stood ready to help them. "Already since the reopening of the community," they wrote, "over 30,000 questionnaires regarding emigration have been distributed, some have been filled out and filed... as soon as a larger percentage of the questionnaires are returned, the community will begin to work on the emigration more

---

[19] Ibid.
[20] The report is dated May 1938, but the exact day is illegible, looks like the 15th. See USHMM film #742, IKG-A/W 300, *Besprechung des Amtsdirektors mit Vereinsvertretern betreffend die Aufloesung bzw. die weiteren Aktivitaeten von Vereinen. 11.05.1938.*

fervently."[21] Then they turned to the main problems the community faced regarding emigration:

"The number of questions from people who are seeking to leave the Reich multiplies.... People

who have a set date in mind when they want to leave but do not know where to turn for help to

obtain an immigration visa.... Requests for information...come unceasingly and we...are not in

the position to give these people information or to help them."[22] Although the IKG had begun to

correspond with various consulates concerning immigration possibilities, it needed further

assistance with these matters and looked to the German-Jewish community for advice. They

therefore asked the German authorities to schedule a meeting with the leaders of the

Reichsvertretung and the *Hilfsvereins* in Berlin.[23]

If the IKG was to prepare its community members for emigration, it needed to sustain

them through the process. Thus, the authors also asked the Germans to approve the funding and

operation of certain Jewish organizations in Vienna essential to the functioning of the

community. They requested that a number of organizations under German authority since

Anschluss be free to operate normally, such as the *Philanthropia* old-age home (Vienna 13,

Lainzerstrasse 172), the Krueger-Heim home for Jewish girls over 14 (Vienna 2, Malzgasse 7),

and a soup kitchen in the sixteenth district. In these cases, they stressed how allowing such

organizations to continue operatations would expedite the emigration process. The *Krueger-*

Heim, for example, could be used to train Jewish girls in trade and handiwork skills, which

would help prepare them for their new lives abroad. Permitting the old-age home to operate

---

[21] USHMM film #742, IKG- A/W 300, *Besprechung des Amtsdirektors mit Vereinsvertretern betreffend die Aufloesung bzw. die weiteren Aktivitaeten von Vereinen. 11.05.1938*
[22] Ibid.
[23] The Reichsvertretung (RV) or national association of all Jewish communities and organizations in Germany was founded in September 1933, on the initiative of the Berlin community. In the aftermath of the November Pogrom the the agency was renamed the *Reichsvereinigung.* Similar to the IKG, the RV was responsible for emigration, education (retraining), and welfare, and looked to establish "a bearable relationship between the Germans and the Jewish people." See Arendt, *Eichmann in Jerusalem,* 35. For more see Lucy Dawidowicz, *The War against the Jews, 1933-1945.*10th ed. (New York: Bantam Books, 1986), 105.

would provide for the increasing number of elderly people whose children sought to emigrate. And the soup kitchen, on Wurlitergasse 11, which had been occupied by an SA unit since 13 March, could feed an additional five hundred hungry people daily if it were reopened. Lastly, the IKG stressed the need for financial assistance to help sustain the despairing Jewish population as its members prepared to emigrate. Having lost their jobs, thousands of individuals could not pay their rent and turned to the IKG for financial support. An even greater percentage of the population depended upon the community for their daily meal. The IKG, however, only had the means to run nine soup kitchens (feeding some 9,000 people daily) and this was not sufficient.[24]

The Community leadership tried to reason with the German authorities, explaining that it could expedite the emigration of Austrian Jewry only with certain permissions and monetary allowances. Eichmann, backed by the Nazi administration, agreed to these and other small concessions, as they conduced to his own objective to rid Austria of Jews.[25] He had reopened the offices of the IKG so the Jewish leaders could promote and advance their own expulsion and he realized that certain Jewish organizations had to be allowed to function for the mass emigration process to be organized and to run smoothly. He also understood the power he could gain and hold over his victims if he kept them in a close and vulnerable situation, in a relationship where they felt they needed him. And the IKG leaders felt they needed Eichmann.

---

[24] USHMM film #742, IKG- A/W 300, *Besprechung des Amtsdirektors mit Vereinsvertretern betreffend die Aufloesung bzw. die weiteren Aktivitaeten von Vereinen. 11.05.1938*
[25] For more on this issue see Chapter 8. See also Rabinovici, *Instanzen der Ohnmacht,* 85; USHMM, RG-60.5009, Tape 3158-3190, *Claude Lanzmann Shoah Collection, Interview with Benjamin Murmelstein* (Rome: 1975).

They felt he was listening to them, that they could reason with him, and that they could in turn make some advances on behalf of their community and themselves.[26]

Hope and deception encouraged IKG cooperation and obedience, becoming decisive steps toward the rescue and the destruction of the community. As Loewenherz and the other leaders of the IKG concluded that emigration was the solution to the misery of the Jews in Austria, they determined to effect this goal. The leadership began to carry out its work with three main objectives in mind: get the community out of Austria, provide social care prior to departure, and care for the sick and elderly who proved unfit for emigration.[27] Not one of these tasks was simple. To organize, finance, and manage the emigration process, the IKG needed to learn about all foreign countries to which immigration was a possibility; to develop a full retraining program for all persons planning to emigrate to make them more suitable and prepared for their country of destination; to begin a working relationship with all Jewish foreign aid committees to obtain funding/sponsorship for emigration; and to keep the community members in compliance with all Nazi decrees -- financial and otherwise -- so they could be granted permission to exit the state. Its other main duty was to maintain the social welfare of the community; to provide soup kitchens, cash support, shelters, hospitals, old-age homes, schools, and orphanages. To fulfill the latter it needed to look beyond cooperation with the German

---

[26] Eichmann testified that the Jewish functionaries ran to him with all their grief and sorrow, whenever they encountered difficulties, and that he helped them. Dr. Franz Meyer, a German-Jewish Zionist, worked with Eichmann and stated that his relationship with members of the Jewish councils was "a kind of cooperation." He recalled that Eichmann not only heard their plea, but "was genuinely listening ... sincerely trying to understand the situation." See Arendt, *Eichmann in Jerusalem*, 59.

[27] The IKG continuously describes its task as threefold. See the following reports drawn up for the foreign aid committees: USHMM film # 295, IKG- A/W 124, *Report of the Vienna Jewish Community, March-April 1939* [slide 0182] and IKG- A/W 119, *Auswanderung, Umschichtung, Fuersorge 02.05.1938-31.07.1939 (Bericht, deutsch, englisch, franzoesisch)* [Slide 0744].

authorities: it needed funding from foreign aid committees and independently wealthy Austrian Jews, and the full support and cooperation of its community workers and members.[28]

As director, Loewenherz oversaw the general administration of the entire community, but he had several leaders operating directly below him. Dr. Benjamin Murmelstein was in charge of the Education and Culture Division of the Community (later, head of the Emigration Department); Dr. Karl Schenk offered legal advice; and Dr. Karl Kapralik ran the Foreign Exchange Office. Under their supervision, Emil Engel stood as head of the Central Office for Social Care and the Emigration Department. Under his supervision, Rosa Schwarz took charge of managing general social care, which oversaw private welfare organizations and youth welfare organizations. Dr. Nahum Blauer oversaw the Emigration Department, which ran offices for emigration advice, registration, correspondence, and final clearance, and Dr. Abraham Schmerler supervised the Retraining Department, which facilitated industrial, agricultural, and youth retraining. In addition, the community maintained offices for education, for unions and societies, for the cemetery, and for the Rabbinate. Then there were the technical offices which handled everything from general registration, to bookkeeping, taxes, auditing financial accounts, and liquidating personal property. Each office had its own director and staff.

---

[28] Note: The IKG managed to obtain all of the above and was able to get people out and care for the community. The number of soup kitchens jumped from nine to fifteen between May 1938 and April 1939; in this same period the number of old-age asylums increased from one to five.

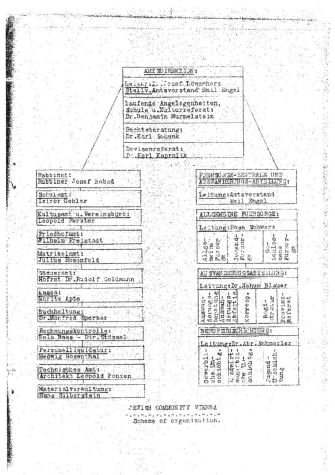

Source: USHMM film # 295, IKG- A/W 121, *The Budget of the Jewish Community of Vienna for the months of November and December 1938* [slide 0058].

To operate such a vast network of services the IKG needed a large, dedicated, and competent staff. When the community reopened on 2 May there were three hundred volunteers at its disposal, eager to help serve.[29] There was also a large staff of paid employees, some of whom had worked previously for the community, others newly appointed. Most of the latter came to work for the community after they lost their former posts or were dismissed from school. Doctors, nurses and medical students could apply for work in the Jewish hospital, teachers and professors could work in Jewish schools or newly established retraining courses, and help was always needed to care for the homeless, to run the soup kitchens, and maintain the orphanages and the homes for the elderly. These men and women, young and old, labored ten to twelve hours a day. Those who were employed worked practically for free. They received no overtime pay, no summer leave, and no pension. But most individuals did not work for the IKG for the money to help sustain themselves; they worked because they saw it as an opportunity to be part of something. Hopelessness ran rampant, and working for the community provided people with a welcome opportunity to keep busy. For example, after twenty-four-year-old Erika Spitzer was fired from the fashionable hat store where she worked on Vienna's most famous street in the first district, am Graben, she decided to volunteer for the IKG, handing out food at one of the soup kitchens. This new job was certainly an adjustment for her, but she found it preferable to the alternative. Erika explained that after Anschluss her mother simply sat around all day and did nothing.[30]

---

[29] USHMM Film # 295, A/W 120, *The Budget of the Jewish Community Vienna for the months of September and October 1938 (Bericht).*

[30] Erica, B., 1996. "Interview by Survivors of the Shoah Visual History Foundation," Upminster, Essex, UK, October 15. Interview Code 20825, Tapes 1-6.

Other people worked for the IKG to ameliorate their chances for emigration, hoping they would be given first priority when it came to being selected and obtaining funding.[31] Hans Morawetz, for example, worked for the technical department of the IKG as a shorthand secretary and typist, receiving a weekly salary of RM 10 and his brother Franz volunteered in the tax office. They lived in very poor financial conditions but did not turn to the community for assistance until they saw a chance to flee to America. In January 1940, Franz wrote a letter on behalf of his brother and himself to the emigration department requesting the funds for two ship tickets from Rotterdam to New York. He stressed their commitment to the work of the IKG and that they had never been a burden before. In response, a handwritten note was placed in his file suggesting that their cases would be granted special attention due to their work for the IKG. Directed to the dispatch office of the emigration department the notice stated: "employees of the IKG can be dispatched for emigration as soon as instructed by the personnel office."[32] Not all IKG employees were able to flee from the country because of their service to the community, but for some, like the Morawetz brothers, this hope fueled their tireless work. Others, by contrast, turned down the opportunity to leave, for they found it their duty to stay and aid the community. All employees and volunteers, regardless of position or how long or how short a time they served the IKG, played an important role providing immediate relief for Vienna's despairing Jews and helping to advance the long-term goal of emigration. At the same time, serving the community affected people's own day-to-day existence positively, offering them a sense of purpose in the midst of the ongoing catastrophe.

---

[31] USHMM film # 295, A/W 120, *The Budget of the Jewish Community Vienna for the months of September and October 1938 (Bericht)*.

[32] See USHMM film #Alpha M7, *Auswanderungsfrageboegen der Israelitischen Kultusgemeinde Wien (IKG), Franz Joseph Morawetz, #12,767* [slide 0867], document dated 18 February 1940 addressed to the dispatch office of the Emigration Department, suggesting that workers of the IKG be given priority regarding emigration. This notice can be found on numerous other questionnaires belonging to IKG employees.

How the IKG Changed Daily Life for the Jews

The IKG warned and advised: try to obey their demands!
~Fred Herlinger, Viennese Survivor

The reopening of the community offices also changed daily life for Jewish people looking for advice and aid. The IKG soon became the central lifeline for Vienna's Jews. As per Eichmann's orders, the IKG began managing all Jewish affairs, public and private. New offices were established to answer all questions about emigration and to encourage, organize, and fund the process strategically. Having a unified body to manage Jewish affairs made life far more manageable for Vienna's Jews than it had been during the previous weeks since Anschluss. As the IKG reorganized the community, it also rebuilt individual people's daily lives, supplying the basic elements of food, shelter, clothing, work, schooling, medical care, and leadership. Equally important, the IKG offered Vienna's Jews hope for the future. This practical and moral support provided renewed strength among the population and unified the people behind the work of the IKG.

Shortly after the IKG reopened its offices, a rush of people flooded the building urgently seeking to emigrate. They all declared with equal vigor: "I just want to get away - where to, does not matter."[33] The majority did not know or care where they went; they did not know which countries would accept them as refugees or what steps they needed to follow to be admitted; they looked to the IKG for help. The IKG leaders, who had no idea how to organize such an extensive operation as emigration en mass, turned to the Jewish Community in Berlin (RV) for

---

[33] See USHMM film #U52, IKG- A/W 2591, *Berichte ueber die Organisation und die Taetigkeit der Auswanderungsberatungsstelle.*

guidance. Before long, the IKG had established its own central office to handle emigration and

had contacts in Jewish relief agencies around the world.[34] The Emigration Advisory Office

provided literature on the different host countries, including the preconditions for entering each,

making the entire process more manageable for the average person.[35] The office offered written

and verbal advice -- information on everything emigrants needed to know -- including the

requirements to get out of Austria and into other countries. Additionally, the central office

ensured that all other offices involved with emigration were privy to the same information, so

that potential emigrants had the opportunity to obtain information in many different locations.[36]

Motivated by the firm belief that it could rescue each and every Austrian Jew from Nazism via

orderly emigration, the IKG took this important step in organizing the emigration process. In

turn, emigration became an equal opportunity for all members of the community, rich and poor

alike.[37]

    With the reopening of the community offices and in particular the establishment of the

Emigration Advisory Office, the IKG offered a message of hope to all of Austria's Jews, rich and

poor, young and old, religious and non-religious: prepare for the future of Austrian Jewry outside

of Austria! The IKG explained that leaving Austria was the only solution to their misery. They

---

[34] By December 1938 the emigration offices were in regular contact with the following agencies: Council for German Jewry, German Jewish Aid Committee, International Student Service, Inter Aid Committee, and National Coordinating Committee in London; American Joint Distribution Committee (Joint), HICEM, and Comité Central d'Assistance in Paris; EZRA in Anvers; HIDAG in Brussels; Fuersorgekommission der Iraelitische Kultusgemeinde and Hilfsverein fuer juedische Fluechtlinge in Zurich; EZRA in Luxembourg; Comite voor Joodsche Vluchtelingen in Amsterdam; Komitet Miedzyorganizacyjny in Warsaw; Det Mosaiska Troessamfund in Copenhagen; Commissao Portuguese de Assistenca in Lisbon; Australian Jewish Welfare Society in Sidney; the Victorian Committee in Melbourne; and the Jewish Colonization Association in Rio de Janeiro. USHMM film # 295, IKG- A/W 121, *The Budget of the Jewish Community of Vienna for the months of November and December 1938.*

[35] Wealthier individuals could hire a lawyer to research immigration options and handle paperwork for them but, this was not the case for the average person seeking to emigrate.

[36] USHMM film #U52, IKG- A/W 2591, *Berichte ueber die Organisation und die Taetigkeit der Auswanderungsberatungsstelle.*

[37] For more information on emigration/immigration expenses and on how the rich financed the poor, see Chapter 5: *Rescue and Destruction: Daily Life During a Mass Exodus.*

also stressed that this could be accomplished only through carefully planned emigration with the IKG and by following all of the IKG's instructions. The community begged Jews to support emigration and to support one another, and to obey. In return, they showed uninformed Jews who wanted to emigrate how to do so, and urged ambivalent Jews to take flight. They encouraged children who were reluctant to leave their parents behind to go ahead, and, persuaded parents to let their children go.[38] Suddenly, the voice of the IKG rang strong among Austria's Jews, pleading with the previously diverse and multifaceted community to set aside their differences and cooperate with the IKG: "To all members of the Jewish community! Our community, formed by a common past and a common fate, will only by a firm union be able to prepare for our future. It is our duty to do the best in order to diminish the misery and to support all those who are suffering from hunger. Only in conscience of having fulfilled our duty, we will bring up the necessary force and calm to begin a new life. Therefore the community calls up all her members to collaborate and to help."[39] Driven by fear and hope, the persecuted members had no alternative but to adhere to the instructions of the IKG, which meant they were actually following Eichmann's orders.

The Voice of the IKG

> *All Jews living in Vienna should be aware the* Zionistische Rundschau *is the only Jewish paper permitted by the authorities. All announcements will appear in this paper only.*
>
> ~Zionistische Rundschau, 3 June 1938: 5

---

[38] For an example of this message, see: "Der Weg der Jugend," *Zionistische Rundschau*, 27 May 1938: 1. "An honorable and good mother would suffer to secure her child's safety -- not keep the child by her side out of fear that she could not live without him."

[39] This is the original English as printed in the report *The Budget of the Jewish Community of Vienna for the months of November and December 1938.* According to this report, the call for unity was not only published in the *Zionistische Rundschau* in October 1938, but an additional 25,000 copies were privately distributed to the certain community members. USHMM film # 295, IKG- A/W 121:5.

In the wake of the reestablishment of the IKG, the Germans permitted the community to publish

a weekly newspaper. It quickly became the mouthpiece of the IKG. Its name, the *Zionistische*

Rundschau (Zionist Circular), chosen by Eichmann, was an extension of Nazi ideology,

emphasizing that Jews belonged to the Jewish state, not to greater Germany.[40] And, the

privilege to print a weekly Jewish newspaper was not free; the Germans demanded that the paper

assume full responsibility for publishing all government orders on economic matters, emigration,

and welfare. The newspaper needed to publicize Nazi decrees and anti-Jewish laws, outline how

these orders should be followed, urge people to be attentive and obedient to such regulations, and

warn that full cooperation was necessary to secure emigration. Thus, the paper served two

purposes. It was a Nazi apparatus aimed at expediting the expulsion of Austrian Jewry and

expropriating their assets. At the same time, the IKG sought to use the paper to help rescue

Austrian Jewry. Readers did not know that it was censored by Eichmann himself and that he

considered it "his" paper.[41] For them, the weekly publications were a voice of reason and hope

in the midst of their turmoil, providing advice and possible solutions to their common questions

and concerns.[42] Idealistic articles -- adorned with cheerful photographs from Palestine --

encouraged emigration, while other articles called for unity within the community and

cooperation with the German enemy. As they began following the IKG's instructions, they

---

[40] Cesarani, *Becoming Eichmann*, 65.
[41] See letter from Eichmann in, Yitzhak Arad, Israel Gutman, and Abraham Margaliot, *Documents On the Holocaust: Selected Sources On the Destruction of the Jews of Germany and Austria, Poland, and the Soviet Union.* (Jerusalem: Ktav Pub. House in association with Yad Vashem [and the] Anti Defamation League, 1981), 93-94.
[42] People read the *Zionistische Rundschau* to stay informed, see note from Dr. Max Jerusalem to medical advisory board of the IKG, 8 October 1938. USHMM film #T1, IKG- A/W 2612, XXIV. *Aerzteberagtung, Verpflichtungserklaerungen zugelassener Aerzte,auch Spitalsaerzte.* Also note: In Germany the circulation of the Zionist weekly (die *Jüdische* Rundschau) increased from approximately five to nearly forty thousand readers in the first months of the Hitler regime.

began to follow the instructions of the Nazi administration. Thus, the paper was a significant method of extending Nazi policy, from the Germans to the Jewish leaders to the Jewish people.

Starting with the first issue on 20 May 1938 and continuing throughout the six months of its operation, the *Zionistische Rundschau* sought to secure Jews' cooperation with the IKG's mission. First and foremost, it informed everyone that emigration was the future of Austrian Jewry, the one and only solution to increasing hardship. The paper explained that the community was in the process of rebuilding its infrastructure specifically to help facilitate the emigration process and help all willing Jews leave the country. The IKG also stressed that it intended to help everyone, regardless of age, gender, income, or previous profession. Children were a priority. Articles on emigration covered the standard twelve pages, ranging from instructions for emigration, advertisements by ship companies, foreign language lessons, information about retraining courses, and information from foreign countries. Special articles by Viennese Jews who had already escaped highlighted the positive aspects of starting a new life abroad. These pieces often included personal letters and cheerful photographs of children and families settled in their new homes. The émigrés addressed the potential emigrants' top concerns; they spoke about work hours, pay packets, and the cost of basic items. They also discussed the climate.[43]

An appeal by IKG director Loewenherz and Chief Rabbi Dr. Taglicht for unity covered the front page of the first issue. They declared that all Austrian Jews, regardless of previous political party or degree of religious observance, were members of one family; they should be proud of their faith and try to revive Judaism.[44] Other articles stressed the community leaders' request for cooperation and unity. "To Those Who Stand Apart" called out specifically to

---

[43] *Zionistische Rundschau*, 20 May 1938: 2.
[44] "Aufruf der Israelitischen Kultusgemeinde: An die Juden Wiens," *Zionistische Rundschau*, 20 May 1938: 1.

assimilated Jewish adults to return to their Jewish brethren.[45] The editors turned to the wealthier Jews in the community and asked them to remember their poor coreligionists and support their emigration and welfare by donating money to the IKG.[46] Still other articles addressed the staff and students of the Jewish schools in the second district, reminding them to welcome the Jewish children from districts all over Vienna now attending their schools.

The IKG used the paper to explain matters of common interest. An article in the inaugural issue, for example, reported on immigration to America. The editors pointed out that in the first ten days after Anschluss (21 March to 1 April) over 25,000 people inquired at the American consulate.[47] The overwhelming number seeking to enter the US had prompted the American government to combine the Austrian quota (1,413) with the German quota (25,957). This improved Austrian Jews' immigration prospects.[48]

Week after week, the editors asked people to be patient in their struggle to flee Austria and with the work of the IKG.[49] Meanwhile, the paper urged individuals not to be hasty and attempt to slip over the green border. People who fled without proper exit and entrance papers would be denied help from Jewish relief agencies abroad, turned back to Vienna, and then refused help from the IKG also, they warned.[50] The repeated message was clear and unequivocal: follow the strategic and organized emigration process developed by the IKG. Register with the community, and from that point on all emigration matters would be handled

---

[45] *Zionistische Rundschau*, 20 May 1938: 2.

[46] USHMM film # 295, IKG- A/W 121, *The Budget of the Jewish Community of Vienna for the months of November and December 1938.*

[47] For more on entry to USA, see USHMM film # 294, IKG-A/W 126, *Report of the Vienna Jewish Community. A description of the activity of the Israelitische Kultusgemeinde Wien in the period from May 2ⁿᵈ 1938- December 31ˢᵗ 1939 (2 Exemplare):156.*

[48] "Auswanderung-Wohin? Die Auswanderungsberetischaft," in *Zionistische Rundschau*, 20. May 1938: 3.

[49] "Der Arbeit der Kultusgemeinde: Errichtung einer zentralen Auswanderungsabteilung," *Zionistische Rundschau*, 20 May 1938: 3.

[50] "Wichtige Mitteilung fuer die Auswanderung," *Zionistische Rundschau*, 20 May 1938:4.

through the centralized Emigration Department of the IKG. Individuals should not attempt to contact relief agencies or organize emigration on their own.

Emigration Questionnaires

Registration began with presenting a request to the Emigration Department. This office assumed responsibility for immigration to all lands, with the exception of Palestine for which there was a separate office called the Pal-Amt (Palestine Office) on Marc Aurelstrasse 5, a few blocks away. The initial registration process was a short four-page questionnaire, free of charge, to be filled out one per family. The department made the forms available for pick-up on the ground floor of the main IKG office and, after completed, they were to be returned to that same office. These instructions were detailed in the *Zionistische Rundshau*, among other rules that applied to carrying out an "organized emigration."[51]

Filled out by the head of household, the form included the applicant's name, address, birth date, birth place, marital status, nationality, residency status in Vienna, and whether and how long the applicant had resided anywhere else. What were the applicant's profession and last held position, financial circumstances, and monthly income? Addressing the technicalities of the emigration process, was the applicant able to procure all the necessary documents for exit, entrance, and travel? What financial resources did the applicant have at his/her disposal to cover these costs? Was passport information updated and available? Could he/she provide personal references for

---

[51] People already in possession of an immigration visa could obtain a personal meeting with a staff member of the Emigration Department. They were given priority over others so that their visas would not expire during the process of acquiring other necessary documents. Since the goal of the IKG was to facilitate the greatest possible number, preference for a given file was not necessarily dependent upon one's background and qualifications, but due to timing. One could be pushed ahead in the process simply because one's papers were ready. For such cases, a special section of the Emigration Department was open daily from 9:00 to 1:00 and the applicant was asked to bring all required documents and verification in preparation for the meeting. See "Planmaessige Auswanderung," *Zionistische Rundschau*, 3 June 1938.

the case? Where did the applicant want to go and why? What languages did the applicant speak, and had he/she learned any new profession with the intent of taking it up abroad? What were the applicant's personal plans for settling abroad? Did the applicant have relatives and friends whom he/she would join? People who would sponsor his/her stay? If so, what were their names, addresses, and relationships to the applicant? Finally, the questionnaire asked for information about dependents: names, ages, birth place, profession, and relationship to the applicant. There was space to enter up to ten people. The last question asked "Who among these people should emigrate now, and who later?" With these questions, most Jews began a long and complicated struggle to flee Vienna. At the same moment, they began to set their sights on the future.

Illustration 9: "Sample Emigration Questionnaire, Harry Gruenberg"[52]

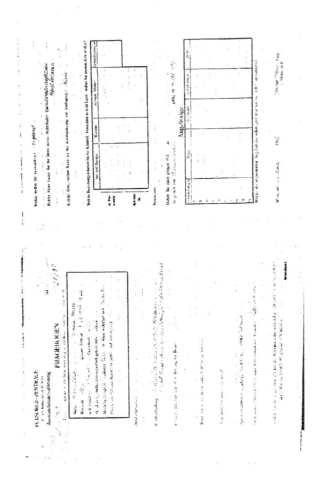

Source: USHMM, Emigration Questionnaires, Alphabetical. CAHJP, IKG Archiv, Aktenverzeichnis 2.Teil -B, A/W, XXV. Auswanderung, H. Fragebogenausgabe, (2337) 2590, 1-274 *Über die Auswanderungwilligen angelegte Akten (Von den Parteien ausgefüllte Emigrationsfragebögen, alph.; mit Bearbeitungsvermerken und diversen Unterlagen)....1938- (1940).*

---

[52] See appendix for English translation.

Retraining

Jews eager to leave needed skills to earn a living elsewhere. Thus, retraining surfaced as a top priority for the IKG, emphasized by the *Zionistische Rundschau*, the Emigration Advisory Office, and through private communications, such as word of mouth and letters. Those who worked in the Emigration Office, who were in constant contact with all the consulates and foreign relief agencies, quickly learned that the pre-Anschluss occupations of most Jews were not suitable for building a life abroad. Most overseas countries sought agricultural work and qualified craftsmen. England, Holland, and Sweden sought positions for domestic help, for example, but few Jews had held such positions. The IKG therefore established retraining courses in farming, domestic service, cosmetics, leather industry, building industry, clothing industry, graphic industry, chemical industry, metal industry, and foreign languages.[53] The newspaper informed people what trades were desirable in which countries and when they could visit the IKG to receive occupational advice, education, and retraining: Monday through Thursday afternoons, 2 to 6 pm, on the second floor, Seitenstettengasse 4. For certain professional groups, like doctors and lawyers, an expert advisor would be in the same place from 6 to 8 in the evenings.[54]

Retraining began in the advisory office in the IKG, and thousands of people came to sign up for courses. Potential emigrants were examined with regard to physical suitability and then advised according to the requirements of his/her desired country of destination. The participants did not pay for the courses or the materials used; the IKG covered these costs with funding from foreign aid committees. People often applied for a class recommended to them by a relative or

---

[53] For photos of IKG retraining courses, see appendix. Also See USHMM film # 294, IKG-A/W 126, *Report of the Vienna Jewish Community. A description of the activity of the Israelitische Kultusgemeinde Wien in the period from May 2nd 1938- December 31st 1939 (2 Exemplare)*; *Zionistische Rundschau*, 2 September 1938.
[54] "Planmaessige Auswanderung" *Zionistische Rundschau*, 3 June 1938.

acquaintance who had already taken the course. Some people received letters from relatives abroad explaining that they would need to learn a new trade to earn their living in their country of destination and they opted for any course with space available.[55] Many people signed up for a course but had the opportunity to leave before training began. Within the first three months the IKG established 240 retraining courses. Language courses in Hebrew, English, Spanish, French, and Portuguese were particularly popular and educated 2,700 participants. Agricultural retraining courses were more difficult to establish because the IKG had little access to suitable agricultural industries or necessary legal licenses, and they were more expensive than most classes because the IKG had to pay for the lodging and support of the participants. Still, the IKG established seven agricultural courses with one hundred participants each. The IKG also developed other retraining courses for youth between the ages of fourteen and seventeen who had been thrown out of school.[56]

Courses kept people occupied, providing many with classes and homework and others with the opportunity to teach. They also kept people focused on the future, filling them with hope of gaining entry to a foreign country and obtaining work abroad. The IKG understood the value of these courses and their positive effect on the community. In a report they drew up for the foreign aid committees, the leadership explained how the retraining program boosted morale:

> All persons concerned, i.e. masters and pupils are aware of the following: Retraining teaches to become happier through working, gives confidence and self-consciousness, knowledge and earnings, facilitates the entrance of emigrants, working manually and productively, enables their accommodating to new

---

[55] USHMM film # 295, IKG- A/W 125, *Report of the Vienna Jewish Community, May-June 1939.*
[56] USHMM film # 295, IKG- A/W 120, *Verwaltung: Taetigkeitsberichte der Gemeindefuehrung, The Budget of the Jewish Community Vienna for the months of September and October 1938 (Bericht).*

professions in new countries, avoids superabundance of certain professions, furthers and perfects abilities and grants values, nobody will able to destroy, to be used everywhere. Retraining will help middle-classes gaining a new point of view towards handicrafts. It helps building a new kind of human being in honoring and loving the handicrafts. Professions learned by retraining are not meant to be professions of secondary meaning but a new one enabling people to earn a new livelihood.[57]

Course participants also understood the significance of retraining. Thousands sent letters to the

IKG expressing their thanks: "I am convinced that we all will be able to earn our lives in a

foreign county, by means of these knowledges acquired in the courses... I am thoroughly

convinced not to be a charge to that country which should be willing to take me up, but to be a fit

worker who would not be afraid of the struggle of life, for I have been excellently shaped out in

my trade. Therefore I say warmly my thanks to the 'Jewish community' for its great work of

training professions and its real aid."[58] By July 1939, over 45,000 people had come to the

Emigration Advisory Office to inquire which course they should take, and over half (24,000) had

actually participated.[59] The retraining program had restructured the community over the course

of one year. The male population, for example, had transformed from professors, lawyers,

physicians, merchants, journalists, students, officials, tradesmen, and clerks... into farmers,

butlers, chauffeurs, shoe makers, and industrial workers. Due to the organization and diligence

of the IKG, these men were made suitable for emigration.

---

[57] USHMM film # 294, IKG- A/W 119, *Auswanderung, Umschichtung, Fuersorge 02.05.1938-31.07.1939 (Bericht, deutch, englisch, franzoesisch)* [Slide 0743].
[58] USHMM film #UZ/2, IKG-A/W 2623, *A. Schmerler, The action for change of profession of the Emigration Department of the Jewish Headquarters in Vienna and its success during the year 1938.* English Original.
[59] Ibid. For more on education and retraining see Lucy Dawidowicz, *The War against the Jews, 1933-1945.*10th ed. (New York: Bantam Books, 1986); Marion Kaplan, *Between Dignity and Despair: Jewish Life in Nazi Germany* (New York: Oxford University Press, 1998).

Preliminary Results of Organized Emigration: Rescue or Destruction?

The first questionnaires registered and filed by the Emigration Office were signed and dated by

the applicants on 9 and 10 May 1938. As each was submitted, it received a number, hand-

written or stamped in the upper right corner, and was filed. As each case was processed, the

questionnaire was transferred to an alphabetical register. The IKG could not distribute, receive,

or process the emigration questionnaires fast enough. On an average day between two and three

thousand people rushed to the Emigration Office. By the beginning of June the *Zionistische*

Rundshau estimated that over 25,000 Jews had picked up a form and begun their "organized"

quest to leave the country.[60] Forty-five-year-old Fritz Czuczka, who registered to immigrate to

Great Britain or the United States with his wife Charlotte and twelve-year-old son George,

signed and dated his questionnaire on 20 May 1938. Still very early in the process, his file was

assigned number 21,297![61]

The overwhelming number of questionnaires filled out in such a short time span

demonstrated Austria's Jews' desperation to get away. It also showed that they had taken a

decisive step -- in unison -- supporting organized emigration through the institution of the IKG.

Practically all Jews, females as well as males, young and old, from different class backgrounds,

religious backgrounds, and professions, were willing to cooperate with the IKG in order to

secure escape. As of October 1938, the community records calculated that 34,730 men and

8,606 women with 28,404 male and 46,239 female dependents had registered to emigrate,

making a total of 117,979 individuals, 63,134 of whom were male and 54,845 female. People

born in 1901-1904 (aged 34-38) filled out the greatest number of forms (7,286) and the elderly,

---

[60] *Zionistische Rundschau,* 3 June 1938.
[61] USHMM film #Alpha C, *Auswanderungsfrageboegen der Israelitischen Kultusgemeinde Wien (IKG), Fritz Czuczka, # 21,297* [slides 0183-0189].

born in1850-1860 (aged 78-88), filled out the fewest (51). The second smallest number of forms

(403) was filled out by children born in 1921-1925 (aged13-17). People aged 43-47 filled out

almost a thousand more forms than people aged 18-22.[62] Although almost four times as many

men as women filled out forms, still a significant number of women took on the role of head of

household.

Table 4: "Who Filled out the Emigration Questionnaires?"

Head-Registered Emigrants:							
			Men				Women
			34,730				8,606
Date of Birth:				Nationality:			
1850-1860	51	1861-1870	588	Germany	33,466	Romania	299
1871-1880	2688	1881-1890	6757	Poland	4,231	Hungary	278
1891-1895	5022	1896-1900	5362	Stateless	3,851	Various	52
1901-1905	7286	1906-1910	7221	C.S.R.	1,132	S.H.S.	27
1911-1915	4815	1916-1920	3143				
1921-1925	403						
Professions:							
	Trade		10,855				3,139
	Employees		10,914				3,314
	Merchants		7,995				420
	Free Professions		4,183				870
	Agriculture		443				821
	Various Professions		340				42
		Total Head-Registered					43,336
Dependants:							
			28,404				46,239
Total Registered for Emigration with IKG:			117,979				

Source: USHMM film # 295, A/W 121, *The Budget of the Jewish Community of Vienna
for the months of November and December 1938.*

[62] USHMM film # 295, A/W 121, *The Budget of the Jewish Community of Vienna for the months of November and December 1938.*

Emigration questionnaires also demonstrated Austria's Jews' desperate willingness to travel anywhere and learn new trades in order to be accepted into a country. As Leo Spitzer explained, "To find a haven from the madness was what mattered."[63] Forty-eight-year-old Erwin Wellwarth, a decorated officer in World War I and the general manager and financial secretary of the movie theater union, retrained in artificial flower production and ceramic manufacturing in order to get his wife Marta, six-year-old son George, and himself to Argentina or the USA.[64] Forty-four-year-old Dr. Hans Grabkowicz retrained from dentistry to portrait photographer as he registered for his sixty-five-year-old mother Anna and himself to immigrate to Australia, South America, New Zealand, Holland, British India, English Dominicans, Egypt, England, France, Belgium, or Switzerland.[65] Thirty-five-year-old Sandor Ultmann hoped to receive his international driving license as he registered for his wife Sefi (Josephine) and himself to immigrate to any of the English colonies, the USA, or South America.[66] Karl Deutsch spoke for his community when he explained that life at that time revolved around one primary concern: "How do we get out, because we have to get out." Karl was thirty-four when he registered to leave with his mother Laura, in-laws Johann and Olga, wife Gertrud, and two-year-old son Heinrich, to anywhere overseas with a climate suitable for a small child or where he knew the language (German/French/English): the Dominions, USA, Europe, or Norway. He was the

---

[63] Leo Spitzer, *Hotel Bolivia: The Culture of Memory in a Refuge from Nazism.* (New York: Hill and Wang, 1998) 185. Leo Spitzer immigrated to Bolivia.

[64] USHMM film #10, *Auswanderungsfrageboegen der Israelitischen Kultusgemeinde Wien (IKG) (Numerisch geordnet): Erwin Wellwarth-Velwart, file #5,871.* Erwin, Marta, and George Wellwarth immigrated to the United States.

[65] USHMM film #Alpha T3, *Auswanderungsfrageboegen der Israelitischen Kultusgemeinde Wien (IKG), Dr. Hans Grabkowicz, #12,630* [slides 1111-1112]. The Germans permitted his older brother Dr. Joseph Grabkowicz to continue his dental practice, although exclusively for Jews. Joseph did not register for his wife, two daughters, and himself to emigrate until much later than most, 21 August 1938. Dr. Hans Grabkowicz emigrated successfully, his brother did not.

[66] USHMM film #Alpha U1, *Auswanderungsfrageboegen der Israelitischen Kultusgemeinde Wien (IKG), Sandor Ultmann, # 1,458* [slides 0371-79]. Sandor and Josephine immigrated to Shanghai.

manager of a small business in Vienna's first district that specialized in the import/export of technical and commercial accessories to large manufacturers. He was still working in this store, although a Nazi "commissioner" had been appointed to it, but he was also taking beginning courses in optical trade and music history, and he was teaching first-aid to Jewish youth aged fourteen and younger preparing to immigrate to Palestine.[67]

The IKG calculated that in the six weeks from 1 September - 15 October 1938, they distributed over RM 551,550.80 to support the immigration of 5,476 men and 4,089 women (10,585 persons) to all the peopled continents, Europe, North America, Central and South America, Asia, and Africa, and to seventy-six different countries. The top ten (in descending order) were the USA (2000), Palestine (1384), England (1321), Switzerland (681), Czechoslovakia(480), Argentina(444), France (316), China (289), Italy (263), and Luxembourg(248).[68] Many of these emigrants departed with a great sigh of relief, seeing their escape as temporary exile and planning to reunite with their relatives and return to Austria as soon as the air had cleared. Others left with a heavy heart, fearful of the future.[69] Still, people were getting out and for the IKG employees who labored day after day to make this mass exodus possible, such positive results kept them motivated to dispatch the next waiting emigrant. The IKG's goal to organize immigration for as many Jews as possible, in the shortest amount of time, was being achieved due to cooperation between the community leadership, workers, and members -- and their ability to carry out German demands.

---

[67] USHMM film #31, *Auswanderungsfrageboegen der Israelitischen Kultusgemeinde Wien (IKG) (Numerisch geordnet): Karl Deutsch, file #19,940* [frame 0720-0721]; Karl, D., 1997. "Interview by Survivors of the Shoah Visual History Foundation," Hasting-on-Hudson, NY, USA, February 5. Interview Code 25520, Tapes 1-4.
[68] USHMM film # 295, IKG- A/W 121, *The Budget of the Jewish Community of Vienna for the months of November and December 1938.* Karl Deutsch and his extended family immigrated to the United States.
[69] See Spitzer, *Hotel Bolivia,* 185.

Illustration 10: "Original IKG Emigration Chart"

Source: USHMM film # 294, IKG-A/W 126, IKG *Report May 2nd 1938- December 31st 1939*.

Conclusions

As political scientist Hannah Arendt put it, Dr. Josef Loewenherz "was the first Jewish

functionary actually to organize a whole Jewish community into an institution at the service of

the Nazi authorities." Driven by fear but motivated by hope, the IKG quickly instituted and

began to operate a mass emigration system sending Viennese Jews to all parts of the world.

The leaders believed in the wisdom of their strategy and that they could save their community;

the employees and volunteers worked day in and day out -- offering advice, retraining, financial

aid, and moral support to facilitate the process.[70] In every bulletin and newsletter, the IKG

expressed its intention to arrange for the exit of all Jews who wanted to leave. All they asked for

in return was cooperation. It was a great irony: as they set out to rescue and preserve the future of

their community, they were also facilitating its destruction. They asked people to stop thinking

---

[70] In an IKG report on the organization and duties of the Emigration Department, the following quote is emphasized: "An old Jewish saying goes: The most expensive thing in the world is good advice." USHMM film #U52, IKG-A/W 2591, *Berichte ueber die Organisation und die Taetigkeit der Auswanderungsberatungsstelle.*

and reacting as individuals, and to conform to the marking their enemies had given them, "Der Jude."[71] With the reopening of the IKG, the Germans co-opted the Jewish leadership to implement such compromising demands.

Doron Rabinovici is one of few historians to have analyzed the IKG's position and recognize its significance to our understanding of the Holocaust and other genocides.[72] In his work, *Instanzen der Ohnmacht, Wien 1938-1945, Der Weg zum Judenrat*,[73] he highlighted the fact that "the prototype of a Jewish administration functioning under National Socialist domination" was established at this time. "[The IKG was] a test model [vorlaufsmodel] of the Judenrat."[74] He explained, moreover, that the administration had no alternative other than collaboration with the Germans. Any strategy it used, whether protest or cooperation, was powerless to protect the Jews of Austria.[75] Hannah Arendt, whose scholarship pre-dates Rabinovici's by almost thirty years, also held that Austria's Jews had no other alternative. At the same time, however, she emphasized that the IKG cooperated with the Germans in 1938 because it was enabling the rescue of their community: "The Jews 'desired' to emigrate, and he, Eichmann, was there to help them, because it so happened that at the same time the Nazi authorities had expressed a desire to see their Reich Judenrein. The two desires coincided...."[76] Arendt also made the important distinction that this wish to emigrate developed only *after* the

---

[71] Leo Spitzer addresses the loss of individuality among the Jews after the Nazi takeover and in relation to the refugee experience. See Leo Spitzer, *Hotel Bolivia*, 21, 57.

[72] Other recent works recognize the importance of the "Vienna Model." See Dan Michman, *Holocaust Historiography: A Jewish Perspective, Conceptualizations, Terminology, Approaches and Fundamental Issues.* (London, Vallentine Mitchell: 2003); see, too, David Cesarani, *Becoming Eichmann*, 64.

[73] Translation: *Instances of Powerlessness: The Path of the Jewish Council, Vienna 1938-1945.* Note: all translations by the author unless otherwise specified.

[74] Rabinovici, *Instanzen der Ohnmacht*: 82.

[75] See Doron Rabinovici, "Die Wiener Judenraete unter der NS-Herrschaft," Vortrag am 14. Februar 2002 in Ebensee, in *Eine Zeitschrift des Zeitgeschichte Museums under der KZ-Gedenkstaette Ebensee* (Ebensee, Austria) 2002:20.

[76] See Arendt, *Eichmann in Jerusalem*: 58 (emphasis added).

Germans had inflicted such great terror upon the Jews that they had begun to fear for their lives. She urged her readers to consider the term "mass emigration" to describe what was in fact a "forced expulsion," reminding them how one never chooses to uproot oneself -- to leave ones home, family, and country is a desperate measure.[77]

Two days after Eichmann reopened the community offices, American Consul General Wiley warned the US government not to be fooled by the lull in violence against the Viennese Jews: "Outright terror will merely be replaced by the 'cold pogrom,'" he wrote in a report called "Intensified Persecution of the Jews in Austria (4 May 1938)." He continued, "[I]t may be forecast that the campaign of physical terror against the Jews is perhaps in its last stages but that the legal measures which will follow will in no way lighten the Jews' burdens."[78] Wiley was correct: it was in fact during this quiet time at the start of the 'cold pogrom' that the seeds of genocide were planted one foot deeper. When Loewenherz, Murmelstein, and the other leaders began to cooperate with Eichmann, and called on their people to cooperate as well, a dangerous perpetrator/victim relationship formed. At the time neither the Jewish leaders, nor ordinary Jewish citizens, nor Nazi authorities understood how this relationship would affect the future. Wiley suggested that the US government keep a close watch on German-Jewish affairs in Vienna and not be deceived by what looked like a restoration of order, but his lonely voice went unheard. It was a decisive moment in history for the Jews of Austria and for European Jewry as a whole, but a key democracy, like its peers, did not understand its significance, took no notice, and let a critical turning point pass. Would anyone recognize the next one?

---

[77] See Arendt, *Eichmann in Jerusalem*, 43.
[78] NARA, US State Dept. Records, RG 59/M1209/Reel 7: 863.4016/177. See Report No.217, "Intensified Persecution of the Jews in Austria" Vienna, 4 May 1938: 15 (John C. Wiley, American Consul General to Mr. Messersmith, Secretary of State).

Chapter Four

Turning Point: From Vienna to Dachau

As an American born citizen reared in a land of culture, freedom and justice, I place this document in the hands of my American Consulate with the firm hope that a thorough inquiry and investigation into my case will be instituted by my government. I solemnly swear that what I have herewith set forth is true in every detail -- and can be corroborated by eye-witnesses inside (officials and prisoners) as well as outside the prison walls within which I was confined.[1]

~Harry Loomer, Vienna, April 1938

Harry P. Loomer, an American citizen completing his medical studies at the University of Vienna in March 1938, was caught amidst the terror of the Anschluss Pogrom. He was subjected to a spontaneous, unanticipated, and forceful arrest carried out by Austrian uniformed and plainclothed officials on the evening of Friday, 8 April 1938. After dinner with his fiancée and her parents at their home, Harry was just descending the stairs of the apartment building when he was accosted by two Gestapo men. They pushed him into a stranger's apartment and arrested him on the spot without stating a reason. Then they took Harry and the three other men in the apartment to the large Rosauerlände prison in the ninth district. There they interrogated him and accused him of Communist activities. Harry was Jewish, but there was no mention that he was arrested for being a Jew. They forced him to spend a night in this prison, in a long and gloomy chamber on the third floor, where men of all ages and professions crouched together in the dark on hard mattresses lined from wall to wall on a stone floor. Harry made a futile attempt to get some rest amidst the horror of his situation. He searched for a space to squeeze into and then lay down next to an elderly grey-haired man bundled up in an overcoat and listened to "the mournful

---

[1] NARA, US State Dept. Records. RG 59/M1209/Reel 7: 863.4016/175. See Enclosure No. 1 to report No.206, "Statement by Harry P. Loomer," Vienna, 19 April 1938: 1-5.

snoring" of his fellow victims. For Harry, the experience was "ghastly." "I chilled to the bones at this spectacle of humanity so distorted and out of its element,"[2] he wrote some days after his release.

Thanks to the intervention of the U.S. consulate in Vienna, Harry was released and permitted to return to his fiancée in their flat on Beethovengasse, a short twenty-two hours after his arrest. Unlike almost all of the other innocent men in this prison, Harry was thus spared further hours or days of torture in Vienna and, ultimately, deportation to Dachau. Nevertheless, his arrest and experience in prison were so frightful that he wrote a detailed five-page report on the injustice he had witnessed and suffered and submitted it to the American General Consul in Vienna the day after his release (Monday, 11 April). Describing his arrest and imprisonment, he requested that the American government do its best to look into his case and consider the sheer lawlessness erupting in Austria. Clearly, if this happened to him, a foreign citizen, no one was safe under this new government authority. He recounted his persistent attempts to reason with various German officials during his imprisonment -- attempts to explain that he was guilty of no crime and to remind them that he was a foreign guest in this country who, according to standards of basic international law, deserved a fair trial. Harry, much like the other innocent men arrested at this time, responded to the authorities according to a rule of law and social order that he believed was still intact: initially he cooperated with their demands; after that, he attempted to reason with them. He did not expect the treatment -- the absolute disrespect -- that he received, and he feared trouble if he objected to their orders.

Complete anarchy had already claimed Austria, however; the rule of law had been eclipsed, and the Nazi officials responded to Harry as they did to the rest of the prisoners: they

---

[2] NARA, US State Dept. Records, RG 59/M1209/Reel 7: 863.4016/175. See Enclosure No. 1 to report No.206, "Statement by Harry P. Loomer," Vienna, 19 April 1938: 3.

disregarded his voice completely. They were unwilling to listen to a word he said, American citizen or not. Harry witnessed this collapse of civil law as it unfolded, but stood as a helpless victim. He endeavored to explain to the American government what was happening, and to warn it: "We were asked nothing; we were told nothing," he wrote. "I found around me men of every age and profession, who, like myself, had been imprisoned without notice and without cause ... and there we were, like mute cattle being led away to slaughter, doomed to an unknown fate."[3] Harry's report had no impact. Nor was he personally able to forewarn, protect, or aid other men in danger. But he tried. Harry was not the first innocent man to be arrested and exposed to this party-sponsored anarchy; he certainly was not the last. Some seven weeks later, these arrests occurred *en masse,* and by this time the Nazis had fine-tuned their torture methods aimed to dehumanize and weaken their victims.

Background and Context

The scale of Nazi terror unleashed against the Jews of Vienna peaked for the first time after Anschluss in late May and early June of 1938. Large-scale raids swept throughout the city, the Austrian police arrested hundreds of Jews, and SS men loaded them into special trains headed for the first German concentration camp, Dachau, near Munich. Two separate transports, carrying approximately six hundred men each, left on 31 May and 3 June. Smaller transports of both Jews and non-Jews followed in mid- to late June (15 June [24 prisoners], 17 June [96],[4] and on 24 June [330] and 25 June [155]).[5] These transports followed in the wake of the

---

[3] NARA, US State Dept. Records, RG 59/M1209/Reel 7: 863.4016/175. See Enclosure No. 1 to report No.206, "Statement by Harry P. Loomer," Vienna, 19 April 1938: 2-4.

[4] Brothers Max, Adolf, and Fritz Bomze were arrested on 24 May 1938 and held in Vienna for close to three weeks before being sent to Dachau on this transport. Ellen Minkwitz, private email correspondence with author, 16 April 2008.

[5] Figures from: Jonny Moser, "Österreich," in Wolfgang Benz, ed., *Dimension des Völkermords, Die Zahl der jüdischen Opfer des Nationalsozialismus* (Munich: Oldenbourg Verlag, 1991), 88; Wolf Gruner, *Jewish Forced*

Prominententransport, the first deportation, which carried 151 prominent Austrian Jews and

non-Jews to Dachau on 1 April 1938.[6]

The arrests and transports in May and June increased the turmoil in the already panic-

stricken Jewish community. If the political and social figures rounded up after Anschluss might

have anticipated their arrest due to the shift in government, the second wave of men could not.

Like Loomer, they were caught off guard, brutally uprooted from their daily activities, seized

from their families and community. The arrests were so sudden and random that when they

occurred, many victims did not even know or understand at first that they were being arrested,

nor did their families, or the community at large. According to one survivor of the operation,

Herbert Zipper (arrested on 29 May and incarcerated in Dachau until September 22 when he was

transferred to Buchenwald), it seemed that not even the Austrian police carrying out the detail

knew exactly "what was happening and what process they were helping along."[7] Zipper wrote a

letter to a friend a few months after his release from Buchenwald and subsequent escape from

Vienna in the spring of 1939 in which he attributed this confusion and uncertainty to "the overall

fog which enveloped Vienna" at the time. But the arrests, on the contrary, were an officially

orchestrated measure, ordered directly by Hitler and planned and carried out by the Austrian

police, Gestapo, and SS. Wanting manpower, Hitler expressed his wish to have all "criminal"

Labor Under the Nazis, Economic Needs and Racial Aims 1938-1944 (Cambridge: Cambridge University Press, 2006), 109; and the *Dokumentations Archiv des Österreichischen Wiederstandes, www.doew.at.*

[6] On 1 April 1938 the first transport, known as the *Prominententransport,* left for Dachau with 151 prisoners, including Jewish and gentile Communists, Socialists, and known opponents to National Socialism. About 60 Jews were on the transport. Most prisoners had been arrested weeks earlier, immediately following Anschluss, and held in "protective" custody up to this point. These were members of the government, mayors, senior civil servants, parliamentary delegates, officials in the police force or ministerial positions, Christian trade-unionists, former members of the conservative and anti-Communist paramilitary organization known as the Austrian "Heimwehr," and many members of the "Fatherland Front." Famous names include political figures such as Friedrich Bock, Robert Danneberg, Richard Schmitz, Josef Reither, Leopold Figl, Alfons Gorbach, Franz Olah, Viktor Matejka, Ludwig Soswinski, the judge Alois Osio, artists Fritz Beda Löhner, Heinrich Sussmann, members of the IKG Robert Stricker, Desider Friedmann, and Jacob Ehrlich. George E. Berkley, *Vienna and Its Jews: The Tragedy of Success: 1880s-1980s* (Cambridge: Abt Books, 1988), 262.

[7] Paul Cummins, *Dachau Song: The Twentieth Century Odyssey of Herbert Zipper* (New York: Peter Lang Publishing, Inc., 1992), 7.

and "asocial" Jews arrested and used for forced labor to help rebuild Germany.[8] Gestapo

headquarters in Vienna issued and distributed a *Schnellbrief* (urgent circular) dated 24 May 1938

to all the police district precincts in Vienna:

> It has been ordered that unpleasant Jews, especially those with prior criminal
> convictions, are to be arrested and transported to Dachau Concentration Camp.
> The arrests are to be carried out through the individual district police
> commissioner's offices. Only Jews of German (Austrian) nationality and stateless
> Jews are to be considered. Jews over fifty years old are only to be arrested if they
> have a particularly heavy charge against them. Jews clearly unfit for arrest are not
> to be considered. Directly following the arrest, the apprehended Jews are to be
> questioned using the enclosed interrogation forms at the police commissioner's
> office and then transferred to the confinement spot Karajangasse.[9]

This command led to the unprecedented arrest and deportation of some 1,800 Viennese Jewish

men -- and, ultimately, to the end of their lives in Austria.

This transition, from secure life at home to incarceration in Germany, did not happen

overnight. A long and painful journey stretched between the point of initial arrest and the men's

arrival in Dachau. The unjust and cruel measures implemented by the Austrian police and

Gestapo, starting with the initial arrests, carried over into police stations and holding spots in

Vienna and climaxed on the train journey. By the time the men arrived in the camp, the

authorities had stripped them of their most basic civil rights and turned them into helpless beings.

Somewhere during this experience they reached a breaking point where they realized life in

---

[8] Hitler ordered that "asocial and criminal Jews would be arrested to perform important excavation work." Quote in Wolf Gruner, *Jewish Forced Labor Under the Nazis: Economic Needs and Racial Aims 1938-1944* (Cambridge: Cambridge University Press, 2006), 109.

[9] See Jonny Moser, "Die Verfolgung der Juden," in Wolfgang Neugebauer, ed., *Widerstand und Verfolgung in Wien 1934-1945, Eine Dokumentation, 1938-1945, Band 3* (Vienna: Oesterreichischer Bundesverlag fuer Unterricht, Wissenschaft, und Kunst, 1975), 263. See also, Wolf Gruner, *Jewish Forced Labor Under the Nazis: Economic Needs and Racial Aims 1938-1944* (Cambridge: Cambridge University Press, 2006), 109.

Vienna had come to an end, but this harsh reality was difficult to accept and registered with them at different points along the way, usually not until they were on the train or set foot in the camp.

Why did it take the men so long to realize the danger they were in? First, at no point were they given information about what was happening, why, or what was yet to come. And as they did not understand the perilousness of the situation, they did not try to run, hide, or resist in any way. They did not anticipate their arrest or consider themselves criminals. They had no way of recognizing their last moments of freedom quickly slipping through their hands. Once arrested they maintained false hope and they were often deceived -- encouraged to believe -- that they might be released and permitted to return home soon. Surviving victims documented their harrowing arrest and deportation experience in letters, diaries, testimonies, and legal statements in the days, months, and years following their release from concentration camp. Each victim described the piercing injustice he had encountered and feelings of frustration, anger, disbelief, and helplessness. While each victim experienced the arrest and transport differently -- depending on age, health, previous war experience, and personal background -- all agreed that this arrest marked a pivotal moment in their lives. Herbert Zipper wrote to a friend in June 1939, one year after his arrest, that the train ride to Dachau was the single most drastic turning point in his life. From that time forward he would divide his life in two segments, B.D. and A.D.; before Dachau and after Dachau.[10] These men's lives were irreparably altered during this experience, and so too were the lives of the family members and community they left behind. Close scrutiny of these histories, individually and collectively, reveals not only how the arrests affected the daily lives of the Jewish community but sheds new light on the perpetrator/victim relationship that formed during this early point in the history of the Holocaust.

---

[10] Paul Cummins, *Dachau Song: The Twentieth Century Odyssey of Herbert Zipper* (New York: Peter Lang Publishing, Inc., 1992), 35.

Illustration 11: "A Jewish Bookstore Locked Up and Defaced with the Message: 'Is in Dachau!!!'"

Source: George E. Berkley, *Vienna and Its Jews: The Tragedy of Success: 1880s-1980s*
(Cambridge: Abt Books, 1988); original, Yivo Institute for Jewish Research, NY.

Behind One Family's Doors

> *I had heard about Jews being arrested in previous*
> *days, but I had never thought about them taking me.*
>
> *~Fritz Czuczka*[11]

A short ten days after Fritz Czuczka filled out his emigration questionnaire with the IKG and

began his organized struggle to escape from Nazi Austria with his family his life took a dramatic

turn for the worse. On the evening of 30 May 1938, Fritz was home alone with his son George

when someone unexpectedly knocked on the door. Fritz had heard about Jews in Vienna being

---

[11] Fritz Czuczka, BMS GER91(45), Houghton Library, Harvard University.

arrested in the previous days, but had never thought about someone coming for him. At age forty-five, he had no criminal record and he had nothing to hide; the knock at the door came without warning or warrant. Thirteen-year-old George answered the door and recognized the man standing there from a previous encounter with the family. Dressed in normal civilian clothing, he was polite when he asked for Fritz. Although George sensed that the situation could not be positive, he was not particularly frightened and called for his father. When Fritz came to the door, the man said: *"Kommen Sie mit. Nehmen Sie einem Mantel mit und a bissel Geld."* (Come with me. Bring a coat and a little cash)."[12]

Fritz did not question or dispute the man's orders and left the house within minutes, following him to the local police station for questioning. He had no idea why he was being taken or when he would return. He left his young son behind, shaken and burdened with the task of relaying to his mother what had happened. Fritz thought about this as he left their house that day, and for many days and nights thereafter. George and his mother Charlotte also lost sleep over Fritz's absence; Charlotte worried incessantly. They heard from him days later, while he was still held in Vienna, but they learned nothing from him other than that he was alive. Fritz had nothing to tell, for he knew nothing; the prisoners were told nothing. He did not realize that the school in the twentieth district where he was being held captive had officially (following the order of 24 May 1938) been transformed into a holding station for prisoners prior to their deportation to Dachau (Karajangasse Sammellager).[13] Neither did his wife or child.[14]

---

[12] George Czuzcka, private interview with author, May 2007. Washington, D.C.

[13] The street was named after a doctor who was the personal physician of the Emperor Franz Joseph and was also the father of the late conductor Herbert von Karajan. Paul Cummins, *Dachau Song: The Twentieth Century Odyssey of Herbert Zipper* (New York: Peter Lang Publishing, Inc., 1992), 7.

[14] Fritz Czuczka, BMS GER91(45), Houghton Library, Harvard University.

Arrests around the City

Similar horror scenes occurred during the final week of May throughout the entire city. Fritz's sudden arrest -- which instantly changed the current situation and future of the whole Czuczka family -- was not an isolated occurrence; hundreds of other families faced the same dilemna. In the ninth district, twenty-four-year-old Hans Bandler heard a forceful knock on the door at six o'clock in the morning. It was the civilian Austrian police, and he knew these men because he lived very near the police station. Although he was surprised to see them standing at his doorway, he followed them down the street to answer questions.[15] In the fifth district, twenty-six-year-old Walter Deutsch was at his parents' home, shaving, when the doorbell rang. A man dressed in civilian clothes said very nicely, "Will you come down to the police station so I can ask you a few questions? No need to finish shaving, just wash it off and come as you are." Walter's parents, Rosa and Edmund, were at home, and they had heard rumors of what was going on, but they did not know the danger their son was in as he walked out the door.[16]

In the thirteenth district, thirty-four-year-old Fritz Herlinger went downstairs to set out for his work day and saw his landlord talking with a man in civilian clothing. The man asked, "Are you Jewish?" and told him to come to the police station for a "short interview."[17] It was evening when the Austrian police knocked on the door of twenty-four-year-old Raoul Klugmann's home on Tittelgasse, also in the thirteenth district. The officers came dressed in civilian clothes and asked first to speak with Raoul's father and then with his brother-in-law. As neither was home, the police officer opted to take Raoul instead: "Maybe *you* can help us. We

---

[15] Hans, B., (date currently unavailable). "Interview by Survivors of the Shoah Visual History Foundation," (location currently unavailable). Interview Code 04421.

[16] Walter, D., 1995. "Interview by Survivors of the Shoah Visual History Foundation," White Plains, NY, USA, September 15. Interview Code 06673-3, Tapes 1-6.

[17] Fred, H., (date currently unavailable). "Interview by Survivors of the Shoah Visual History Foundation," (location currently unavailable). Interview Code 08022.

just need to ask you some questions.... You may want to take a toothbrush and a towel because you might have to stay overnight."[18] Also in the thirteenth district, a plainclothesman arrived in the evening at the Zipper home and knocked at the door. Without explanation, the man told Herbert Zipper and his two brothers, Otto and Walter, that they were "criminals"[19] and needed to follow him to the local police station for questioning. Herbert's father was not in Vienna at the time or he would have been taken as well.

On Favoritenstrasse in the tenth district, thirty-year-old Walter Knie and his wife, Blanka, lived with his parents, Hersch (Hermann) and Hilda, in a large apartment above his father's store, Knie and Co. Shortly after Anschluss someone had come to seize Hermann's store, but he had refused to give it up, stating again and again that he "was born in Austria and served in the army." Hermann might have anticipated that the police would come to talk with him about this matter, but when they showed up at his door prepared to arrest and deport him and his son to Dachau, he was caught totally unprepared.[20] In the sixteenth district twenty-six-year-old Otto Linder lived near his parents with his wife, Klara, and ran his parents' general store. He started hearing about people being arrested at the end of May, specifically that a friend of the family and his four sons had been arrested all together. When he discussed this with his father, the latter quickly eased his worries: "'They wouldn't arrest anybody if you're not guilty of something. They must have done something.'" But this logic no longer applied to the situation in Nazi Austria. Days later there was a knock at the door and two people dressed in civilian clothing

[18] Raoul, K., 1996. "Interview by Survivors of the Shoah Visual History Foundation," Great Neck, NY, USA, April 23. Interview Code 14413, Tapes 1-3.

[19] Paul Cummins, *Dachau Song: The Twentieth Century Odyssey of Herbert Zipper* (New York: Peter Lang Publishing, Inc., 1992), 7. Also see Herbert, Z., 1995. "Interview by Survivors of the Shoah Visual History Foundation," Los Angeles, CA, USA. Interview Code 00833.

[20] Walter, K., 1997. "Interview by Survivors of the Shoah Visual History Foundation," Allentown, PA, USA, November 19. Interview Code 35772, Tapes 1-4. Also see USHMM film #Alpha K, *Auswanderungsfrageboegen der Israelitischen Kultusgemeinde Wien (IKG)*, Walter K., # 9324/25882.

politely said to Otto, "Mr. Linder, we'd like to ask you a few questions at the police station." Otto's first thought was, "Okay, I have nothing to hide. I had never done anything wrong,"[21] and he followed the men to the local precinct.

Like Fritz Czuczka, all the men arrested at this time were caught off guard and given little or no information. Many were also deceived. Approached by men in civilian dress, treated decently, and asked politely to go to their local police station for questioning, they went. Others, like Dr. Fritz O., were approached by the secret police in full uniform, but even to these men, the situation remained unclear. The twenty-eight-year-old doctor had no way of knowing if, how, when, and where the Gestapo would come looking for him, so he carried on with his regular daily routine. He was preparing a lesson for his anatomy class in the café right around the corner from his apartment on Waagasse 17/19 in the fourth district, when the Gestapo came to look for him on 29 May. It was broad daylight, 1:30 in the afternoon, when they entered the Theatercafé on Favoritenstrasse and said to the host, "Where is the Jew?" After finding him upstairs, they told him to come along for questioning and Dr. Fritz O., like the other men arrested, did just as he was told, not knowing that this was the beginning of the end of his life in Vienna.[22]

The terror ignited by this first large wave of arrests affected far more Jewish families than those of Dr. Fritz O., Fritz Czuczka, Walter Deutsch, Raoul Klugmann, Hans Bandler, Herbert Zipper, Fritz Herlinger, Otto Linder, Walter Knie, and the rest of the men who were taken into custody at this time. All able-bodied men capable of performing forced labor for the Germans were equally susceptible to arrest, but few understood, or were willing to accept the strength of this threat. Rumors spread quickly through the community, and most Jewish households --

[21] Otto, L., 1997. "Interview by Survivors of the Shoah Visual History Foundation," Valley Stream, NY, USA, February 27. Interview Code 26151,Tapes 1-6 . Also See USHMM film #Alpha L7, *Auswanderungsfrageboegen der Israelitischen Kultusgemeinde Wien (IKG)*, Otto L., # 42838/23409.
[22] OstA/AdR/BMF/06/AHF 08124.

whether or not they admitted it -- lived with a constant fear of the "dreaded knock on the door." At the same time, most were also blinded by hope and a false sense of security that lingered from the days before Nazism. People continued to rationalize the situation and make sense of the Germans' actions; they told themselves and one another not to worry, the Nazis would not arrest people who were not guilty of some crime. These logical arguments, most often adduced by the older generation (like Otto Linder's father), remained in play. As fear intensified, so did these men's efforts to keep their families calm. But it was not just the older generation that was in denial; as Czuzka and the other men explained, no one believed that the Austrian police might come for him. They believed in justice and did not understand that they could be arrested at any moment simply for being a Jew. Because of this, few forestalled seizure by staying away from home; most opted to carry on with their daily lives as usual and were taken completely off guard. Even when they tried to stay away, as Herbert Zipper did, they could still be caught.

At the Police Station

The situation began to change for the prisoners at the local police stations. The danger of their current predicament became more evident, although the parameters still far from clear. Fritz Herlinger noted that he was now surrounded by Austrian police in uniform, as opposed to the police who had arrived at his door in civilian dress.[23] Fritz Czuczka had to answer more than a couple of questions, and was forced to sign an affidavit including personal information such as his name, occupation, and history. Czuczka recognized that no one would listen to him or explain why he had been brought there, only that it was on order of the Gestapo.[24] And the police needed no other justification to carry out an arrest than that it was Gestapo orders; if they

---

[23] Fred, H., (date currently unavailable). "Interview by Survivors of the Shoah Visual History Foundation," (location currently unavailable). Interview Code 08022.

[24] Fritz Czuczka, BMS GER91(45), Houghton Library, Harvard University.

needed one more body to fill their count, they went ahead with the arrest and invented the crime. At the local police stations they cross-examined their victims, probing them to come up with some action that could ultimately serve as the cause for arrest. For example, when Walter Deutsch got to the police station the first thing they asked him was, "Who is your girlfriend? Do you have any Christian girlfriends...?" They tried to arrest him for *Rassenschande* (race defilement) a crime the Nazis had invented.[25] Other questions they asked prisoners were: "Did you during the last five years have an affair with an Aryan girl?" or "Do you belong to a Freemason Lodge?" or "Have you been supporting Communist activities?" If one did not answer yes to one of these questions straightaway, the interrogator repeatedly asked, "Why are you here? Why were you arrested?" until the victim unveiled some information that could be fabricated into a crime.[26] Walter Deutsch explained that he was never given any reason for his arrest, but on the train he realized it was because the Germans wanted a labor force. Deutsch was right. The Germans wanted men able to work, and it was easy enough for the police to find something under Nazi law that would mark them as enemies of the state.

In district precincts around the city, Austrian police questioned Jewish men, forced them to sign papers, and gave them no answers. Then they held them for an indeterminate period, depending on when the prisoner was arrested and the transport schedule to Dachau. Some were held overnight; others kept for a matter of hours. Some were taken directly to the train station; most were shuffled along to the next holding spot. Otto Linder was fortunate to be one of the last men arrested and therefore kept at the local police station in the sixteenth district for only some hours before the police took him directly to the West Bahnhof. He was fortunate in the

[25] Walter, D., 1995. "Interview by Survivors of the Shoah Visual History Foundation," White Plains, NY, USA, September 15. Interview Code 06673-3, Tapes 1-6.
[26] George E. Berkley, *Vienna and Its Jews: The Tragedy of Success: 1880s-1980s* (Cambridge: Abt Books, 1988), 262; also see NARA, US State Dept. Records, RG 59/M1209/Reel 7: 863.4016/175, Enclosure No. 1 to report No.206, "Statement by Harry P. Loomer," Vienna, 19 April 1938: 2-3.

sense that he had less time than the majority of the men to contemplate his situation. Most were not deported to Dachau for days. Raoul Klugmann and the three Zipper brothers (Herbert, Otto, and Walter), for example, were transferred from their local police stations to a larger district police station, joining Jews already gathered there, before being delivered to the main holding station in the twentieth district and then brought to the train station.

Hermann and his father Walter Knie were taken directly from their local police station to the West Bahnhof, but only after two days and three nights of internment, sleeping on the floor, with nothing to eat, and with absolutely no information about how long they would be there, why they were there, or where they were going. Hermann recalled how slowly time passed for them as they sat there, father and son, in the local police station just around the corner from their home, and worried. They worried about the future and thought of their wives, down the street, shocked and frightened.

Fritz Czuczka was held overnight in his local police station before being transferred to another collection spot and then to the train station. During that first night of his arrest he too worried about his wife and unknown fate. His thoughts ranged from fear and worry to sheer frustration: "I spent a night in a cell in this prison without knowing anything. They would not give me any information and so my future was completely up in the air.... And I thought about how bizarre it was that for the first time in my forty-five years I was arrested and in the police station. I thought about my wife, who worried when I came home late from work, and who now had no idea where I was and would be worried sick."[27] The transition from security to vulnerability occurred quickly during the Viennese imprisonment period. An ominous sense of worry -- about families and futures -- characterized the prisoners' experience already during the very first stage of their arrest.

---

[27] Fritz Czuczka, BMS GER91(45), Houghton Library, Harvard University: 1.

"Sammellager" Karajangasse

The Austrian police delivered most prisoners in dark closed police wagons from the local police stations to a school on Karajangasse in the twentieth district. There, the Nazis set up a collection point for arrested Jews to await deportation to Dachau, and it became Vienna's first *Sammellager* (collection camp). From points all over the city, the men were delivered to this school. Otto Linder was taken from the sixteenth district, Raoul Klugmann, Fritz Herlinger, and brothers Herbert, Walter, and Otto Zipper from the thirteenth, Walter Knie from the tenth, Fritz Hans Bandler and Fritz Czuczka from the ninth, Walter Deutsch from the fifth, Dr. Fritz O. from the fourth. Upon arrival they were registered again, received something minimal to eat -- coffee, bread, some soup -- and slept on straw scattered on the floor. Sanitary conditions were poor. The prisoners sat and waited from hours to days until the Austrian police had collected a sufficient number for a transport to Dachau.[28]

Still, the prisoners got no information: they were told nothing more about why they were there or where they were going. Walter Deutsch remembered how slowly the hours passed -- the men did not do anything, just sat there, wondered, worried, and waited to meet an unknown fate.[29] Hans Bandler looked around and saw many men of all ages -- about sixty men in his immediate vicinity -- and he noted that they all pondered the same thoughts: "What are we doing here and where are we going?"[30] The fear and worry that set in during the first stages of the prisoners' arrest (at home, in the police station) continued through each step thereafter. And yet, despite the odds that faced these men, Fritz Czuczka noted that many prisoners in the school still had hope. Since they had not been given any information at all, the glass could be seen as half

---

[28] Fritz Herlinger, one day; Hans Bandler, several days; Fritz Czuczka, one overnight; Fritz O., one day.

[29] Walter, D., 1995. "Interview by Survivors of the Shoah Visual History Foundation," White Plains, NY, USA, September 15. Interview Code 06673-3, Tapes 1-6.

[30] Hans, B., (date currently unavailable). "Interview by Survivors of the Shoah Visual History Foundation," (location currently unavailable). Interview Code 04421.

empty or half full. Thus, even in the terrible conditions of the collection camp on Karajangasse, some men believed there had been some sort of mistake and they would be sent home soon.[31]

Gather and Transfer

Fritz Czuczka found it particularly puzzling when the guards suddenly ordered the prisoners in the school to divide into groups of twenty and separated them among the various classrooms. At this point he could sense that change was imminent, but he and the other prisoners were still not provided any information. Soon a policeman began to call out names and then they were herded, again, into covered police wagons that stood waiting outside the door. They were not allowed to bring anything with them, just the clothes they had on.[32] Unbeknownst to them, they were headed to Vienna's main railway station, the West Bahnhof in the fifteenth district. The transfer from the school to train station should have been only a short ride, but it was an all-day process. Raoul Klugmann was among those awoken first thing in the morning, brought to the station, and forced to wait on the train until it was filled to capacity.[33] Others, like Fritz Czuczka, were not transferred until late in the evening. For all, the transfer to the train station marked yet another turning point in their lives. Czuczka noted that since the men still did not know where they were going as they rode, some remained hopeful, assuming that they were only being transferred to another collection point or prison in Vienna. Hope shattered -- quickly and completely -- when they arrived at the West Bahnhof. The young man sitting next to Czuczka broke down and started to cry bitterly, and Fritz recalled that he himself had become indescribably numb at this

---

[31] Fritz Czuczka, BMS GER91(45), Houghton Library, Harvard University.

[32] Otto, L., 1997. "Interview by Survivors of the Shoah Visual History Foundation," Valley Stream, NY, USA, February 27. Interview Code 26151,Tapes 1-6 . Hans, B., (date currently unavailable). "Interview by Survivors of the Shoah Visual History Foundation," (location currently unavailable). Interview Code 04421.

[33] Raoul, K., 1996. "Interview by Survivors of the Shoah Visual History Foundation," Great Neck, NY, USA, April 23. Interview Code 14413, Tapes 1-3.

moment. He put his arms around the young man to try to console him, but the bleakness of the situation suddenly struck him. He thought of how many times in the past his wife, child, and he had come to this train station to travel on vacation. Now he sat among helpless men, facing an ominous fate.[34]

Arrival at the West Bahnhof

Upon arrival at the West Bahnhof, the situation took another drastic turn. The Austrian police turned the prisoners over to the SS. Fritz Herlinger recalled the last words of the Austrian police as they left him off: "Just do as you are told."[35] Hans Bandler recalled that while the Austrian police had seemed uncomfortable with their duties (although they had fulfilled them scrupulously), these SS men showed no compunction.[36] When the men arrived at the station, a third-class passenger train awaited them on an outside track, not in the main part of the station.[37] The men were forced to exit the police wagons quickly and saw the SS men ready for them. Young in age, the SS were nevertheless big, tough, and intimidating. They stood in a chain leading to the train, and the prisoners had to move at a trot along this line, harassed and beaten, sometimes until bloody.[38] Czuczka recalled that even his most frightening experiences from World War I could not have prepared him for the fear he felt at this time. He was stunned by the thought of all the men deported. And as Raoul Klugmann explained, these men were not only innocent, they were utterly ignorant of what was going on, even after the train was fully loaded

---

[34] Fritz Czuczka, BMS GER91(45), Houghton Library, Harvard University.

[35] Fred, H., (date currently unavailable). "Interview by Survivors of the Shoah Visual History Foundation," (location currently unavailable). Interview Code 08022.

[36] Hans, B., (date currently unavailable). "Interview by Survivors of the Shoah Visual History Foundation," (location currently unavailable). Interview Code 04421.

[37] Testimonies of Walter Deutsch, Herbert Zipper, and Fritz Czuczka. The evidence suggests that this was not done as a matter of secrecy, but more as a matter of convenience, so as not to disturb the regularly scheduled passengers.

[38] Testimonies of Otto Linder and Herbert Zipper. See also Fritz Czuczka, BMS GER91(45), Houghton Library, Harvard University.

and had left for Munich. Still, he explained, nobody knew where they were going. They were

not told anything.[39]

The Train from Vienna to Dachau

> *Could you describe what you saw when you arrived in Dachau? Well, one of the*
> *most memorable things I think was the transport itself....*
>
> ~*Walter Deutsch*[40]

> *It was the most beastly, most terrifying, most ugly, most inhumane, most ghastly*
> *experience of my life... the ride itself. Those thirteen hours from Vienna to*
> *Dachau are the worst thing I can experience.*
>
> ~*Herbert Zipper*[41]

> *The trip itself was a horror. They terrorized the people on the train. You had to sit*
> *absolutely still... the minute you make the slightest motion they hit you.*
>
> ~*Raoul Klugmann*[42]

> *It was terrible. They hit me. Without a reason, on the train.*
>
> ~*Walter Knie*[43]

A normal journey from Vienna to Munich takes about five hours by train, but the men deported

to Dachau spent well over one night, enduring between twelve and thirteen hours of torture.

They were transported on a normal third-class passenger train, but shoved into the compartments

like sardines. Facing each other on benches meant for about three on either side, they sat twice

---

[39] Raoul, K.,1996. "Interview by Survivors of the Shoah Visual History Foundation," Great Neck, NY, USA, April 23. Interview Code 14413, Tapes 1-3.

[40] Walter, D., 1995. "Interview by Survivors of the Shoah Visual History Foundation," White Plains, NY, USA, September 15. Interview Code 06673-3, Tapes 1-6.

[41] Herbert, Z., 1995. "Interview by Survivors of the Shoah Visual History Foundation," Los Angeles, CA, USA. Interview Code 00833.

[42] Raoul, K., 1996. "Interview by Survivors of the Shoah Visual History Foundation," Great Neck, NY, USA, April 23. Interview Code 14413, Tapes 1-3.

[43] Walter, K., 1997. "Interview by Survivors of the Shoah Visual History Foundation," Allentown, PA, USA, November 19. Interview Code 35772, Tapes 1-4.

as many.[44] There were some seven hundred prisoners on the train, but to the victims it seemed that there were many more.[45] Raoul Klugmann believed there must have been at least one thousand people, sixty people to a car.[46] Walter Knie thought there were at least two thousand prisoners on the train with him.[47] The men were given no food or water; they were not allowed use the toilet, speak to each other, move, or sleep; and they were given no information as to where they were going, why, or how long the trip would be.[48] Aside from these prohibitions, there was a whole range of torture methods that the SS unleashed on the prisoners, starting while the train was still waiting in the station. Their first maneuver was to close the windows in the compartments and draw the curtains.[49] Someone turned up the heat.[50] The men were squeezed together on the hard seats of these small compartments and told to sit still with their hands on their laps/knees. They were told to keep their heads up, eyes open, and stare into the neon electric light. Otto Linder explained that since the "heat was on, and the light was on, and from the beating and from what was going on, everybody was soaked in sweat."[51]

---

[44] The men's descriptions of the seating situation differ slightly; most say there were twelve packed into a compartment intended for six. See testimonies of Walter Deutsch and Edward Weiss.

[45] This is the number adduced by the *Documentations Archiv des Oesterreichischen Widerstandes* in Vienna and historians such as Wolf Gruner.

[46] Raoul, K., 1996. "Interview by Survivors of the Shoah Visual History Foundation," Great Neck, NY, USA, April 23. Interview Code 14413, Tapes 1-3.

[47] Walter, K., 1997. "Interview by Survivors of the Shoah Visual History Foundation," Allentown, PA, USA, November 19. Interview Code 35772, Tapes 1-4. Also see USHMM film #Alpha K, *Auswanderungsfrageboegen der Israelitischen Kultusgemeinde Wien (IKG),* Walter K., # 9324/25882.

[48] One prisoner stated that it was possible to bribe a guard to let you use the bathroom. It is possible that this occurred in his wagon, but it was not standard for the guards to allow the men to use a bathroom. For further information see Walter, D., 1995. "Interview by Survivors of the Shoah Visual History Foundation," White Plains, NY, USA, September 15. Interview Code 06673-3, Tapes 1-6.

[49] The evidence does not suggest that the windows were closed and the curtains drawn for secrecy purposes. The train departed from an outside track and traveled overnight; few people would have had looked into the train windows. These techniques were used to terrorize and frighten the prisoners and prevent them from looking out.

[50] For further details see Otto, l.., 1997. "Interview by Survivors of the Shoah Visual History Foundation," Valley Stream, NY, USA, February 27. Interview Code 26151,Tapes 1-6 . Interview Code 26151; Fritz Czuczka, BMS GER91(45), Houghton Library, Harvard University.

[51] Otto, L., 1997. "Interview by Survivors of the Shoah Visual History Foundation," Valley Stream, NY, USA, February 27. Interview Code 26151,Tapes 1-6 . For further descriptions also see Walter, D., 1995. "Interview by Survivors of the Shoah Visual History Foundation," White Plains, NY, USA, September 15. Interview Code 06673-3, Tapes 1-6, and Fritz Czuczka, BMS GER91(45), Houghton Library, Harvard University..

Before the train left the station the guards forced the prisoners to sing cheerful songs while looking into the light. Herbert Zipper decided to sing the Beethoven masterpiece, "An die Freude" (Ode to Joy). He recalled the look on the guards' faces when he reached the line, "alle Menschen werden Brüdern" (All men will become brothers).[52] Written in 1785 by the beloved German poet Friedrich Schiller, these words clearly condemned the actions the guards were perpetrating against the men on this train. Fritz Czuczka had a different musical experience in his compartment. He arrived at the station from Karajangasse rather late in the evening, so he was exposed to this torture for only about an hour until the train departed. The guards forced Fritz and the prisoners around him not only to sing joyful tunes, but to sing Hebrew songs such as "Lecha Dodi" or "Shalom Aleichem" normally sung to greet the Sabbath. Fritz recalled how the religious men among them sang, while others struggled to remember the words from their childhood or to join in these songs they never had known. They sat shoved together, full of fear and drenched in sweat until they were ordered to continue singing but now to kneel between the rows of benches with their arms raised in the air above their heads, all the while staring at the light. When Fritz looked into the faces of the men around him he felt helpless. "The great tragedy of our situation really only hit me when I first peered into the faces of my comrades," he wrote twelve months later.[53]

When the train left the station the men were ordered back to their seats, where they had to remain with their hands on their knees while staring up at the light. The heat was unbearable and they were not permitted to take off their coats until many hours later. An SS man stood with a gun and bayonet at the front of each compartment to ensure that the prisoners cooperated fully. The SS kept a close watch on them the entire time and hit them in the shoulder or chest with their

---

[52] Paul Cummins, *Dachau Song: The Twentieth Century Odyssey of Herbert Zipper* (New York: Peter Lang Publishing, Inc., 1992), 10.
[53] Fritz Czuczka, BMS GER91(45), Houghton Library, Harvard University: 2.

guns if they failed to comply with orders. But it was impossible to comply with such demands; it was impossible to keep one's head up, stare into this light, and remain calm.

All failed and everyone was beaten at some point. Young and old, no one was spared. According to Hans Bandler, if a prisoner fell asleep he was forced to get down and do push-ups between the seats while being hit with a gun butt.[54] According to Otto Linder, the Nazis walked through with a whip and hit the prisoners for fun.[55] Walter Deutsch recalled that when one of the guards got bored, he took a cigarette and put it out on the back of the neck of one the prisoners. "That was entertainment for them," he said.[56] Herbert Zipper, who believed the train trip to Dachau was "the most terrifying and shocking event in his life,"[57] recalled that the guards spoke the exact same words, with the same exact sentence structure, and that "when the shock wore off [he] learned how beastly people can be made."[58]

Fritz Czuczka was beaten on three separate occasions. The first time, he had to lie bent over the knee of his comrade while he received twenty-five blows from the butt end of a bayonet. He was also on the periphery of a beating given to his neighbor, who was struck in the chest with the flat of the gun's blade; Fritz's upper lip was cut and blood dripped from it until he finally was allowed to use his handkerchief to staunch the bleeding. His lip was split and took over a week to heal. When he reflected on the ordeal a year later, Fritz explained that the guards not only entertained themselves by torturing the prisoners, but the torture was part of their plan to squelch all thought of resistance. It seemed to him that it was these young SS guards' duty to give the

[54] Hans, B., (date currently unavailable). "Interview by Survivors of the Shoah Visual History Foundation," (location currently unavailable). Interview Code 04421.

[55] Otto, L., 1997. "Interview by Survivors of the Shoah Visual History Foundation," Valley Stream, NY, USA, February 27. Interview Code 26151,Tapes 1-6 .

[56] Walter, D., 1995. "Interview by Survivors of the Shoah Visual History Foundation," White Plains, NY, USA, September 15. Interview Code 06673-3, Tapes 1-6.

[57] See Paul Cummins, *Dachau Song: The Twentieth Century Odyssey of Herbert Zipper* (New York: Peter Lang Publishing, Inc., 1992), 12.

[58] Herbert, Z., 1995. "Interview by Survivors of the Shoah Visual History Foundation," Los Angeles, CA, USA. Interview Code 00833.

Jews a taste of what lay ahead and to kill any remaining hope and inner strength they might have had when they boarded the train. He recalled that they had a long list of torture methods and as they exercised each one, they intended to show the Jews that they were now powerless: they were toys at the disposal of the SS guards' whims, to be played with as the guards wished, depending upon their mood.[59]

The guards' efforts to break these men were successful. A number of prisoners attempted to commit suicide. The journey to Munich stretched out more than twice as long as it normally would -- because the train kept stopping. According to Otto Linder, it came to a halt about twenty times. Perhaps, Bandler, Linder, and Czuczka believed, because the guards had to deal with the attempted suicides. Some men went completely crazy and tried to jump through the closed glass windows of the moving train. Linder recalled the terrified young man, eighteen or twenty years old, sitting next him:

> We were talking like ventriloquists. He said to me, "I can't take it anymore," without moving his lips. And I took my finger and touched his leg and said, "Don't worry everything is going to be okay."
> "No, No!" he said.
> I see this now, with my own eyes, and I could cry until I die -- that that young fellow jumped up and went right through the glass... out the window in the train. And the train stopped. Well, they brought him back and put him right in front of the door, but he was not dead. He kept on saying, "*a bissel Wasser*. A little water, a little water, a little water." Whenever he spoke, the Nazi hit him with the rifle. He broke his ribs. The train stopped so many times, so I don't know what happened in the other cars.[60]

---

[59] Fritz Czuczka, BMS GER91(45), Houghton Library, Harvard University.
[60] Otto, L., 1997. "Interview by Survivors of the Shoah Visual History Foundation," Valley Stream, NY, USA, February 27. Interview Code 26151,Tapes 1-6 .

Hans Bandler witnessed a similarly horrific scene. "One fellow could not take it and jumped straight through the glass window while the train was moving. The train was stopped, he was shot, and the train kept on moving."[61] Czuczka remembered screams, a lot of excitement, a stop, guards moving about, and then the train would keep going. Days later, in Dachau, he learned from the other inmates that a person had tried to jump through a closed window and then was shot.[62] Although many prisoners on the train, like Fritz, did not personally witness this horrendous spectacle, they all felt its repercussions: the extended journey, the extra hours of torture. And they all felt the extreme desperation as those men who attempted to end their lives by suicide.

As the train neared Dachau, it stopped in Bavaria where new German guards boarded. With them they brought a fresh wave of energy and new methods of torture. Czuczka was beaten again, this time receiving five blows with a rubber whip. He clenched his teeth while he was beaten in order to keep quiet, praying that this response, this cooperation, would spare him further torture and help him withstand the journey. But ultimately there was no response, no action that Fritz or any of the other men could have taken that would have minimized the abuse they endured or changed their fate. They had boarded the train in Vienna as men, bruised but still hopeful; when they were thrown off the train at Dachau, they were powerless beings, physically and spiritually broken. To the Nazis, they were not human beings; they were sub-human slaves to be used by the German state. It was on the train that the men first began to understand this. After reaching a turning point where they realized they could no longer defend themselves, they began to absorb that their lives in Vienna had come to an end and that their fate -- and the fate of their families -- was out of their control. Czuczka remembered arriving in

---

[61] Hans, B., (date currently unavailable). "Interview by Survivors of the Shoah Visual History Foundation," (location currently unavailable). Interview Code 04421.
[62] Fritz Czuczka, BMS GER91(45), Houghton Library, Harvard University.

Dachau, contemplating the thirteen hours of horror he had just endured, and asking himself which part had been worse: the physical or the spiritual torture? Both continued to intensify. Upon entry into Dachau, the prisoners came face to face with an unrecognizable world with which not even the horror of the train compared. Herbert Zipper recalled, "[We were] stripped of everything. But not just hair, our entire past. What we had been, our education, social standing, friends, how we lived -- that all fell apart. We didn't even have names, we had numbers. So what we were facing was naked humanity; you were what you were: a piece of human. And there you could see how low this could go, to a depth you had never imagined."[63]

Effects of the Dachau Deportations on the Community at Large

False hope and a psychological inability to grasp the reality they faced prevailed. Vienna's Jews carried on with their daily lives despite waves of random arrests in spring 1938. Still, most people could not completely repress the fear caused by this forceful and unexpected Nazi attack. For the nuclear families, relatives, and friends of men taken into custody, the threat of Nazism suddenly became very real, and the number of those seeking to emigrate multiplied significantly. Some individuals who had previously been hesitant to leave were now afraid to stay and wished to go at any cost. Among them was Fritz Herlinger's father Leopold, an old Austrian patriot who declared after Anschluss that he would never leave his homeland. Now, his son's incarceration prompted him to begin the emigration process. Overnight, his top concern became selling his furniture business on Porzellangasse and paying his taxes, so he could immigrate to Palestine

---

[63] Herbert, Z., 1995. "Interview by Survivors of the Shoah Visual History Foundation," Los Angeles, CA, USA. Interview Code 00833.

where his daughter had already settled some months earlier.[64] He was one of many men and women for whom the spring transports to Dachau served as a catalyst for flight from Austria.

The IKG tried to keep the community calm in response to the arrests. Recognizing that widespread fear had increased desire for emigration, it became more determined than ever to secure emigration possibilities. It sped up its current work and moved into a more collaborative relationship with the Germans and foreign aid committees. The result: emigration more than doubled in June (8,034) as compared to May (3,668). Of the total 11,707 emigrants, some 2,161 received full financial aid, with the IKG expending RM 25,632 in May and RM 83,392 in June. These sums continued to increase steadily in the following months, reflecting not only the IKG's hard work but also its dependence upon funding from abroad. Of the 8,804 persons who emigrated from 4 July to the end of the month, 2,001 received financial aid from the IKG -- train tickets, ship tickets, and landing fees -- costing a total of RM 157,240. This number increased in the following month: of the 9,729 persons who emigrated, 3,422 (almost one-third) received aid from the community, amounting to RM 323,000.[65] The IKG arranged immigration wherever possible. The United States, England, Switzerland, Palestine, Czechoslovakia, Argentina, Italy, France, Luxembourg, and Finland were the top ten countries to which Jews fled between 3 May and 31 August, but they were not limited to these destinations. Other nations offered

---

[64] OstA/AdR/06/ BMF/ VVst/ VA 16802 and St. 273; Fred, H., 1995."Interview by Survivors of the Shoah Visual History Foundation," Bronx, NY, USA, October 26. Interview Code 08022, Tapes 1-4.
[65] USHMM film # 295, IKG- A/W 121, *The Budget of the Jewish Community of Vienna for the months of September and October 1938*: 2-4. Also based on an in-depth study and analysis of hundreds of emigration questionnaires from *USHMM, Films #Alpha A-Z, Auswanderungsfrageboegen der Israelitischen Kultusgemeinde Wien (IKG)*. For further details see Chapter 5. For graphs and monthly emigration statistics, see USHMM film # 294, IKG-A/W 126, *Report of the Vienna Jewish Community. A description of the activity of the Israelitische Kultusgemeinde Wien in the period from May 2ⁿᵈ 1938 December 31ˢᵗ 1939 (2 Exemplare)*: 81-82.

opportunities as well: China, Mexico, Turkey, Panama, Haiti, Trinidad, Syria, Iraq, Iran, Morocco, Egypt, Sudan, Cuba, Gibraltar, Uganda, Liberia, Costa Rica, Peru, and Estonia.[66]

Table 5: "Original IKG Emigration Statistic, March 1938- December 1939"

TOTAL EMIGRATION FROM THE OSTMARK
MARCH 1938 – DECEMBER 1939

117.409 persons

listed month by month:

March – April 1938	4.700
May	3.668
June	8.038
July	8.804
August	9.729
September	8.094
October	5.643
November	4.786
December	9.496
January 1939	5.628
February	5.993
March	7.846
April	5.416
May	5.058
June	3.768
July	4.359
August	4.624
September	957
October	4.697
November	4.254
December	1.811

Source: USHMM film # 294, IKG-A/W 126, IKG *Report May 2ⁿᵈ 1938- December 31ˢᵗ 1939.*

[66]USHMM film # 295, IKG- A/W 121, *The Budget of the Jewish Community of Vienna for the months of September and October 1938*: 3.

On an individual level, people began to seek emigration routes. Family members and friends of those arrested set to work immediately. Often, those now in charge had not previously considered it their responsibility to attend to such matters. But now women and children assumed the roles formerly played by husbands and fathers. To ease the situation, brothers, uncles, grandfathers, and male friends came to the aid of a despairing wife and mother whose husband had been arrested, but this assistance could not last. Most often, such a presence was only temporary, and the women and children needed to accept their new roles. For example, after Fritz Czuczka's arrest, his brother Artur came to stay with Fritz's wife Charlotte and his son George. But however comforting Artur's presence may have been, it was only temporary, and Charlotte had to accept that she was now on her own, in charge of organizing the emigration of her son and herself from the country and, if possible, the release and subsequent emigration of her husband. As for thirteen-year-old George, his childhood days had become a distant memory. He was now treated as an adult, entrusted with the family's most important documents, the emigration papers, and responsible for having photographed copies made -- a task his mother could not manage while she continued to work so she could put food on the table.

In other families, the wives alone had to assume the role of their husbands in arranging emigration.[67] In cases concerning unmarried men, it was most often elderly fathers and sometimes mothers who tried to secure exit papers for the family, first and foremost for their imprisoned sons, then for themselves.[68] Sometimes, as in the case of Raoul Klugmann, it was an older sister: Edith made a concerted effort to arrange her brother's emigration before securing her own, traveling to Berlin to meet with top Gestapo officials to beg for his release from

---

[67] For more on married men, see cases of Walter Knie, Otto Linder, and Joseph Pichler.
[68] For more on unmarried men, see cases of Fritz Herlinger, Herbert and Walter Zipper, and Dr. Fritz O.

Dachau.[69] Rarely, a Christian friend helped, but such was the good fortune of Walter Deutsch, also unmarried, whose friend helped his parents, Rosa and Edmund.[70]

These role reversals were an unanticipated result of the spring arrests. Not only were the men's lives changed by their arrest and deportation, but so were the lives of the families they left behind. The family structure shifted on its axis, and life revolved around one prospect: how to get loved ones back and get out of Austria. Everyone worried incessantly about arrested loved ones and they were given little or no information. News came, tragically, in the form of an urn with ashes. Those much more fortunate received a postcard from Dachau that typically said little; it only assured them that their loved one was alive and asked for money.[71] Still, neither the men in the camp nor their families knew what the future held for Viennese Jews. But day after day they hoped to reunite and live somewhere in freedom. As families were torn apart and their futures dangled, the IKG and individual people grew more and more desperate, and thus more and more willing to work with the German authorities for a chance to secure the prisoners' release and to get out of Vienna.

Conclusions: Addressing the Question of Resistance

The Germans and their Austrian allies transformed some 1,800 ordinary Viennese Jewish men into hopeless and powerless slaves to the Nazi state in only a matter of days, sometimes in less than twenty-four hours. How did they manage to break these men so quickly and make the entire Jewish community of Vienna even more vulnerable, willing to do anything to promote the

---

[69] Men could be released from Dachau on the grounds of their immediate emigration from Germany. Often this release was arranged through the Gestapo in Berlin. See case of Raoul Klugmann, USHMM film #Alpha G7, *Auswanderungsfrageboegen der Israelitischen Kultusgemeinde Wien (IKG)*, Raoul K., # 36524/19807. See also Chapter Six, "Escape! Further Complications Come in November, but Emigration Continues."

[70] Walter, D., 1995. "Interview by Survivors of the Shoah Visual History Foundation," White Plains, NY, USA, September 15. Interview Code 06673-3, Tapes 1-6.

[71] OstA/AdR/BMF/06/AHF 08124.

chances of the men's release and the community's emigration from the country? Why did the men not try to resist orders?

During the course of their arrest and deportation, there were moments in the life of each of the men in which, even in their subordinate victim position, they might have resisted their tormentors and attempted to forge their own fate. Herbert Zipper was one of the men who did. The day after his two brothers and he were arrested, Herbert approached an Austrian Nazi guard in the Karajangasse Sammellager and attempted to persuade him to release his brother Otto from the detention center and send him to a local hospital for medical treatment. Herbert was successful in this endeavor; Otto was released to the hospital, and ultimately spared deportation and incarceration in Dachau. Paul Cummins, author of Zipper's biography, *Dachau Song*, explained that by doing this, Herbert exercised "one of the last acts of a middle class Jew asserting his authority over a Viennese working class gentile."[72] Cummings also noted that Herbert's action had little to do with his physical strength, and more with his ability to think rationally at this time. Cummings wrote, "Zipper still believed he had the social power and status and rights to issue warning and to assert himself."[73] In this last statement, Cummings draws our attention to an initial Jewish response to Nazi oppression: disbelief. Herbert Zipper, like other Jewish victims, had not accepted his new status. He did not believe that his class was no longer recognized. He did not feel physically or spiritually broken (yet), he still felt secure in his bourgeois status. Thus he felt capable of questioning Nazi orders and reasoning with Nazi officers. This belief, however, did not guarantee the outcome it had. His actions were risky, naïve, and dangerous, considering the odds against him. His brother could have been shot or tortured instead of saved, and he might have put his other brother, Walter, and himself (and his

---

[72] Paul Cummins, *Dachau Song: The Twentieth Century Odyssey of Herbert Zipper* (New York: Peter Lang Publishing, Inc., 1992), 7.
[73] Ibid.

extended family at home) in even greater danger. Zipper's response in this situation was out of the ordinary and he was very lucky that it had the outcome it did. He did not consciously or strategically plan to resist Nazism, to exercise his last minutes of freedom before they were taken away; he just reacted normally at a moment in which he still felt entitled to assert himself -- a moment when he still believed that some inkling of justice remained in the Nazis' realm.

If more men had asserted themselves and tried to challenge Nazi orders at this early stage, as Herbert Zipper did, perhaps the future would have been significantly changed for Vienna's Jews. However, resistance was not a realistic option in this situation. Few men chose to resist or question the authorities' demands for a number of rational reasons. First, the men had no way of recognizing their last moments of freedom as they slipped away -- just as they could not see their last moments to spend with family members or friends, their last moments in their homes or at work. They did not recognize these moments as the end of their lives in Austria and as the last time they would be treated as human beings able to defend themselves against the terror of Nazism. They did not have the ability to comprehend what was happening as it was transpiring, nor could they anticipate what would happen in the future -- that the danger would only intensify. The nature of the assault they endured -- the randomness, and the deception which accompanied the arrests -- blinded the victims from recognizing the need to run, hide, or refuse what was being asked of them. From the initial knock on their doors to the moment the train unloaded them in concentration camp, the men did not know the extent of the danger they were in. They were taken off guard by their arrest and could not anticipate the injustice they would encounter in the Viennese prisons, on the train ride to Dachau, or in the concentration camp. They did not realize what was at stake, what they were about to lose, and that the consequences of their acquiescence could possibly outweigh the repercussions of an immediate and unprepared revolt. In their eyes, any response other than obedience to authority put family members at risk and themselves in danger. Since the men believed they were innocent, they rationalized the situation, waited for misunderstandings and false arrests to be rectified, and they never openly questioned the rule of higher authority; this was not the way things were properly done, especially without legal representation. Rational thinking, the social contract they assumed, and human nature led these men to hope for the best and to deny acknowledgement of the violent situation that entrapped them.

Interviewed in 1996, Walter Deutsch was asked how he and other prisoners behaved on the train to Dachau. His response: "I think the whole system was set up from the beginning to intimidate you so you didn't revolt."[74] His answer provides another reason why resistance was so sparse, even in the early stages of Nazi persecution. When the men realized the danger they faced, for example on the train to Dachau, they were too intimidated by the strength of the Nazi force and the odds against them to resist. German and Austrian terror masked by decency (i.e., officers in civilian dress requesting politely for the Jews to come along for brief questioning) had encouraged them to cooperate up to that point, instead of revolting -- and this reaction paved the way for the future. The men who sat in prison doomed to an unknown fate were not "mute cattle waiting to be led to the slaughter," as Harry P. Loomer put it in 1938 (and as many have said about Jews deported to gas chambers). Rather, these people were uninformed victims responding to their situation in the only way they knew how: as law-abiding citizens whose duty it was to cooperate with government orders. As ordinary human beings, innocent of all crimes, they were caught off guard and had no point of reference for the naked aggression they would encounter. Not only did they have hope and faith in humanity, they were weakened by their love

---

[74] Walter, D., 1995. "Interview by Survivors of the Shoah Visual History Foundation," White Plains, NY, USA, September 15. Interview Code 06673-3, Tapes 1-6.

for Austria, and believed that the rule of law under which the Austrians had lived for centuries would return. Their denial of the present situation, and their hope that the terror would cease on its own, discouraged them from attempting resistant behavior. For some survivors, like Raoul Klugmann, who believed at the time that there must have been some sort of mistake, it took decades before they could come to terms with the government-sponsored terror that had gripped Austria in 1938. When asked during an interview in 1996 why he had been arrested, he struggled to get the words out and to rationalize what had actually transpired: "I was arrested strictly on the basis of being a Jew."[75] These factors help to explain how a pivotal moment to challenge Nazism in its early stages -- which might have altered future Jewish responses to Nazism -- proved impossible to seize.

The transports to Dachau in May-June 1938 heightened the preexistent fear within the Jewish community, pushed the IKG's emigration efforts to a new level, and encouraged further cooperation between the Jewish Community and the Nazi authorities. At this time, the Jews were weakened again -- stripped of their strength, courage, and will to resist -- and the Germans exploited their vulnerability. The lower the perpetrators pushed their victims, the stronger and more confident they became in their ability to solve the "Jewish question." Increased terror led to further desperation, encouraging further cooperation. It became a vicious cycle that would prove impossible to break. In the months following the deportations, the Germans managed to drive more than double the number of Austrian Jews from their homes as had left to that point. As we have seen, from March through April 1938, 4,700 had emigrated, and in May another 3,668 left. In June this number jumped to 8,083, in July to 8,804, and in August it peaked at

---

[75] Raoul, K., 1996. "Interview by Survivors of the Shoah Visual History Foundation," Great Neck, NY, USA, April 23. Interview Code 14413, Tapes 1-3.

9,729.[76] This drastic increase in emigration occurred partly because the IKG had figured out how to arrange and finance the process more efficiently and *also* because the Dachau deportations frightened the community into flight. The western democracies watched this next shift of power take place, yet still stood silent. As they disregarded the deportations and their aftermath, they missed a crucial moment to take action -- a moment which we can now identify as another warning sign of the genocide ahead.

---

[76] USHMM film # 294, IKG-A/W 126, *Report of the Vienna Jewish Community. A description of the activity of the Israelitische Kultusgemeinde Wien in the period from May 2nd 1938 December 31st 1939 (2 Exemplare).*

Chapter Five

Rescue and Destruction: Daily Life during a Mass Exodus

New tensions and worries spread throughout the Jewish community after the Dachau

deportations in May and June 1938. The way many people thought about life in Vienna and

about the prospect of emigration shifted anew. Fear of a recurrence of such arrests spread in

Jewish households throughout the city, making daily life more uneasy for everyone, and

particularly for those families with males between the ages of 18 and 45 who were most at risk

for forced labor. Equally troubling was the predicament for the relatives of those men already

arrested. They now faced a new dilemma. On the one hand, they felt a new urgency to escape; on

the other, it became difficult to consider emigration for themselves while their loved ones were

incarcerated for an indeterminate period.[1]

During this time of heightened uncertainty, as desperation and panic grew, people set

their sights on the single solution to their common problem: escape, no matter the cost.

Determined to get out of Austria as quickly as possible, they searched assiduously for advice and

aid, flocking to the offices of foreign consulates and the IKG, but also occasionally to Gestapo

headquarters to try to negotiate with the enemy.[2] All the while, they hoped that the outside

world might show some sympathy for their situation. U.S. President Franklin D. Roosevelt had

called for an international meeting to discuss solutions to a growing refugee problem, and a

major conference was scheduled in Evian, France on 6 July 1938. Jews in Austria and Germany

paid close attention to this conference as it drew near, and they held great hopes that other

---

[1] Fred, H., 1995. "Interview by Survivors of the Shoah Visual History Foundation," Bronx, NY, USA, October 26. Interview Code 08022, Tapes 1-4. See also, case of Hugo Spitzer in Erica, B., 1996. "Interview by Survivors of the Shoah Visual History Foundation," Upminster, Essex, UK, October 15. Interview Code 20825, Tapes 1-6.
[2] See USHMM Film #V10, IKG-A/W 2696, *Deutsche Staatsbuerger: Abgelegte Akte, Enthaftet - Gestorben von A-Z, Josef Pichler*.

nations would recognize and empathize with their situation.[3] To their disappointment, the

international conference proved a complete failure. Thirty-two countries attended the meeting

and nearly all were unwilling to open their borders, extend their visa policies, or enlarge their

quotas to help the despairing Jews seeking refuge.[4] With this failure, it became evident to IKG

leadership that it was up to them to rescue their people, to arrange and facilitate their emigration

and immediate departure. They could not depend on help from governments elsewhere. During

this time of crisis, under close supervision by the German authorities and intense pressure from

the terrified Jewish community, the IKG would have to organize, cooperate, and put up a great

fight if it wanted to preserve the future of Viennese Jewry.

IKG Looks to Jews outside Austria for Help

There was one place the leaders of the IKG found they could turn for support during this time:

Jewish aid committees in countries around the world, most of which were united under the

umbrella organization of the Jewish Joint Distribution Committee (JDC).[5] The IKG, which

continued to seek advice from the German Jewish community (RV) and looked to it as a model,

now began reaching farther afield to work closely with foreign aid committees. It soon

discovered that with their help it was able to explore a multitude of options for immigration, the

core (though not the only) factor in emigration and even ways to speed up the departure process.

The IKG initially believed that group immigration would be the most efficient way to get

160,000 Jews out of Austria. This plan soon failed, and the leadership turned to individual

---

[3] Newspapers document their hopes. See article, "Die Bemuehungen um Auswanderung," in *Zionistische Rundschau*, 20 May 1938.

[4] For further information on US immigration policy, see Richard Breitman, *American Refugee Policy and European Jewry 1933-1945* (Indiana, Indiana University Press, 1987).

[5] For more on the JDC, see Yehuda Bauer, *American Jewry and the Holocaust: the American Jewish Joint Distribution Committee, 1939-1945.* (Jerusalem: The Institute of Contemporary Jewry, Hebrew University , 1981).

departures.[6] As the IKG experienced how long the process took, the many difficulties involved with immigration, and the great danger of staying in Vienna, they realized that all options had to be explored. Some of these meant making sacrifices and compromises and taking risks. It was under these circumstances, for example, that together with foreign aid committees, the IKG started a transmigration system. Transmigration enabled people to leave as quickly as possible.[7] If the family or individual had a final destination secured, the IKG was able to organize a transit stay for somewhere else first, which was far safer than waiting in Austria. For example, after the Hebrew Immigrant Aid Association (HIAS) managed to procure 12,000 affidavits for people to enter the United States, the IKG, collaborating with foreign Jewish agencies, helped provide a transit stay for these people by finding them work places through which they could gain temporary admission to the countries in which those short-term employment opportunities were located.

The IKG conducted written negotiations, on a case-by-case basis, with individual committees in countries around the world to arrange for refugees to enter temporarily. While the countries themselves refused to help the refugees, making it nearly impossible for them to reside permanently, the local Jewish aid committees helped with their maintenance during stay.[8] The IKG managed to organize a system in which many persons desperate to emigrate immediately, including children and former concentration camp inmates, were able to utilize transmigration. Although the IKG did not want to split up families, it encouraged individual immigration when options for all to emigrate became limited, viewing it as a necessity.[9] The IKG dispatched 3,188

---

[6] USHMM film # 294, IKG-A/W 126, *Report of the Vienna Jewish Community. A description of the activity of the Israelitische Kultusgemeinde Wien in the period from May 2nd 1938- December 31st 1939 (2 Exemplare).*
[7] Ibid: 49.
[8] Ibid: 50.
[9] For example, Leopold Vulkan took his two daughters to Paris (September 1938) where they waited for him to return with their mother and grandmother, intending to travel on as a family to the US. Dr. Grabkowicz agreed to send his thirteen-year-old daughter Alix alone on a train to Antwerp, where she would stay with a friend. Letter from

children to European transit countries between May 1938 and December 1939 to wait for their

parents before traveling on to the final country of destination.[10] This was a major risk, but the

IKG aimed to expand its rescue mission to greatest capacity and get all able-bodied Jews out of

the country.

The support of foreign aid committees enabled the IKG to explore all immigration

options, and helped foster the belief that the rescue of its community was within its reach.

Distant communities gave the IKG hope. Family and friends who had already emigrated during

previous decades paved a path for their loved-ones entry.[11] In these far-flung communities,

relatives, friends, and complete strangers worked together to raise money to help bring their

coreligionists to a safe haven. The IKG was grateful. In a progress report to the JDC (December

1939) it expressed its deep appreciation: "The IKG thanks first and foremost the Joint and the

Council for German Jewry for providing landing money in foreign currencies which permitted

entrance into these places enabling emigration."[12] The IKG understood that the emigration was

completely dependant upon these agencies' financial and strategic support.[13]

Alix G. Kowler to the author, 1 August 2003; see also Alix , K., 1997. "Interview by Survivors of the Shoah Visual History Foundation," Lenox, MA, USA, October 16. Interview Code 34544, Tapes 1-5; Gertrude, S., 1998. "Interview by Survivors of the Shoah Visual History Foundation," Cranbury, NJ, USA, May 28. Interview Code 42400, Tapes 1-7.

[10] USHMM film # 294, IKG-A/W 126, *Report of the Vienna Jewish Community. A description of the activity of the Israelitische Kultusgemeinde Wien in the period from May 2nd 1938 December 31st 1939 (2 Exemplare)*: 72.

[11] The IKG concluded that emigration was enabled by the preceding waves of immigration to the overseas-countries. See USHMM film # 294, IKG-A/W 126, *Report of the Vienna Jewish Community. A description of the activity of the Israelitische Kultusgemeinde Wien in the period from May 2nd 1938–December 31st 1939 (2 Exemplare)*: 77.

[12] USHMM film # 294, IKG-A/W 126, *Report of the Vienna Jewish Community. A description of the activity of the Israelitische Kultusgemeinde Wien in the period from May 2nd 1938–December 31st 1939 (2 Exemplare)*: 50. Original English.

[13] Funding from abroad also helped cover the cost of the community's welfare expenses. Wealthy Jews purchased foreign currency from the IKG, supplying it with reichmarks in exchange, financing the welfare of the community, including the emigration of the poor. See the cases of Otto Goetzl and Alfred Tausky, mentioned at the end of this chapter. For more information on this topic, see David Cesarani, *Becoming Eichmann: Rethinking the Life, Crimes, and Trial of a "Desk Murderer"* (Cambridge: Da Capo Press, 2004) 66; also see Doron Rabinovici, *Instanzen der Ohnmacht: Wien 1938-1945 Der Weg zum Judenrat* (Frankfurt am Main: Jüdischer Verlag, 2000) 78,108.

Jews outside Austria could help, and external support provided hope, but neither help nor hope solved the problem. For all parties in the emigration process -- emigrant, sponsor, social worker, volunteer -- the red tape involved in exiting Austria and entering a foreign country was overwhelming; many times the hurdles proved insurmountable. Arranging the process was time consuming and stressful for everyone. IKG workers expressed the difficulty of this process in their progress report to the JDC. "Each single case required an intense correspondence until all necessary files were in such a state that the permits could be granted."[14] Sometimes even the most concerted efforts to arrange emigration could not secure an escape, for luck and timing were also factors in flight.

More often than not, however, the emigration efforts of the IKG proved successful. These positive results encouraged aid committees to continue to help the IKG, and the IKG was able to continue to help its people. In addition to exploring all emigration possibilities, and every option to raise funds, the IKG, as we have seen, turned to training people in new professions and languages to make them desirable to destination countries. Then, through its offices and announcements, it tried to ease the looming uncertainty that came with emigration by making the process as functional and smooth as possible.[15] And it provided dependents who remained in Vienna food, clothing, and shelter. The IKG gave people hope, and people cooperated with it and placed their trust in it because of this. This cooperation and hope in turn allowed the IKG's workers to continue their difficult daily work. They understood that Vienna's Jews needed to get out and quickly learned that there was no place too far, no city too impoverished or desolate, and no climate too unsuitable for Vienna's potential emigrants -- they could send them anywhere

---

[14] USHMM film # 294, IKG-A/W 126, *Report of the Vienna Jewish Community. A description of the activity of the Israelitische Kultusgemeinde Wien in the period from May 2nd 1938–December 31st 1939 (2 Exemplare)*: 50. Original English.
[15] See the IKG's calls for community unity expressed in the advertisements for "Winterhilfe," in *Zionistische Rundschau*.

because Jews were willing to go anywhere. IKG workers understood this cooperation and

mutual dependence as a key factor in acquiring help from the outside. Knowing that people were

getting out, that the IKG could work within the boundaries of the Germans' authority and

actively arrange a process that could help save its community, prompted both the struggling

Jews in the community and IKG workers to carry on day after day. Neither the IKG nor the

Jews of Vienna sat back passively and let the Germans determine their future; they worked with

one another and with the foreign aid committees to rescue as many members of their community

as they could via emigration.

The Struggle, Step by Step

Jews typically spent their summers in Vienna bathing on the Danube Canal, strolling through the

Prater and taking long walks in the Vienna woods, or traveling to the lakes and mountains of the

Austrian countryside. The summer of 1938, however, was markedly different. "I spent a long

summer 1938 not knowing what to do," thirteen-year-old Alix Grabkowicz recalled. "All parks,

swimming pools, even public benches on streets... movies were forbidden for Jews."[16]   Her

classmate, twelve-year-old Elizabeth Malkin, also experienced this change. She never forgot the

moment when she went to the local public swimming pool and saw a sign that read: "No dogs

and no Jews!"[17] Life during the summer of 1938 was about acclimating to Nazi laws while

figuring out how to get out of Nazi-occupied territory as quickly and easily as possible:

cooperation and emigration.

The day that the trains delivered the second transport of Viennese men to Dachau (3 June

1938), the *Zionistische Rundschau* (ZR) warned the rest of the community members about their

---

[16] Letter from Alix G. Kowler to the author, 1 August 2003.

[17] Liz, M., 1996. "Interview by Survivors of the Shoah Visual History Foundation," New York, NY, USA, March 8. Interview Code 12674, Tapes 1-8.

new status as non-Aryan citizens. The *ZR* printed the full text of the Nuremberg Laws in "Race Laws Expanded to Include Austria"[18] and published an article entitled "Organized Emigration" in which it detailed the steps to follow.[19] Serving as the IKG's main tool for keeping the community informed, the *ZR* was fulfilling its twofold responsibility: ensuring that the people knew how to cooperate from day to day within the Nazis' realm, and that they knew how to exit the country properly and as quickly as possible. Notwithstanding the violence of deportation, the *ZR* emphasized that cooperation and emigration went hand in hand. There were many instructions to be followed and prerequisites to be covered prior to emigration, and the IKG used the *ZR* to try to ensure that everyone was aware of what was prohibited and what was expected. It published all pertinent information regarding emigration as well as the newest Nazi restrictions and requirements. As we have seen (Chapter Three), the IKG warned its readers repeatedly not to try to leave on their own -- that they would never succeed and that when they returned to Vienna they would be denied aid from the IKG.[20]

---

[18] See article, "Die Rassengesetze auf Österreich ausgedehnt," in *Zionistische Rundschau*, 3 June 1938.

[19] See article, "Planmaessige Emigration," in *Zionistische Rundschau*, 3 June 1938.

[20] *Zionistische Rundschau*, 3 June 1938; 17 March 1939; and 17 February 1939.

Source: *Zionistische Rundschau*, 3 June 1938 [21]

---

[21] See appendix for full translation.

Private Decisions

To exit Austria, people needed to identify somewhere to go -- a country in which they could

envision themselves and one willing to take them in. This was no easy task. Every country had

different requirements for immigration, making some easier to enter or more suitable than others.

While the IKG helped guide people to what land was best for them and helped with immigration

preparations, Jews first entertained these questions privately, inside their own homes. Where can

and should I go? How can I get there, financially and strategically? Who will I, can I, take with

me and whom must I leave behind? Can I stay there, and how long? Can I find work? A second

set of questions followed. What will I take with me, and how will I say goodbye to my home,

my life, my family, my native tongue?

Contemplating these matters, people turned to each other -- family, friends, and

colleagues -- for advice and support. As the latter had little knowledge of the many technicalities

of immigration and emigration, people soon turned to the IKG for help. First and foremost,

however, most turned inward, each asking: In which countries safely outside the Reich do I

where do I have family or friends who might offer temporary housing and assistance, as well as

financial help to arrange immigration and travel? [22] Additionally, the thought of family and

friends settled abroad served as a link to Austria and to the past, making the foreign country less

intimidating. Knowing that other Austrians had acclimated before them made the transition less

frightening and gave them hope that it would be possible to adjust and start life anew. Of course

not everyone had kin or acquaintances overseas, but almost all had relatives in continental

Europe, particularly in regions of the former Austro-Hungarian Empire. While many hoped to

---

[22] The IKG summarized that emigration was enabled by family and friends in a report to the JDC: "It has been repeatedly proved by figures that the emigration from the Ostmark up to this time has for the most part been enabled by the preceding waves of emigration to the overseas countries." See USHMM film # 294, IKG-A/W 126, *Report of the Vienna Jewish Community. A description of the activity of the Israelitische Kultusgemeinde Wien in the period from May 2nd 1938–December 31st 1939 (2 Exemplare)*: 77. Original English.

quit Europe entirely, they still looked first to these relatives and friends in their search to emigrate.[23] Most did not intend to stay in these European countries permanently, but long enough to make arrangements for travel to another destination.[24] Family and friends paved the way for the transmigration process that was strongly encouraged by the IKG.[25]

Jews looked too for a country that needed a skill they practiced or could learn quickly. They turned to the IKG for guidance -- to the representatives in the emigration offices on Seitenstettengasse, to information brochures provided by foreign aid committees, and to the Jewish newspaper -- to learn what opportunities were available. At the end of May 1938 the *ZR* announced new possibilities for agricultural and industrial workers in Central and South America. Ecuador, for example, was looking specifically for men over eighteen who could help in industry or manufacturing, if they could provide the hefty sum of $400 to invest in an agricultural or industrial enterprise in that country. Men who felt qualified for such work and had the financial means (or wanted to request it from the IKG) needed to apply to the Ecuadorian Consulate. A man who was approved for immigration could obtain a visa not only for himself but for his wife and children as well.[26]

If leaving together with family was the top priority and if one could adjust to the new climate, did not fear the new language and culture, could handle the tough labor, and could procure the funding, this opportunity to immigrate shone bright. For many people this was not

---

[23] The emigration questionnaires indicate that Jews were willing to go anywhere. Most applicants listed a handful of possible immigration destinations and always included countries outside of Europe.
[24] For example, some applied with the IKG to immigrate to Poland. See USHMM film #Alpha H4, *Auswanderungsfrageboegen der Israelitischen Kultusgemeinde Wien (IKG), Rafael Haut., #53265* and *Alpha B?, Aron Binsztok # 50372.*
[25] USHMM film # 294, IKG-A/W 126, *Report of the Vienna Jewish Community. A description of the activity of the Israelitische Kultusgemeinde Wien in the period from May 2nd 1938–December 31st 1939 (2 Exemplare)*: 72.
[26] See *Zionistische Rundschau*, 20 May 1938: 4.

the case.[27] Thus the IKG continuously publicized all emigration opportunities and tried to place

people in different countries on the basis of their personal, professional, financial, and familial

background. For example, different categories of certificates were granted to Vienna's Jews who

wished to immigrate to Palestine. The candidates included religious functionaries, parents of

persons already residing there, and persons who practiced certain professions that were

particularly needed. Palestine also stood as a prime destination for wealthy Jews, those with the

equivalent of £1,000 English pounds in reichmarks to purchase a "capitalist certificate." These

people could enter Palestine on the grounds that they would help to improve the Palestinian

economy.[28] Palestine was also a place for young Zionists, the next generation who could build

the Jewish state.[29]

For highly qualified engineers and technicians, the IKG advertised that Australia was the

place to go, and from 500 applicants selected 150 who emigrated in October 1938.[30] Continental

Europe, by contrast, was most suitable for Jews over sixty with friends or relatives who could

provide for them. Continental Europe was suitable also for professionals who could improve the

---

[27] Climate, language, employment, and funding were top concerns for potential emigrants when seeking a country. See USHMM, Films #Alpha A-Z, *Auswanderungsfrageboegen der Israelitischen Kultusgemeinde Wien (IKG)*.
[28] The Palestine option for wealthy Viennese Jews was an extension of negotiations that started in 1933 between German Zionists and the Nazi government. For more on this system know as the Transfer Agreement, see Yehuda Bauer, *Jews for Sale? : Nazi-Jewish Negotiations, 1933-1945* (New Haven: Yale University Press, 1994); Edwin Black, *The Transfer Agreement: the Untold Story of the Secret Agreement Between the Third Reich and Jewish Palestine* (New York: Macmillan, 1984). For more on the granting of Capitalist Certificates and the specific situation in Vienna, see Rabinovici, *Instanzen der Ohnmacht*, 105-107.
[29] The IKG recognized the value and importance of Jewish youth immigrating to Palestine and it assisted in developing an agricultural and industrial retraining programs. It also helped create and provide special training places for children ages 14-18 who prepared to emigrate with Youth Aliya. Aside from helping the Youth Aliya and the Hechaluz, the IKG's retraining program also helped a great many other Jews receive certificates of immigration to Palestine. See USHMM film # 294, IKG-A/W 126, *Report of the Vienna Jewish Community. A description of the activity of the Israelitische Kultusgemeinde Wien in the period from May 2nd 1938–December 31st 1939 (2 Exemplare)*: 68. Also see, Erica Simmons, *Haddassah and the Zionist Project*. (Lanham: Rowman and Littlefield, 2006); Recha Frier, *Let the Children Come: The Early Story of Youth Aliyah*. (London: Weidenfeld and Nicolson, 1961); Marian G. Greenberg, *There is Hope for Your Children: Youth Aliyah, Henrietta Szold and Hadassah*. (N.p.: Haddassah, the Women's Zionist Organization of America, 1986); Marvin Lowenthal, *Henrietta Szold: Life and Letters* (New York: Viking, 1942).
[30] USHMM film # 294, IKG-A/W 126, *Report of the Vienna Jewish Community. A description of the activity of the Israelitische Kultusgemeinde Wien in the period from May 2nd 1938–December 31st 1939 (2 Exemplare)*: 67.

economic situation of a host country, such as engineers, technicians, and domestic servants.[31] For

people who had nowhere else to go, Shanghai appeared a promising option. No visa was needed

for this destination and no medical examination (as the United States required for entry); rather,

one had to sign a waiver that one understood the medical risks associated with immigration to

this city in the Far East.[32] In short, people made private decisions about where to attempt to flee,

but could not make any arrangements on their own: they needed the help of the IKG. The IKG

advertised emigration possibilities, vetted applications, chose whom to send, offered retraining

courses, and provided financial assistance. After May 1938, everyone had to register with the

IKG to emigrate.

Waiting in Lines at the Consulates

At the same time as Jews wrote to family members and friends abroad, they stood on line at the

consulate of the country of destination to apply for an immigration visa. Some began this

process days after Hitler invaded Austria.[33] While corresponding with far-flung kin carried its

own challenges (sometimes communicating in a second language), it did not rival the difficulty

of trying to speak with a representative at a foreign consulate. Applying for a visa was a major

ordeal that lasted anywhere from hours to days, and it exposed applicants to danger. While the

---

[31] Ibid: 72. Also see: Amy Gottlieb, *Men of Vision: Anglo-jewry's Aid to Victims of the Nazi Regime, 1933-1945.* (London: Weidenfeld & Nicolson, 1998); Frank Dawes, *Not In Front of the Servants: Domestic Service In England 1850-1939* (London:Wayland Publishers, 1973); Pamela Horn, *The Rise and Fall of the Victorian Servant* (New York: St. Martin's Press, 1975); Werner Mosse, *Second Chance: Two Centuries of German-speaking Jews In the United Kingdom.* (Tübingen: J.C.B. Mohr [Paul Siebeck], 1991).

[32] See standard document printed by the IKG to be signed by the applicant seeking emigration to Shanghai, USHMM microfilm #Alpha U1, *Auswanderungsfrageboegen der Israelitischen Kultusgemeinde Wien (IKG), Sandor Ultmann,* # 1,458 [slides 0371-79]. For more on Jewish emigration to and life in Shanghai, see: Franziska Tausig, *Shanghai Passage: Emigration Ins Ghetto.* 2. Aufl. (Wien: Milena, 2007); Steve Hochstadt and Gerda Neu-Sokol. *Shanghai Geschichten: Die Jüdische Flucht Nach China.* 1. Aufl. (Teetz: Hentrich & Hentrich, 2007); James Ross, *Escape to Shanghai: a Jewish Community In China.* (New York: Free Press, 1994); Ernest G. Heppner, *Shanghai Refuge: a Memoir of the World War II Jewish Ghetto.* (Lincoln: University of Nebraska Press, 1993); Evelyn Rubin, *Ghetto Shanghai.* (New York: Shengold, 1993).

[33] For a personal example, see the testimony of Alois, G., 1996. "Interview by Survivors of the Shoah Visual History Foundation," Los Angeles, CA, USA, February 23. Interview Code 12444, Tapes 1-2.

lines were certainly longer outside the American consulate than the Ecuadorian consulate, for example, they stretched beyond all consulates' doors, because people wished to go anywhere and everywhere. In summer heat or winter snow, Jews stood hours awaiting entry to these offices. And as the consulates offered them no protection while they waited outside the doors, they stood as easy targets for Nazi thugs and random Gestapo arrests.[34] Sometimes people came the night before and slept outside; other times they arrived very early in the morning. It was not uncommon to stand all day only to reach the entrance just as the office closed. Then one had to return the next day and start the process all over. Some people, particularly the elderly, could not stand in these lines at all, and so they paid or bribed someone younger to stand for them.

Illustration 13:"Lines Outside the Consulate"

Source: Documentation Center of the Austrian Resistance (DÖW): *www.doew.at*

---

[34] See case of twenty-year-old Erika Betts, arrested for "Rassenschande" while trying to get a visa from the office in the Belvedere Palace. Erika was imprisoned and deported to Dachau in the summer of 1938. Erica, B., 1996. "Interview by Survivors of the Shoah Visual History Foundation," Upminster, Essex, UK, October 15. Interview Code 20825, Tapes 1-6.

All of this waiting and anticipation was just to get inside these consulates where, for ten minutes, even Jews might still be treated as full human beings and offered the chance of getting out. This was not always the case, however. Sometimes people waited and waited and learned only when they got inside that they were not even eligible for emigration to that country, or that their chances of getting a visa were extremely slim.[35] For those potential emigrants who found hope within the walls of the foreign consulates -- hope that they would be able to obtain a visa sometime in the near future -- life seemed brighter for a brief moment. But they exited with no guarantees at all of getting out, and little more than perhaps a number of their file-in-process. As they stepped off the grounds of foreign sovereignty and back onto the streets of Nazi Vienna, they returned to a hostile environment that was no longer their home.

Affidavits, The United States

Jews needed to do a lot more than get through the doors of a consulate in order to receive an immigration visa. This was the case for all countries and applied particularly to immigration to the United States, which stood "as one of the most important countries of destination," according to an IKG report to the JDC.[36] The *ZR* noted a huge demand for immigration to the United States, reporting that in the ten days immediately following Anschluss (21 March and 1 April) over 25,000 people inquired at the US consulate for immigration visas.[37] This did not mean that the United States was opening its doors to the refugees or easing any of its immigration policies.

---

[35] See USHMM film #Alpha A5, *Auswanderungsfrageboegen der Israelitischen Kultusgemeinde Wien (IKG), Walter Austerlitz, #8194*.
[36] USHMM film # 294, IKG-A/W 126, *Report of the Vienna Jewish Community. A description of the activity of the Israelitische Kultusgemeinde Wien in the period from May 2nd 1938–December 31st 1939 (2 Exemplare)*: 65. Original English.
[37] *Zionistische Rundschau*, 20 May 1938: 3.

Rather, as Helen Herz remembered, the United States was not only the most desired country of immigration, but the most difficult into which to gain entry. [38]

A major difficulty of immigrating to the United States that did not apply to other countries was that in order to register for a visa, one needed a financial guarantor in the US to send an official written statement, an affidavit, to the consulate or the IKG on one's behalf. [39] This condition for entering the US was established by law in 1924.[40] "Owing to the large number of Jews (three million) that went to the USA between 1880-1937 many people managed to get affidavits to the USA from relatives and friends who had settled there in the previous decades," the IKG reported to the JDC.[41] However, many people were unable to get there -- not due to lack of effort on the part of the IKG, the potential emigrant, or even the American citizen trying to procure an affidavit. America's strict immigration laws stood as a barrier.[42] Few relatives and friends were willing and able to offer their assurances.

Guarantors had to prove their financial standing to the US government and provide a notarized document with this information for the refugee. Mrs. Postman, for example, an American citizen, a married mother of two living in Waltham, Massachusetts, went to great lengths to help procure an affidavit for a Viennese refugee whom she did not know personally

---

[38] Helen, H., 1995. "Interview by Survivors of the Shoah Visual History Foundation," Newbury Park, CA, USA, February 21. Interview Code 00903, Tapes 1-2. For more on this subject see: Richard Breitman, *American Refugee Policy and European Jewry 1933-1945* (Indiana, Indiana University Press, 1987); Henry L. Feingold, *The Politics of Rescue: The Roosevelt Administration and the Holocaust, 1938-1945* (New York: Waldon Press, Inc., 1970); J. Jenks and J. Lauck, *The Immigration Problem: a Study of American Immigration Conditions and Needs* (New York: Funk & Wagnalls Co.,1922).

[39] For visual samples of affidavits see file of Ernst Gerstenfeld in *Ernst Gerstenfeld Archival Collection*, courtesy of Ted Shealy; also see Simon Grossmann in USHMM film #Alpha G10, *Auswanderungsfrageboegen der Israelitischen Kultusgemeinde Wien (IKG)*.

[40] *Zionistische Rundschau*, 20 May 1938: 3.

[41] Original English as printed by the IKG, see USHMM film # 294, IKG-A/W 126, *Report of the Vienna Jewish Community. A description of the activity of the Israelitische Kultusgemeinde Wien in the period from May 2nd 1938- December 31st 1939 (2 Exemplare)*. Original English.

[42] See Henry L. Feingold, *Bearing Witness: How America and Its Jews Responded to the Holocaust.* (New York: Syracuse University Press, 1995); David Wyman, *The Abandonment of the Jews: America and the Holocaust, 1941-1945.* (New York: New Press,1998); Bat-Ami Zucker, *In Search of Refuge: Jews and Us Consuls In Nazi Germany, 1933-1941* (Portland: Vallentine Mitchell, 2001).

but with whose situation she empathized. "I am... a Jewess of German nationality, born and still living in Vienna. I am compelled to leave my country," Dr. Hochsinger wrote to Mrs. Postman on 14 July 1939.

> As I do not know any relations of mine living in America, I come to beg you to help me to get an affidavit... I am Dr. [of] Philosophy, I took my degree at the University of Vienna in the year 1910. I was a teacher of mathematics at the "People's Highschool Volksheim" in Vienna, where I taught thirty-two years. I had, more over, many private lessons, I conducted a Home for children in Vienna, and a summer-home for children in the country. I was a pupil of Dr.Alfred Adler's, when he still lived in Vienna, so I know individual psychology. I know all sorts of needle-work, I know to knit pullovers, to crotchet gloves and collars, to make hats, belts, brooches and different other hand-made works. Would you, dear madam, lend me a helping hand, to achieve my longed-for aim? ...Should my request be successful, I shall certainly do my very best to satisfy my employers. On no account I should ... become a burden to you nor to anyone else. Will you, then, be kind enough as to help me to get an affidavit? Hoping that I am so lucky as to find in you a rescuer, I remain, thanking you beforehand. [43]

When Mrs. Postman learned that she and her husband did not have enough money to prove to the American government that they could support this refugee and prevent her from becoming a burden on the state, she tried to open her own home to Dr. Hochsinger and provide work for her as a governess for her own children. But this was not enough to satisfy the government's demands. "Believe me, Dr. Hochsinger, if I were financially able to sign an affidavit and bring you here we would be happy to have you stay in our home until a more profitable occupation was offered you. From what you wrote about yourself I am sure you would be a fine influence over our two young children and be of assistance to me," Mrs. Postman explained. [44] As she could not bring Dr. Hochsinger to the United States on her own,

---

[43] *Harriet Postman letters, 1939-1941*, Crane, Evelyn P., donor. USHMM: Archives, Acc. # 2000.32: 1-2.
[44] Ibid: 22.

she began writing letters to family, friends, colleagues, and various aid organizations -- even to the First Lady, Eleanor Roosevelt -- looking for help. "I would like to have her in our home as I think she would be a fine influence over our two children while I am occupied in assisting my husband in his work [but] we are not qualified financially to apply for an affidavit." [45]

Mrs. Postman sent copies of Dr. Hochsinger's original letter to the Refugee Committee Council for Jewish Women, the Boston Committee for Refugees, the Refugee Aid Department of B'nai B'rith, a Hollywood film director in California, the president of the B'nai B'rith magazine in Ohio, the head of the *Worcester Evening Gazette* in Massachusetts, and to a famous actor at the Wilbur Theatre in Boston. She suggested to these people and organizations that Dr. Hochsinger work as a governess and repeated that while she was a stranger to her, she was highly qualified to work in various positions and a woman in desperate need of help. Writing to Dr. Hochsinger in Vienna, Mrs. Postman explained her efforts: "In all I have sent out eight copies of your letters to persons and organizations likely to answer your appeal." [46] Then she added, "I certainly hope your wish will come true soon....When you come to America I shall be very glad to hear from you."[47]

Quotas

Obtaining an affidavit was just one of the problems Jews faced in their struggle to enter America. Those fortunate enough to have one in hand sought a number on the American

---

[45] Ibid: 25.

[46] Ibid: 18.

[47] Dr. Hochsinger still had hopes that the IKG could help arrange her emigration from Vienna, as late as 1941, if only she could get an affidavit. Mrs. Postman received her last letter from Vienna on 24 May 1941, in which Dr. Hochsinger made her last desperate plea for help: "I beg you to excuse me for writing you once more and to feel sure that I should be very thankful if you would be as kind to try once more to interest somebody so as to secure an affidavit for me." After almost three years of correspondence, Mrs. Postman realized that she had been unable to find anyone who would provide an affidavit of support for Dr. Hochsinger. She had waited for one of the persons or organizations to help, but for various reasons none of the avenues she tried provided an affidavit for this refugee in need. Mrs. Postman's sincere efforts had proved futile and Dr. Hochsinger, like so many Jews searching for a home in the United States, was still trapped in Nazi Vienna.

consulate's waiting list or quota. Each year a designated number of people were given permission to enter the US if they satisfied all the regulations. With the start of the new fiscal year on July 1, a new quota was opened, starting at zero.[48] One hoped that by the time one made it to the top of the queue at the American consulate, there would still be room in the current year quota, but this was rarely the case. The quotas were too small and always over-subscribed.[49] For example, the quota established by the United States for Austria in the beginning of 1938 had only 1,413 slots; 25,000 Jews lined up outside the American consulate in the first two weeks following Anschluss.[50]

Even after the Austrian quota was combined with the quota for Germany, making for a total of 25,957 openings, it was still insufficient to accommodate the tens of thousands of desperate Jews trying to leave. Combining the Austrian and German quotas gave Viennese Jews born within the borders of the First Austrian Republic significantly better chances of getting a US visa than Viennese Jews born elsewhere, but the problem was not solved.[51] None of the quotas was large enough, and this prevented the immigration of many willing and able refugees. Trapped Jews prayed that the US would have pity on them, introduce more flexible immigration policies, and increase its quotas, but to their dismay Washington did not move.

---

[48] USHMM film # 294, IKG-A/W 126, *Report of the Vienna Jewish Community. A description of the activity of the Israelitische Kultusgemeinde Wien in the period from May 2nd 1938–December 31st 1939 (2 Exemplare)*: 151.
[49] See standard notice from American General Consulate to applicant stating that affidavit has arrived. This notice explains to the applicant that he or she still must wait for the quota number. See USHMM film # VZ48, IKG-A/W 2689, 2, *Ansuchen um Aufnahme in das Transitlager Richborough (Alphabetisch), A-B, 1939: Dr. Ernst Adler, 15 May 1939; Edwin Bibring, 17 October 1938*. For more on US immigration policy see: Herbert Arthur Strauss and Steven W Siegel, *Jewish Immigrants of the Nazi Period In the USA* (München: K. G. Saur, 1978); Edwin Gilbert Flittie, *The Quota System: a Study In Immigration, 1913-32* (Stanford University: Thesis [M.A.], 1947).
[50] *Zionistische Rundschau*, 20 May 1938: 3.
[51] Paul Berger wrote in his application to the transit camp, "since I am registered on the German quota, I am sure to receive a visa within the next half a year." He actually was not estimated to have his quota called until one year from the time he registered, July 1939, but this was still much sooner than if he were registered on another quota. See USHMM film # VZ48, IKG-A/W 2689, 2, *Ansuchen um Aufnahme in das Transitlager Richborough (Alphabetisch), B, 1939: Paul Berger.*

Raising the quota figures would have helped, but could not solve a greater issue at hand: family separation. The American quota system registered Jews on the basis of their nationality, thus Austria's Jews were forced to apply as natives of many European countries. Because of the geographic history of the Austrian region, the territorial losses and border changes which resulted after World War I, the IKG faced a situation unlike other Jewish communities when it came to family emigration. To be specific, in November 1939, of 10,000 Viennese Jews registered on waiting lists to get into the United States, only 2,818 women and 1,866 men waited on the Austrian (German) quota, while the rest (over half) waited on the Romanian, Czech, Polish, Slovakian, or Hungarian quota-- countries that had formerly been part of the Austrian monarchy.[52] Thus, a large percentage of Viennese Jewry was not qualified to register on the Austrian/German waiting list.

Table 6:"National Quotas for Vienna's Jews Waiting to Enter the USA, November 1938."

National Quotas for Vienna's Jews Waiting to Enter the USA, November 1938

MEN				
	Germany	Protectorate[53]	Poland	Other Quotas
0-14 years	428	1	10	5
15-24	175	3	4	6
25-39	249	12	120	30
40-60	813	277	957	269
Over 60	201	210	373	109
Total	**1856**	**503**	**1464**	**419**
WOMEN				
0-14	385	--	11	4
15-24	359	7	16	4
25-39	640	54	335	76
40-60	1159	452	1262	320
Over 60	275	244	336	114
Total	**2818**	**757**	**1960**	**518**

Source: USHMM film # 294, IKG-A/W 126, IKG *Report May 2nd 1938- December 31st 1939.*

---

[52] USHMM film # 294, IKG-A/W 126, *Report of the Vienna Jewish Community. A description of the activity of the Israelitische Kultusgemeinde Wien in the period from May 2nd 1938–December 31st 1939 (2 Exemplare)*: 65.
[53] The Czech provinces Bohemia and Moravia.

Each national quota offered different chances of getting registered and obtaining an immigration visa, depending on how large the quota for the particular country was set for that year and how long the waiting list. Some quotas offered the refugees a much better chance than others. The quota for Poland, for example, was set very small, with only 6,524 openings (about one-fourth the Austrian/German quota)[54] but there were many Viennese Jews of Polish descent trying to get to the US. In fact, in November 1938 more Viennese Jews over the age of sixty were waiting to go to the US on the Polish quota than on the Austrian/German quota: 375 men and 336 women, compared to 201 men and 275 women.[55]

Once registered, the complications of the quota system did not let up. Each quota list had a different number of spaces and a different waiting period, presenting a particular problem for Viennese families who sought to get out of the country all together. A typical Viennese family consisted of members born in different countries and the quota system could therefore divide their paths. For example, the Romanian quota was much smaller than the Austrian/German quota and the wait was much longer. Dr. Michael Albert Milch, a former lawyer and a veteran of World War I, considered himself Austrian by nationality, but neither the new German state nor the US government recognized him as such. Dr. Milch, his wife Emma, and his mother Regina, were born in the formerly Austrian cities of Czernowitz and Oszechlib and needed to register on the Romanian quota; meanwhile, his fifteen-year-old daughter Kitty, born in Vienna, was able to register on the Austrian quota. All four family members had the same sponsor in New York, a cousin named Harry J. Rudick who supplied them with an "excellent" affidavit. They assumed they would immigrate to the United States together as a family until they learned of the strict US quota regulations. In a standard notice from American general consulate they learned that

[54] *Zionistische Rundschau*, 20 May 1938: 3.
[55] USHMM film # 294, IKG-A/W 126, *Report of the Vienna Jewish Community. A description of the activity of the Israelitische Kultusgemeinde Wien in the period from May 2nd 1938–December 31st 1939 (2 Exemplare)*: 65.

"affidavits are good for one person only. It is possible to have one affidavit for one family as long as the whole family is on the same quota and plans to leave together – meaning parents and their underage children. If the family members are on different quotas and if they apply for emigration separately, then they must have separate affidavits."[56]

With this knowledge, in response to the IKG's final question on the emigration questionnaire: "Which dependent should emigrate together with you now and which later?" Kitty wrote, "Only I shall emigrate now, my dependents belong on the Romanian quota and can only emigrate much later, at which time exactly is still unknown to them."[57] In this statement Kitty marked the moment when the emigration process started to sever ties between parents and children. Both Dr. Milch and his daughter explained to the IKG on several occasions, beginning on 13 May 1938 that, as the family had no money or assets at its disposal and was living on the welfare support of the IKG, their only remaining hope was to emigrate and start life anew elsewhere.[58] In their desperation to flee Austria, the members of the Milch family, like so many others, decided to go ahead with a process that offered them and their loved ones completely different odds for leaving via emigration to the US, just for the sake of getting out. The uncertainty of their situation required them to take separate paths. When Kitty boarded the ship in Rotterdam on 26 August 1939 she left alone, with the rest of her family waiting in Vienna for their chance to leave. She never saw them again. [59]

---

[56] USHMM film # VZ48, IKG-A/W 2689, 2, *Ansuchen um Aufnahme in das Transitlager Richborough (Alphabetisch), A-B, 1939: Dr. Ernst Adler, 15 May 1939; Edwin Bibring, 17 October 1938.* Original English.
[57] USHMM film #Alpha M6, *Auswanderungsfrageboegen der Israelitischen Kultusgemeinde Wien (IKG), Kitty Milch, # 9843.*
[58] 13 May 1938 [Dr. Milch], 13 July 1939 [Kitty], Aug. 1939 [Hausreseresche, IKG]. See USHMM film #Alpha M6, *Auswanderungsfrageboegen der Israelitischen Kultusgemeinde Wien (IKG), Dr. Michael Albert Milch, #7339,* and USHMM film #Alpha M6, *Auswanderungsfrageboegen der Israelitischen Kultusgemeinde Wien (IKG), Kitty Milch, # 9843.*
[59] The Germans deported Dr. Michael Albert Milch and Emma Milch on transport #36 from Vienna to Minsk, Maly Trostinets on 17 August 1942. The fate of Regina Milch is unknown. See *Documentation Center of the Austrian Resistance (DÖW):*DOEW-Project Registration by Name: The Austrian Victims of the Holocaust, 2001. (Database

Uncertainties: Waiting and Looking Elsewhere

Those fortunate enough to receive a place on the quota list left the American consulate with a

number but without a clue as to when that number would be called. Waiting was the next major

challenge potential emigrants faced. Twenty-nine-year-old Dr. Ernst Adler, a former lawyer,

lived alone in a small apartment in Vienna's seventh district. Both his mother and father had

passed away before Anschluss, and now he existed only for his chance to emigrate. He had no

job, no income, and no assets at his disposal. But he possessed an affidavit and was registered on

the German waiting list to enter the United States. On 21 April 1939, he received the following

notice:

> The American General Consulate of Vienna, Germany, informs you that papers
> have arrived regarding the subject of your visa....It should be brought to your
> attention that visas to the United States will only be granted after the quota
> number is reached and that presently all quotas for middle Europe are exhausted,
> so it will be months before you can expect the number to be called. If, at the time
> when the quota is reached and your documents are reviewed, not all your papers
> are in order, you will be informed at once to bring the missing documents to us.
> Until that time, however, verbal and written notices, as well as visits are
> pointless.[60]

All applicants hoped that their number would be called as quickly as possible but, like

Ernst, received only a vague estimate of when that might be. The local American consulate

general refused to provide official information regarding the receipt of the visa. They simply

could not pinpoint the date a visa would be granted, or when the medical examination (a final

---

available online: *http://www. doew.at*). For an additional example of a family divided by nationality in the
emigration process, see Helen, H., 1995. "Interview by Survivors of the Shoah Visual History Foundation,"
Newbury Park, CA, USA, February 21. Interview Code 00903, Tapes 1-2.
[60] Standard notice from American General Consulate to applicant stating that affidavit has arrived. Original English.
USHMM film # V7.48, IKG-A/W 2689, 2, *Ansuchen um Aufnahme in das Transitlager Richborough (Alphabetisch),
A-B, 1939: Dr. Ernst Adler, 15 May 1939; Edwin Bibring, 17 October 1938.*

prerequisite) could be scheduled. Instead, the IKG published a list of approximate dates for people listed on the German, Polish, Czechoslovakian, Italian, Russian, and Romanian quotas. These lists allowed candidates to estimate when their number might be reached, based on when their application was submitted.[61] Then people prayed that the quota number was called in good timing with the rest of the required emigration/immigration documents -- i.e., not too long *before* the other documents were in order (because then it could expire and be given away to someone else) and not too long *after* the rest of the documents were in order (or else they might expire). In short, they had to sit, wait, and accept that they had no control over into which nation's quota they fell or how soon their number would be called. This took a great psychological toll and was another significant factor in their struggle to move the process forward.

Strategic coordination of documents and their timing was such a daunting prospect that it drove some families and individuals to explore other countries for immigration, even when they had an affidavit and quota number for the United States. The Feiden family, for example, was among some ten thousand Jews already in possession of strong affidavits and registered on a quota to immigrate to the US in July 1938.[62] Still, they had troubles getting to the US. Ten-year-old Walter Feiden and his parents Moses and Emilie had affidavits supplied by a niece in Brooklyn. They had expected to register on the Austrian/German quota, but they discovered they would have to register on the Polish quota. This quota was so small and the number of applicants so large, that the wait was estimated at three years! Thus their chances of leaving Vienna were uncertain, notwithstanding their affidavit and quota number. With this news they decided to explore other destinations with far more lenient immigration policies, such as

---

[61] The consulate provided estimations in August 1938 and the IKG published an updated list six months later. USHMM film # VZ48, IKG-A/W 2687, *Report from the Reichsvertretung der Juden in Deutschland to the German Jewish Aid Committee, 29 January 1939*: 3.

[62] USHMM film # 294, IKG-A/W 126, *Report of the Vienna Jewish Community. A description of the activity of the Israelitische Kultusgemeinde Wien in the period from May 2nd 1938–December 31st 1939 (2 Exemplare)*: 65.

Shanghai and Hispaniola, the island on which the countries of Haiti and the Dominican Republic are located.[63]

Transmigration

Thirty-nine-year-old Paul Berger, like the Feiden family and so many others registered and in possession of affidavits, still felt uncertain of his chances to get to the US. Paul was single, living in Vienna's seventh district, attending a retraining course in electrical engineering at the IKG, and desperate to flee. Fortunate to have two cousins living in the US with enough money to sponsor him, he received two strong affidavits in the spring of 1938 and managed to register for a visa to the US on the Austrian/German quota that summer (3 July 1938), but this was not enough to guarantee his safety. He believed he could not survive in Nazi Germany one more day and sought immediate assistance. Looking to the IKG emigration advisory office for help, he learned about the possibility of transmigration. Thanks to the IKG and foreign aid committees, people could apply for temporary stay in the transit camp Richborough established in Kent, England.[64] Certain qualified individuals, including males who could prove "1) that their emigration is urgent, 2) that the continuation of their journey from England to overseas seems to be secured and that the same is not possible before 3 months, but can be executed at any rate

---

[63] When their quota numbers had still not been reached in May 1940, these leads gave them hope, but the Feiden family did not manage to secure emigration. Moses, Emilie, and Walter were deported to Lódz in 1941. Walter was the only survivor. USHMM microfilm#49, *Auswanderungsfrageboegen der Israelitischen Kultusgemeinde Wien (IKG) (Numerisch geordnet): Moses Feiden,* file #39554. See also, Walter, B. F., 1997. "Interview by Survivors of the Shoah Visual History Foundation," Jackson Heights, NY, USA, April 10. Interview Code 27974, Tapes 1-7.
[64] The Richborough Transit Camp existed from March to August 1939 and served as a temporary stay for some 1,600 people between the ages of 18 and 45, particularly men who were released from Dachau with a warning to leave the country within weeks. The IKG helped to erect this camp together with the Council for German Jewry in December 1938. The IKG strongly advocated that another such place be set up in another neutral foreign city. See USHMM film # 294, IKG-A/W 126, *Report of the Vienna Jewish Community. A description of the activity of the Israelitische Kultusgemeinde Wien in the period from May 2ⁿᵈ 1938–December 31ˢᵗ 1939 (2 Exemplare):* 65. For more information on Richborough, see Norman Bentwich, *They Found Refuge: An account of British Jewry's work for victims of Nazi oppression.* (London: Cresset Press, 1956) 102-114; Amy Gottlieb, *Men of Vision: Anglo-jewry's Aid to Victims of the Nazi Regime, 1933-1945.* (London: Weidenfeld & Nicolson, 1998).

after 9 months,"[65] could wait for their quota numbers to be reached (or for their visa to enter another country) from this safe haven. Paul Berger sent a letter to the IKG requesting admittance to Richborough: "My departure is of the upmost urgency," he wrote, "because I have no way to live here anymore, I have no income. Also, spiritually, I can not manage living here anymore.... My soul simply cannot bear to be so degraded."[66]

News about the Richborough opportunity was disseminated to all emigration representatives in Germany on 26 January 1939;[67] the IKG published advertisements about the camp in the renamed Jewish newspaper, *Jüdisches Nachtrichtenblatt*[68] on 10 February and 10 March 1939.[69] For Jews whose primary concern was immediate flight, a safe place to wait shone bright. Transit stay appeared to be the best option, so they followed the instructions printed in the paper, sending their request letters to the IKG, clarifying their situations, and pleading to be accepted for this transit camp. Each applicant tried to explain why his situation was more urgent than the next and how they could be useful at Richborough. Many boasted of their skills and offered to lead retraining courses in their specialties if they were chosen.[70] Some also referenced their long commitment to the IKG, hoping that this would improve their chances of being selected. The majority documented their arrest, the length of their incarceration, and the date the Gestapo threatened they must leave greater Germany. Then too, there were men who were never

---

[65] USHMM film # VZ48, IKG-A/W 2687, *Report from the Reichsvertretung der Juden in Deutschland to the German Jewish Aid Committee, 29 January 1939*: 1.
[66] USHMM film # VZ48, IKG-A/W 2689, 2, *Ansuchen um Aufnahme in das Transitlager Richborough (Alphabetisch), B, 1939: Paul Berger.*
[67] Rundschreiben, USHMM film # VZ48, IKG-A/W 2689, 2, *Ansuchen um Aufnahme in das Transitlager Richborough (Alphabetisch), B, 1939: Alfred Barbsch.*
[68] The IKG newspaper name changed from *Zionistische Rundschau* to *Jüdisches Nachtrichtenblatt* after the pogrom in November 1938.
[69] *Jüdisches Nachtrichtenblatt*, 10 February 1939: 5. Paul Berger and Ernst Breuer respond to the newspaper notice. USHMM film # VZ48, IKG-A/W 2689, 2, *Ansuchen um Aufnahme in das Transitlager Richborough (Alphabetisch), B, 1939: Ernst Breuer, 16 February 1939.*
[70] Moritz Bluman (carpenter) and Isidor Blatt (watchmaker, gold and silversmith), application letters to the IKG for entrance to Richborough, USHMM film # VZ48, IKG-A/W 2689, 1-2, *Ansuchen um Aufnahme in das Transitlager Richborough (Alphabetisch), A-B... 1939.*

imprisoned but still desperate to get out of Vienna, writing that they simply could not handle life inside anymore.[71]

Thus, while the United States remained the most desirable country of immigration, people looked to other countries where they could find shelter, often places far from their mental universe. For example, on the same page of the *Jüdisches Nachtrichtenblatt* that the IKG published advertisements about Richborough, they listed important immigration facts about British Guiana, Rhodesia, and Manchukuo.[72] Jews had to make sacrifices and compromises to go to these countries too, but their primary goal was simply to find a place of refuge. For example, Samuel Jekel could not consider the US as a potential country of immigration for his family because (as he explained to the IKG on 24 June 1938) the Gestapo had ordered him and his whole family -- his wife Blima, and their two sons Julius and Berthold -- to leave Germany by 1 September 1938, and he could not organize immigration to America for the four of them in so short a time. [73] While the two sons, born in Vienna, were eligible for the Austrian quota, he and his wife were born in the former Austro-Hungarian city of Dolina and would therefore have to register on the Polish quota. If they were on the list by June 1938, when Samuel received this Gestapo notice, the children's quota could be reached approximately 9 to 12 months later (March–June 1939). But, only by being among the very first registered on the German quota in March 1938 would it have been possible for them to receive a quota number as of September

[71] Paul Berger and Dr. Ernst Adler, application letters to the IKG for entrance to Richborough, USHMM film # V748, IKG-A/W 2689, 1-2, *Ansuchen um Aufnahme in das Transitlager Richborough (Alphabetisch), A-B... 1939.*
[72] *Jüdisches Nachtrichtenblatt*, 10 February 1939: 5.
[73] USHMM film #Alpha J1, *Auswanderungsfrageboegen der Israelitischen Kultusgemeinde Wien (IKG), Samuel Jekel, # 33401.* Private interview with Elli Caroll (Ella Jekel), USHMM, December 2006.

1938, and even then, these dates were only estimates.[74] Samuel and Blima's numbers on the

Polish quota would not be called for some three years.

Samuel's brother, David Jekel, faced some of the same troubles. Although he was not

under Gestapo threat, he was eager to get his family out as quickly as possible and understood

that this was not an option if they applied for immigration to the United States. David and his

wife Klara were born in Dolina also and their two children, Margit and Ella, in Vienna. They

could split the family up, as the Milch family chose to do, sending the children ahead and hoping

to follow them later, or stay together as the Feidens did and seek alternative immigration

destinations. David chose not to waste any time applying for immigration to the US and instead

applied for permits to enter Trinidad. Trinidad, a country with a very different climate, language,

and culture than Austria, also had a steep financial requirement for a family of four to provide as

a landing fee. But Trinidad did not have the strict immigration requirements of the US which

risked splitting families apart. Applying for and obtaining immigration visas to a destination as

exotic as Trinidad may have seemed absurd to the Jekel family and their friends (even to David)

at first, but these types of decisions soon became commonplace. Fleeing to Trinidad enabled the

Jekels to stay together and leave the country as quickly as possible.[75]

---

[74]Quota Estimations: German, Polish, Czechoslovakian, Italian, Russian, Romanian. USHMM film # VZ48, IKG-A/W 2687, *Report from the Reichsvertretung der Juden in Deutschland to the German Jewish Aid Committee, 29 January 1939*: 3.

[75] USHMM film #Alpha J1, *Auswanderungsfrageboegen der Israelitischen Kultusgemeinde Wien (IKG), David Jekel, # 24196;* Elli Caroll (Ella Jekel), private interview with author, December 2006. Washington, D.C.

Table 7: "Original IKG Emigration Statistics, Countries of Destination, March 1938-December 1939."

51.501 Persons

Countries of Destination:

E u r o p e:		A s i a:		Australia	584
Albania	36	Palestine	4.820	Fiji Islands	1
Belgium	974	Afghanistan	7	New Zealand	32
Bulgaria	36	China	5.488		
Cyprus	127	Iraq	17		
Denmark	143	Japan	32	C e n t r a l	
England	14.492	Brit.India	86	and S o u t h	
Esthonia	23	Neth.India	30	A m e r i c a :	
Finland	213	Manchukuo	4	Argentine	765
France	717	Persia	14	Barbados	22
Greece	172	Philippines	34	Bolivia	1.428
Ireland	3	Siam	20	Brazil	171
Italy	1.800	Syria	18	Chile	144
Yugoslavia	111			Columbia	222
Latvia	284			Costa Rica	26
Lithuania	68	A f r i c a :		Cuba	229
Luxemburg	337	Abyssinia	5	Ecuador	72
Malta	7	Algeria	2	Guatemala	5
Monaco	32	Belg.Kongo	3	Guyana	3
Netherland	503	Egypt	26	Haiti	29
Norway	31	Guinea	1	Honduras	10
Poland	991	Kenya	23	Jamaica	4
Portugal	137	Marocco	18	Mexico	316
Protectorat	848	Rhodesia	36	Nicaragua	3
Sweden	293	South-Africa	44	Panama	114
Switzerland	967	Sudan	2	Paraguay	1.052
Turkey	65	Tanganjika	3	Peru	30
Hungary	347	Tunisia	28	Porto Rica	3
Rumania	70	Ughanda	27	San Domingo	105
Liechtenstein	6	Liberia	4	San Salvador	6
Gibraltar	2			Trinidad	172
Spain	4			Venezuele	86
Slovacia	4			Uruguay	176

N o r t h
A m e r i c a
Alaska	2
Canada	54
U.S.A.	10.980

Source: USHMM film # 294, IKG-A/W 126, IKG *Report May 2nd 1938- December 31st 1939*

Table 8: "Original IKG Map, Total Emigration to Various Countries, as of 31 October 1939"

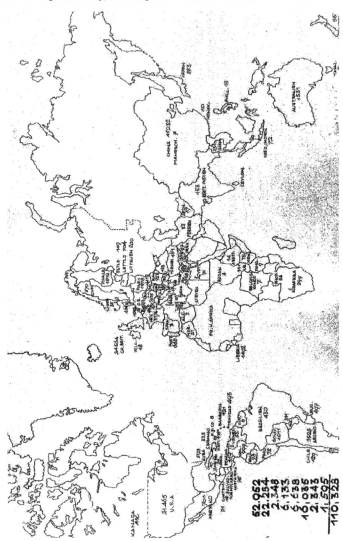

Source: USHMM film # 294, IKG- A/W 119, *Auswanderung, Umschichtung, Fuersorge 02.05.1938-31.07.1939 (Bericht, deutsch, englisch, franzoesisch).*

Struggle Continues: Exit Papers and Emigration

For many people, the greatest hurdle was not getting permission to immigrate but clearance to emigrate. Jews needed a visa to enter a foreign country, and they needed official government clearance to leave Austrian soil. Obtaining exit papers was as difficult as securing immigration permissions. The Germans made the exit process particularly difficult, imposing steep financial demands upon Jews and instituting special tax requirements for them to fulfill prior to their departure. Although their aim was to make the country "Judenrein," their policies remained exigent, even when these requirements held Jews in Austria. As a result, some eight hundred people with permission to enter over forty countries in Europe and overseas (other than the United States) were stuck in Vienna in November 1939, and this was not an isolated occurrence.[76]

Table 9: "Original IKG Emigration Statistics, 809 Jews with Permission to enter over 40 Countries, November 1939"

Argentine	87	Liberia	2
Belgium	20	Luxemburg	3
Belgian Congo	1	Manchukuo	4
Bolivia	178	Mexico	9
Brazil	12	Panama	12
Bulgaria	12	Paraguay	18
Chile	78	Persia	3
Columbia	20	Portugal	4
Cuba	8	Roumania	17
Denmark	13	Philippines	16
Ecuador	15	San Domingo	6
Finland	2	Siam	1
Guatemala	1	Slavakia	10
Haiti	3	South-Africa	
Holland	12	(Colonies,neubr.	
Dutch-India	4	States)	60
Honduras	5	Sweden	9
Italy	11	Turkey	2
Japan	5	Switzerland	10
Yougoslavia	30	Hungary	82
Latvia	5	Uruguay	16
		Venezuela	2
	together		809

Source: USHMM film # 294, IKG-A/W 126, IKG *Report May 2nd 1938- December 31st 1939.*

---

[76] USHMM film # 294, IKG-A/W 126, *Report of the Vienna Jewish Community. A description of the activity of the Israelitische Kultusgemeinde Wien in the period from May 2nd 1938–December 31st 1939 (2 Exemplare)*: 76.

Jews were unable to obtain emigration clearance for a variety of reasons. Some did not have a valid passport, and could not get one. Before the establishment of the *Zentralstelle*, Eichmann's Central Office for Jewish Emigration, only the head of police, located in Vienna's fifth district, could issue passports. This office was insufficient to serve the tens of thousands of Jews needing a passport to emigrate. And the long lines stretching the length of the city block stood as prime targets for vicious Nazis. Chances of receiving a new passport improved after the Zentralstelle began its operation on 20 August 1938.[77] Designed to expedite the emigration process, the new office housed booths with representatives from all relevant offices inside its walls, the former palace of Lord Rothschild on Marc Aurelstrasse in the third district. A conveyer belt system handled all paper requirements of potential emigrants and dispensed passports on the other end.[78] This scheme simplified the emigration process, yet some of the same fundamental issues persisted.

Passport regulations, for example, were particularly problematic for Austrian Jewry due to the region's history. As people entered the IKG and filled out emigration questionnaires, they encountered the following questions: Do you have a valid passport? Where was it issued? What is the date of expiration? The answers to these straightforward questions revealed that the new German passport legislation on passports was confusing and that few people understood exactly what it meant and how important it was to have a valid passport. Many people replied that they had a valid passport, issued by the head of police in Vienna, which they believed was valid for up to five years. The expiration date, however, indicated that it was an old passport for Austria

---

[77] Yitzhak Arad, Israel Gutman, and Abraham Margaliot, *Documents On the Holocaust: Selected Sources On the Destruction of the Jews of Germany and Austria, Poland, and the Soviet Union.* (Jerusalem: Ktav Pub. House in association with Yad Vashem [and the] Anti Defamation League, 1981), 55 .

[78] Gabriele Anderl, *Orte der Täter. Der NS-Terror in den "Arisierten" Wiener Rothschild-Palais.* (Wien, Band 15 der Schriftenreihe des Instituts zur Erforschung der Geschichte der Gewerkschaften und Arbeiterkammern, 2005); also see Cesarani, *Becoming Eichmann.* 68,69,73.

that was actually not valid anymore. This kind of confusion complicated the strategic process of emigration and obstructed one's ability to get out.

When Germany annexed Austria, it was understood that Vienna was now part of Germany, that the citizens of Austria would soon become Germans. And indeed, Austrians got German citizenship on 3 July 1938. If they were interested in traveling out of the country they needed to replace their Austrian passports with German documents. This was also the case for the thousands of Jews seeking to emigrate; they too needed German passports. These passports would not be granted to everyone, however, because many people had been born outside the First Austrian Republic and did not qualify for a German passport. If one was born in a region of the former Austro-Hungarian Empire but obtained Austrian citizenship after World War I, one could reapply and get a German passport. But if one had not acquired Austrian citizenship during the interwar period -- and many people simply had not -- one now had to apply for a passport at the consulate of one's respective country of birth. In some cases, these people were temporarily more fortunate than others, as they could travel to their native country on their old passports.[79]

In August 1938 a new German law prompted by negotiations with Switzerland, required all German passports held by Jews to be stamped with a red "J". So marked, Jews were barred from entering neighboring countries. This new passport requirement presented new obstacles to in the emigration. The date the passport was issued or modified with the "J" was printed next to

---

[79] This passport issue did not apply to all Jews right away. Many persons living in Vienna did not have a passport from the First Austrian Republic and therefore did not need to reapply for the new German Reich passport. Many Viennese Jews born outside the 1918 borders considered themselves Austrians, but on paper they were citizens of the country in which they were born. After WWI and the collapse of the Empire these people lived on in Vienna, but quite often did not officially register for Austrian citizenship. When the Germans marched into Austria, these Jews were more fortunate than most. Leopold Vulkan, for example, decided to apply for Czech citizenship for his family and he after WWI, and embraced this decision some two decades later. Carrying their Czech passports, Leopold, his wife Mathilde, and his two daughters Gertrude and Edith were less susceptible to random persecutions and attacks. As Czech foreigners they were to be protected and most importantly, they could move in and out of the country until Germany invaded Czechoslovakia a year later on 15 March 1939.

the stamp and the passport bearer was given exactly 365 days to leave. In contrast to previous passports and passports held by Aryans which were valid for five years, these new passports were valid for one. This created an added layer of difficulty regarding timing and coordination of documents. Then too, for those who had already gone through the process of exchanging an Austrian for a German passport since Anschluss, and whose immigration papers were close to being dispatched, this new requirement was a major setback which could prove detrimental to their chances of emigrating. When people appeared at the passport office for this modification to be applied, it was possible that their other documents would be found to have expired, or that some other problem would be found. For example, when Josefine Kaufmann, born in Vienna in 1882, went to have her passport stamped, it was taken away from her, making her chances of leaving Austria very slim.[80] It is unclear exactly why Josefine Kaufmann's passport was confiscated, but it is likely that someone recognized an irregularity in her record: perhaps that she had not paid all her taxes or had failed to comply with some German order that was a prerequisite for receiving a German passport and exit visa.

The flood of regulations the Nazis imposed on Jews, and especially financial restrictions, posed a great challenge in the struggle to get out. The German principle was that the Jews should leave the country, but only after they forfeited their assets to the German state. In order to obtain permission to leave the country, people needed to go through a bureaucratic obstacle course to provide proof that they were in good financial standing, had handed over all their assets, and paid all their taxes.[81] Only with proof of completion -- after they received a tax clearance certificate

---

[80] USHMM film #Alpha K2, *Auswanderungsfrageboegen der Israelitischen Kultusgemeinde Wien (IKG), Josefine Kaufmann, # 51224.*
[81] There was a series of different taxes imposed on Jews seeking to emigrate, beginning with the Capital Flight Tax or *Reichsfluchtsteuer (1931)* which totaled 25% of one's total assets. For more information, see Martin Dean, *Robbing the Jews: The Confiscation of Jewish Property in the Holocaust, 1933-1945* (Cambridge: Cambridge University Press, 2008); also see website, *http://home.arcor.de/kerstinwolf/gesetz.htm.*

(Steuerunbedenklichkeitsbescheinigung) from their local district tax office -- could emigrants be issued a passport from the head of police and dispatched with funding and assistance from the IKG. It was very important that once the document had been received the person did not let it expire, but the tax clearance certificate -- like the quota number, affidavit, visa, and passport -- was valid only for one year. As time passed and the Germans imposed further taxes,[82] Jews' financial situations deteriorated, making it more difficult, if not impossible, to receive this essential document. Obtaining and preserving a tax clearance certificate was thus another tricky factor in the twisted route to departure.[83]

How Did Nazi Germany Account for the Wealth of All the Jews?

The first steps in the Germans' plan to expropriate the Jews and to "dejewify" the economy was to find out exactly how great an influence they had in the financial sector by appraising their total assets. On 26 April 1938, the major economic decision makers for the Reich, Goering (in charge of the Four Year Plan) and Frick (Reichsminister of the Interior) released the "Law on the Registration of Jewish Assets." Arthur Seyss-Inquart (Austrian Governor of the Reich) implemented this decree in Austria the following day. This decree called for the registration of all Jewish property in Austria. Part of the Four Year Plan to rebuild the German economy, this new decree aimed to file, monitor, and expedite the transfer of all Jewish assets into Aryan

---

[82] After the 1938 November Pogrom, the Germans introduced a punitive tax or *Sühneleistung*, which demanded 20% of one's total assets to be paid to the state in reparations for the destruction. See chapter six.

[83] There were other factors that added difficulty and confusion to the emigration process and disrupted the coordination of documents. For example, as of 15 May 1938 the Germans demanded that all emigrants provide their local currency office with a full list of everything being shipped out of the country two weeks prior to packing. See *Zionistische Rundshau*, 20 May 1938: 4. Also, purchasing tickets for travel was a particular problem. Tickets needed to be purchased far in advance, especially ship tickets to distant destinations such as Shanghai, and the ships and trains did not wait for passengers, nor did they reimburse them if they could not make their scheduled travel date. People bought the tickets well in advance because the ships got booked quickly. They hoped that their immigration visas and exit papers would be in proper order by the time of their departure, but often this was not the case and they had to give up their tickets and start all over again.

hands. It also aimed to control corruption within the Nazi system and to make sure that all proceeds from the aryanization of the German economy went to the Nazi state. Under no circumstances could an ordinary citizen be permitted to gain privately from Jewish assets as had occurred during the wild-aryanization period in Vienna; the expropriation process would be carried out in an organized and timely fashion.[84]

This order resulted in the establishment of a special office in Vienna's first district, the Assets Transfer Agency (*Vermögensvehrkehrstelle*), headed by Walter Rafelsberger, a member of the Nazi party since 1933. Initially the agency was created as part of the Ministry for Trade and Transfer, but by the end of May it became integrated into the new division of Economics and Labor. It functioned as the registration office for Jewish assets and as the approval office for the divestiture or leasing of business, land, or forestry enterprises. Its main task was to calculate all assets and enterprises owned by Jews and organize their transfer into "Aryan hands." This relied on the distribution, receipt and processing of "Assets Registration Forms."

The Germans ordered that all persons who qualified as a Jew under the Nuremberg Racial Laws and possessed more than 5,000 RM detail the type and sum of his/her total assets in an official four page questionnaire. Filling out the assets registration form (*Vermögensanmeldung*) began by declaring the following:

> I am a Jew (according to the 5th paragraph of the first order of the Reich Citizens Law from 14 November 1935, Reich Law 1, page 1333), and I am of German nationality/ other nationality/ or without nationality. Since I am a __ (Jew of German nationality) __ (a Jew without nationality) I have evaluated and declared in the following Assets Declaration Form my total domestic and foreign assets.[85]

---

[84] Gauleiter Burkel ordered that all commissars who had taken control of businesses or industries owned by Jews during the Anschluss pogrom report their full actions and those who were found guilty of taking assets for themselves were sentenced to prison. See Martin Dean, *Robbing the Jews: The Confiscation of Jewish Property in the Holocaust, 1933-1945* (Cambridge: Cambridge University Press, 2008).
[85] Austrian State Archives: OstA/AdR/06/VVst/VA.

After the forms were complete they were to be reproduced in triplicate and returned to the Assets

Transfer Agency no later than 30 June 1938. The agency offered extensions for Jews who

already lived outside the Reich and for those imprisoned in Dachau, but no one was exempt. If

one was not physically in Vienna to fill out the forms, a representative agent undertake the task.

The process demanded more of the victims' time and energy. The forms needed to be filled out

carefully, completely, and honestly. Failure to do so carried risk of imprisonment or other severe

punishment and jeopardized one's chance of successful emigration.

The *ZR*, as well as other newspapers like the *Neue Freie Presse* and the *Wiener Zeitung*,

informed Jews of their duty to register their total domestic and foreign assets with the state.[86] In

late May 1938, as random arrests were occurring around the city the *ZR* explained: "According

to the law for the protection of the Austrian economy and the rules pertaining to the Registration

of Jewish Assets, an Assets Transfer Agency has been established that will begin seeing people

on 24 May.... All must see to it that their assets are officially transferred with approval of the

Assets Transfer Agency."[87] The newspaper instructed Jews to go to the Assets Transfer Agency

and to fill out the paperwork carefully and accurately, again warning them that only through such

cooperation would emigration be possible.[88] An estimated 47,768 Viennese Jews and their

families, over one-quarter of the total population at the time, were affected by this new law. The

---

[86] Other newspapers ran articles as well. As receivers of property and assets owed by Jews, gentile Austrians were directly affected by this decree. There were many regulations they needed to follow. *Neue Freie Presse*, 19 May 1938.

[87] *Zionistische Rundschau*, 27 May 1938: 1.

[88] The article in the Jewish newspaper copies direct language from the announcement "Kundmachung from Gauleiter Buerkel and Reichstatthalter Seyss-Inquart," published in the *Neue Freie Presse*, 19 May 1938. The totalitarianism of the Nazi regime is documented in the final part of this article, as the government also threatens the Austrian people with arrest, should they fail to cooperate. "This is a notice to the Austrian people that an Assets Transfer Agency has been opened in the former Anglobank in the 1st district and that this office, which will be part of the government ministry for labor and economics, will be run by Walter Rafelsburger. This office will handle the aryanization or transfer of Jewish assets into Aryan hands. All requests to take over Jewish property or assets should be turned to the agency and as of 24 May, people can begin visiting the office to make these requests directly. People are strictly warned that all transfers must be approved by the agency and people who try to make transfers without following these orders will be punished severely. Transfers that have already been made still need to seek this approval and people have up to 31 June to do this."

Vulkans, Hastens, Gerstenfelds, Spitzers, and Grabkowiczs were among the many who now added the Assets Transfer Agency to the long list of offices they needed to enter to receive permission to emigrate.[89] And, for these families, following the newspaper's instructions -- picking up the standard assets declaration forms, filling them out, and returning them to the agency -- was only the tip of another iceberg. After registering with the Assets Transfer Agency, the expropriation process began, and a new set of complications was added to the emigration process.[90]

There proved no way around these regulations. The Gestapo, the head of the police, and the financial administrations worked together and shared information. Post offices, tax offices, moving companies, notaries, banks, and insurance companies worked in cooperation with and in complete subservience to the Nazi state. The newspaper printed the names of successful emigrants who had outstanding taxes and threatened them with arrest if they were found on German soil.[91] With such threats, the Germans drove their victims into full willingness -- if not eagerness -- to comply with their demands. If they wanted to get out, they simply needed to follow the rules and pay close attention to the long and complicated financial obstacle course required of all "wealthy" Jews. And, for the most part, they did. Rafelsberger, declared on 1 February 1939 that the sum of the registered assets in Austria equaled approximately two billion Reichsmarks, comprising about one-quarter of the total registered assets in the Greater German

---

[89] The archives of the Austrian Republic hold the original files of approximately 50,000 Jewish victims who were forced to declare their assets in April 1938. These names have been alphabetically indexed (1993) by two historians in the Austrian State Archives, Dr. Hubert Stein and Christian Kucsera, in *Recht als Unrecht. Quellen zur wirtschaftlichen Entrechtungder Wiener Juden durch die NS-Vermögensverkehrsstelle. Teil 1: Privatvermögen-Personenverzeichnis* (Right as Wrong: Sources to the Economic Dispossession of Vienna Jews by the Nazi Authority for the Transfer of Assets).

[90] Some privileged people fled illegally -- evading taxes and smuggling out money and assets -- even after initially registering their assets with the Assets Transfer Agency. See the case of Lili and Karl Fuchs, two Czech citizens living in the nineteenth district who fled to Prague "for vacation" in July 1938. See OstA/AdR/VVst/VA #998, 999.

[91] These tax citations were called *Steuersteckbriefe*. See Martin Dean, *Robbing the Jews: The Confiscation of Jewish Property in the Holocaust, 1933-1945* (Cambridge: Cambridge University Press, 2008).

Reich.[92] Broken down by category: land and forestry assets comprised approximately 30 million RM; real-estate 500 million RM; business and enterprise 300 million RM; and other assets totaled 1.5 billion RM. After subtracting the liabilities and encumbrances (253,257,000 RM) the total registered Jewish assets equaled 2,041,828,000.[93] In 1938, one German Reichsmark (1.0 RM) equaled forty American cents ($ 0.40); thus the sum of registered Jewish assets in Austria was equal to roughly one billion American dollars.[94] Through the work of the Assets Transfer Agency, over the course of months, the state had efficiently obtained precise records of all assets owned by Jews in Austria. This provided the information required for systematic expropriation and future incorporation into the Nazi state.

---

[92]This figure is significantly large considering that Germany's Jewish population still totaled approximately 400,000 in spring 1938.
[93] These figures are derived from the work of Gertrude Fuchs: 12-29. Gertrude Fuchs' Master's Thesis on the Assets Transfer Agency for the University of Vienna was one of the only works to address this topic in detail before the *Historikerkommision* in 2002. Her figures match the estimates provided by the Historians' Commission in 2003, as well as the Nazi-estimate given by Walter Rafelsberger on 1 February 1939. The Historikerkommision has estimated this amount between 1.842 and 2.9 billion, depending on various methods and assumptions. See *htttp./www.historikerkommission.at*: Press Release on Final Report of the Historikerkommision, p. 3.
[94] Due to inflation, $1,000,000,000.00 in 1938 would equate to $15,367,872,340.00 in 2010. See http://www.bls.gov/data.

Illustration 14: "Assets Declaration Form"[95]

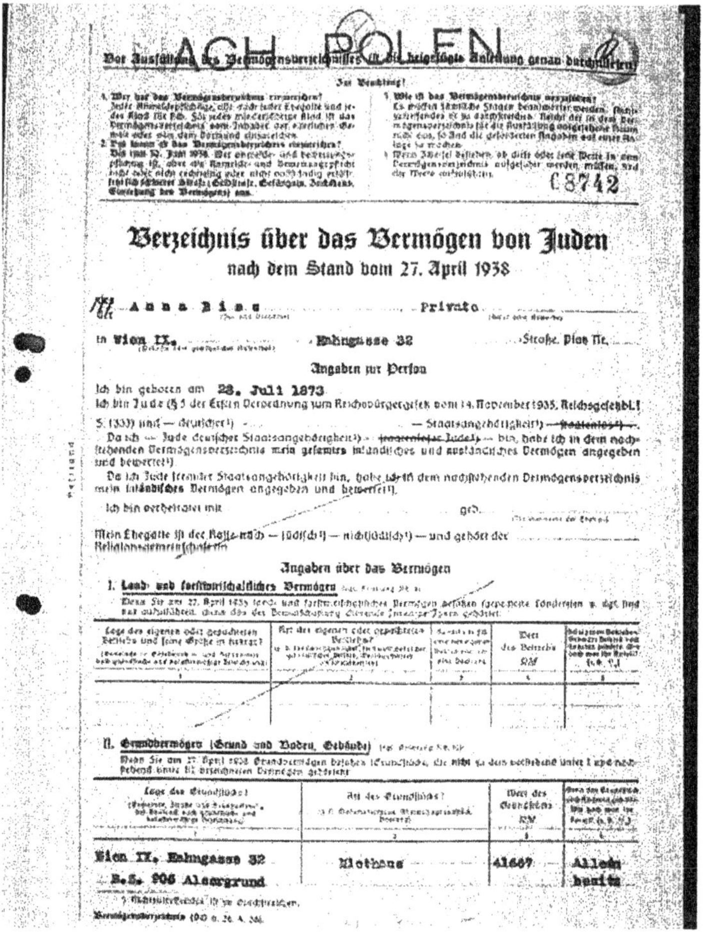

Source: Austrian State Archives: OstA/AdR/06/VVst/VA

---

[95] See appendix for English translation. Also see Lucy Dawidowicz,. *A Holocaust Reader*. (New York: Behrman House. 1976), 50.

The Struggle to Emigrate and the IKG's Struggle to Facilitate Emigration

Jews feared leaving the language, culture, family, friends, and country they knew. And they were anxious about the uncertainties ahead. But they had little choice. They needed to emigrate. The IKG offered what help it could. People walked into its offices hoping to immigrate to one place and the IKG wound up helping them go somewhere else completely, often somewhere they had never imagined starting a new life. Similarly, people applied to leave with their families, or at least with certain dependents, and ended up leaving alone, or with only one sibling, one parent, or relative.[96] Very rarely did things work out as people hoped or expected. But they took what they could get, made difficult decisions and compromises, and continued to follow the IKG's instructions and to maintain hope. They turned to the IKG with their troubles and their desperate need for help, and the IKG workers continued their unceasing efforts to help the community escape.

Forty-one-year-old Elisabeth Fellner, divorced, born in Vienna, residing on the popular Taborstrasse in the second district, wrote a desperate letter to the IKG in the summer of 1938 requesting financial aid. She begged that they help pay for her train ticket to Constantinople, where she intended to stay with a friend's family who would provide her with employment. She had already gathered the funds she could and had paid RM 50 toward the ticket, but she needed a total of RM 155 to cover the cost of the trip. She had lost her job as a bookkeeper on 1 July 1938 and after twenty-four years of employment had been released with no final pay. She had no money at her disposal and had to give up her apartment in one week (31 August 1938); she had been selling her furniture to sustain herself. To bolster her plea, she explained that she had always paid her taxes to the Jewish Community on time and that she had never before requested

---

[96] Based on an in-depth study and analysis of hundreds of emigration questionnaires from *USHMM, Films #Alpha A-Z, Auswanderungsfrageboegen der Israelitischen Kultusgemeinde Wien (IKG)*.

aid from the Community's welfare services. Additionally, her father had served the Community for over twenty years, working in the cemetery office. All she needed was RM 100 for continental travel to Turkey. Could the IKG help her?[97]

Forty-eight-year-old Helene Herz, wife of Oskar Herz and mother of Susanne (sixteen) and Elenore (twelve), submitted a similarly desperate letter to the Community offices almost eighteen months later. Helene had begun her quest to get her family out of Austria shortly after Anschluss but had encountered numerous difficulties along the way. First, she could not obtain affidavits from her family in the United States because of their financial problems, and only later managed to procure an affidavit from friends. Next, she had to register her two daughters and herself on the German quota to enter the US (as of 30 June 1938), while her husband Oskar had to register on the Russian quota. Then, convinced that their quota numbers would be called within the next year, she had managed to procure funding from friends and purchased four ship tickets for travel to New York, well in advance because she knew that the ships filled up quickly. To her great misfortune and surprise, the family's quota numbers were still not reached eighteen months later. She had to return her ship tickets to the company, as advised by the staff of the IKG. Meanwhile, Oskar had been arrested and deported to Nisko in October 1939 and the family had been forced to turn to the IKG for welfare. In January 1940 she received word that her quota number was reached and she was called for a medical examination at the American Consulate on 12 February 1940. This was the final step in her emigration process, but she had lost her ship tickets, her funding, and her husband. Helen was in desperate need of help from the IKG. She explained her situation, emphasizing her husband's long commitment and service to the IKG,

---

[97] USHMM film #Alpha F3 [slide 0471-76], *Auswanderungsfrageboegen der Israelitischen Kultusgemeinde Wien (IKG)*, Elisabeth F., # 42110/15701. It appears that Elizabeth emigrated from Vienna in 1939, but further details are unknown.

and she begged for three tickets (for her daughters and herself) from Vienna to New York on the earliest possible date. Could the IKG help her?[98]

Illustration 15: "Inside the IKG Offices"

Source: Documentation Center of the Austrian Resistance (DÖW): *www.doew.at*

Dr. Oskar Gottfried, facing a situation resembling yet different from Helene Herz's, also turned to the offices of the IKG begging for immediate financial help. He wrote to the IKG on 10 October 1939 asking for four tickets in less than three weeks on an Italian ship line to New York,

---

[98] On 21 January 1940 her case was approved and she was granted RM 1,000 for three ship tickets on the Holland-Line to New York. USHMM film #Alpha H7 [slide 0931-42], *Auswanderungsfrageboegen der Israelitischen Kultusgemeinde Wien (IKG)*, Oskar H., # 28729.

explaining his unfortunate situation. His wife, child, and he, all German citizens, were granted

visas for entry to the US on 17 August 1939, but his seventy-eight-year-old father was held back.

He was registered on the Hungarian quota and did not receive his visa until 20 September. The

problem was twofold: on 18 August Oskar had reserved four seats on the Untied States ship line

departing from Hamburg on 20 September 1939. He had had to forfeit these seats because he

would not leave Vienna without his father and now he was encountering another problem

regarding the timing of their documents as his tax clearance certificate would expire on 29

October.[99] The difference between him and Helene Herz was that Dr. Gottfried was not living

on the IKG's welfare service but had close to RM 5,000 to offer the IKG in exchange for these

ship tickets, which needed to be paid in foreign currency provided by the foreign aid committees.

His problem was getting out of Vienna with his father and his family, and obtaining the travel

tickets to do so, before his other documents expired. Would the IKG grant him the necessary

travel money within two weeks? Was his case any more or any less compelling than that of

Helene Herz? [100] Was the IKG more willing to help him because he could provide it with

funding?

The IKG could help some, but not all. The officials had to make impossible decisions

weighing one person's request against another's and balancing help given to one to emigrate

against resources to sustain the community. Some applicants, struggling to get their papers

together, while encountering myriad frustrations and difficulties, understood this and jockeyed

for advantage. Out of desperation many would have done anything to escape their current

---

[99] See also the cases of Hugo Sommer (born in lower Austria in 1894) and Simon Grossmann (born in Poland in1884). Both faced the same problem regarding the expiration of the tax clearance certificate. See USHMM film #Alpha S7, *Auswanderungsfrageboegen der Israelitischen Kultusgemeinde Wien (IKG)*, Hugo, S., # 437/11982 and #Alpha G10 [slide 0268], *Auswanderungsfrageboegen der Israelitischen Kultusgemeinde Wien (IKG)*, Simon, G., # 14864/18663.

[100] On 25 October 1939 it appears he was granted his request for four tickets to the US. See USHMM film #Alpha G7 [slide 1147-1158], *Auswanderungsfrageboegen der Israelitischen Kultusgemeinde Wien (IKG)*, Oskar, G., # 36537.

condition, perhaps even exaggerate their circumstances to the IKG, in hopes of making their cases appear more compelling. Did others lie or cheat? For example, some people listed in the Jewish newspaper as having received approval to immigrate and with documents waiting for them in the British Passport Office, were also listed as "Missing Persons."[101] Did someone try somehow to steal or forge the missing person's papers and assume his/her identity?

While it was in everyone's best interest to follow the guidelines set forth by the IKG, the situation pitted people against each other. And as valiantly as the IKG worked, it could not solve the problem the Nazis created. Many applicants unleashed frustration and anger on the IKG. Thirty-six-year-old Otto Glaser, for example (born in Heidenreichstein, Lower Austria, an airplane engineer and mechanic) felt that the IKG was responsible for jeopardizing his chances to emigrate. "It is unfathomable to me that the IKG not only did not help me with my case," he wrote to the community office, "but caused serious harm to it."[102] He worried about his wife, and their eleven-month-old child. He had procured all of the travel money on his own, so as to not bother the IKG. Further, he managed to come up with RM 2,000 to offer the IKG in exchange for landing money. However, he wound up losing all his money and blamed it on the negligence of the IKG.[103] Determined to obtain immediate action, Otto went straight to the IKG offices every day for a week try to get information on his case. This only caused him further aggravation, as he was unable to get "any useful information" from these visits. When he finally managed to speak to the man handling his files, the latter promised he would have an answer for him the following day. But, when Otto returned, the answer was postponed yet another day.

---

[101] *Jüdisches Nachtrichtenblatt* (Ausgabe Wien, 24 February 1938): 1.
[102] USHMM film #Alpha G4, *Auswanderungsfrageboegen der Israelitischen Kultusgemeinde Wien (IKG)*, Otto, G., #24866.
[103] It is unclear exactly how Otto G. lost his funding, although it is likely that he paid for train and ship tickets and was unable to get his papers ready in time to use them. In such a case (which happened often) the ship company would not refund the tickets and the IKG would assign them to another waiting Jew.

Otto sat down and wrote a letter to the IKG explaining his frustration: "Tomorrow is cutting it too close, if they don't make a decision to help me by tomorrow, the whole thing will be pointless because my tax clearance certificate will have expired.... No one is paying special attention to my file and since one must have an invitation to speak with someone at the IKG," he wrote mockingly, "I will have to stand there all Monday morning, at different times, to try to talk with someone -- prior to my scheduled meeting at 4 pm." Otto was insistent that the Community do everything it could to make up for the previous damage it caused to his case. He had lost his money, his ship tickets, and his papers were about to expire -- all due to what he saw as the incompetence of the IKG.[104] He understood that his family's future was dependent upon the IKG's support, so he had cooperated with its instructions and followed its advice. However, when the IKG was unable to dispatch his case in return, he was livid. From his standpoint, in his fear, he was unable to see the hard work the IKG was doing to process not only his request for emigration but the requests of so many other individuals and their families. While people like Otto turned to the IKG in desperation, the latter could do only so much in return.

Jews requiring help from the IKG needed patience and an ability to pay attention to new regulations, fill out forms correctly, carefully, and punctually, and do everything in their power to avoid tension with the German authorities.[105] They needed to be willing to make sacrifices and compromises, and understand that where they went and with whom they went was secondary to getting out at all. Many people -- the 117,409 who managed to emigrate by December 1939 -- made these sacrifices and conformed to these news standards. Ultimately, they had no other alternative than to work with the IKG. And for the most part, they did.

---

[104] Other people expressed frustration with the IKG. See case of Elias and Heinrich Verstandig, USHMM film #Alpha V5, *Auswanderungsfrageboegen der Israelitischen Kultusgemeinde Wien (IKG), Heinrich Verstandig, #13404.*

[105] *Zionistische Rundschau,* 3 June 1938; *Jüdisches Nachtrichtenblatt* 17 March 1939; 17 February 1939.

The IKG, for its part, carried a terrible burden. The leaders had to establish a careful balance between working with the foreign aid committees (FACs), and for the German authorities, while maintaining its focus on assistance and rescue. IKG workers had to look at the particulars of each plea with a seasoned eye; they worried about the support of the FACs, and feared the capricious Nazi authorities. They had to adapt to these conditions of distrust and uncertainty and find a way to stay optimistic and move forward. They did not know how to, but learned step by step. They did not throw their hands up in the air, but continued to persevere in their mission to rescue the Jews of Vienna. Day after day they read desperate letters, one after the next, and tried to decide who was worthy of funding, who took first priority, and who needed to wait -- often times at the expense of separating family members in the process. While they hoped to rescue all of Vienna's Jews, they simply could not; they could not even manage to keep families together. Still, they continued their work relentlessly.

Rescue and Destruction

The results of their efforts were evident immediately. Between May 1938 and December 1939, exactly 117,409 Jews fled Vienna through the organization and efforts of the IKG; 51,501 of these also relied on financial support arranged through the community. Following the first deportations to Dachau in May/June 1938, emigration figures soared. The IKG moved almost three times as many Jews out of Austria during the summer of 1938 as had managed to get out on their own that spring. Close to 27,000 Jews left in the months of June through August, an average of 9,000 emigrants per month. Emigration numbers peaked in August 1938, when almost 9,729 individuals left in a single month. In June alone, nearly as many people left Vienna (8,038) as had left in the three months of March through May (8,368). As of January 1940, the

IKG calculated that only 54,000 Jews remained in Vienna, 24,000 of whom were not to be considered for emigration due to illness or old age, but they intended to rescue the other 27,000.[106]

Notwithstanding its impressive results, the IKG's job was wrought with difficulties; while the rescue was highly successful, the cost and consequences of compromise were grave. The IKG as an institution -- its leaders, workers, and volunteers -- played a vital role in shaping the future of Viennese Jewry, both its rescue *and* destruction. Under the circumstances, the leaders believed that full cooperation -- cooperation between Jews and the Jewish leadership, and between the leadership and the Nazis -- was the only way to move the most people out of Austria in the shortest time. Thus they called for and enforced this cooperation, asking people to respond as a collective rather than as individuals. Time and again they backed German efforts to frighten Jews and dissuade them from resisting or attempting illegal flight, explaining that these types of rebellious actions not only jeopardized a individual person's chances for emigration, but undermined the emigration efforts of the entire community. In its eyes, such feckless behavior only showed the Germans that the IKG did not have a strong hold on its members and that the Community was not taking advantage of the opportunity to run the emigration process from the inside and complete the rescue of its members. In order to receive permission from the authorities to continue its work, the IKG needed all Jews to cooperate with its demands and they needed to demonstrate results: that it was creating a mass exodus of Viennese Jewry -- fulfilling the German prophecy, helping make the Reich "Judenrein."

Equally important in this process was the IKG's relationship with the foreign aid committees, which were pumping money into the IKG to facilitate emigration. To send people to

---

[106] USHMM film # 294, IKG-A/W 126, *Report of the Vienna Jewish Community. A description of the activity of the Israelitische Kultusgemeinde Wien in the period from May 2nd 1938 - December 31st 1939 (2 Exemplare).*

countries in Central and South America, for example, the IKG depended upon financial aid from abroad. These countries accepted only foreign currency, which the IKG could not obtain on its own. The IKG looked to the JDC and other foreign aid committees to pay the travel and landing fees. In order to continue to receive aid from them, it also needed to provide regular statistical tabulations as to how well the emigration system was working: how their funds were allocated between welfare, retraining, and emigration, and how many Viennese Jews were making it safely to countries abroad due to this funding. The IKG supplied these statistics month after month. Pleased with its own efficiency and steady accomplishments, the IKG felt entitled to ask for further assistance and explained in a report to the Council for German Jewry and the JDC in January 1940: "The existing possibilities have been too low to suffice to the will for emigration of the Jews residing in Vienna." "It is necessary to look for and find new possibilities with the aid of the foreign organizations in order to finish the last part of the emigration not yet settled." The IKG continually requested further financial aid from the foreign aid committees, writing that "[t]he task of the IKG [is] taking care that no Jew, who is in position to emigrate, be kept back because of lack of funds."[107]

Conclusions

From the moment the IKG began the emigration operation, it became entangled in the web of Nazism, forced to make terrible sacrifices in exchange for the rescue of its community members. Nazi domination required the IKG to enforce cooperation among the victims, offer subservience to the perpetrators, and coerce Jews from the outside world to offer aid. This working system of cooperation between the Germans and their Jewish victims came into full

---

[107] USHMM film # 294, IKG-A/W 126, *Report of the Vienna Jewish Community. A description of the activity of the Israelitische Kultusgemeinde Wien in the period from May 2nd 1938–December 31st 1939 (2 Exemplare)*: 68; 75; 77. Original English.

swing during the pre-genocidal years in Vienna and its result was double-edged: cooperation

allowed almost two-thirds of Austrian Jews to escape from Nazism, but also aided the permanent

destruction of the community. As people scattered around the globe, their culture and society

vanished with them, never to be resurrected. And irreparable family divisions began to occur

with the move to mass exodus in 1938. Most families did not leave together, and many were

separated permanently. For those families in which all members managed to flee, they rarely got

visas to the same destination. And it was not as though they ended up in neighboring cities or

towns; they were separated by continents and oceans. In Charlotte Czuczka's family, for

example, family members immigrated to six different continents in less than a year.[108] Which

continent would this family call home? For her family and so many others, Vienna was no

longer home; they were subject to life in permanent exile.[109] They had survived, but their

families and community had not; thus, their "home" had vanished. Viewed from this angle, the

mass exodus of Viennese Jewry that began in spring 1938 marked a heroic rescue effort, but also

its tragic implication: the beginning the community's permanent destruction.

---

[108] Charlotte's case is representative of many Jews. See, USHMM microfilm #Alpha C, *Auswanderungsfrageboegen der Israelitischen Kultusgemeinde Wien (IKG), Fritz Czuczka,* # 21,297 [slides 0183-0189] and USHMM microfilm #Alpha U1, *Auswanderungsfrageboegen der Israelitischen Kultusgemeinde Wien (IKG), Sandor Ultmann,* # 1,458 [slides 0371-79]; see also Erna, G., 1995. "Interview by Survivors of the Shoah Visual History Foundation," Miami Beach, FL, USA, May 16. Interview Code 02588, Tapes 1-4.

[109] Alfred Polgar, a well-known Viennese-Jewish writer and émigré (1873-1955), spoke to the common refugee experience in his works. In 1949 he concluded: "Die Fremde ist nicht Heimat geworden, aber die Heimat Fremde," (the foreign country did not become home, but home became foreign). His sentiment was shared by many.

Chapter Six

November Complications, but Emigration Continues

Illustration16: "Postcard: Erwin Lencz and his younger sister Erika on the Ship to America, October 1938"

"Oh, how quick it was, and yet how deeply it will always remain ingrained in our hearts --
the memory of our departure, Antwerp, three o'clock, 22 October 1938."

Source: Lencz Family Archive, Sharon, Massachusetts

Introduction (Fall 1938)

The IKG continued to relay Nazi orders to its community members and encourage the people to

obey them if they wanted to get by, get out, and support their ailing community. The system had

caught on quickly and was working. Following the summer of 1938, hopes ran high as people

held faith in rescue through emigration. Jewish men and women of all ages and backgrounds

were retraining in new professions to prepare for their new lives abroad, while also volunteering

to help the community.[1] People were getting by in Vienna with the aid of the IKG's soup

kitchens, cash-support system, hospitals, and old age homes, and people were continuing to

---

[1] For detailed statistics on the retraining effort in October 1938, USHMM film # 295, IKG-A/W 122, *Financial and Statistical Report of the Jewish Community Vienna, December 1938 (2 Exemplare).*

emigrate on a regular basis.[2] By the end of October 1938, IKG figures showed that 48,676 individuals had fled Vienna since March,[3] of whom 12,475 had received aid from the IKG totaling RM 1,212,571.[4] In October alone, 5,643 people had managed to depart,[5] of whom 1,858 had received financial support from the community totaling RM 309,261.00.[6] The top destinations in October were China, with 471 persons, and the United States, with 467 (the largest number since Anschluss), including twenty-six-year-old Erwin Lencz and his younger sister, twenty-year-old Erika. Next were Palestine, accepting 334; England, 305; and Liberia, 162.[7] Of the 493 persons who left Vienna with financial support from the IKG during the week of 16-22 October, 413 fled to safety (336 overseas and 77 to England), but 70 departed for other European countries that would soon be occupied by or allied with the Germans. Based on these figures, on an average week in October, while some 1,400 Jews were managing to flee, approximately one-third of them received financial help from the community, and of these, 500 persons, approximately one-seventh (70 persons) were not truly safe from Hitler's grasp.[8] Although they did not know it then, getting out of Vienna did not guarantee survival.[9]

---

[2] For detailed statistics on the distribution of cash support, soup kitchen, and old-age asylum, USHMM film # 295, IKG-A/W 122, *Financial and Statistical Report of the Jewish Community Vienna, December 1938 (2 Exemplare)*.
[3] USHMM film # 294, IKG-A/W 126, *Report of the Vienna Jewish Community. A description of the activity of the Israelitische Kultusgemeinde Wien in the period from May 2nd 1938-December 31st 1939 (2 Exemplare)*.
[4] USHMM film # 907, IKG-A/W 2532, *Statistische Berichte der Auswanderungsabteilung ueber die Auswanderungsbewegung (gegliedert nach den die Emigranten aufnehmenden Ziellaendern)*.
[5] USHMM film # 294, IKG-A/W 126, *Report of the Vienna Jewish Community. A description of the activity of the Israelitische Kultusgemeinde Wien in the period from May 2nd 1938-December 31st 1939 (2 Exemplare)*.
[6] USHMM film # 907, IKG-A/W 2532, *Statistische Berichte der Auswanderungsabteilung ueber die Auswanderungsbewegung (gegliedert nach den die Emigranten aufnehmenden Ziellaendern)*.
[7] USHMM film # 295, IKG-A/W 122, *Financial and Statistical Report of the Jewish Community Vienna, December 1938 (2 Exemplare)*.
[8] USHMM film # 907, IKG-A/W 2532, *Statistische Berichte der Auswanderungsabteilung ueber die Auswanderungsbewegung (gegliedert nach den die Emigranten aufnehmenden Ziellaendern)*.
[9] Approximately 15,000 Jews who emigrated from Vienna between March 38 and October 41 were caught in another Nazi occupied territory and deported and murdered. Figures based on George Berkley, *Vienna and Its Jews: The Tragedy of Success: 1880s-1980s* (Cambridge: Abt Books, 1988), 297; Walter B. Mass, *Country Without A Name: Austria under Nazi Rule 1938-1945* (New York: Frederick Ungar Publishing Co., 1979) 47.

Jews had also gone to great lengths to try to procure emigration/immigration papers for

their loved ones who had been incarcerated in Dachau the previous spring or summer; they had

learned that this could enable their release from the camp and subsequent escape from Austria.

On 11 October 1938 efforts were advanced when Franz van Gheel-Gildemeester's emigration aid

committee composed a list of 150 men imprisoned in Dachau whose emigration papers were

fully in order and financially secured by the agency itself. Operating parallel to the IKG's

emigration office, the Gildemeester Auswanderungshilforganisation focused on assisting persons

who the Germans defined as Jews by Nazi standards, but it helped those belonging to the Jewish

faith as well. All of these 150 men had been among those arrested in Vienna between March and

July of 1938, and while they were incarcerated, their families looked to the IKG and to

Gildemeester's organization for special help. Together, they managed to organize emigration

papers for them.[10] While half had visas for entry to the United States (42 persons), Palestine (17)

and England (17), it was evident that the family members of the rest had explored all options:

they were listed with visas to over thirty different countries, on six continents.[11] A month later,

on 30 November, a note was attached to this list which stated that under the order of Gauleiter

Bürckel they were to be released from Dachau within three to five days.[12]

[10] For more on Gildemeester, see Gabriele Anderl, *Orte der Täter, Der NS-Terror in den "Arisierten" Wiener Rothschild-Palais.* (Wien: Band 15 der Schriftenreihe des Instituts zur Erforschung der Geschichte der Gewerkschaften und Arbeiterkammern, 2005) 22-23; Theodor Venus and Alexandra-Eileen Wench, *Die Entziehung jüdischen Vermögens im Rahmen der Aktion Gildemeester: Eine empirishe Studie über Organisation, Form und Wandel von "Arisierung" und jüdischer Auswanderung in Österreich 1938-1041* (Vienna and Munich: Oldenbourg verlag, 2004); Peter Berger, "The Gildemeester Organization for Assistance to Emigrants and the Expusion of Jews from Vienna, 1938-1942," in Terry Gourvish, ed., *Business and Politics in Europe, 1900-1970: Essays in Honour of Alice Teichova* (Cambridge: Cambridge University Press, 2003) 215-245; Doron Rabinovici, *Instanzen der Ohnmacht: Wien 1938-1945: der Weg zum Judenrat* (Frankfurt am Main, Juedischer Verlag, 2000). 76, 182.

[11] Albania 1, Argentina 5, Australia 5, Belgium 2, Bolivia 3, Ceylon 1, China 5, Colombia 1, Cuba 1, Cyprus 2, Czechoslovakia 2, Denmark 2, England 17, Finland 1, France 3, Holland 1, India 1, Latvia 1, Liberia 2, Mexico 5, Palestine 17, Panama 2, Paraguay 4, St. Domingo 2, Switzerland 5, Tangier Zone 1, Turkey 1, United States 42, Uruguay 2, Yugoslavia 3. *Documentation Center of the Austrian Resistance (DÖW)*:21.830/4, E-21.621, 21.10 1991: *Sammlung von Dokumenten-Kopien aus dem Ost/AdR betreffend 1938 (Bestand: Bürckel-Akten).*

[12] Ibid.

Jews got by in Vienna, sustaining themselves and their families with help from the community, but also choosing to serve the greater community. People of all ages, from various former professions and different religious, political, and financial backgrounds, not only benefited from the soup kitchens, schools, hospitals, old-age homes, and the cash support offered by the IKG, but also volunteered in these welfare institutions, making the continued service possible. This required compromise and humility on their part, as former university professors offered to teach in the Jewish grade schools, former professionals and intellectuals offered to instruct retraining courses, and former society women learned to distribute meals in a soup kitchen.[13] Then, too, some lawyers and doctors were permitted to continue their practices, as long as they served only Jews. The *Zionistische Rundschu* continued to operate as the voice of the IKG, carrying advertisements addressed to former professionals and recruiting them for these positions. The IKG also contacted people directly. For example, all Jewish doctors who had been permitted to continue their practice since Anschluss were recruited again on 6 October 1938 via a notice mailed to them, which read:

> In accordance with the National Socialist Medical Fraternity we turn to you once again to see if you are willing to continue the medical position you currently hold for the next six months. If you are, please send a written statement with your signature by mail to the IKG no later than 11 October 1938. If we do not have it in our hands by then we will assume that you are no longer interested in continuing your practice. We request that you refrain from any further enquiry on these affairs, whether verbal, written, or by telephone -- it is pointless.[14]

---

[13] As testimonies from the Survivors of the Shoah Visual History Foundation reveal, former aristocrats and wealthy individuals also volunteered to help sustain the community. See also Norman Bentwich, "The Destruction of the Jewish Community in Austria 1938-1942," in Josef Frankel, ed., *The Jews of Austria: Essays on their Life, History and Destruction* (London: Valentine Mitchell, 1967); and Rabinovici, *Instanzen der Ohnmacht.*

[14] USHMM film #T1, A/W2612, XXIV: *Aerzteberatung, Verpflichtungserklaerungen zugelassener Aerzte, auch Spitalsaerzte:* slide 0098.

While some declined this offer, Dr. Joseph Grabkowicz agreed to continue his dental practice for another six months. As directed, he asked no questions and made no further inquires to the IKG; he simply sent the IKG a written notice on 7 October 1938 stating that he accepted the position.[15] Dr. Grabkowicz saw security in this offer to continue his practice, the security that he could continue to provide for his family and therefore that his life in Vienna could carry on. He was among the few optimistic Jewish men left in Vienna who were still praying for the Nazi storm to blow over. Job security held great value among elderly men in the community and for those few who could hold on to their profession, the future appeared far less grim.

"Kristallnacht," 9-10 November 1938: "The Night of Broken Glass" and Its Aftermath

Dr. Grabkowicz's outlook shifted a month later as life for Jews under Nazi occupation took another turn for the worse. Over the course of two days, on the 9th and 10th of November, the Germans staged a nationwide pogrom in which they assaulted and pillaged Jewish people, their businesses, their religious sanctuaries, and their homes. Terror levels peaked for Jews throughout greater Germany, and desperation followed.[16] Everyone was affected, if not by the immediate violence perpetrated by the Germans and their Austrian allies, then by the aftermath of the pogrom.

---

[15] USHMM film #T1, A/W2612, XXIV: *Aerzteberagtung, Verpflichtungserklaerungen zugelassener Aerzte, auch Spitalsaerzte*: slide 0098. Other doctors from across the city included: surgeon and urologist Dr. Robert Bachrach; Dr. Leo Rapoport, the X-ray Institute; Dr. Artur Bergel, specialist for internal disease; Dr. S. Steiner, orthopedic specialist; Dr. Otto Maier, radiology specialist; and general practitioners Dr. Otto Lang, Dr. Adolf Schaller, and Dr. Jakob Altschiller.

[16] For example, the IKG soup-kitchens shut down for the week following the pogrom (November 11-17). In the month of November it only operated a total of 23 days, but still managed to serve a total of 326,526 persons, 16,067 daily, more than any month since Anschluss. The kitchen distributed food to everyone, although women professionals received less food than their male counterparts, and persons between the ages of 1-10 and 21-30 received the least amount of food. The items distributed consisted of flour, vegetable grease, sugar, potatoes, peas, lentils, rice, tomatoes, oil, semolina, plums, jam, cacao, salt, onions, and other tinned goods. For further details, see USHMM film #295, IKG-A/W 122, *Financial and Statistical Report of the Jewish Community of Vienna, December 1939(2 Exemplare)*. Original English.

Dr. Grabkowicz may have been more shocked on the evening of 9 November 1938 than most Jews in Vienna. Although his life had been far from worry-free over the past months -- his car, for example, had been confiscated in October by his neighbor, the owner of the bakery in front of which he parked every day -- he had nonetheless felt somewhat protected by his status as a practicing dentist. His thirteen-year-old daughter Alix was already planning a trip to Antwerp to stay with a friend, but it had been arranged more or less against his wishes. Dr. Grabkowicz still believed in Austria and was waiting for order to be restored. When the SA entered his expensive flat on Suttnerplatz 1 in Vienna's fourth district on the evening of 9 November, they "herded" the doctor, his wife Hilde, and their two daughters Vera and Alix into one room, looked everywhere in the apartment for weapons, and finally threw furniture and belongings out the window. Although Dr. Grabkowicz was spared arrest, nothing was the same from this moment forward. Alix recalled that the family began to speak only in whispers and that her father had finally realized that "he wasn't immune anymore, but treated like everybody else."[17]

Thirty-year-old Rudi Tausz was not hoping for a restoration of order in Austria like Dr. Grabkowicz. He knew he had to get out and was working on his emigration papers. Still, the events of 9-10 November took him by surprise. "Nothing interfered with me prior to the November Pogrom," he recalled. "I even went to the movies before that time." Rudi had recently married (on 31 July 1938, one of the last days Jews were permitted to marry), and although it was not a huge public celebration (fifteen other couples were married on the same day), it was a major leap toward a better future: he and his bride Julie intended to leave the country together and start anew in the United States.[18] That plan changed on the evening of 9 November. When

---

[17] Letter from Alix G. Kowler to the author, 1 August 2003. See also, Alix K., 1997. "Interview by Survivors of the Shoah Visual History Foundation," Lenox, MA, USA, October 16. Interview Code 34544, Tapes 1-5.
[18] Walter and Irma Austerlitz married on 31 July 1938 as well. Walter was arrested during the November Pogrom, spent a couple nights in the cellar of the *Elisabethpromenade* police station and then was deported to Dachau.

Rudi opened his parents' department store, Tausz, on Wallensteingasse 6 in the twentieth district he was suddenly arrested. Brought to the police station, he was held for a couple of days, and then taken to a collection camp, where he was interrogated. Where were you born? Who are your parents? Are you applying for a visa to another country? Waiting in this *Sammellager* "was a terrible situation," he recalled some decades later. The guards would not let the older men go to the toilet; the inhumane and unsanitary conditions were accompanied by a lack of food and information. "There was no food but it didn't affect me because I was so upset I wasn't hungry anymore." Rudi remained in this second holding spot with other 18-to 60-year-old men for another three to four days waiting to learn whether they would release him and send him home to his wife and parents (as they did with a couple of foreigners) or would call out "Dora" -- their code name for Dachau -- and deport him.[19] Meanwhile, his parents Albert and Sidonie were confined to their house on the evening of the pogrom, forced to watch as their bank account books and all the jewelry in their house and their safe were confiscated and their Stradivarius violin was smashed into pieces.[20]

Pre-genocidal Tragedies

Seventy-one-year-old Theodor Rechnitzer directed the following complaint to the IKG on 3 December 1938:

> On 10.11 the key to the apartment belonging to my wife, my son, and myself was taken away. [...] On 26.11, according to one of our former neighbors in the apartment house, ten people went through the apartment, including one woman

---

Walter A., 1995. "Interview by Survivors of the Shoah Visual History Foundation," Glenview, IL, USA, May 31. Interview Code 02907-0, Tapes 1-6.

[19] Rudolf T., 1997. "Interview by Survivors of the Shoah Visual History Foundation," Margate, FL, USA, April 9. Interview Code 27990, Tapes 1-3.

[20] Ibid; see also, OstA/AdR/06/VVst/VA # 2770, 2771, Albert and Sidonie Tausz.

who claimed to be the new renter. They also said that two suitcases belonging to my son, filled with unknown contents, were taken out. Since 28.11 there is a woman by the name of Fraulein Olga Gaertner living in the apartment, who has an official document that the apartment now belongs to her, that she has taken it over including all of it contents. ...Our personal documents are all inside.

The Grabkowicz and Tausz families were not alone in their horror. Thousands of Jewish homes and stores were entered by force and looted during the pogrom, thousands of men were arrested, and many families were simply forced out of their homes, their keys taken away and their residences taken over fully furnished with all their personal belongings inside.[21] In some, like the Grabkowicz family's, the criminals entered and left without causing much physical harm or making any arrests.[22] Sandor Ultmann viewed this as his miracle. While describing a searing memory of furniture thrown out of windows and explaining that November 9 was "a very happy day for the Austrians, who could do what they liked," he recognized that his own life was little affected. The three strangers who showed up at his flat at 2 a.m. looked through everything and did not cause any physical damage to his apartment or to him, nor did they turn him in for arrest.[23] Walter Hacker experienced a similar fate, although the two men who entered his flat were familiar faces, former customers at his parents' restaurant across the street -- and greedy.[24] These men left Walter physically untouched but did not leave empty-handed; they enjoyed their

---

[21] USHMM film # 281, IKG-A/W 442, *Beschlagnahmungen (Schadensmeldungen) 11.1938* [frame 0273-4].

[22] Letter from Alix G. Kowler to the author, 1 August 2003.

[23] Sandor U., 1997. "Interview by Survivors of the Shoah Visual History Foundation," Bondi, AU, July 20. Interview Code 04144, Tapes 1-4. Sandor Ultmann describes this moment when his parents were forced out of their home as a tragedy. "You can imagine what it was like for my old parents to share an apartment with people from different ways of life... including my step-sister and her family... it was a tragedy."

[24] Walter H., 1995. "Interview by Survivors of the Shoah Visual History Foundation," Los Angeles, CA, USA, May 23. Interview Code 02787, Tapes 1-4.

new freedom to enter his home by force and openly search for and confiscate gold and other valuables.[25]

In other Jewish homes and stores across the city, there were other men who were fortunate to avoid arrest but still suffered greatly from the aftermath of the pogrom. In the case of Leopold Vulkan, the invasion of his home on Gersthofferstrasse 166 in the thirteenth district and the destruction of his personal property were detrimental not only to his immediate situation but to his chances of getting out and reuniting with his family.[26] Although he had been spared arrest upon the invasion, the Nazi supporters who looted and destroyed the contents of his home caused irreparable damage to his future.[27] In a letter to the Assets Transfer Agency dated 23 November 1938 he wrote, "On 10 November of this year at three o'clock in the afternoon a group of eight to ten men under the leadership of Herr Johann Aschauer appeared in my home and in the adjacent flat belonging to my eighty-year-old mother-in-law and they demolished in both flats the following items…" There followed a detailed list of the damage. The men began their rampage by smashing the glassware, crystal, and porcelain, before turning to cover the bedding and towels with ink, and confiscate the silverware, gold watches and jewelry, clothing, theater glasses, leather goods, a typewriter, and other valuable goods, including over three thousand Reichsmarks in cash. Then they proceeded to burn a number of his books, his business records, and other papers: "To my greatest regret practically all of my personal documents, identity papers and many, many very important documents of all kinds have been burned."[28] At six

---

[25] Individual profiteering was not permitted by Nazi policy, but it started with Anschluss and continued through the November Pogrom and after, demonstrating the corruption within the Nazi administrative system.

[26] This was the second time Leopold Vulkan's house was invaded and his property was stolen. Staffel IV of the Brigade X entered the Vulkan home immediately after Anschluss (14 March), confiscated jewelry, foreign currency, gold coins, shillings, and his model 503 Fiat automobile. He first documented this crime in July 1938 in his Assets Declaration Form. He reported it for the second time on 18 August 1938, sending letters to Gauleiter Burkel, the Assets Transfer Agency, and the Secret Police (Gestapo). OstA/AdR/06/VVst/VA # 33074, Leopold Vulkan.

[27] Leopold Vulkan was most likely spared arrest because he held foreign citizenship.

[28] OstA/AdR/06/VVst/VA # 33074, Leopold Vulkan. Letter to VVst, 23 November 1938.

o'clock that same evening, Leopold was arrested by the NSDAP Gruppe Spittelau on Althanplatz in the ninth district, and the rest of his necessities were taken away: his typewriter, and RM 50, his passport, and three cash-vouchers he carried in his pocket.[29] When he was released a short time later, these items were not returned to him, although both he and his wife sent a number of letters to the Assets Transfer Agency begging for them.[30]

Illustration 17:"General Store and Home of Leopold and Mathilde Vulkan (née Trepper), Gersthofferstrasse 166, Vienna 13"

Source: Gertrude S., 1998. "Interview by Survivors of the Shoah Visual History Foundation," Cranbury, NJ, USA, May 28. Interview Code 42400, Tape 7.

The immediate consequence of this theft and destruction was that he could not travel out of the country to meet his two young daughters Gertrude and Edith whom he had taken to Paris

---

[29] The original German term is *Versatzschein*, which can best be translated as "a receipt or certificate for an item waiting to be sold at a pawn-shop." This is an Austrian term. OstA/AdR/06/VVst/VA # 33074, Leopold Vulkan, Letter to the Assets Transfer Agency, 23 November 1938.
[30] OstA/AdR/06/VVst/VA # 33074, Ha #951, Leopold Vulkan; OstA/AdR/06/VVst/VA # 5889, Mathilde Vulkan.

just two months earlier (20 September 1938), promising to return as soon as possible with their mother and grandmother.[31] Spared physical injury, Vulkan was spiritually wounded. After working so hard to protect his family and enable their emigration, he now had to start the process all over again. He was not alone. He was one of many fathers whose property had been destroyed and whose chances of protecting his family were now limited due to the pogrom.

The scale of violence during the pogrom varied from district to district and from home to home. While some families and individuals managed to emerge from the pogrom with no arrests and little physical damage to their property or otherwise, others were left destitute.[32] As in the first wave of arrests in May 1938, men were taken without warning or warrant, brought to a holding prison in Vienna, and then deported to Dachau within a matter of hours or after a number of days. Some, like forty-year-old Oskar Herz, heard rumors of the arrests, anticipated his own, and tried to escape it by avoiding his home and place of work; he walked around the streets of the ninth district with his ten-year-old daughter Eleanor at his side to make him less conspicuous.[33] Others, like twenty-year-old Leo Deutsch, could not help but walk straight into danger. When Leo saw the synagogues on fire that evening of 9 November, he ran to his parents' home, only to find that his two brothers had already been arrested and that his father was being threatened.[34] He insisted that he be taken in place of his elderly father.[35] Most men, however,

---

[31] Gertrude Silberstern, private interview conducted by Ilana Offenberger, Washington, D.C., May 2007. Gertrude S., 1998. "Interview by Survivors of the Shoah Visual History Foundation," Cranbury, NJ, USA, May 28. Interview Code 42400, Tapes 1-7.
[32] There was less public violence and destruction in districts that were less populated by Jews. Helen H., 1995. "Interview by Survivors of the Shoah Visual History Foundation," Newbury Park, CA, USA, February 21. Interview Code 00903, Tapes 1-2.
[33] Helen H., 1995. "Interview by Survivors of the Shoah Visual History Foundation," Newbury Park, CA, USA, February 21. Interview Code 00903, Tapes 1-2.
[34] Forty-two synagogues were torched in Vienna during the November Pogrom. David Cesarani, *Becoming Eichmann: Rethinking the Life, Crimes, and Trial of a "Desk Murderer"* (Cambridge: Da Capo Press, 2004) 71.
[35] Leo D., 1997. "Interview by Survivors of the Shoah Visual History Foundation," San Francisco, CA, USA, May 17. Interview Code 29174, Tapes 1-5.

like Franz Bauer, who was arrested while standing on the steps of the American consulate,[36] were simply taken off guard; they were carrying on their normal daily activities and neither volunteered for arrest nor managed to avoid it. The SA, SS, and Gestapo arrested thousands of Jewish men during the November pogrom. Overnight they became not only useless members of Vienna's already struggling Jewish community, but a heavy burden upon it.

As with the first wave of deportations in the spring, the families of the arrested men (together with the help of the IKG) were left behind: to manage the difficulties of the emigration process. Many of those arrested in November had applied for emigration in May and June 1938 and their efforts were coming close to fruition -- quota numbers on the horizon, ship tickets paid. But now their plans and efforts came to a halt and suddenly their relatives faced a daunting challenge. Families had to work quickly to arrange the release of their loved ones, and they now faced new and constraining difficulties. Families who had lost men to Dachau the previous spring, had explored options to get their loved ones' emigration papers in order during the summer. Families who lost men in November had an additional series of problems in their daily lives created by the pogrom.

Perhaps surprisingly, Vienna's wealthiest Jews found their chances of managing emigration (for themselves or their loved ones) greatly impaired. Jews who had registered their assets with the state the previous spring and summer were plunged ever deeper into the process of the bureaucratically camouflaged, "legalized" robbery. All businesses not already confiscated or put under the direction of a Nazi Kommisar [superintendent] [37] during the wild Aryanization period were plundered and liquidated in the November pogrom. In addition, apartments and homes were rampaged and looted, whatever occupations Jews still practiced were forbidden, and

---

[36] Frank, B., 1996. "Interview by Survivors of the Shoah Visual History Foundation," Los Angeles, CA, USA, March 14. Interview Code 13282, Tapes 1-4.

[37] Komissar applications are found in the archives of the Assets Transfer Agency: OstA/AdR/06/VVst/VA, H, Lg,St.

whatever assets they still possessed were subject to confiscation. Any savings they might have put aside, or were depending on to defray emigration costs, were vulnerable. And this was not all. The pogrom depreciated existing Jewish assets and added new financial impositions.[38]

Holding the Jews responsible for the damage caused during "Kristallnacht," the Nazis imposed an "Atonement Tax" or fine of one billion marks on the entire Jewish community in greater Germany.[39] By official government decree, as of 12 November 1938, they demanded that all Jews whose total assets had exceeded 5,000 RM in April 1938 (when the original Assets Declaration Forms were circulated) re-register their assets with the Assets Transfer Agency and pay one-quarter of the total to the state in the form of a new tax called the *Sühneleistung*.[40] This tax had to be paid in addition to the standard Weimar-era flight tax (*Reichsfluchtssteuer*), introduced in 1931, which required people to pay one-quarter of their assets to the state prior to emigration.[41]

Where would despairing persons such as Dr. Grabkowicz, Albert Tausz, and Leopold Vulkan find the means to pay such taxes -- required for themselves and their family members to emigrate -- after their assets had been confiscated or destroyed? Confronted by the demand to pay *more* to the state when they suddenly had less, the victims not only re-registered their assets, but appealed to the Assets Transfer Agency. Paula Popper, sixty years of age, wrote the agency a letter headed "Concerns Assets Adjustment." In it, she documented the destruction wrought by the November pogrom and stressed her duty to abide by government policy and update the

---

[38] German Insurance companies would not pay for the destruction of the pogrom. See David Cesarani, *Becoming Eichmann*, 71.

[39] For more on Goering's "expiation payment," see David Aretha, ed., *The Holocaust Chronicle* (Lincolnwood, Illinois: Publications International, Ltd, 2000) 142-47; Dawidowicz, Lucy. *A Holocaust Reader.* (New York: Behrman House, 1976), 53; Martin Dean, *Robbing the Jews: The Confiscation of Jewish Property in the Holocaust, 1933-1945* (Cambridge: Cambridge University Press, 2008).

[40] The Jews who filled out the forms most often referred to the *Sühneleistung* as the "Jewish Tax," using the terms *Judenkontribution, Judenvermoegensabgabe*, or *Judensteuer*. OstA/AdR/06/VVst/VA.

[41] See Dean, *Robbing the Jews, 68.*

relevant authorities of her financial changes. "Approximately RM 2,400, as well as silverware and jewelry and rugs were confiscated and taken away from me during the raiding of my house, which occurred on 10 November 1938. I inform you of this condition because I declared these assets under section IV, c, g, h, and i, in the Assets Declaration Form per the decree of 27 April 1938. I therefore dutifully bring this change in my assets to your attention." [42] Leopold Berl also informed the Assets Transfer Agency of the reduction of his assets due to the damage from the pogrom: "The RM 6,800 cash I declared in my original Assets Declaration Form is inaccurate because it was confiscated on 15 November."[43] Forty-three-year-old Melanie Fuchs wrote to fulfill her duty and explained how her assets decreased since 27 April 1938. "I take this opportunity to stress that what I declared at that time about my assets is no longer accurate." In her letter, Melanie further described exactly what she had spent her money on in the last months: "general living expenses, emigration preparations, occupational retraining, and aid for a sick relative."[44] She added that she had already sold clothing and other items from her dowry to defray these expenses.

---

[42] There are no records that the Nazis deported Paula Popper from Vienna, but her exact fate is unknown. OstA/AdR/06/VVst/VA # (NA), Paula Popper.

[43] See OstA/AdR/06/VVst/VA # 0872, Leopold Berl, letter from 12.12.38.

[44] A little over two years later Melanie Fuchs was sent on one of the Nazis' earlier transports from Vienna to the Opole ghetto in the Lublin district of German-occupied Poland. She was deported on 15 February 1941 and subsequently her Assets Declaration Form was stamped in red ink: NACH POLEN (to Poland). Her ultimate fate is unknown, but of the 2003 Viennese Jews deported to the Opole Ghetto, only twenty-eight are known to have survived. The ghetto was liquidated in the spring of 1942 and most Jews were transported to the newly developed annihilation camps, Belzec and Sobibor. OstA/AdR/06/VVst/VA # (NA). For more on Opole see chapters 7 and 8.

Illustration 18:"Leopold Berl Informs the Assets Transfer Agency of the Reduction of his Assets due to the Damage from the November Pogrom (12 December 1938)."

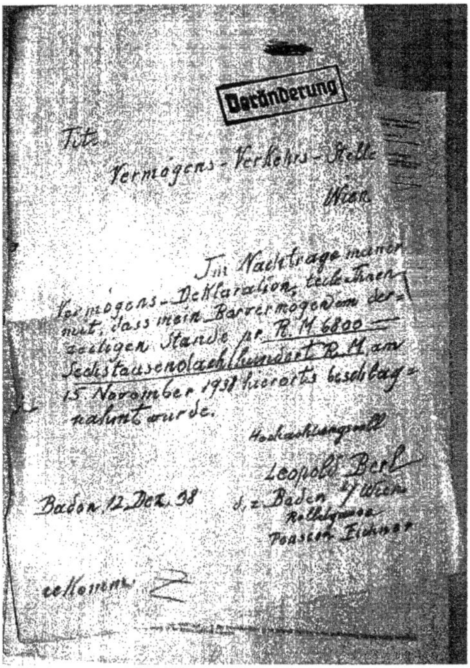
Veränderung

Vermögens-Verkehrs-Stelle
Wien.

Im Nachtrage meiner Vermögens-Deklaration, teile Ihnen mit, dass mein Barvermögen dem derzeitigen Stande per R.M. 6800.— Sechstausendachthundert R.M. am 15. November 1938 hierorts beschlagnahmt wurde.

Hochachtungsvoll
Leopold Berl

Baden, 12. Dez. 38

"The 6,800Rm cash I declared in my original Assets declaration form is inaccurate because it was confiscated on 15 November."
Source: OstA/AdR/06/VVst/VA # 0872

Glimpses of Resistance

While most people complied with the order to update their assets, many went beyond this requirement and not only listed their financial reductions but addressed their difficulty -- if not sheer inability -- to pay the new "Jewish tax." During the last weeks of November and the beginning of December 1938 people wrote to the agency documenting the destruction of their property due to the pogrom and requesting extensions for or exemptions from paying the new tax.[45] Their letters were carefully written, some by hand and others by typewriter. For the most part they were devoid of emotion. While the information they reported was traumatic as well as devastating to their current and future situations, their letters were dry and to the point. For example, sixty-eight-year-old Therese Friedman requested an extension to pay the first installment of the tax. Her letter stated that she had absolutely no cash to pay the first or following installments of the Jewish tax, but that she was part-owner of a house in Vienna's first district, which had no outstanding debts. She suggested that the money could be deducted from her share of the real estate, as long as she was allowed more time so this process could be approved.[46]

Sidonie and Albert Tausz, whose son Rudi had been arrested two weeks earlier and deported to Dachau, submitted a similar request. Albert informed the Assets Transfer Agency that he had sold the last of his stocks in an attempt to cover the tax, and Sidonie appealed to their mortgage company *Landeshypothekanstalt*, stating that they had no cash or other valuables to sell in order to pay the first installment of the Jewish tax; they needed to secure the mortgage. They, too, were seeking an extension on payment of the tax and were exhausting all avenues to procure funds.[47]

---

[45] For letters, see Finance Ministry archive, Assets Transfer Agency/ Registration Forms (OstA/AdR/06/VVst/VA). The fate of the victims is determined either from the files or from the DOEW-Project Registration by Name: The Austrian Victims of the Holocaust, 2001. (Database available online: *http://www. doew.at*).

[46] It is unclear whether or not Therese Friedman was granted her requested extension of time to pay the tax. She was deported to Theresienstadt on 10 July 1942, and died there on 1 September 1942. OstA/AdR/06/VVst/VA # 00972.

[47] OstA/AdR/06/VVst/VA # 2770, 2771, Albert and Sidonie Tausz.

Illustration 19: "Letter to the Assets Transfer Agency Reveals Inability to Pay First Installment of Jewish Tax"

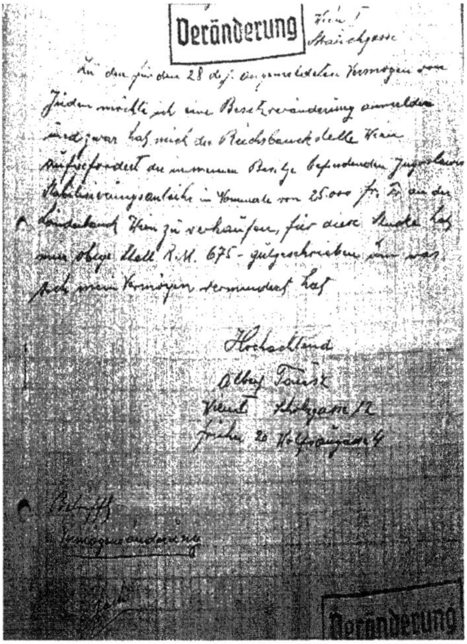

Albert Tausz explains that he has sold his stock and that his assets have been reduced by RM 675.

Source: OstA/AdR/06/VVst/VA # 2770, 2771, Albert and Sidonie Tausz.

Fifty-four-year-old Wilhelm Monias had no cash, capital assets, or real estate at his disposal and was forced to take a different approach. Wilhelm typed a letter on 12 December 1938 to the Assets Transfer Agency in which he summarized his precarious situation with three key points: he had lost his job as supervisor at a major Austrian firm; he was a pensioned veteran of WWI; and he had no money or anything else to sell to cover the tax. He requested "to be exempt from the tax against the Jews: 'Judenkontribution.'"[48] Fifty-one-year-old Ludmilla Fritz

went one step further. She requested no exemption from the agency; nor did she request an

extension to pay the tax over a longer period. Ludmilla simply wrote: "You have taken

everything I have. The last thing that I had was this piece of property, which was taken by the

Secret Police. And you have records of this. I have no more money. I am simply not eligible to

pay the contribution."[49]

Illustration 20: "Wilhelm Monias, Italian Front, WW1"

Source: Offenberger Family Archive, Beverly Farms, Massachusetts.

---

[48] OstA/AdR/06/VVst/VA # 15142, Wilhelm Monias, letter of 12.12.38. Approximately three years later (20 August 1942), the Germans deported Wilhelm and his wife Elisabeth (20.10.1891) from Vienna to Theresienstadt. Neither survived the war. See DOEW-Project Registration by Name: The Austrian Victims of the Holocaust, 2001. (Database available online: *http://www. doew.at*).
[49] The Nazis deported Ludmilla Fritz with her husband Jakob to Theresienstadt on 20 August 1942. Her husband died just days after their arrival; there is no record of Ludmilla's exact date of death. OstA/AdR/06/VVst/VA # (NA)

Theresa Friedman, the Tauszes, Wilhelm Monias, Ludmilla Fritz, and other formerly

wealthy Jews who wrote to the Assets Transfer Agency during November and December 1938

regarding damage from the pogrom, struggled to withstand the unjust measures imposed upon

them while simultaneously trying to cooperate with their enemy's demands. When compared

with the letters sent to the emigration offices of the IKG, these letters were remarkably

straightforward. Although they took orders from both parties, they approached the Nazi

government authorities differently, disclosing little or no emotion, but nevertheless insisting that

their voices be heard. Leopold and Mathilde Vulkan, for example, wrote to the Assets Transfer

Agency requesting the return of some important household items that were confiscated during

the pogrom. They requested these items only so that they could sustain themselves until they left

the country. Their letter was also devoid of emotion but, to support their plea, they listed

Leopold's military honors from World War 1 in the top left corner. Perhaps this would help their

case. The Assets Transfer Agency was not at all interested in Leopold's military record, and a

large X was penned over the list of awards. Leopold and Mathilde were informed that they

could not be helped.[50] And yet they had tried. Leopold and Mathilde were among many who

courageously tried to negotiate with the Nazi authorities although the odds weighed heavily

against them. Most people accepted their situation as unfortunate and simply complied with

demands, but there were those who requested the restitution of confiscated possessions[51] or

asked for more time, and some, like Ludmilla Fritz, chose to refuse orders.

---

[50] OstA/AdR/06/VVst/VA # 33074, Ha #951, Leopold Vulkan; VA # 5889, Mathilde Vulkan.

[51] See, for example, letter from Theodor Rechnitzer to the IKG, 3 December 1938, USHMM film # 281, IKG-A/W 442, *Beschlagnahmungen (Schadensmeldungen) 11.1938* [frame 0273-4]. "On 23.11 my son appealed to the NSDAP and explained to them that I am 71 years old, my wife is 65 years old and that he himself is prepared to immigrate to USA, where he will arrange for us to follow shortly after. He asked that the apartment be returned to us or at the least our possessions inside. We have received no answer."

Trapped in Vienna after the November Pogrom, formerly wealthy Jews were not in a privileged situation relative to the rest of the community. What might remain of their wealth only strapped them with additional obligations to fulfill before exiting the country. They sank to a new level of insecurity, fearing an inability to keep loved ones safe; to free loved ones from the camps; or to enable their emigration. Further, the community as a whole was negatively affected: wealthy Jews who previously helped sustain the community by supplying Reichsmarks in exchange for foreign currency, or paying taxes to the IKG which went directly to supporting the welfare institutions, no longer had the fiscal means nor as much ambition to do so.

Analysis

In Vienna, the November pogrom in many ways repeated the Anschluss terror. Historian Beate Meyer points out that Vienna's Jews responded differently than German Jews because of this. She notes that it was not as shocking to them because it was not the first time they had endured physical destruction perpetrated by the Nazis in the public sphere:

> A few years ago I asked a Jewish man from Hamburg who had witnessed the pogrom of November 9/10, 1938 whether he felt those events constituted a caesura, a turning point in the persecution of the Jews. No, he answered, not as he saw it. In the spring of 1938, he had gone with his parents to Vienna, and a half year later they had returned to Hamburg. After all they had experienced in Vienna during those six months, the rowdy gangs of Nazis, the Jews being manhandled on the street, burning Torah scrolls, and synagogues set ablaze seemed to him quite everyday and commonplace.[52]

Meyer notes the important and often overlooked fact that Vienna's Jews encountered the November Pogrom differently than most other German-Jewish communities. It was not the first

---

[52] Beate Meyer, "The Restructuring of a Jewish Gemeinde into the 'Prototype' of the Judenrat" in *Yad Vashem Studies, XXX* (Jerusalem: 2002) 451-464.

wave of arrests to strike their community randomly and suddenly, nor was it the first time they suffered public humiliations, or had their homes/stores seized, looted, and vandalized (see chapter 2). Nevertheless, the pogrom constituted another major turning point for Vienna's Jews and the impact it had on their future should not be minimized. Different from Anschluss, the November Pogrom revealed to Vienna's Jews (and the outside world) the might and scope of the Nazis' racial antisemitism and terror. Likewise, its aftermath -- the arrests, destruction, and financial regulations -- turned an already difficult situation into a horrific one. Desperation to save themselves and their family members made Jews even more vulnerable and willing to cooperate with the German authorities. Thus, in the aftermath of the November pogrom, the Germans pulled the Jews deeper into the vicious -- and growing -- cycle of victim/perpetrator cooperation, which would eventually assist the genocide, but that in the meantime continued to enable emigration.

Emigration Continues

The onslaught of setbacks brought by the pogrom might have discouraged individual hopes, but it did not deter the IKG from continuing its mission to get all able-bodied Viennese Jews out of Austria as quickly as possible. The IKG offices faced new difficulties, but the community as a whole did not lose hope. People continued to cooperate with the IKG and the Nazi authorities, and in turn the IKG managed to continue its emigration activities throughout November, dispatching 4,524 persons.[53] Emigration continued in the months that followed, and certain foreign actors helped sustain its efforts. Whereas the outside world had been most apathetic to Hitler's invasion of Austria and the ensuing Anschluss pogrom, media coverage following the

---

[53] USHMM film # 294, IKG-A/W 126, *Report of the Vienna Jewish Community. A description of the activity of the Israelitische Kultusgemeinde Wien in the period from May 2nd 1938-December 31st 1939 (2 Exemplare).*

November pogrom against all of German Jewry lit a small fire in some corners of the world, particularly Great Britain.

England was one country that made a difference in the future of Viennese Jewry, opting to ease its immigration policies by allowing for the immediate admission (although not permanent residence) of an increased number of Jews via the *Kindertransport* action,[54] the erection of transit camps, and permitting Jews to enter if they had secured positions as domestic help.[55] The British government by itself could not help everyone, but its willingness to provide massive assistance kept hope alive in the despairing community. After witnessing the terrors of the November pogrom, Vienna's Jews did not collapse under German demands, but became ever more determined to find ways to get out of Austria. It was at this time, in their bleakest moment since the invasion, that through cooperative efforts with each other and the IKG, Vienna's Jews managed to resist Nazism and organize to enact some small miracles. Together, the people and the IKG arranged the release of many arrested and deported men from concentration camps.

---

[54] For further information on Kindertransports and emigration of children with the aid of the IKG, see USHMM film # 295, IKG- A/W 123, *The Household of the Jewish Community of Vienna for the months of January- February 1939*. For more on Kindertransports, see Norman Bentwich, *They Found Refuge* (London: Cresset Press, 1956); Alan Gill, *Interrupted Journeys, Young Refugees from Hitler's Reich* (Pymble, NSW: Simon & Schuster Australia, 2005); Mark Jonathan Harris and Deborah Oppenheimer, *Into the Arms of Strangers* (New York: Bloomsbury Publishing, 2000); Christine Berth, *Die Kindertransporte Nach Grossbritannien 1938/39: Exilerfahrungen im Spiegel Lebensgeschichtlicher* (Munich: Dolling und Galitz, 2005); Bernard Wasserstein, Britain *and the Jews of Europe 1939-1945* (Oxford: Oxford University Press, 1988); Ernst Goodman, "How the Kindertransports were Born," Kinderlink (KTA Journal, 1994). For personal histories see Mona Golabek, *The Children of Willesden Lane: Beyond the Kindertransport: A Memoir of Music, Love, and Survival* (New York: Grand Central Publishing, 2003); Liz, M., 1996. "Interview by Survivors of the Shoah Visual History Foundation," New York, NY, USA, March 8. Interview Code 12674, Tapes 1-8; Alix , K., 1997. "Interview by Survivors of the Shoah Visual History Foundation," Lenox, MA, USA, October 16. Interview Code 34544, Tapes 1-5.

[55] For more on the role of the British at this time see, "From Kristallnacht to the Outbreak of the War, November 1938 to September 1939," in Louise London, *Whitehall and the Jews, 1933-1948: British Immigration Policy, Jewish Refugees, and the Holocaust* (New York: Cambridge University Press, 2000) 97-142. Also see: See Amy Gottlieb, *Men of Vision: Anglo-jewry's Aid to Victims of the Nazi Regime, 1933-1945*(London: Weidenfeld & Nicolson, 1998); Yvonne Kapp and Margaret Mynatt, *British Policy and the Refugees, 1933-1941* (London: Frank Cass, 1997); Frank Dawes, *Not In Front of the Servants: Domestic Service In England 1850-1939* (London:Wayland Publishers, 1973); Pamela Horn, *The Rise and Fall of the Victorian Servant* (New York: St. Martin's Press, 1975); Werner Mosse, *Second Chance: Two Centuries of German-speaking Jews In the United Kingdom.* (Tübingen: J.C.B. Mohr [Paul Siebeck], 1991).

These releases coincided with the German policy of the time, expulsion, but they also revealed

the struggle and sacrifices that ordinary Viennese Jews together with the IKG made during the

pre-genocidal period to defend themselves, hold their families together, and preserve the future

of their community.

Concentration Camp Releases

And so I spoke with the Secret Police about how to obtain the release of my second son, Ernst. I received word from a competent consultant that a request for release would only be taken into consideration if a ship ticket, paid in full to an overseas country, was attached.

~ Leopoldine Maas,
Letter to the IKG for her son Ernst

He could be set free from the concentration camp if he could show some kind of entry visa.

~ Klara Apfelgruen,
Letter to the IKG for her husband Osias

I plead with you most respectfully to intervene on behalf of my son Fritz Bleichfeld: to allow him to wait in England [transit camp] for his entry visa to the USA to be granted. It is understood that in this case, he would be released from protective custody in Dachau.

~ Simon Bleichfeld,
Letter to the IKG for his son Fritz[56]

The Germans deported over 7,000 Jewish men from Vienna to Dachau from the Anschluss

through the November pogrom. More than 5,000 were released between December 1938 and

March 1939 due to the combined efforts of their loved ones and the IKG, and the ability of both

to cooperate with and function under the increasingly oppressive German authorities.[57] Inmates

[56] USHMM film # VZ48, IKG-A/W 2689, 2, *Ansuchen um Aufnahme in das Transitlager Richborough (Alphabetisch), A-B, 1939; Mass; Apfelgruen; Bleichfeld.*
[57] Jonny Moser, *Demographie der jüdischen Bevölkerung Österreichs 1938-1945* (Vienna: DÖW, 1999); Gertrude Schneider, *Exile and Destruction: The Fate of the Austrian Jews, 1938-1945* (Westport: Praeger, 1995), 29, 40.

who could prove that they could emigrate immediately could be released from the camp. When this word spread through the Viennese Jewish community, family members and community workers did all they could to aid this most threatened sector of their community. For the most part, family members came to these men's aid. Prisoners who did not have family at home to take over the emigration process for them had the option to empower the IKG to assume full responsibility over their case.[58] The IKG emigration offices then gave these men's files priority and did all it could to arrange and expedite their papers to facilitate immediate release.

The Richborough refugee camp in Kent, England stood as an important destination, a short-term transmigrant haven for persons who urgently needed to get out of the Reich -- primarily, although not limited to, men trapped in Dachau and Buchenwald.[59] Richborough offered an opportunity to wait in safety while their papers were processed. Thirty-year-old Walter Austerlitz, for instance, who had been registered on the Austrian/German quota for entrance to the U.S. since July 1938, but was arrested during the November pogrom and deported to Dachau, yearned desperately to wait in a British transit camp for his quota number to be called.[60] He wrote to the IKG on 29 January 1939, the day after he returned from Dachau, to

---

[58] See for example: "Vollmacht," signed 25 October 1939 by Josef Pichler, Buchenwald inmate. Pichler authorizes the IKG to take full charge of his case. USHMM Film #V10, IKG-A/W 2696, *Deutsche Staatsbuerger: Abgelegte Akte, Enthaftet - Gestorben von A-Z, Josef Pichler*. He died in Buchenwald on 7 June 1940.

[59] Approximately 3,500 refugees from Germany, Austria, and Czechoslovakia took shelter from Nazi persecution in the camp at Richborough in Kent, England. The Kitchener camp, which was later established, published a monthly journal that can be accessed via the following website: *http://sandwicharchive.homestead.com/KCJ.html* . For further information on these transit camps see Louise London, *Whitehall and the Jews, 1933-1948: British Immigration Policy, Jewish Refugees, and the Holocaust* (New York: Cambridge University Press, 2000); Norman Bentwich, *They Found Refuge: An account of British Jewry's work for victims of Nazi oppression*. (London: Cresset Press, 1956) 102-114.

[60] See USHMM film # VZ48, IKG-A/W 2689, 2, *Ansuchen um Aufnahme in das Transitlager Richborough (Alphabetisch), A-B, 1939: Walther Austerlitz*, 29 January 1939; USHMM film # Alpha A5. *Auswanderungsfrageboegen der Israelitischen Kultusgemeinde Wien (IKG)*, Walter A., # 1894; USHMM film # 7, *Auswanderungsfrageboegen der Israelitischen Kultusgemeinde Wien (IKG) (Numerisch geordnet)*: Irma (Spitzer) Austerlitz, file # 3510; and Walter A., 1995. "Interview by Survivors of the Shoah Visual History Foundation," Glenview, IL, USA, May 31. Interview Code 02907-0, Tapes 1-6.

explain his situation. [61] Or Arthur Andersmann, who was released from Dachau on 11 January 1939 and ordered to leave the Reich by 23 January 1939, received an extension to leave on 28 February 1939, but the first ship ticket he could book to his final destination (Peru) was not until July 1939.[62] Selig Adler, arrested on 10 November 1938 and deported to Dachau, was released on 6 May 1939 and ordered by the secret police to be out of the country by 14 June 1939. He wrote a letter on 12 May stating that he was healthy and ready to work and hoping to be admitted to Richborough: "Please select me for the camp as I am in a desperate situation, I have always led an honest life, and this is the only chance I have to be saved."[63] Then too, men like Otto Heilpern and Heinrich Arzt were spared arrest and deportation but, frightened to remain in Vienna, begged for entry into a camp, viewing their situation as desperate. Heilpern explained that he had been registered on the Austrian quota since 3 September 1938 and had three strong affidavits, was the son of a war veteran, and was without income and struggling to live under these most difficult circumstances.[64] Arzt wrote on 20 May 1939 that he had been registered on the Polish quota for America since 1 April 1938 but knew that his number would not be called until the fall. He explained that he just could not wait in Germany that long: "my only chance [to get out] is to be admitted to the camp.[65]

There was not room in Richborough to accommodate everyone. The IKG, which received the thousands upon thousands of letters begging for acceptance into these camps, was again

---

[61] For more examples, see thirty-year-old Josef Broad who also wrote to the IKG the day after he returned from the camp, USHMM film # VZ48, IKG-A/W 2689, 2, *Ansuchen um Aufnahme in das Transitlager Richborough (Alphabetisch), A-B, 1939: Josef Brod*, 21 February 1939 or Fritz Adler, USHMM film # VZ48, IKG-A/W 2689, 2, *Ansuchen um Aufnahme in das Transitlager Richborough (Alphabetisch), A-B, 1939: Fritz Adler.*

[62] See USHMM film # VZ48, IKG-A/W 2689, 2, *Ansuchen um Aufnahme in das Transitlager Richborough (Alphabetisch), A-B, 1939: Arthur Andersmann.*

[63] USHMM film # VZ48, IKG-A/W 2689, 2, *Ansuchen um Aufnahme in das Transitlager Richborough (Alphabetisch), A-B, 1939: Selig Adler,* 12 May 1939.

[64] USHMM film # VZ48, IKG-A/W 2689, 2, *Ansuchen um Aufnahme in das Transitlager Richborough (Alphabetisch), A-B, 1939: Otto Heilpern,* 30 January 1939.

[65] USHMM film # VZ48, IKG-A/W 2689, 2, *Ansuchen um Aufnahme in das Transitlager Richborough (Alphabetisch), A-B, 1939: Heinrich Arzt,* 20 May 1939.

faced with the heavy burden of determining which case was more pressing than the next. As of

February 1939 it reported to the foreign aid committees that together with the Council for

German Jewry they had selected 1,119 applicants for Richborough; 642 intending to immigrate

to the US, 380 to Palestine, 70 to Australia and 27 to other countries.[66] In their report they

stressed the need for an additional 1,000 persons to be admitted to the camp within the next

weeks, and suggested that more such transit sites be built: "It appears indispensable to admit

additional persons from Vienna to the Richborough and especially to establish other camps for

the same purpose."[67] The next community report revealed that this was only a hope. In April

the IKG reported that still only approximately 1,150 Viennese Jews had been admitted to the

camp: 655 of whom were already sent there, while further transports were still in preparation.[68]

The IKG understood that while transit camps allowed some to leave immediately, they could not

help enough.

Some men, like those above, wrote to the IKG on their own, but most often family

members of men in concentration camps wrote to the IKG on their behalf.[69] The authors once

again detailed their desperate situations: they explained how the men suffered injustice in

Dachau, Buchenwald, or another prison in Vienna, and stressed that the case was urgent. Some

also tried to show how they had offered the IKG service in the past. This was just one part of

taking over the emigration process to enable the rescue of these men; these same family

---

[66] USHMM film # 295, IKG- A/W 123, *The Household of the Jewish Community of Vienna for the months of January- February 1939.*

[67] USHMM film # 295, IKG- A/W 124, *The Household of the Jewish Community of Vienna for the months of March- April 1939.* Also see USHMM film # 294, IKG-A/W 126, *Report of the Vienna Jewish Community. A description of the activity of the Israelitische Kultusgemeinde Wien in the period from May 2nd 1938-December 31st 1939 (2 Exemplare).*

[68] Ibid.

[69] Most letters were written by mother, fathers, and wives, but extended family members and in-laws also contacted the IKG on behalf of their loved ones. See USHMM film # VZ48, IKG-A/W 2689, 2, *Ansuchen um Aufnahme in das Transitlager Richborough (Alphabetisch), A-B, 1939.*

members also filled out the IKG emigration questionnaires on their behalf,[70] as well as the assets

declaration forms and other financial documents; met with Gestapo in Vienna or traveled to

Berlin to meet with Gestapo; and spent hours upon hours writing letters and dealing with various

officials from banks, insurance agencies, ship companies, and consulates.

Although the separation and destruction of Viennese Jewish families began to occur as

early as Anschluss, and reached a new level in November, so too did a remarkable struggle to

save one another. Jewish families responded to the Nazi's assault with practical and spiritual

resistance. Perhaps because their actions have not been scrutinized before, this aspect of the pre-

genocidal period in Vienna has been overlooked. While Nazi German law increasingly

constrained families and the IKG, they fought back -- within the means at their disposal -- to

save themselves and their loved ones. Their persistent efforts could not save everyone, but they

did enable many to flee. If cooperation with the German authorities was one part of the equation,

so too were resilience and determined action. Practically all family members, with the exception

of arrested men, fought to save their loved ones: they assumed responsibilities and adopted

familial roles they may have been unfit and unprepared for but were willing to take on in order to

help. Women -- wives, daughters, sisters, and mothers-- suddenly had a very new and important

role in the family.[71] Still, gender roles continued when possible. Men who were spared arrest

---

[70] Emigration Questionnaires at the IKG were filled out by all family members. Wives filled out questionnaires for their husbands: e.g., Engel, numerical film #74, #54915, 13.8.39. Sisters for their brothers: e.g., Zita Feger for her brother Otto Feger, who was taken in May 1938 to Dachau, then transferred to Buchenwald; she was arranging his flight to Shanghai. See alpha film F1, #21354 20.12.38. Mothers for their sons: e.g., Loewy, numerical film #74, #54864, 12.8.39; Leopoldine Mass filled out the form for her two sons, who were taken to Dachau on 21 June 1938, one of whom she has learned died in the camp (Buchenwald on 22 December 1938), while the other, she has heard, would be released if she paid in full for a ticket overseas. She borrowed money to buy this ticket for her son and now is asking the IKG to reimburse her. See alpha film M10, #48326.

[71] See, for example Raoul Klugmann, *USHMM film #Alpha G7, Auswanderungsfrageboegen der Israelitischen Kultusgemeinde Wien (IKG), Raoul K., # 36524/19807*, for the role of his sister Edith.
See Czuczka, Fritz: Manuscript, BMS GER91(45), Houghton Library, Harvard University, for the role of his wife Charlotte. For further examples of the role of wives, see testimonies of Franz Bauer, Stephan Shifferes, or Wilhelm Jellinek in Survivors of the Shoah Visual History Foundation. For a discussion of the same phenomenon in

and imprisonment were left in charge. Fathers arranged for their sons to emigrate, sometimes risking their own lives. Joseph Brod's father, Emil, organized for him to go to a transit camp in England on 21 February1939;[72] and Leopold, Karl, and Alexander Deutsch were released from Buchenwald and on a ship to Shanghai in April 1939 due to the efforts of their father Geza. Elias Verstandig, seventy-two years old and ill with angina pectoris, got special permission from the German authorities to travel to Hamburg to arrange for an extension of his son Heinrich's Bolivian visa,[73] while Leopold Herlinger postponed his immigration to Palestine where he would join his daughter until his son was released from the camp.

Illustration 21: "Recently-Released: Brothers Leo, Alexander, and Karl Deutsch Pose with Parents Rosa and Geza, Sister Irene, and Niece Ingeborg, for the Last Time before Departing to Shanghai, April 1939"

Source: Leo, D., 1997. "Interview by Survivors of the Shoah Visual History Foundation,"
San Francisco, CA, USA, May 17. Interview Code 29174, Tape 5.

Germany proper, see Marion Kaplan, *Between Dignity and Despair: Jewish Life in Nazi Germany* (New York: Oxford University Press, 1998).
[72] Joseph B., 1996. "Interview by Survivors of the Shoah Visual History Foundation," Encinitas, CA, USA, March 15. Interview Code 13315, Tapes 1-4. Also see, USHMM microfilm #31, Auswanderungsfrageboegen der Israelitischen Kultusgemeinde Wien (IKG) (Numerisch geordnet): Josef Brod, file #19,882 [frame 0626-27].
Fred, H., (date currently unavailable). "Interview by Survivors of the Shoah Visual History Foundation," (location currently unavailable). Interview Code 08022
[73] See Elias Verstandig in *USHMM film #Alpha V5, Auswanderungsfrageboegen der Israelitischen Kultusgemeinde Wien (IKG), Heinrich Verstandig, #13404*.

The English Zionist Norman Bentwich, who had dedicated himself to refugee work during the Nazi years, commented upon the tragedy Vienna's Jews faced during the pregenocidal years: "One of the most pitiful aspects of the destruction of the community was the breaking-up of families: children separated from parents, wives from husbands, and the old left behind."[74] Bentwich's observation is correct, but it does not capture the familial unity that achieved those departures. Were it not for the sacrifices and difficult decisions families made, they would not have managed to save one another. Many persevered in their struggle to get themselves and their loved ones out of Austria until 1941, when the Germans prohibited all emigration from the Greater German territory.

Daily Life: Little Miracles, Lots of Goodbyes

Five days before Christmas, late on the evening of 20 December 1938, the Gestapo in Berlin ordered the release of twenty-nine-year-old Dr. Fritz O. from Buchenwald. Eleven o'clock the next morning, camp officials returned Fritz his civilian clothing and had him sign a document stating that he received the briefcase, notebook, papers, keys, and pocket watch that he surrendered upon entrance to Dachau the previous spring.[75] Then they gave him a stamped dismissal certificate that included his name, date of birth, address, and term of imprisonment, stating that upon the order of the secret police in Berlin, he was to be released to his home in

---

[74] Norman Bentwich was the first British attorney general in Palestine. He was a life-long Zionist and during the 1930s played an active role in the welfare efforts of Jewish refugees, working for the Council for German Jewry, established in 1936. See Norman Bentwich, "The Destruction of the Jewish Community in Austria1938-1942," in Josef Frankel, ed., *The Jews of Austria: Essays on their Life, History and Destruction* (London: Valentine Mitchell, 1967) 475. See also Louise London, *Whitehall and the Jews, 1933-1948: British Immigration Policy, Jewish Refugees, and the Holocaust* (New York: Cambridge University Press, 2000) 40-41.
[75] It is unclear whether he actually received these items. Effektenkarte 8624, December 21, 1938, ITS Digital Collection, Individual Documents Male Buchenwald, 1.1.5.3, 6737405, USHMM.

Vienna.[76] That same day, ninety-nine other prisoners were spared, and the commandant in Buchenwald calculated that the total number of camp inmates had been reduced from 11,527 to 11,427.[77] Over the next months the camp continued to release prisoners who could guarantee they would leave the Reich, in order to make more room for new inmates.

Illustration 22: "Release Certificate from the Buchenwald Concentration Camp, Authorized by the Gestapo in Berlin (20.12.38)"

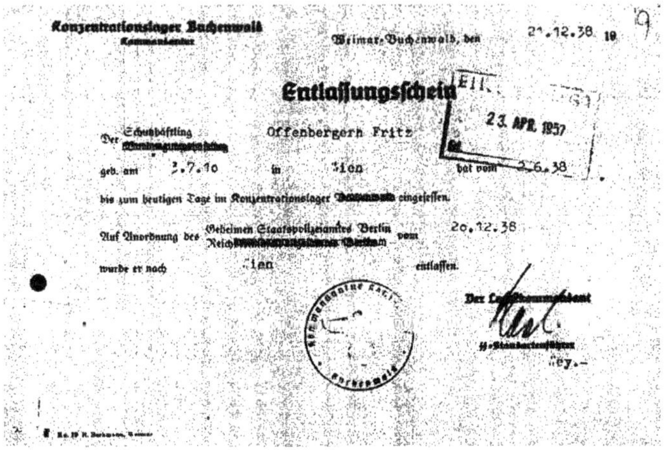

Source: File #08124, *Alte Hilfsfonds.* Austrian State Archives: OstA/AdR/BMF/06/AHF/08124.

Twenty-five-year-old Raoul Klugman was also released from Buchenwald that December. He was told to report to a certain station in the camp where he met with an attorney who said, "'I am here for you to sign papers, your family has applied for a passport for you and

[76] Gedenkstaette Buchenwald Archiv: Datenbank -Haeftlingsnummernkartei, Enlassungscheine, 8624. See also, Fred, H., 1995. "Interview by Survivors of the Shoah Visual History Foundation," Bronx, NY, USA, October 26. Interview Code 08022, Tapes 1-4. Edward, W., 1996. "Interview by Survivors of the Shoah Visual History Foundation," Chicago, IL, USA, April 21. Interview Code 14235, Tapes 1-3.
[77] Gedenkstaette Buchenwald Archiv: Datenbank -Haeftlingsnummernkartei, Enlassungscheine; Thueringisches hauptstaatsarchiv Weimar; Geldkartei; and NARA- Washington: RG 242, Film 3.

you have to sign.'" He signed and the next day was called to the same office and told: "'You are going home today.'" Raoul had to certify that he would leave the country within six weeks after he arrived in Vienna and that he would report to the Gestapo once a week. The police returned the clothing he had been forced to hand over when he had entered Dachau some seven months earlier.[78] It had been dry cleaned and, although it was winter, the summer coat he had worn there seemed like a gift compared to the striped uniform he had stuffed with newspaper against the cold.[79] For Otto Linder, who was released from Buchenwald some three months later (March 1939), the return of his civilian clothing was not such a pleasant experience. Although the clothes had been dry cleaned, his white shirt still carried the blood stain of the boy who had sat next to him on the train when they were deported to Dachau some nine months earlier. As Otto boarded the train headed back to Vienna, he could not shake the memory of the boy. That young man had already lost hope in June 1938 before even getting to the camp and had jumped out the train window.[80]

Upon arrival in Vienna, most newly released men were forced to say their final goodbyes to family members almost immediately.[81] They had been freed upon condition that they would leave the Reich within a specific period of time, ranging from a fortnight to six weeks.[82] Extensions were sometimes granted to men whose papers were in order and awaited a U.S. quota

---

[78] For more on this process, see: "The Camp Laundry" in David A. Hackett, *The Buchenwald Report* (Boulder: Westview Press, 1995), 182.

[79] Raoul K.,1996. "Interview by Survivors of the Shoah Visual History Foundation," Great Neck, NY, USA, April 23. Interview Code 14413, Tapes 1-3. See USHMM film #Alpha G7, *Auswanderungsfrageboegen der Israelitischen Kultusgemeinde Wien (IKG), Raoul K., # 36524/19807.*

[80] See chapter 4, "Turning Point: Vienna to Dachau;" Otto, L., 1997. "Interview by Survivors of the Shoah Visual History Foundation," Valley Stream, NY, USA, February 27. Interview Code 26151,Tapes 1-6; USHMM film #Alpha L7, Auswanderungsfrageboegen der Israelitischen Kultusgemeinde Wien (IKG), Otto L., # 42838/23409.

[81] Erica B., 1996. "Interview by Survivors of the Shoah Visual History Foundation," Upminster, Essex, UK, October 15. Interview Code 20825, Tapes 1-6.
Sandor U., 1997. "Interview by Survivors of the Shoah Visual History Foundation," Bondi, AU, July 20. Interview Code 04144, Tapes 1-4.

[82] See USHMM microfilm #4, *Auswanderungsfrageboegen der Israelitischen Kultusgemeinde Wien (IKG) (Numerisch geordnet): Heinrich Akselrad,* file #1893.

number but, more often than not, people left within the predetermined time or they were picked up and incarcerated again.[83] Ordered to report to the Gestapo until their departure, some had to go to headquarters on Morzinplatz once a week, others every day, or every other day.

While the prisoners were fortunate to have been released, their return to Vienna was fraught with peril. Most had hoped that they would reunite with their families sooner or later -- that their families would either be secure living in Vienna until they returned, or that they would join them abroad as soon as they could. These illusions quickly melted away. Thirty-five-year-old Fritz Herlinger, for example, was released from Buchenwald on 9 February 1939 and sent back to Vienna with exactly two weeks to leave the Reich. Focused on leaving so that he would not be arrested again, he said very few goodbyes; in any case most of his friends were gone already. Still, parting from his father Leopold -- the man who had enabled his release and had stayed in Vienna to wait for him -- was a particularly unpleasant time. The two men did not speak much during Fritz's short return to Vienna, because it was too painful for both of them "I didn't want to hurt my father and he didn't want to hurt me."[84] [He weeps.] "He could see by the way I looked," Fritz recalled, "[and] I could tell how bad it was, what happened to him. [I] tried not to ask too much, he was too depressed. [His] home was taken away...everything taken away." Such was the experience for many men who came home from the camps as wounded and beaten individuals and encountered the destruction that had occurred while they were gone. They had been unaware of what had transpired in Vienna during their absence -- how severely their families had been hurt while they were away, unable to do anything to help.

---

[83] Isidor Blatt, who was a veteran, received extensions. Heinrich Verstandig was picked up and deported a second time. Fred, H., 1995. "Interview by Survivors of the Shoah Visual History Foundation," Bronx, NY, USA, October 26. Interview Code 08022.

[84] Fred, H., 1995. "Interview by Survivors of the Shoah Visual History Foundation," Bronx, NY, USA, October 26. Interview Code 08022.

The departure and goodbyes were a different experience for former camp inmates like Fritz Czuczka, who was greeted at the train station by his wife and son and who left with them weeks later. While in Buchenwald, Fritz received a letter from his wife explaining that she had spoken on the telephone with the Gestapo in Berlin and had learned his release would be arranged in matter of days. She had purchased ship tickets to New York, had the tickets photographed, and included the copies in her letter. Fritz waited anxiously the following days and nights. He feared contracting the typhoid virus then spreading through the camp and, knowing he would not be released if ill, wondered if his chance for freedom would come in time. As it happened, he was in one of the last groups of men discharged from Buchenwald that winter. He and some thirty other men got their civilian clothing and a superficial medical examination by the camp doctor. Then he received his release certificate, on the back of which he was instructed to report to the Gestapo in Vienna, room 229, immediately upon arrival. He and other men were called into a locked room where a Gestapo officer gave them strict instructions. They were to board the bus waiting for them outside the camp gates and go directly to the Weimar train station. They were forbidden to consume any alcohol, and they were to take the first train home. They were threatened that if they uttered a word of what happened in the camp to anybody, the Gestapo would find them and arrest them and their families.[85]

Three Jewish women in Weimar greeted Fritz and the other men at the train station, gave them coffee, bread, and cigarettes, and sent telegrams to their families to say that their men were on their way home.[86] Every day local Jewish women volunteered to help liberated inmates, and Fritz recalled their kindness and the way it made him feel in his first moments of freedom: "The Jewish women were the first human beings [Menschen] to greet us and speak to us kindly... I

---

[85] Fritz Czuczka: BMS GER91(45), Houghton Library, Harvard University.

[86] These women's actions were not clandestine; they were supported by the local Jewish community of Weimar. For more about their work, see Thueringisches hauptstaatsarchiv Weimar, *www.thueringen.de/de/staatsarchive/weimar.*

would like to repay them a thousand times, for during this first half hour of my freedom they restored my faith in humanity." Fritz's train stopped two hours later in Leipzig, where he was greeted again by kind members of the Jewish community. After eating a hearty dinner, he boarded a fast train to Vienna with a reserved compartment for him and the other men. He tried to sleep, but could not; his mind was filled with thoughts of what was yet to come and what he had left behind -- his wife and son who awaited him, his comrades in Buchenwald who were still in the camp. "I was free from the camp and yet the horror of the war that I was about to return to struck me. I understood that I had not truly reached freedom yet."[87]

Not For Everyone

Despite family efforts, the work of the IKG, and relaxed regulations to enter Britain, not everyone was released and not everyone was fortunate enough to arrange to emigrate. Even persons who qualified for the more privileged categories (children and former camp inmates) were not guaranteed a chance to emigrate. There were just too many people seeking to get out and not enough slots on the *Kindertransport* to rescue all the children who needed it, or sufficient space in the transit camp to house all the men who sought temporary shelter.[88] Despite intensive efforts to effect the emigration of a loved one, people failed. Helene Pichler, an Aryan woman married to a Jewish man incarcerated in Buchenwald, did all that she could to set him free. Writing 3 July 1939 "to the Secret Police in Vienna, Franz Josefskai 33... Concerning: Protective Prisoner Nr. 2074, Block 20a Buchenwald, Josef Pichler," she pleaded:

---

[87] Fritz Czuczka, BMS GER91(45), Houghton Library, Harvard University: 90.
[88] Richborough intended to keep 5,000 refugees, but a lower limit of 3,500 was agreed upon. When war broke out some 3,350 and 220 women and children were lodged at Richborough. See Louise London, *Whitehall and the Jews, 1933-1948: British Immigration Policy, Jewish Refugees, and the Holocaust* (New York: Cambridge University Press, 2000) 116.

I am a pure Aryan woman and have two children ages 3 and 11, who are both of mixed race (Mischlinge). My husband is in protective custody since 20 June of this year and I am writing to request that he be released from prison. I base my plea upon the following: My husband never was politically active. He fought in the world war and volunteered to register in the army of the lieutenant general Fischer. My husband is a war veteran and has an injured foot. I myself live with both of our children in the poorest condition and I am supported by the public welfare system. My husband is a printer and can immigrate to Switzerland, find work there and support our family, so that we should no longer be a burden on the public welfare system. The funding for the emigration will be loaned to him. With attention to these matters, I beg you to release my husband so that my two young and innocent children can once again receive their daily meals." [89]

Despite her status as an Aryan woman, Helene's plea yielded nothing. Her husband never got out of Buchenwald, although both the IKG and his wife made concerted efforts on his behalf.

Many other people who were fit to emigrate and had the means to do so also were trapped. Persons with connections overseas, such as Ernst Wengraf, a cousin of the famous director Max Reinhardt who was settled Los Angeles, was still unable to escape.[90] And what about thirteen-year-old Mia Gruenberg, who was in perfect health, practicing English, learning how to sew, and desperately seeking entrance to England? Her older brother Harry (see chapter 2), had left Vienna in 1938 and was in England. Mia sent him letters begging him to find her a home. In July 1939, shortly before the war started, she thanked him for the English dictionary he had sent her and asked him to help correct her English mistakes.

I am 13 years old, and was born in Vienna on the 26th of January 1926. I am German nationality. I finished four classes of the elementary school and two of the higher school classes with very good result and now I visit the 3rd class of the

[89] Letter from Helene Pichler to the Secret Police in Vienna, 3 July 1939. USHMM Film #V10, IKG-A/W 2696, *Deutsche Staatsbuerger: Abgelegte Akte, Enthaftet - Gestorben von A-Z, Josef Pichler.*
[90] He was deported to Lodz in 1941 and his brother was deported to Minsk, Maly Trostinec in 1942. USHMM microfilm #NA, *Auswanderungsfrageboegen der Israelitischen Kultusgemeinde Wien (IKG) (Numerisch geordnet), Ernst Wengraf, #NA.*

normal school because it is not allowed for Jews to visit higher school. I can a little English and Hebrew and I understand good to keep company with little children. Also I have talent to draw and to hand-needleworks.[91]

Even children like Mia Gruenberg, who worked their hardest to make themselves more desirable for emigration, who had family members outside Nazi Germany pulling for them, and whose parents were willing to send them away, could still be caught inside.

Illustration 23: "Thirteen-year-old Mia Gruenberg Practices her English,
Seeking the Opportunity to Immigrate to England, July 1939"

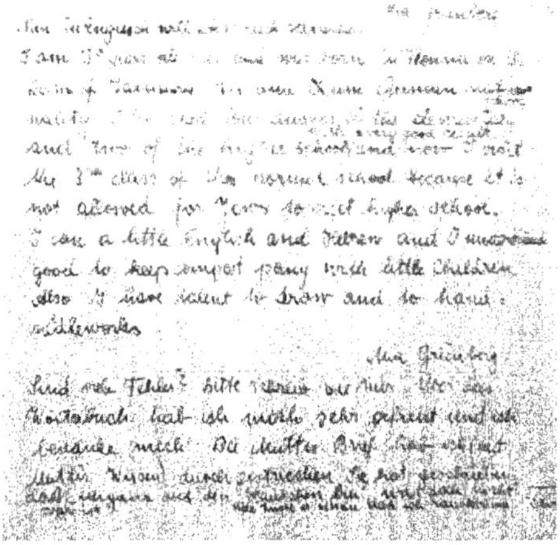

Source: Gruenberg Family Archive, Weston, Massachusetts.

---

[91] Gruenberg Family Archive, Weston, Massachusetts. Letter from Mia, July 1939. Original English. Mia Gruenberg did not escape from Vienna; she was deported with her parents Leo and Elka to Minsk, Maly Trostinec on 27 May 1942. For family photograph, see illustration 5. For more details on deportation see Chapter 8.

Conclusions

With the outbreak of World War 2 on 1 September 1939, emigration slowed, but did not

cease. As the months passed and country after country joined battle, important immigration hubs

shut down -- countries were either conquered by or at war with Germany, their ports closed or

unavailable, and communication and immigration opportunities withered. Still, approximately

20,000 Jews fled from Vienna to points around the world between September 1939 and October

1941, when the Germans forbade emigration from the Reich.[92] The majority departed in last

months of 1939 (12,000), some left in 1940 (6,378), and even fewer in the first six months of

1941 (1,194).[93] These people, who left in small numbers at these late dates, were very fortunate

to make it out, and their journeys were far more difficult than those who had left earlier. [94] They

were desperate to go, and the last to leave; they took what they could get. And some did not

survive the treacherous journey.

Hope endured among the Jews of Vienna through 1941 and the few people still getting

out validated it. Although diminished in number and in spirit, the Jewish community did not lose

sight of its ultimate goal: emigration and social assistance -- to rescue and care for its people.[95]

Despite the odds against them, people kept trying to get themselves out, and family members

already abroad kept trying to get out their loved ones. Although chances were slim and people

---

[92] This will be discussed further in chapters 7 and 8.

[93] USHMM film #295, IKG- A/W 113, *Bericht in Tabellenform betreffend Auswanderungsangelegenheiten, Bevoelkerungsstand, Fuersorgeangelegenheiten und Umschulung, Janner-December 1940; IKG- A/W 131, Israelitische Kultusgeminde Vienna. Activity During Twelve Months of War, 01.09.1939-31.08.1940;* IKG-A/W 132, *Israelistische Kultusgeminde Vienna. Survey on Nineteenhundredforty.* Of the 6,378 Jews who fled in 1940, 4,588 depended upon the community for financial aid, a much larger percentage than in previous years.

[94] For example: Lucie Benedikt left on a Kindertransport to England in 1938; her parents left on one of the last ships from Barcelona, Spain to the United States in 1941 (before the U.S. joined the war). Sick cattle, in addition to the extreme overcrowding, made for a most treacherous journey that lasted six weeks. The ship was comparable to the SS-Navemar, which left from Seville, Spain on 6 August 1941 and arrived in New York on 12 September 1941. The ship was fit for 28 passengers and held over 1,000. See photo above: *http://www.narrow-gate.net/jeffking/archives/002665.html.* Lucy Benedikt, private interview with the author, October 2008. Orlando, Florida.

[95] As of March 1940 the IKG was preparing 175 families (370 persons total) for immigration to San Domingo. USHMM film # 1264, IKG-A/W 2686, *San Domingo "C" (Listen der Transportteilnehmer).*

often met with failure, they kept trying until the end.[96] Even after trapped Jews were listed for deportation to the east, and were waiting at the collection point for deportation, their family members did not desert them. Enoch Mandel, for example, a middle-aged graduate engineer born in Vienna and residing in Berlin, learned on 9 February 1941 that the previous day the IKG had ordered his elderly mother Melanie to report to the school in Vienna II, Castellezgasse 35 with 50 kilograms (110 pounds) of hand luggage for the purpose of resettlement to Poland. Upon receiving this news, Enoch looked to the Council of German Jewry in Berlin for help and then to the IKG in Vienna, through which he sent telegrams to his brother Ernesto, who, safely overseas in Mexico, might be able to help. "I'm writing to request that she [Melanie Mandel] be taken off the transport to Poland and given the opportunity to wait in Vienna just a little bit longer, until my brother Ernesto, currently living in Mexico, can arrange her passage over Lisbon, Portugal," he wrote to the IKG. "My mother already has her entry visa to Mexico, but has had trouble with her passage. First she was booked on a Holland ship, but then Holland was occupied.... Then she had a ticket on an Italian ship, but then Italy joined the war.... Since the opportunity to travel out of Lisbon has only recently become an option, she had not arranged this yet." Enoch wrote to the IKG on 9 and 10 February and 12 February asking them to act on behalf of his mother, and to confirm that they had forwarded his request to his brother for help. Too late. Melanie Mandel (b.1872) was on the first mass transport from Vienna to the Opole ghetto in the Lublin district of Poland, with approximately one thousand other persons, five days later (15 February 1941). The IKG made a note that Melanie -- and one other person on the deportation list -- had her

---

[96] Attempts were made as late as November 1941 to secure transit visas through Spain for Heinrich and Berta O. and to bring them to the U.S. USHMM film #U50, IKG A/W 2572, 11, *Korrespondez*, 20 November 1941. By this date emigration from Germany was already prohibited: see Chapter 7.

emigration documents in order, but this was not enough to get her off the list.[97] Nothing ever came of her sons' attempts to free her. One wonders whether she knew how they tried to save her.

People like Enoch Mandel continued to try to rescue family members until communication was cut off completely -- until the letters stopped, the telegrams stopped, and nothing was left to be done. When this dead end became evident, the Viennese Jewish community began to crumble internally.[98] This stark realization came to each family on an individual basis and at a different time, but the entire community was permanently and irreparably scarred by this, too. Thirty-six-year-old Sandor Ultmann, a recent immigrant to Shanghai, received a despairing letter from his parents, Ida (seventy-six years) and Heinrich (sixty-seven years), still in Vienna, in October 1939. The letter, written by his father, read:"Mother is for the last few weeks full of sorrow -- she cries and cries -- she can't take the loss of you and your sister -- and her worry is that she fears she will never see you again."[99] Heinrich continued to explain that life in Vienna had become grayer and grayer in their children's absence, and that their letters were the only ray of light left. Emigration was still a possibility for Heinrich and Ida, but it seemed they already felt hopeless. It was at this turning point, when Jews remaining in Vienna lost hope of getting out and reuniting with family, and Jews abroad lost

---

[97] It is unclear whether the IKG, Melanie, or an outside party informed Enoch Mandel of this news. It was possible for people to write letters in the Sammellager, so it may have come directly from Melanie. USHMM film # V10, IKG-A/W 2697, 6, *Bemuehungen, die Auswanderung von in Abwanderungstransporte eingeteilten Personen und deren Angehoerigen in die Wege zu leiten, 1. Transport (Opole ue/Pulawy)*. See *also, Documentation Center of the Austrian Resistance (DÖW):* DOEW-Project Registration by Name: The Austrian Victims of the Holocaust, 2001. (Database available online: *http://www.doew.at*). The fate of Enoch Mandel is unknown.

[98] The destruction of the community continued overseas. After emigration, life was all about trying to get the rest of the family out. One was not completely free, the story was not over. Rather, it was the start of a new chapter that continued to be filled with fear and longing. Secher, Pierre H., *Left behind in Nazi Vienna: Letters of a Jewish family caught in the Holocaust, 1939-1941* (Jefferson: McFarland & Co., 2004) 25.

[99] Sandor, U., 1997. "Interview by Survivors of the Shoah Visual History Foundation," Bondi, AU, July 20. Interview Code 04144, Tapes 1-4.

hope in freeing their family members and seeing them again, that the destruction of this community reached a new level.

The Germans drove the Viennese Jewish community into a state of desperation beginning in March 1938, ultimately forcing it into submission, compromise, and collaboration, and gradually tearing it apart -- using tactics of persecution, expropriation, and expulsion. Over the course of three years, the efforts of the IKG, family members, and foreign aid committees managed to rescue 136,000 Jews, over two-thirds of Vienna's Jewish community, sending them to six different continents and over fifty different countries.[100] These numbers marked both a heroic rescue effort and a great tragedy: the Jewish community of Vienna reduced from 181,778[101] souls in March 1938 to a mere 44,000[102] in October 1941. Emigration constituted an achievement for the Germans too; helping them accomplish their goal of making Austria "Judenrein." Still, Vienna's Jews did not understand this then, and they persevered, keeping hope alive for as long as they possibly could. They did not sit by passively in this time of confusion and turmoil; they were engaged in a constant struggle to promote rescue, while resisting the destruction of their families and community.

---

[100] The final IKG report lists a total of 136,000 Jews for emigration between 1938-1941, see USHMM film # 294, IKG- A/W 116, *Taetigkeitsbericht fuer das Jahr 1942 (2 Exemplare)*. 117,409 Jews emigrated between 1938-1939, see USHMM film # 294, IKG-A/W 126, *Report of the Vienna Jewish Community. A description of the activity of the Israelitische Kultusgemeinde Wien in the period from May 2ⁿᵈ 1938-December 31ˢᵗ 1939 (2 Exemplare)*. From this total of 136,000, an estimated 15,000 Jews were caught in another Nazi occupied territory and deported and murdered. See: Berkley, *Vienna and Its Jews*, 297; Mass, *Country Without A Name*, 47.

[101] According to IKG figures, 181,778 Jews belonged to the community as of 15 March 1938. USHMM film # 294, IKG-A/W 126, *Report of the Vienna Jewish Community. A description of the activity of the Israelitische Kultusgemeinde Wien in the period from May 2ⁿᵈ 1938-December 31ˢᵗ 1939 (2 Exemplare)*, 17.

[102] According to four separate IKG reports, approximately 44,000 Jews lived in Vienna in the fall of 1941. See: USHMM film #295, IKG- A/W 115, *Tatigkeitsberichte in Tabellenform [Anschlag?] fuer die Zeit vom 01. Jaenner-30. Juni 1941*; IKG- A/W 132, *Israelitische Kultusgeminde Vienna. Survey on Nineteenhundred-forty*; film #UZ27, IKG- A/W2663, slide 0628; film #288, IKG- A/W 466, 1-2. *Ausgabe von Judenkennzichen. 09.1941-10.1941*.

Chapter Seven

Transition to Deportation

Illustration 24: "Original IKG Diagram,
Population Figures of the Jewish Community of Vienna, 1934-1939"

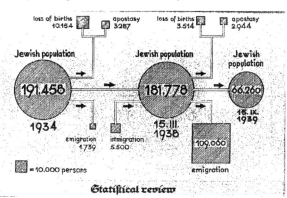

Source: USHMM film # 294, IKG-A/W 126. IKG *Report May 2nd 1938- December 31st 1939:* 10

Introduction

A third wave of deportations devastated Vienna's Jewish community shortly after the

outbreak of war in September 1939. The Germans sought to establish a 'Jewish

Reservation' in newly occupied territory in Poland, ordering (October 1939) the

immediate deportation of able-bodied males to a tiny town called Nisko, in a sparsely

populated wetland near the San river. Again, it was men who were targeted for removal,

further skewing Vienna's already disproportionally gendered community[1] of 39,238

---

[1] These numbers draw attention to the atypical aspects of the crisis that Viennese Jewry faced under Nazi
tyranny. Typically, in an emergency situation relief workers focus their efforts upon saving the women and
children. According to the International Committee of the Red Cross (founded in 1863), basic rules of
international humanitarian law, 3.9, "Vulnerable groups, such as pregnant women and nursing mothers,

females and 27,702 men and aged: 47,000 of a total of 67,000, of whom were over forty-five years old.[2] But this "aktion" differed greatly from the sudden arrest and deportation of Jews to Dachau in the spring and fall of 1938. In this case, the German authorities instructed the IKG to organize and carry out the process, giving them three days to gather the first 1,000-1,200 deportees. They assured the IKG that the selected men would be sent somewhere they could work and that their families would soon follow. They encouraged the IKG to select poor Jews and former KZ inmates, those who were desperate to get out immediately. They emphasized that this was a chance to "resettle."

The IKG fulfilled its orders. It informed the community of the decree, encouraged men to volunteer for the transports, compiled the lists, and organized the departures. The IKG leadership knew little about the final destination,[3] and men who volunteered to go to Nisko did not have any idea of what awaited them, but they nevertheless followed German orders. Two transports carrying a total of 1,584 Jewish men left Vienna that fall: 912 persons on Friday 20 October and 672 persons on Thursday 26 October 1939.[4] The trains carried passengers as well as freight cars filled

---

unaccompanied children, the elderly, etc., must be given special protection." See:
http://www.redcross.org/images/pdfs/RCOBasicRules.pdf. On the seas, a naval tradition of "Women and children first" began in 1852 after the shipwreck of the H.M.S. Birkenhead, one of the first iron-hulled troopships in the British Royal Navy. There were few survivors of the tragedy (193 of 638) but all women and children were saved. "The incident captured the world's imagination and the story was read aloud to every regiment in the Prussian Army as an example of supreme discipline, courage and self-sacrifice. The disaster gave rise to the 'Birkenhead Drill' meaning 'women and children first'." http://www.national-army-museum.ac.uk/exhibitions/shortVisits/iconic/page11.shtml.
[2] USHMM film #295, IKG- A/W 131, Israelitische Kultusgeminde Vienna. Activity During Twelve Months of War, 01.09.1939-31.08.1940.
[3] It is evident that the IKG leaders did not understand the conditions in Nisko because they did not try to hide information of transports to this destination. They made reference to the Nisko deportations, reporting to the JDC in October 1939: "Moreover 1,584 have left for Poland." USHMM film # 294, IKG-A/W 130, Report of the Vienna Jewish Community. July- October 1939 (2 Exemplare).
[4] USHMM film # 294, IKG-A/W 130, Report of the Vienna Jewish Community. July- October 1939 (2 Exemplare). See also, Jonny Moser, Demographie der jüdischen Bevölkerung Österreichs 1938-1945 (Vienna: DÖW, 1999) 80; Documentation Center of the Austrian Resistance, 2536, Report by the Central Office for Jewish Emigration, October 18, 1939.

with building equipment, tools, and a food supply to last at least a couple weeks. The

Germans' plan was to send multiple transports to the reservation, each transport was to

carry 1,000 Jews, to depart bi-weekly on Tuesdays and Fridays from the Aspang Banhof

at 10 o'clock in the evening,[5] but there were no further deportations that year, or

throughout the entire following year of 1940: the German plan to expel and resettle Jews

in Poland had proved impractical.[6] Those Jews deported to Nisko were left stranded in

this desolate reservation with little chance to survive. Few ever saw their families again;

many died of disease or starvation, the SS and police guards forced many to cross into

Soviet territory, some few escaped and returned to Vienna. "Resettlement" had not

proved a viable solution to the Jewish Problem, but during this experiment the Germans

had managed to set a new system in motion that would sustain the genocide: they had

acquired Jewish cooperation and collaboration in the deportation process.

Over half of Vienna's community had fled the country prior to the Nisko

deportations, an average of 5,000 persons emigrating each month during 1938 and the

first half of 1939, for a total of 105,759.[7] After the war started, these numbers fell

precipitously, but Jews still sought assistance from the IKG's emigration office,

ultimately depending on it for their preparations and the final dispatch. The IKG

---

[5] Rabinovici, *Instanzen der Ohnmacht: Wien 1938-1945: der Weg zum Judenrat* (Frankfurt am Main, Juedischer Verlag, 2000), 197; also see George E. Berkley, *Vienna and Its Jews: The Tragedy of Success: 1880s-1980s* (Cambridge, MA. Lanham, Md., Abt Books; Madison Books, 1988).
[6] For more information on the failed Nisko venture, see David Cesarani, *Becoming Eichmann: Rethinking the Life, Crimes, and Trial of a "Desk Murderer"* (Cambridge: Da Capo Press, 2004), 78; Gertrude Schneider, *Exile and Destruction: The Fate of the Austrian Jews, 1938-1945* (Westport: Praeger, 1995) 41; Hans Safrian, *Eichmann's Men*. (Cambridge: Cambridge University Press, 2010). For oral histories see Wilhelm. K, 1996. "Interview by Survivors of the Shoah Visual History Foundation," East St. Kilda, AU, August 28. Interview Code 19014, Tapes 1-5; Helen, H., 1995. "Interview by Survivors of the Shoah Visual History Foundation," Newbury Park, CA, USA, February 21. Interview Code 00903, Tapes 1-2.
[7] USHMM film #295, IKG- A/W 113, *Bericht in Tabellenform betreffend Auswanderungsangelegenheiten, Bevoelkerungsstand, Fuersorgeangelegenheiten und Umschulung, Janner-December 1940*; IKG- A/W 131, *Israelitische Kultusgemeinde Vienna. Activity During Twelve Months of War, 01.09.1939-31.08.1940*; IKG- A/W 132, *Israelitische Kultusgemeinde Vienna. Survey on Nineteenhundredforty*.

continued to face an enormous task, too. The leaders presented it to the JDC as threefold: "1) The organization of the emigration of the Jews of the Ostmark, 2) Social Care for all the families who have to wait for the moment when they will be able to leave the country, 3) Care for the old and sick people."[8] Although the war had begun, emigration had not stopped completely, nor had funding from abroad which enabled the community to continue supporting its welfare institutions. Hope for a brighter future remained among the IKG leadership and was passed to Vienna's Jews. On the last page of a statistical report the IKG compiled for the JDC in December 1940 was written in very large print: "Help to continue and conclude the work [of the Jewish Community of Vienna]!"[9] The leadership expressed its continued intention -- and determination -- to save each and every Viennese Jew from Nazism, despite the elevated level of terror and the Germans' new demand that they cooperate with their plan to "resettle" Jews in the east.

Mass Deportation and Family Division

Even after the situation darkened in the winter of 1941, the IKG tried to remain hopeful. The Germans commenced the first deportations from Vienna to the Lublin district of Poland in February and March 1941, and again they turned to the IKG. They ordered the leaders to organize transports of Jews to be "resettled," only this time they would not have to select the deportees, the *Zentrallstelle* compiled the lists in advance.[10] With no alternative, the IKG leadership did as it was told. During those two months, five transports from the Aspang Banhof headed to the ghettos of Opole, Kielce, Modliborzyce, and Lagow/Opatow, each carrying approximately one thousand prisoners.

---

[8] USHMM film #295, IKG-A/W 142, *Report of the Vienna Jewish Community, March-April1939 (2 Exemplare)*. Original English.
[9] USHMM film # 295, IKG- A/W 132, *Israelitische Kultusgeminde Vienna. Survey on Nineteenhundredforty*. Original English.
[10] Rabinovici, Instanzen der Ohnmacht: 226, 234.

But this time the Germans demanded the deportation of entire families and they made it clear that these people were not coming back -- or at least not any time soon.[11] Those selected for the transport were summoned to the local school on Castellezgasse 35 in the second district, where they presented their papers and were registered while they waited for transfer to the train station. The deportees were ordered to bring their food ration cards and the keys to their apartments with an attached piece of paper recording their name, address, and date of birth -- all of which they were required to turn in to the authorities. To keep the situation under control and to keep the people calm, Lowenherz arranged with Brunner for IKG workers to provide the deportees with food and water. Also, a representative from the local bank was called to the site to convert what little money they took with them into Polish zloty.[12]

For the community of some 46,000 Jews remaining in Vienna in the winter of 1941, still struggling to emigrate or to just get by, news of the deportations again took a toll.[13] The result: lost hope. Family members -- both in Vienna and abroad -- began to doubt that they would see their loved ones again and, for some, this thought sapped their energy to carry on. The IKG, however, did not waver, nor did it stray from the mission and work before it, which now stretched beyond emigration and welfare to include forcibly "resettling" thousands of persons in the east. It continued to carry on with its work.

---

[11] The transports also carried many single persons whose family members emigrated previously. See previous chapter for case of Melanie Mandel, USHMM film # V10, IKG-A/W 2697, 6, *Bemuehungen, die Auswanderung von in Abwanderungstransporte eingeteilten Personen und deren Angehoerigen in die Wege zu leiten, 1. Transport (Opole ue/Pulawy).*

[12] Rabinovici, *Instanzen der Ohnmacht:* 227.

[13] According to IKG figures, 46,000 Jews lived in Vienna as of January 1941. See USHMM film # 294, IKG- A/W 113, *Bericht in Tabellenform betreffend Auswanderungsangelegenheiten, Bevoelkerungsstand, Fuersorgeangelegenheiten und Umschulung, Jaenner- Dezember 1940*; USHMM film # 295, IKG- A/W 132, *Israelitische Kultusgeminde Vienna. Survey on Nineteenhundredfourty.*

Personal Experiences

Herbert and Maximillian Kaufmann were among the first 5,000 Jews the Germans deported from Vienna in the winter of 1941. The brothers were eleven and thirteen respectively when Hitler marched into Austria in March 1938 and in their life under Nazi occupation had endured various hardships: their father was deported to and released from Dachau and died in Vienna shortly thereafter; they had been forced out of two different schools; had moved from two different apartment buildings; and their immigration papers to Colombia had fallen through at the last minute. In February 1941, the boys, now fourteen and seventeen, faced the most significant upheaval in their daily lives, although it did not appear that way at the time. By way of postcard they learned they would need to move again, this time away from Vienna. The IKG sent them a notice in the mail which instructed them to bring fifty kilos of their belongings and to report to the local school in the second district. They were told to wait at this assembly point "to be resettled in the east" and soon gained knowledge that this meant they were being evacuated to work camps in Poland. Days later, on 26 February 1941, Herbert and Maximillian were brought to the train station, given food, and loaded into regular passenger trains with some 1,000 other Jews from the city, including Harry and Mia Gruenberg's aunt Berta and uncle Isidor Helwing, and Gertrude Vulkan's parents, Leopold and Mathilde Vulkan. They were sent out with the third mass transport of Viennese Jews to Poland, the second and last transport from Vienna to the ghetto Opole, to which in the month of February 1941 the Germans deported a total of 2,003 persons.[14]

---

[14] A few deportees managed to escape from these ghettos and return to Vienna, but the majority died of starvation or disease or were later transferred to a concentration camp or death camp and murdered. There were twenty-eight known survivors from the Opole ghetto. Elizabeth Guttmann (b. 1925), Regine Tuter (b. 1923), and brothers Herbert (b. 1927) and Maximillian Kaufmann (b. 1925), along with their mother

News of their transport came suddenly and without warning, but neither brother became too anxious about this major transition in their lives; it appeared to be just another unpleasant change, when they had already been forced to move many times, "first to move in with one other family, then all of us in with other families." By February 1941 they were living crammed together with almost forty other people. They also did not worry about leaving anything behind because they did not have much to bring with them, almost everything had already been taken. Finally, the boys did not fear their new and unknown destination because they had received mail from aunts and uncles who had gone before them -- explaining that they were in a Jewish town, a sort of ghetto. This correspondence with family reassured them that they would manage wherever they were being sent.[15]

While for some deportees, particularly younger individuals like Maximillian and Herbert, the transport to Opole was just another unpleasant event, for others it marked their destruction: the point at which their entire family unit began to unravel. Most deportees as well as their immediate and extended family members experienced panic and terrible unrest due to these sudden notices to "resettle in the east." The deportation of Isidor and Berta Helwing, for example, and the letters which followed, did not ease the

---

Jeanette Kaufmann, were five of the twenty-eight known survivors. Regine, Elizabeth, Herbert, and Maximillian were the only four survivors of this ghetto to have recorded oral testimonies with the Survivors of the Shoah Visual History Foundation (SOSVHF) in Los Angeles, California. See, Regine, C., 1995. "Interview by Survivors of the Shoah Visual History Foundation," Los Angeles, CA, USA, January 10. Interview Code 00751, Tapes 1-3 and Elizabeth, G., 1996. "Interview by Survivors of the Shoah Visual History Foundation," Dobbs Ferry, NY, USA, May 16. Interview Code 15247, Tapes 1-5; Maximillian K., (date currently unavailable). "Interview by Survivors of the Shoah Visual History Foundation," (location currently unavailable). Interview Code 07225; Herbert K., (date currently unavailable). "Interview by Survivors of the Shoah Visual History Foundation," (location currently unavailable). Interview Code 01867.

[15] Herbert K., (date currently unavailable). "Interview by Survivors of the Shoah Visual History Foundation," (location currently unavailable). Interview Code 01867 Maximillian K., (date currently unavailable). "Interview by Survivors of the Shoah Visual History Foundation," (location currently unavailable). Interview Code 07225.

family's worries, but prompted an intensification of fear among those relatives left behind in Vienna, as well as those already situated abroad.

Berta Helwing's brother, Simel Blaustein, was among those Jews left behind in Vienna whose daily lives were affected greatly by these first deportations to Poland. Simel had been writing letters to his relative Harry Gruenberg in the United States since 1938 and for three years had focused on the central concern of Viennese Jews during that time: emigration. By the winter of 1941, however, his letters took on a new tone; his life in Vienna had reached a significant turning point. On the very date that his sister Berta and her husband Isidor were deported to Opole (26 February 1941), he sat down to write a letter to Harry. A week later, on 4 March 1941, he wrote again. In these two letters, he showed desperation for the first time. Pleading for strong affidavits and ship tickets to America, he also requested ship tickets and landing money for Shanghai, demonstrating that it was terribly urgent -- anything to get out! Then, in code, he wrote of the recent deportation of his sister and brother-in-law: "Isidor and Berta had been taken *to Uncle Samuel*."[16] Harry understood what this meant, but only to a limited degree. He understood that Isidor and Berta had been forced to leave Vienna and move to Poland, because Uncle Samuel lived in Lemberg (L'vov).[17] However, Harry did not know that his relatives were being deported to a closed Jewish ghetto in Opole, where there was no work and where they would be left either to starve or to die of disease, if they were not transferred to a death camp first. Neither he nor Simel could know or understand that

---

[16] Letters from Simel Blaustein, 26 February 1941; 4 March 1941. Gruenberg Family Archive, Weston, Massachusetts.

[17] Harry Gruenberg, unpublished memoirs. Gruenberg Family Archive, Weston, Massachusetts.

their deportation was part of the Germans' greater plan to solve their Jewish question by means of ghettoization and annihilation.[18]

And yet, while Simel did not know the extent of the danger that he faced, his letters to America revealed that he sensed great terror in connection with his relatives' "resettlement." He feared being selected to make such a move himself; thus the deportations had heightened his already present fear of staying in Vienna. In a letter dated March 4 he expressed that getting out was now a "matter of life and death."[19] Safe in the U.S., Harry sensed the danger that Simel was in and wanted to help him but, a recent émigré himself, was helpless to do so.[20] When no further letters from Simel arrived, and Harry had no way of knowing what had happened to him, this sense of helplessness began to carve its mark on Harry's psyche, too.

News of the transports had traveled far and was taking a toll on relatives in Vienna and in safety elsewhere. Isidor and Berta Helwing had family in Vienna, Harry in the U.S., and their only son, fifteen-year-old Kurt, lived in England. The transfer to Opole forced Berta and Isidor into limited communication with Kurt, who had left on a Kindertransport in 1938. For nearly three years -- until the time of their deportation -- they had struggled to keep in contact with him and it had been a great challenge. They sent numerous letters to which they had not received any reply. About three months before their separation with their son became final, a relative reported Berta and Isidor as

---

[18] The transport carrying Isidor and Berta Helwing to Opole on 26 February 1941 is confirmed by the *Documentations Archiv des Oesterreichischen Wiederstandes* (see, *www.doew.at*) and a recent Holocaust education project, *A Letter to the Stars* (*www.lettertothestars.at*). Both foundations are based in Vienna, Austria.

[19] Harry Gruenberg, unpublished memoirs. Gruenberg Family Archive, Weston, Massachusetts.

[20] These letters mark Simel's final words. Simel and his wife Gittel were deported sometime in August or September of 1942, according to family letters and other documents sent to Harry Gruenberg. There are no official listings for Simel Blaustein (16 June 1869) or Agathe (Gittel) Blaustein, nee Menkes (2 February 1872) in the Central Database at Yad Vashem, or at *www.doew.at*. The exact date and destination of their transport is unknown.

"inconsolable about Kurtl."[21] In February 1941, like so many other parents on the transport to Opole, they were finally forced to face a parent's greatest fear: losing a child. The ability to establish contact with relatives outside the Reich would be even more restricted from Opole than it had been in Vienna, and Isidor and Berta boarded the train without word from their son.

The Helwings feared lost communication with their only son; Leopold and Mathilde Vulkan mourned the separation from their two teenage daughters, Gertrude and Edith. Leopold had moved the girls to France in 1938 in order to provide them with a safe haven, envisioning at the time not only their immediate safety but that by the end of the year he and his wife would join them in Paris. He could not know that his return to Vienna would ultimately cost him his life, nor the effect this would have on his children: that for a period they would consider themselves abandoned. By the time the Germans deported Leopold and Mathilde to Opole in February 1941, Gertrude and Edith were safe and living in the United States, but like Kurt Helwing and so many other children forced into separation from their parents, they did not have an easy time of it; they struggled to carry on. The girls lived with a relative who was not prepared for the responsibility of providing for two teenagers but had nevertheless agreed to do so because of the dire situation in Nazi-occupied Vienna. Leopold had bribed this relative to send affidavits for his daughters and to shelter them. Still, the relative could not or would not cope. The girls were charged rent and were forced to leave the house on the eve of Rosh Hashanah, 1941. This was almost six months after Leopold and Mathilde had been deported from Vienna, utterly ignorant of the difficulties their daughters faced as foreigners in the United States.

---

[21] Gruenberg family letters 1938-1941, 4 November 1940. Gruenberg Family Archive, Weston, Massachusetts.

In any case, there was absolutely nothing they could have done. Communication between the parents and their daughters had ceased: deportation to Opole had made the separation permanent.[22]

Responses: Private vs. Community

The transports created another sudden and unexpected rupture in the daily lives of those who were deported and their immediate and extended families. The Germans were in the process of changing their policy from ghettoization and expulsion to deportation. While neither the deportees nor the relatives in Vienna or abroad knew exactly what the future held, they sensed great danger. By the winter of 1941 those left in Vienna had little chance to emigrate. Ports were closed, funding was limited, and many were simply too ill or elderly. Until this time, they had lived off the dream of getting out and reuniting with their families. Suddenly this prospect shattered. People did not know if, when, or how they would see or contact their family members again. With these persisting uncertainties, daily life became an increased struggle for many of Vienna's Jews.

The IKG, an institution, was affected by the deportations differently than the Kaufmanns, Helwings, or Vulkans and their extended families. Throughout the spring and summer of 1941 the Germans ordered no further deportations to the east. On the other hand, foreign aid committees continued to supply the IKG with funding to support emigration and welfare. Emigration hit its lowest total between January and June 1941-- only 1,194 persons were dispatched, the smallest number to emigrate from Vienna in a

---

[22] For Gertrude, the inconsolable trauma set in much earlier. It was not the difficulties of her escape, or of starting a new life abroad that struck hardest. Rather, it was the initial realization that she would never see her parents again. When she heard the news that Hitler took Czechoslovakia, she knew her parents -- both Czech citizens -- would no longer be able to get out of Vienna. "I was terribly unhappy. I cried so much in France, I just can't cry anymore." Gertrude Silberstern, phone interview with the author, Washington, D.C., May 2007. See also Gertrude, S., 1998. "Interview by Survivors of the Shoah Visual History Foundation," Cranbury, NJ, USA, May 28. Interview Code 42400, Tapes 1-7.

six-month period since the Germans had annexed Austria three years earlier (459 fled to other European countries, 429 to the United States, 243 to South and Central America, and 63 to other places overseas) -- but what mattered to the officials of the IKG was that individuals were still getting out.[23] As late as February 1941, as the first deportations rolled to Poland, the IKG remained busy investigating emigration options. On 3 and 6 February trains left Vienna for Siberia carrying Jews (16 persons and 9 persons, respectively) with a final destination of San Domingo.[24] On 9 and 17 February, Murmelstein sent letters to the American consulate in Vienna with the names of Vienna's Jews who had reserved berths on the ships "Sera Pinto" and "Magallanes" departing from Lisbon, Portugal in March 1941 and on the "Heian Maru" and the "Hikawa Maru" to depart from Kobe, Japan in April 1941. As director of the emigration department of the IKG, Murmelstein pleaded with the consulate to expedite the visa process for these people who already had reserved ship tickets; he stressed that the situation was urgent. On 17 March 1941 he asked the consulate to please expand the quota number for Jews in the coming months, and explained that the IKG in turn would see that every person with a visa also managed to obtain a ship ticket.[25]

Although the number of emigrants departing during this time was vanishingly small-- far fewer than the number of Jews deported -- rescuing even one person was

---

[23] These figures are based on the IKG report from July 1941. This is the last IKG report to address emigration and the last report compiled for the Foreign Aid Committees. It is also the first report since May 1938 that is in German instead of English, and it is uncertain whether the report was ever translated and sent abroad. See USHMM film # 295, IKG- A/W 115, *Tatigkeitsberichte in Tabellenform (Anschlag?) fuer die Zeit vom 01. Jaenner-30. Juni 1941.*

[24] USHMM film # 1264, IKG- A/W 2686, Auswanderung, Abfertigung, *San Domingo "C" (Listen der Transportteilnehmer).* For further information on the emigration to San Domingo and a complete nameslist of all applicants, including photographs, see USHMM film # 1264, IKG- A/W 2492, 3, Auswanderung, Abfertigung, *Propositions for the Emigration to San Domingo, March 1940.*

[25] USHMM film # 1264, IKG- A/W 2954, Auswanderung, Abfertigung, *Emigration nach den USA, Amerikanisches Konsulat Wien 1938-1940.*

ample motivation for the IKG to press forward on its mission. In a report complied in July 1941, four months after the last deportation, with emigration at an all-time low, and against terrible odds, the IKG leaders demonstrated this diligence: "The daily duties of the IKG revolve upon the following: 1.) To facilitate the emigration of those Jews belonging to the community who are fit for emigration; 2.) To secure and provide daily bread, shelter, and clothing; and 3.) To offer medical assistance to the sick, and homes for the elderly and disabled."[26] Even after the Germans had ordered the IKG to organize and execute the first mass deportations to the east, the leaders stayed focused on the rescue and expressed hope for the future. They were so focused on the rescue operation that they simply could not see how it had been strangled.

Dependence upon Foreign Aid

Foreign aid played a significant role in the IKG's response to the German oppressors. In fact, foreign aid may have been the single factor that made it possible for the IKG to look past its involvement in the recent deportations and stay focused on rescue. The IKG assumed responsibility for approximately 44,000 Jews[27] as of 30 June 1941. In return, it continued to ask for their complete cooperation and assistance: "Our members should

---

[26] USHMM film # 295, IKG- A/W 115, *Tatigkeitsberichte in Tabellenform (Anschlag?) fuer die Zeit vom 01. Jaenner-30. Juni 1941.*

[27] This number includes up to 4,600 *Nichtglaubensjuden* ("racial" but non-professing Jews). For details see Table 11: "Distribution of Jewish Stars throughout the City." The population count of 44,000 is derived from four separate IKG reports: USHMM film #295, IKG- A/W 115, *Tatigkeitsberichte in Tabellenform [Anschlag?] fuer die Zeit vom 01. Jaenner-30. Juni 1941;* IKG- A/W 132, *Israelitische Kultusgeminde Vienna. Survey on Nineteenhundred-forty;* film #UZ27, IKG- A/W2663, slide 0628; film #288, IKG- A/W 466, 1-2. *Ausgabe von Judenkennzichen. 09.1941-10.1941.*). Jonny Moser provides a different count for this time: 44,000 *Glaubensjuden*, plus an additional 9,000 *Nichtglaubensjuden*, for a total "Jewish" population of 53,000. See Table 31 in Moser, *Demographie der jüdischen Bevölkerung Österreichs,* 46. Moser's figures contradict the number of stars distributed on 18 September 1941, 4,600 of which, went to *Nichtglaubensjuden.*

cooperate with and be willing to make sacrifices for the community."[28] The IKG deemed

almost half the community, some 22,000 persons, unsuitable for emigration because they

were too old or too sick, but it intended to provide for them with full care in old-age

homes and hospitals. By contrast, there were still 2,412 young and healthy boys and girls

under the age of eighteen[29] -- a small percentage of the 32,750 children and young adults

in this community of 181,778 souls in March 1938 -- plus another 18,000 persons whom

the IKG intended to help emigrate.[30] The community was still disproportionately aged

and gendered, with 19,691 persons over sixty years old and almost 10,000 more females

than males (26,657 to 16,343);[31] the single largest demographic was women over forty-

five, comprising almost 21,000 of the total of 44,000 persons in the community. In the

age bracket from forty-five to sixty, the number of females (9,540) was nearly double that

of males (4,835). At this time the community also cared for some *Nichtglaubensjuden*

("racial" but non-professing Jews), *Mischlinge*, and Jews in mixed-marriages.

As long as foreign aid continued to support the IKG's emigration and welfare

costs, the leaders of the community turned a blind eye to how skewed these statistics

were and what they revealed about the past and the future of Viennese Jewry. These

constructive external relationships shielded them from acknowledging the precarious

---

[28] USHMM film # 295, IKG- A/W 115, *Tatigkeitsberichte in Tabellenform (Anschlag?) fuer die Zeit vom 01. Jaenner-30. Juni 1941.*

[29] Parents and the IKG hoped to organized the emigration of nearly all children. Some children who remained in 1941 were physically handicapped or ill. These children were cared for in one of the IKG's homes for children, such as: Orphanage for boys and girls, 19th District- Bauernfeldgasse 40; Emergency-shelter for Jewish babies and little children, 2nd District- Unter Augartenstrasse 35; Creche, 2nd District-Mohapelgasse; Lele Bondi-Heim for children of 6-14 years, 2nd District- Boecklinstrasse; Home "Zukunft" for boys over 14, 9th District- Gruene Torgasse 27; and Krügerheim for girls over 14, 2nd District- Malzgasse 7. See USHMM film # 294, IKG-A/W 126, *Report of the Vienna Jewish Community. A description of the activity of the Israelitische Kultusgemeinde Wien in the period from May 2nd 1938- December 31st 1939 (2 Exemplare).*

[30] USHMM film # 295, IKG-A/W 119, *Auswanderung, Umschichtung, Fuersorge 02.05.1938- 31.07.1939 (Bericht, deutsch, englisch, franzoesisch, 2 Examplare).*

[31] USHMM film #295, IKG- A/W 115, *Tatigkeitsberichte in Tabellenform (Anschlag?) fuer die Zeit vom 01. Jaenner-30. Juni 1941.*

situation in which they had become trapped as they complied with demands from the Nazi authorities by ordering the full cooperation of their community members and begging for financial aid from abroad. They did not know if and when the deportation trains would roll again,[32] nor that they would again be responsible for organizing and financing the transports. Moreover, psychologically, they refused to accept this possible reality.

The IKG's job at that point was to carry on with the rescue work and, to this end, the foreign relief agencies aided them immensely. All forty-four thousand Jews residing in Vienna in June 1941, those hoping to emigrate and those expecting to be cared for, were almost completely dependent upon the support of the IKG, which in turn, was dependent upon support from abroad. Financial support from the two main organizations, the JDC and the Council for German Jewry,[33] had enabled the community to rescue over half the population through emigration and still manage to provide for those left behind. The JDC, for example, between 1938 and 1939 sent $685,461.63 into Vienna for the purpose of emigration, during 1940 it sent another $462,257.08,[34] and between January and June 1941, it sent $302,894.[35] As we have seen, the community used this money to seek out immigration opportunities; to provide retraining and language courses for potential emigrants; and to cover the financial costs of emigration,

---

[32] Pierre H. Secher, *Left Behind in Nazi Vienna* (Jefferson, North Carolina: McFarland and Company, Inc., 2004), 303.

[33] Prior to 1941 the Jewish Community of Vienna was in contact with many foreign aid committees, in addition to the "JDC." For a complete listing of these agencies see chapter three. Original source, USHMM film # 295, IKG- A/W 121, *The Household of the Jewish Community of Vienna for the months of November and December 1938.*

[34] USHMM film # 295, IKG- A/W 132, *Israelitische Kultusgeminde Vienna. Survey on Nineteenhundredforty.*

[35] The JDC funded emigration and welfare for the IKG from 1938 until 1941. USHMM film # 295, IKG-A/W 115, *Tatigkeitsberichte in Tabellenform (Anschlag?) fuer die Zeit vom 01. Jaenner-30. Juni 1941.*

such as travel and landing fees.[36] The IKG also used outside funds to sustain an entire

social welfare system that had been operating since the community organization was

reopened under Nazi supervision in May 1938. External support allowed the community

to expand its resources immensely since 1938, increasing the number of old-age homes

from one (housing 439 persons) to four (1,295) in 1939 and from four to eight (1,584) in

1940.[37] It also expanded the Jewish hospital in 1941 to include a separate children's

wing; maintained kindergartens, elementary schools, secondary schools, and preparatory

courses; and operated six full-care institutions for children (an orphanage for boys and

girls, nineteenth district, Bauernfeldgasse 40; an emergency shelter for Jewish babies and

little children from birth to six years, second district, Unter Augartenstrasse 35; a crèche

for ages zero to six years, second district, Mohapelgasse; a home, Lele Bondi-Heim, for

ages six to fourteen years, second district, Boecklinstrasse; a home, Zukunft, for boys

over fourteen, ninth district, Gruene Torgasse 27; and a home, Krueger-Heim, for girls

over fourteen, second district, Malzgasse 7).[38] At this time in 1941 the IKG also ran

fourteen soup kitchens throughout the city -- feeding twelve thousand people per day –

and provided over thirty thousand persons with regular cash support.[39]

---

[36] USHMM film #295, IKG-A/W 142, *Report of the Vienna Jewish Community, March-April 1939(2 Exemplare).*

[37] USHMM film #295, IKG- A/W 131, *Israelitische Kultusgeminde Vienna. Activity During Twelve Months of War, 01.09.1939-31.08.1940.*

[38] The Krügerheim on Malzgasse later turned into a collection point for Jews deported to the east. See chapter eight. Also see, USHMM film # 294, IKG-A/W 126, *Report of the Vienna Jewish Community. A description of the activity of the Israelitische Kultusgemeinde Wien in the period from May 2nd 1938-December 31st 1939 (2 Exemplare).*

[39] USHMM film # 295, IKG- A/W 132, *Israelitische Kultusgeminde Vienna. Survey on Nineteenhundredforty.* Most of these institutions were shut down in 1943 when the IKG was dismantled in November 1942. See, USHMM film # 294, IKG- A/W 117, *Taetigkeitsbericht fuer das Jahr 1943 (2 Exemplare).*

Table 10: "IKG Relief Work Supported by the JDC"

SOUP KITCHEN

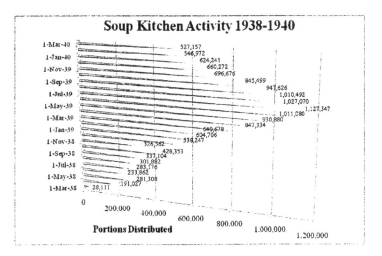

Source: Photograph, USHMM film # 295, IKG- A/W 132, *Israelitische Kultusgeminde Vienna. Survey on Nineteenhundredforty*; Chart by T.Weiss, based on IKG- A/W 119, 120,125,126, 130. 131.

Balancing a careful relationship between the foreign aid committees and the German authorities for three years, the IKG had managed to rescue the great majority of its people. The tightly run social welfare system had helped potential emigrants feel assured that their sick or elderly relatives left behind would be cared for, and this encouraged them to leave.[40] The IKG kept detailed records of how foreign aid was distributed between emigration costs and welfare needs and they sent updates to the JDC regularly. Their astounding results encouraged the JDC and other foreign aid committees to continue sending money, and the IKG, in return, to thank them profusely. In a report compiled in September 1940 they wrote: "The American Joint Distribution Committee have proved comprehension and readiness of help for the Jews living in Vienna likewise in the course of the past year in a special measure, for which ten thousands of emigrated and supported persons are greatly indebted to them."[41] Loewenherz, director of the IKG, and Murmelstein, his direct subordinate, understood that without the financial support from abroad, their community would not have been able to survive. In a second report dated July 1941 they wrote: "It has only been possible to carry on with the emigration and the social care by means of the help of the organizations abroad, who put landing- and show-money at disposal, the counter value of which was used for the fares, for cash support, for the soup kitchen and other institutions of social care."[42]

---

[40] In a community report from Januay 1941, the IKG explained that nurses stood by day and night to aid solitary sick people whose relatives had emigrated. See USHMM film # 295, IKG- A/W 132, *Israelitische Kultusgeminde Vienna. Survey on Nineteenhundredforty.*

[41] USHMM film #295, IKG- A/W 131, *Israelitische Kultusgeminde Vienna. Activity During Twelve Months of War, 01.09.1939-31.08.1940.*Original English.

[42] USHMM film # 295, IKG- A/W 115, *Tatigkeitsberichte in Tabellenform (Anschlag?) fuer die Zeit vom 01. Jaenner-30. Juni 1941.*

Fueling the Aim to Rescue

In the summer of 1941, when the IKG leaders drew their charts documenting the

emigration and welfare activities from January through June 1941, they provided precise

statistics, as usual. During that six-month period, however, the Germans had ordered

them to carry out the "resettlement" of some five thousand community members to

Lublin. There was no mention of this in the report. The reduction of the community by

this number of people was not even calculated in the final count of 44,000 persons.[43] The

IKG officers who compiled the report focused on their past achievements and their

ambition to save the community; they believed that the longer they could receive money

from the outside world, the longer they could facilitate emigration and sustain their

community from within. Their ambition was to rescue the majority. They managed this

successfully. At the same time, they were responsible for having coordinated and carried

out the deportation of some five thousand others. The leaders did not know the

implications of these first deportations to the east, what ultimately would be the fate of

those transported, nor did they have any alternative but to follow this next German

demand. But they knew from the Nisko experience in October 1939 and from the first

letters they received from Jews in Opole, that the conditions in these places were

inadequate for human survival. Still, they continued their work helping the Germans to

forcibly "resettle" Jewish families in the east and sought to conceal this aspect of their

activities from the foreign aid committees.

---

[43] This count, unlike those before it, included approximately 5,000 *Nichtglaubensjuden,* who made up for
the difference of 5,000 persons deported. In a separate report, drawn up explicitly for the Nazi authorities
for an exhibition in March 1941, the IKG listed the total number of community members at 39,984 persons.
See chart, "Die Jüdische Wanderung aus der Ostmark," main exhibition, United States Holocaust Memorial
Museum, Washington, D.C.

The Imposition of the Jewish Star in September 1941

Intent upon rescuing as many Jews as possible, the IKG had learned to endure

various Nazi restrictions, regulations and decrees, and to adapt to the Nazi apparatus. To

facilitate the deportation and ghettoization process, the Germans in September 1941

ordered all Jews in greater Germany to purchase, sew onto their clothing, and wear a

yellow Star of David. Again, the Jewish community would be responsible for ensuring

that this order came into practice and that every Jew cooperated.

For years historians have recognized the imposition of the Jewish Star or

"Judenstern," as one of the most significant measures the Nazis took to dehumanize and

segregate Jews during the pre-genocidal period of the Holocaust. In almost all areas of

Holocaust education the star has become one of the most frequently used images and has

become a symbol for Nazi persecution of Jews. Herbert Rozenkranz, who has written

extensively on the plight of Austria's Jews during the Holocaust, is one of the many

historians who consider the star the turning point of Nazi persecution. In his article, "The

Anschluss and the Tragedy of Austrian Jewry 1938-1945," he referred to the star as "the

hardest blow," suggesting that the mark/badge was not only a highly significant change

for the Jews of Austria, but the most demeaning and discriminatory measure taken

against them through September 1941. "The hardest blow," he wrote, "was the

introduction of the yellow star. On September 8, 1941, Loewenherz was ordered by

Guenther of the R.S.H.A. in Berlin to ensure that the community saw to it that by

September 19, all Jews in the 'Ostmark' … wore the Jewish badge, consisting of a Jewish Star in yellow outlined in black, with the inscription 'Jew' in black."[44]

Illustration 25: "Forced to Wear the Yellow Star of David"

Source: Institut für Zeitgeschichte, Wien; *http://bob.swe.uni-linz.ac.at/vwm/betrifft/58/Rabinovici58.html*

How did Vienna's forty-four thousand Jews react and respond to this newest humiliation in September 1941?[45] How did it affect their daily lives? Was it a critical moment in their historical experience -- "the hardest blow" -- as Rosenkranz stated? Did

[44] See Herbert Rozenkranz, "The Anschluss and the Tragedy of Austrian Jewry 1938-1945," in Josef Frankel ed., *The Jews of Austria: Essays on their Life, History and Destruction* (London: Valentine Mitchell,1967), 480.

[45] In the last report of the Jewish community from July 1941, forty-four thousand Jews are remaining in Vienna. This number is the closest calculation to how many Jews existed in Vienna September 1941. See, USHMM film # 295, IKG- A/W 115, *Tatigkeitsberichte in Tabellenform (Anschlag?) fuer die Zeit vom 01. Jaenner-30. Juni 1941.*

they feel more isolated and endangered, now that they were physically marked? Or was it more, as Ruth Kluger described in her memoirs, that "it almost seemed appropriate at that time?"[46] Had Vienna's Jews adapted to the previous 250 anti-Jewish regulations,[47] and was this just one more to absorb?[48] On a practical level: How did community leaders, employees, and volunteers learn about the order and how did they carry it out? How did an ordinary Jewish family learn about and fulfill the order? What do survivors recall about this in their memoirs and testimonies? Examining the daily lives of the victims, recognizing them as ordinary individuals and not automatons, we begin to understand what transpired at this critical point in the progression of the genocide. Official IKG reports from 1941 shed light on the victims' response to the imposition of the Jewish star.[49]

Community Responses

Like the winter deportations and most other Nazi demands, this new Nazi order was forced upon the victims to carry out and it soon became a planned campaign which required a huge infrastructure. Just as the Germans had forced the Jews to paint a yellow star or the word "Jude" on their storefronts, to adopt the middle name "Sarah" or "Israel," to pay for the destruction wrought by the November pogrom, and to fund their own

---

[46] Ruth Kluger, *Still Alive, A Holocaust Girlhood Remembered* (New York, The Feminist Press at the City University of New York, 2001), 49.

[47] See George E. Berkley, *Vienna and Its Jews: The Tragedy of Success: 1880s-1980s.* (Cambridge, MA. Lanham, Md., Abt Books; Madison Books, 1988), 286.

[48] The Jews had been marked many times before under the Nazi occupation-- as early as April 1938 Jews were forced to designate the windows of their store fronts with large Jewish stars and the word "Jude"; that summer Switzerland saw to it that Jews' identity papers (passports) would be stamped with a large red "J" to avoid further unwanted immigration; and a little over a year later, the Germans decided that all Jews would adopt the "Jewish" middle-name "Sarah" or "Israel." See, USHMM film # N/A, IKG- A/W 134, 2, *Zirkulare der Amstdirektion und des Amtsvorstands an saemtliche Abteilungen bzw. Alle Angestellten und Mitarbeiter, 6 April 1939.*

[49] See USHMM microfilm #288, IKG- A/W 466, 1-2, *Ausgabe von Judenkennzichen. 09.1941-10.1941.*

expulsion -- so too did they force them to carry out this measure of segregation. The IKG leaders kept records of this process in September and October 1941 and they bear witness to how stressful and taxing it was, and to how much organization and cooperation it required.[50]

Responding promptly, the leadership of the IKG devised a plan to carry out Reinhard Heydrich's decree *Reichgesetzbatt 1. S 547, Polizeiverordnung ueber die Kennzeichnung der Juden*. Benjamin Murmelstein held a meeting with community officers on 9 September 1941 which yielded the, "guidelines for the execution of the police order over the marking of the Jews from 1 September 1941."[51] This report showed the overwhelming nature of the task and the great responsibility the community leaders shouldered. Dated 10 September 1941, the guidelines comprised six typed pages of extremely dense and detailed information, broken down into seven main sections: 1. Basics; 2. Provisions for Implementation; 3. Distribution to Institutions and Employees of the IKG; 4. Dispersal outside of Vienna; 5. Announcement; 6. Organization – for Jews and Non-Professing Jews; and 7. Assignment of the Agenda. The leaders circulated the guidelines through all offices and institutions of the IKG, because to fulfill the decree in time required the help of many community employees; they had only eight days before the law was to go into effect on 19 September. Making the task even more stressful, the guidelines revealed that the community would not receive the material for the stars until

---

[50] See"Amtsbetrieb im Zuge der Vernichtung," section 1, "Segregation und Kennzeichnen oder Ein 'Judenstern' fuer 10 Pfennig" in Doron Rabinovici, *Instanzen der Ohnmacht: Wien 1938-1945: der Weg zum Judenrat* (Frankfurt am Main, Juedischer Verlag, 2000), 243-251.
[51] See frame #0086, USHMM microfilm #288, IKG- A/W 466, 1-2. *Ausgabe von Judenkennzichen. 09.1941-10.1941.*

17 September, giving them just over twenty-four hours to make, pack, count, and distribute them to the entire community, 44,000 strong.[52]

Jews in Vienna learned about Heydrich's newest decree as they heard most other news: by word of mouth. Information also traveled via community bulletins or the one remaining newspaper available to Jews, the Vienna edition of the Berlin-based *Nachtrichtenblatt* (which as we have seen, replaced the *Zionistische Rundschau* following the November Pogrom). On Friday, 12 September 1941 the *Jüdisches Nachtrichtenblatt* attracted the attention of its readers with an oversized headline "Official Proclamation!" and released the Nazis' newest regulation: "It is forbidden for all Jews over six years of age to appear in public without wearing a Jewish star (as of 19 September 1941)."[53]

---

[52] "The economic department of the Jewish Community Vienna, that is, the central depot, is being entrusted with the acquisition and safekeeping of the Jewish stars on the 17th of this month. The delivery of the stars to the individual institutions, including the issuing offices, will be processed with delivery orders. The economic department holds each issuing office accountable for providing its fees and will provide the account auditing office with a total summary by the 26th of the month. The central depot is encouraged to count the stars on the evening of the 17th and every 50 stars, meaning every 100 pieces, they should pack up separately." USHMM microfilm #288, IKG- A/W 466, 1-2. *Ausgabe von Judenkennzichen. 09.1941-10.1941.*

[53] *Jüdisches Nachtrichtenblatt* (Ausgabe Wien, 12 September 1941), 1.

Illustration 26: "Official Proclamation! *Jüdisches Nachrichtenblatt*, 12 September 1941"

Source: *Jüdisches Nachrichtenblatt* (Ausgabe Wien, 12 September 1941), 1.

The article in the *Jüdisches Nachtrichtenblatt* focused on what the Nazis demanded of the Jews and advice from community leaders as to how to meet those demands. The front page of the paper reproduced a copy of the decree as it was released in Berlin and published in the *Reichgesetzblatt* on 5 September 1941. The decree concluded with a typed signature from Heydrich, head of the Reich Main Security Office (RSHA). The decree stipulated who was required to wear the new badge. The punishment for attempting to hide the star or circumvent the order was a fine of RM 150 or up to six weeks in jail.

The article presented clear and concise directions for how Jews should comply with the German order. These were similar to Murmelstein's guidelines for distributing the star, which he had circulated through the community offices two days earlier. The head of the household was to locate the issuing office where he would need to pick up stars for his family exactly one week from that date, i.e., on Friday, 18 September. The head of household was to find the appropriate office according to the district he lived in and the first letter of his last name. He would need money, identity papers in the form of current *Reichsfettkarte* (food rations cards), and a signed written statement declaring receipt of the star. The stars were not expensive, only ten pfennig (RM .10) apiece, but they still had to be purchased. To avoid confusion, the newspaper printed an exact model of the written statement that needed to be turned in. [54] On a piece of paper the size of a postcard the recipient was to write: "I hereby confirm that according to the decree of 1 September 1941, I have received one star." It needed to be signed and dated, and include his address.

---

[54] *Jüdisches Nachtrichtenblatt* (Ausgabe Wien, 12 September 1941), 1. See also, USHMM microfilm #288, IKG- A/W 466, 1-2. *Ausgabe von Judenkennzichen. 09.1941-10.1941.*

Illustration 27: "Sample Written Statement as printed in the Jüdisches Nachrichtenblatt"

Ich bestätige, ein Stück des in der Verordnung vom 1. September 1941 vorgeschriebenen Judenkennzeichens erhalten zu haben.

Wien, am 18. September 1941.

Unterschrift:

Adresse:

Source: *Jüdisches Nachrichtenblatt* (Ausgabe Wien, 12 September 1941), 1.

Harry Gruenberg's sister Mia, and parents, Leo and Elka, still lived in Vienna at this time. Mia, now sixteen years old, had been unable to follow her brother to England as she had hoped. Leo and Elka feared selection to "resettle" in the east, as had been the case with their relatives Isidor and Berta Helwing. And Harry by this time had been transferred to an internment camp in Canada and was unaware of much of what was going on in Vienna. During the previous year, the family had been forced to leave their home on Alserstrasse 12/22 (Harry's childhood residence). Fortunately, they had found a new place to live not too far away, on Botzmanngasse 12g (also in the ninth district). When Leo corresponded with his son for the last time, he explained that the family had moved and, to comfort him, added that they had found a "nice apartment" and felt "quite at home."[55] One wonders how they felt over a year later when the Germans imposed *Reichgesetzbatt 1. S 547*. On 18 September 1941, Leo, as the head of the household, was responsible for obtaining stars for his wife, daughter, and himself. After reading the Jewish newspaper, he found that the issuing office for persons living in the eighth and

---

[55] Leo Gruenberg letters to his son Harry do not depict an accurate description of life in Vienna at this time. Leo clearly tried to calm Harry's worries. Gruenberg family letters 1938-1941, 1 August 1940. Gruenberg Family Archive, Weston, Massachusetts.

ninth districts -- whose last names began with the letters E through M -- was the *Waisenhaus* on Grüne Torgasse 26.[56] Grüne Torgasse was also in the ninth district, not far from Boltzmanngasse. Leo also needed to bring thirty pfennig (RM .30) with him, three identity cards, and three written statements, one each from his wife, his daughter, and himself.

If the directions appeared straightforward, fulfilling them may not have been. What if Leo had misread the instructions in the newspaper and showed up at the wrong office, forgot to bring one of the requirements, or filled out the written declaration incorrectly? How might this have affected the lives of his wife, his daughter, and himself, and how would this have affected the entire community? Leo was just <u>one</u> of forty-four thousand individuals for whom the IKG assumed responsibility, who was instructed to obey this order and expected to carry it out properly.

Illustration 28: "Star Distribution at Grüne Torgasse 26, Internal IKG Memo, 17 September 1941"

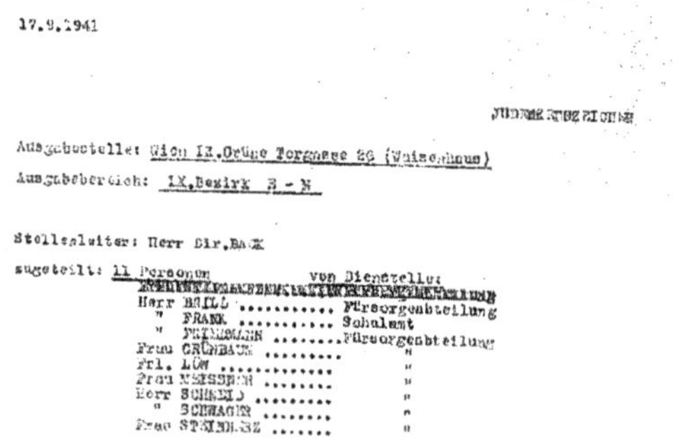
17.9.1941

JUDENKENNZEICHEN

Ausgabestelle: Wien IX.Grüne Torgasse 26 (Waisenhaus)

Ausgabebereich: IX.Bezirk E - M

Stellenleiter: Herr Dir.BACK

zugeteilt: 11 Personen von Dienststelle:

Herr BRILL .... Fürsorgeabteilung
" FRANK .... Schulamt
" FRIEDMANN .... Fürsorgeabteilung
Frau GRÜNBAUM .... "
Frl. LÖW .... "
Frau NEISSNER .... "
Herr SCHMID .... "
" SCHWAGER .... "
Frau STEINBERG .... "

Source: USHMM microfilm #288,
IKG- A/W 466, 1-2. *Ausgabe von Judenkennzichen*. 09.1941-10.1941 (Frame 0081).

---

[56] *Jüdisches Nachtrichtenblatt* (Ausgabe Wien, 12 September 1941), 1.

Details of the Process

According to Murmelstein's "Guidelines" and a series of additional documents
compiled by the IKG in mid-September 1941, the days leading up to the imposition of the
star mark on Friday 19 September took a great degree of planning. By Tuesday 16
September, leaders of the various Jewish institutions throughout Vienna -- the hospitals,
old-age homes, and children's homes -- had to provide the head economic office with a
count of how many stars they needed for the workers and patients in their institutions. For
example, Max Birnstein, administrative director of the IKG's old-age homes, sent a
report to the human resources department on 11 September 1941 requesting 2,857 stars.
Birnstein wrote on behalf of the one main old-age home (located in the ninth district on
Seegasse) and its seven branch institutions, three of which were located in the second
district, and one each in the third, fifteenth, nineteenth, and twentieth. He reported that of
the total, 1,973 were patients and 884 employees.

The community was provided with the material for the stars on Wednesday 17
September. It was responsible for ensuring that all the stars were distributed the following
day so that on Friday 19 September each of Vienna's 44,000 Jews was in compliance
with the new law. The material went to the central depot of the economic office, where
community workers counted and packed in preparation for distribution the next
morning.[57]

The community also compiled a list of all the IKG employees whom they called
up from their various departments to help with the distribution of the stars. The list
included the number of individuals from each of the departments (within the community

---

[57] See "Guidelines for the execution of the police order over the marking of the Jews from 1 September
1941," USHMM microfilm #288, IKG- A/W 466, 1-2. *Ausgabe von Judenkennzichen. 09.1941-10.1941.*

and institutions funded by the community) and their names. For example, two persons, Sucher and Pollatschek, were detailed from the Technical Office; one person, Kasten, from the medical advisory office; five people, Wottitz, Kohn, Lustig, Wolfsohn, and Meisei, from the foreign currency advisory office; and so on.[58] In total, 182 people were seconded for this effort: 92 employees from various IKG offices on Seitenstettengasse, plus 30 schoolteachers, 20 soup kitchen employees, 20 employees from the research offices of the emigration department, and 20 employees from the old-age homes and hospitals. The effort required the assistance and cooperation of the community's employees, regardless of their rank, function, or expertise.

From eight o'clock in the morning until half past eleven at night on Thursday 18 September those 182 workers labored in the locations designated for issuing the yellow stars. They had less than twenty-four hours to provide full compliance with the decree, and one mistake could throw off their entire system. They were prepared with 50 stamps with the letter "K" and with 15,000 postcard size papers for the written confirmations of receipt. First they collected fees (charging ten pfennig for stars that actually cost five, using the difference to cover any financial shortfall). Then they collected the recipients' identity cards (ration cards) and stamped a "K," short for *Kennzeichnen* or "marking" (referring to receipt of the yellow badge), next to the previously stamped "J," for *Jude* or Jew. Last they collected the written confirmations. They needed to keep an exact count of how many stars they sold and to submit this figure to the human resources department and the economic office the next day.[59] As they were charged with the task of distributing

---

[58] Each IKG department drew up a separate list of all employees involved with the star distribution on 18 September. USHMM microfilm #288, IKG- A/W 466, 1-2. *Ausgabe von Judenkennzichen. 09.1941-10.1941.*
[59] USHMM microfilm #288, IKG- A/W 466, 1-2. *Ausgabe von Judenkennzichen. 09.1941-10.1941.*

the stars, and confirming that each person had received one and was obeying the German order, it also fell to them to persuade all community members to cooperate with the order.[60]

Issuing offices were set up in seventeen locations for *Glaubensjuden* (Jews of faith) and three for *Nichtglaubensjuden* ("racial" but non-professing Jews).[61] These distribution sites were dispersed throughout the city's twenty districts-- in soup kitchens, school buildings, children's homes, a homeless shelter, a hospital entrance, and the cemetery. Each location had its own supervisor, appointed by the community, who was responsible for ensuring that the center had all necessary materials to carry out the order. The supervisors were the directors of the different IKG departments and institutions. For example, Dr. Max Birnstein, director of the old-age homes, served as the supervisor of the issuing office stationed in the main old-age home on Seegasse, in the ninth district. This issuing office distributed stars to heads of households from the eight and ninth districts whose last name began with the letters, N through Z. It also appears that this office supplied those in the old-age home with stars. Dr. Birnstein, however, was accountable both for the distribution to the local community members and for those individuals within his old age home. This was a heavy responsibility for one man.

The results of the distribution activities were compiled in two separate reports on Friday 19 September. One, a handwritten chart on graph paper, listed how many stars each location started with and the number dispensed each hour. The second report was a typed summary based on this chart, which was approved by the human resources

---

[60] It is likely that the final number of stars was passed from the human resources department and the economic office to the German authorities. There is no official record of this, however.
[61] USHMM microfilm #288, IKG- A/W 466, 1-2. *Ausgabe von Judenkennzichen. 09.1941-10.1941.* According to Rabinovici, there were nineteen different locations.

department and signed by Murmelstein. According to the statistics in these reports, 44,770 stars were distributed throughout Vienna on 18 September to 43,180 persons.[62] A total of 4,600 of these 44,770 stars were distributed to *Nichtglaubensjuden*, many of whom were in mixed-marriages. The highest number of issuing offices (nine) in one area was in the second district -- the district most densely populated with Jews. These nine locations started with 24,500 stars and distributed 20,100: 15,800 to people living in the second district and 4,300 to people living in the first district. They provided almost half of the population with stars, whereas the location at the Jewish cemetery, which serviced heads of households from the third, tenth, eleventh, and twenty-third districts, gave out only 1,330 stars, and the clothing bureau in the first district, which served Jews living the fourth and fifth districts of the city, distributed only 570.

The distribution of the star was a complex assignment for the IKG leaders, requiring the focused cooperation of its many offices, workers, volunteers, and members -- who, even at this late stage of the Nazi occupation, were living dispersed throughout the city. While most Jewish communities in central and eastern Europe were living in restricted areas when they were ordered to wear the yellow star, Vienna's Jews were not. Although most Jewish apartments had been aryanized by this time, and many Jews had been forced into all-Jewish apartment homes (primarily in the second district) pockets of Jewish life still existed everywhere. On the one hand, this meant that compared to Jewish leaders elsewhere, the IKG exercised a certain amount of additional freedom when it came to obeying Nazi orders. On the other hand, it had a greater task and responsibility

---

[62] The number 43,180 is according to a population count included on the list that is based on the number of food ration cards presently being used. This number is confirmed by the statistical report from July 1941, and the star districbution report of 1941. This number includes *Glaubensjuden* and *Nichtglaubensjuden*, and is the most reliable figure. See USHMM film # 295, IKG- A/W 115, *Tatigkeitsberichte in Tabellenform (Anschlag?) fuer die Zeit vom 01. Jaenner-30. Juni 1941.*

before it: it needed to ensure that all parts of the city were sufficiently covered. If one member of the community misunderstood or challenged the orders, the future of the whole community might be jeopardized.

Table 11: "Distribution of Jewish Stars throughout the City"

District of Vienna	Amount of Stars Purchased by Jews (*Glaubensjude*)
I.	4,300
II.	15,800
III., X., XI., XXIII.	1,330
IV., V.	570
VI., VII., XII-XV., XXIV.-V.	2,900
XIII., IX., XX., XXI.	7, 230
XVI., XVII.,XXVI.	310
XVIII., XIX.	500
Old Age Home	2,370
Hospital	1,690
Orphanage	170
IKG	3,000
Subtotal	40,170
	non-professing Jews (*Nichtglaubensjude*)
All Districts	4,600
Total	**44,770**

Source: Based on IKG Internal Document dated 19 September 1941,
USHMM microfilm #288, IKG- A/W 466, 1-2. *Ausgabe von Judenkennzichen. 09.1941-10.1941.*

The organization and effort of the Jewish community leaders and workers prevailed. On Friday 19 September, 43,180 Jews remaining in Vienna were prepared to meet the Germans' most recent demands. So long as they wore their new yellow badges, they were permitted to go out on the streets and about their business. Daily life resumed, but for some, simple activities like riding the tram or shopping became dangerous. Suddenly

Jews could be recognized a mile away, making them easy prey. The IKG leaders had worked hard to fulfill the German demand and they had done so in three short days. Their efficiency spared the community from additional punishment at the time, but ultimately left it more vulnerable in the face of the Nazi threat. The leaders did not know exactly what the stars would be used for or the impact they would have on the future, but they were also too afraid to question the authorities, or to decide to cease cooperating.

Individual Responses to the Star Marking

Contemporary reports, survivor testimonies, and survivor memoirs indicate that individuals within the community experienced this change similarly to their leadership. These sources suggest that Vienna's Jews did not experience the star as the "hardest blow," but rather as a further humiliation and inconvenience, neither of which were out of the ordinary at the time. Although people responded differently depending on their age and experiences both before and after, Ruth Kluger spoke loud for her community when she stated in her memoirs, "I can't say that I was unhappy about that star....Under the circumstances it seemed appropriate."[63] The disproportionately aged and gendered community of some 44,000 Jews was weak and struggling to get by in September 1941.

---

[63] See Ruth Kluger, *Still Alive, A Holocaust Girlhood Remembered* (New York, The Feminist Press at the City University of New York, 2001), 48. Also see, Siegfried, B., 1996. "Interview by Survivors of the Shoah Visual History Foundation," Baltimore, MD, USA, October 18. Interview Code 21190, Tapes 1-7. Siegfried Buchwalter was fifteen years old when the Germans imposed the decree. His life, like that of most boys his age in Vienna preceding this order, had been difficult. The Germans had deployed Siegfried to a forced labor detail in January 1940 and he filled road potholes with asphalt. The star marking came in September and he was deported to the Lodz ghetto in October 1941. He endured many hardships during those three years in Nazi-occupied Vienna and many more after deportation. He survived and, while reflecting upon his experiences years later, he saw the star as a minor event in his history. In his oral testimony he barely mentioned it and did not offer any comments about it. For the short period of time that he was forced to wear the star (approximately one month) it did not affect him greatly, whereas the events that preceded and followed it most certainly did.

By this time, they had become used to unjust demands, and to the misery of their situation.

The majority of the middle-aged and elderly Jews who remained in Vienna in 1941 were either working for or sheltered by the IKG. We know little about them. Some died of natural causes; the rest were deported to ghettos and concentration camps in the east. Few survived. Thus, we are left to piece together their response to the imposition of the star. The community reports offer a few clues. For example, the 182 individuals working for the community, who had been planning this event for over a week, who were up for many hours counting and packing up stars on the evening of the seventeenth, and who were dispersed throughout the city at the various issuing offices throughout the entire day of the eighteenth, were all ordinary older adults.[64] Most did not survive or leave a written record of their feelings on those days. What we do have from them are the detailed lists they prepared and submitted to the economic office on 19 September. The lists they so carefully and thoroughly compiled -- with the names and numbers of all the people to whom they distributed the stars -- do not tell us anything about their sentiments at this time, but they remind us of the actual situation in which these people found themselves. Simply put, they had a responsibility and a job to carry out. This job had deadlines and repercussions and the community workers had little time to consider moral and ethical dilemmas, or to lament or agonize over the Nazis' newest attempt to demoralize them by branding them. Thus, the reports reveal how people's feelings about this decree may have been repressed by their determination to fulfill the order and avoid additional havoc for their community. The duty before them came first; their thoughts

---

[64] For a full listing of names and departments, see appendix A, frames 0073-0085 from USHMM microfilm #288, IKG- A/W 466, 1-2. *Ausgabe von Judenkennzichen. 09.1941-10.1941.*

about wearing the yellow star were secondary. Perhaps it was a matter of days or weeks or even longer before they considered the inhumanity and possible implications of this order.

This was the case for IKG employees Greta Spainermann, Regina Winter, Fritzi Spitzer, Anne Katz, and Martha Oppenheim. These five women, all in their mid-twenties in September 1941 and thus younger than many of their cohorts, survived to relate their experiences. What they do and do not say in their testimonies reveals that they did not pity themselves or dwell on the inhumane order they faced. They all worked for the Jewish Community -- four of them in the Rothschild Spital (the IKG's main hospital) and one in a children's home -- and each was actively involved in the distribution campaign. Like all Jews, they were humiliated and forced to wear the star, but only one mentioned this in her oral testimony; the others said nothing. Regine Winter remembered "You had to wear the star, you had to stand on the back of the tram, you couldn't go into stores…you couldn't do anything."[65] She recalled the decree, but not as an individual experience that changed her life or affected her directly. She described it as one of the many anti-Jewish laws she had to face while living under the Nazis.

These women were young, healthy, and employed. At the other end of the spectrum stood Vienna's elderly Jews, many of whom, along with the handicapped and the ill, were living in one of the IKG's eight old-age homes or three hospitals by September 1941. According to statistics from January 1941 there were 1,700 people sheltered in the eight nursing homes, 548 male and 1,152 females between 30 and 95

---

[65] Regina, R., 1995. "Interview by Survivors of the Shoah Visual History Foundation," Brooklyn, NY, USA, March 7. Interview Code 01279, Tapes 1-4.

years of age.[66] Their daily lives did not extend beyond the confines of the IKG institution in which they resided, so wearing the star did not ostracize them within their immediate surroundings, nor put them in any great danger. They were not burdened with the task of organizing the distribution of the stars, nor were they responsible for learning about the decree or obtaining the stars. While sheltered in one of these homes or hospitals they received full care from the IKG employees and all bureaucratic work was handled for them. For the sick and elderly, the star was indeed a humiliation, but it was just another antisemitic measure which did not have any immediate repercussions on their daily lives.

Healthy children, teenagers, and young adults experienced the decree differently from those persons who worked for, or who were taken care of by, the IKG. Some 2,412 Jewish boys and girls under the age of eighteen still lived in Vienna in September 1941 and this small portion of the community has reflected upon their youthful naïveté at the time.[67] We can gain a much clearer understanding of these children's, teenager's, and young adult's responses to Heydrich's decree because many survived and their words were preserved in letters, diaries, memoirs, and oral testimonies. The law affected children's daily lives and activities, as it did the lives of the adults who worked for the community. Unlike the adults and the elderly, however, children were not so much humiliated by the star, as they were impressed by their experiences while wearing (or not wearing) it.

Ruth Kluger and Helga Feldner-Busztin were not yet teenagers when the decree was ordered. Ruth was ten and Helga twelve, and the star changed their daily lives in a

---

[66] USHMM film #295, IKG-A/W 132, *Israelistische Kultusgeminde Vienna. Survey on Nineteenhundredforty.*
[67] USHMM film # 295, IKG- A/W 115, *Tatigkeitsberichte in Tabellenform (Anschlag?) fuer die Zeit vom 01. Jaenner-30. Juni 1941.*

way that left both girls with lasting memories of their feelings. Ruth Kluger was embarrassed and angered by the uncomfortable experience she had when she wore the yellow star for the first time. She was riding on the tram and the star drew attention to her, arousing feelings of sympathy among one of her fellow passengers, who was an older man. This man felt so bad for Ruth that when the tram went through a tunnel and nobody was looking, he quickly stuffed an orange into her hand. He apparently thought it was a kind gesture that would make little Ruth happy, but she was not comforted or pleased by this gift from a stranger. Instead, she felt poor, vulnerable, and self-conscious, and she resented her new situation. "He wanted to show his pity for me," she wrote in her memoirs some sixty years later, "the child with the Jew star."[68] As a child, Ruth could not grasp the new physical danger that she was in and she did not understand how lucky she was to receive this gentle and kind response. She revealed in her memoir that the star itself actually made little impression on her, "because discrimination was already rampant, both the legal kind and the joyous popular sort." The star was so much part of that pattern that it was hard for her to remember that the star was not imposed until September 1941: "I tend to think it was earlier, and I have to check the history books to make sure I have the date right."

Like Ruth, Helga Feldner-Busztin received public sympathy for having to wear the star, but she was also teased and ridiculed. For twelve-year-old Helga, the star prompted a range of feelings, from insecurity and confusion to anger and fear. "There were very different responses from the population as I went out with the Jewish star,"

---

[68] Ruth Kluger, *Still Alive, A Holocaust Girlhood Remembered* (New York, The Feminist Press at the City University of New York, 2001), 49.

Helga stated in her testimony. "Some people would tease and torment me, while others would say: '*Oh, du armes Kind...*' (You poor child)." [69]

A significant number of children, teenagers, and young adults tried to avoid wearing the star, either by hiding it, or by taking it off completely. This was a bold and daring move that was mostly a sign of youth and naïveté. The children who did this had vivid memories of the star, because taking it off and defying both their parents and the law provoked feelings of fear and excitement. Liz Sussmann, Betty Ziegler, Kurt Klein, and Walter Hacker all disobeyed the order without getting caught. Liz Sussman was fifteen years old when she was first ordered to wear the star and she remained in Vienna for almost two years after the decree was enacted, until her deportation to Terezin in late 1943. Liz chose not to wear the star and this put the lives of her family members and her at great risk. "Nobody was going to make me wear a mark of shame," she remembered some sixty years later. "I got lucky that I wasn't caught though; I endangered my whole family and I'm not proud of it." [70] Betty Ziegler, also fifteen years old in September 1941, wore the star for almost a year before she was deported to Terezin in 1942. Betty disregarded the law and disobeyed the order, either taking her star off or covering it with a briefcase. She pretended to be an "Aryan," and went into stores all over town (including stores that were prohibited to Jews) buying whatever she wanted. When she walked into a store and a German greeted her with "Heil Hitler," she responded with the nonsensical rhyme "Drei Liter." [71]

---

[69] Helga F. B.1998. "Interview by Survivors of the Shoah Visual History Foundation," Vienna, AT, December 20. Interview Code 48947, Tapes 1-4.

[70] Liz, M., 1996. "Interview by Survivors of the Shoah Visual History Foundation," New York, NY, USA, March 8. Interview Code 12674, Tapes 1-8.

[71] Betty, D., 1995. "Interview by Survivors of the Shoah Visual History Foundation," Del Rey, CA, USA, August 7. Interview Code 05289, Tapes 1-4.

Kurt Klein was the son of a Jewish father and a Christian mother. As a "Mischling" he remained in Vienna until 1944, when he was sent on one of the last transports to Terezin. When the star was introduced, he was eleven years old. He was living at home with his parents and brother and he remembered how his mother and brother had to sew it onto their clothing. In order to help his family, Kurt took off his star so that he could travel into other districts of the city to cash in their food stamps, avoid long lines, and receive better rations.[72] It was an ambitious and threatening task, which left him with a strong impression of the yellow star and its impact on his daily life.

The Germans deported eleven-year-old Walter Hacker and his parents to Terezin in 1942. Like the others, he did not wear the star. Walter did not take it off to help his family, but so that he could continue to partake in social activities that were forbidden to Jews. For example, Walter (like most children) loved going to the movies and his childhood naïveté made him believe that he could continue to do this. He did not understand the consequences of violating the law, just as he did not fear the Nazis as much as being reprimanded by his parents. Walter traveled all the way to the other side of the city, took off his star, and sneaked into movie theaters. He always brought his younger brother Kurt along, encouraging him to remove his star also. He was afraid that if he left Kurt behind he would tattle, and then he would certainly be scolded. Walter made sure that both his brother and he put the stars back on their clothing before they got home, and luckily neither the Nazis nor their parents caught them defying the order.[73]

---

[72] Kurt Klein Bernard, 1994. "Interview by Survivors of the Shoah Visual History Foundation," Los Angeles, CA, USA, December 15. Interview Code 00382, Tapes 1-6.
[73] Walter Hacker, 1995. "Interview by Survivors of the Shoah Visual History Foundation," Los Angeles, CA, USA, May 23. Interview Code 02787, Tapes 1-4.

Walter's young age sheltered him from the danger he faced and shaped his understanding and response to the Nazi order. He, like Ruth, Helga, Betty, Liz, and Curt, was among the final 2,412 Jewish children to remain in Vienna, from a community that originally counted over 33,000. They were among the few members of the Jewish community to disobey the order, only because they were young and naïve. The rest cooperated because they were instructed to do so and they were threatened with the consequences of resistance. Had the Germans imposed the same demand in 1938, when the community was still heavily populated with children, teenagers, and young adults -- and when it was still evenly populated with males -- the Jewish response may have been different. We will never know, but there may have been greater resistance to this order if the community had not already been so broken down, physically and spiritually.

Analysis

For nearly seventy years, the star decree has loomed large as a traumatic measure in the evolution of the Holocaust. Yet it seems to have carried less weight at the time than we may imagine. The star did indeed constitute a crucial change in Hitler's Jewish policy in 1941, but the way Jews experienced this change is different from our present understanding. Contemporary reports from the Jewish community and the testimonies and memoirs from individual community members provide a glimpse of how life was actually lived in September 1941. While daily life changed for Vienna's Jews, according to most survivors the star itself was not perceived as a life-changing experience. Perhaps other racist measures starting in the late thirties desensitized them. Perhaps previous attempts to brand the Jews -- the red "J" in their passports and the middle names "Sarah" and "Israel" -- diminished the intensity of this decree. By the time the Jewish star was

introduced, the Jews of Vienna were not only conditioned to obeying humiliating orders,
but perhaps also impervious to such humiliations.

The official documents also show how the IKG responded quickly and dutifully to
the order it was given. The intricacies of the process suggest that the community had no
time to pause, to reflect upon the injustice and inhumanity of the order it was forced to
carry out. They simply had to get on with it. As scholar George E. Berkley noted in
Vienna and Its Jews: The Tragedy of Success, 1880s-1890s, after the regime ordered all
Jews to wear a yellow star, "The Gemeinde [the IKG] worked day and night to get them
ready in time. [E]arlier experiences had already taught the Jews to take all official
measures seriously."[74]   Berkley is right: by September 1941 the Jewish Community of
Vienna had learned to obey Nazi demands. But they not only obeyed out of fear -- i.e.,
because experience had taught them that failure to do so would result in the unleashing of
rampant and wild violence. They obeyed also because cooperation initially secured a
positive function: it enabled the Jews to rescue nearly two-thirds of their community via
emigration and it allowed them to provide for the sick and elderly who were trapped
behind.[75]

A Question of Resistance

The IKG spent three years unintentionally weaving itself into a codependent relationship
with a racist totalitarian authority and in turn created a similar one with its community

---

[74] George E. Berkley, *Vienna and Its Jews: The Tragedy of Success: 1880s-1980s* (Cambridge: Abt Books, 1988), 286.

[75] 123,490 emigrated as of January 1941 according to USHMM film # 295, IKG- A/W 132, *Israelitische Kultusgeminde Vienna. Survey on Nineteenhundredforty*; this number was slightly lower (122,785) according to USHMM film #295, IKG- A/W 113, *Bericht in Tabellenform betreffend Auswanderungsangelegenheiten, Bevoelkerungsstand, Fuersorgeangelegenheiten und Umschulung, Janner-December 1940.*

members. An IKG report dated June 1941 stated: "our members should cooperate with and be willing to make sacrifices for the community," further explaining that such behavior was necessary "to receive approval from the supervisory board for allowances."[76] Thus, the leaders continued to enforce a deadly relationship. While cooperation initially had enabled the IKG to rescue the majority of the population, it now meant the destruction of the rest. When the mass deportation trains began to roll in February/March 1941 and the star of David was implemented in September of that year, the IKG leadership could see how its labor harmed as well as helped their community. However, there was little it could do. For the IKG, there was no way out.

The great eighteenth-century philosopher Jean-Jacques Rousseau argued that if those in power failed to fulfill their end of the social contract, the people had the right to break their part of the contract as well and establish a new one.[77] Vienna's Jews did not apply Rousseau's proposed response to their situation in 1938, nor three years later when the situation worsened and it no longer stood as a viable solution to their suffering. The community had learned to manage terror by cooperating with the enemy's demands. Questioning or objecting to the rule of law had no place in their history; resistance to authority did not appear to them to be in their favor. They had lived for decades in a society where they had grown accustomed to abiding by the rule of law; they were not prepared to stop doing so. An example: immediately after Anschluss, when thirteen-year-old Walter Feiden suggested to his father Moses, "'Let's just leave! Let's just take the train to Switzerland, sit in a café until it's dark and then walk over the border.'" His

---

[76] USHMM film # 295, IKG- A/W 115, *Tatigkeitsberichte in Tabellenform (Anschlag?) fuer die Zeit vom 01. Jaenner-30. Juni 1941.*
[77] See Jean-Jacques Rosseau, *The Social Contract* (England: Penguin Books, 1968).

father's response: "'We cannot do that mein Kind, DAS IST ILLEGAL!!'"[78] It was precisely this vision of society and mutual obligation that blinkered Moses Feiden and the rest of Vienna's Jews to the vice closing on them. Trapped in a state of denial, they could not see that their assimilation into Austrian civil society had been more apparent than real. They did not belong, and the rule of law no longer applied to them.

If Vienna's Jews had known of their ultimate fate in the Holocaust, they may have attempted to respond differently from the very first day of the Nazi occupation. But they did not know. How could they? Not even the Germans knew what their "final solution" to their "Jewish problem" would be until late 1941, by which time it was way too late for Vienna's Jews to change their response to their oppressors. Reports by the Jewish community in Vienna show that throughout the period from 1938 to 1941, the community intended to provide all Jews who wished to emigrate with the possibility to do so and provide care for the sick and elderly who could not or did not wish to leave. These reports, taken together with the reports on the distribution of the star, prove that neither the leadership nor the rank and file knew that their future would consist of further deportations, ghettos, and concentration camps. On the contrary: they knew that cooperation could promote survival. The first deportations in the winter of 1941 and the introduction of the star the following fall ushered in the final phase of the destruction of Vienna's Jewish community: deportation and annihilation. From this point forward, cooperation with the German authorities could no longer save the Jews of Vienna; it would only help to further their demise. But the IKG could not see that genocide was

---

[78] Walter Feiden, conversation with author, USHMM, Washington, D.C., June 2007. Also see Walter, B. F., 1997. "Interview by Survivors of the Shoah Visual History Foundation," Jackson Heights, NY, USA, April 10. Interview Code 27974, Tapes 1-7. The Germans deported Walter Feiden and his parents to the Lodz Ghetto on 15 October 1941.

unfolding before them and that they had become an essential part of its operation. They tried to keep hope alive for the future.

Conclusions

The year 1941 marked a transitional period for Viennese Jewry. It began with the sudden order to deport selected individuals to the ghettos Opole, Kielce, Modliborzyce, and Lagow/Opatow in the Lublin district of Poland. The year ended with the resumption of deportations, on a much greater scale. The trains began to roll again on 15 October, one month after the star was introduced precisely to aid this process, and this time they did not cease after five transports. In just two and a half months, the IKG transported eight thousand individuals on trains with about one thousand each to ghettos: Lodz, Kaunas, Riga, and Minsk (the only transport to that ghetto) and not to the annihilation site, Maly Trostinecs. At the same time as the deportations resumed, the Germans prohibited emigration from the Greater German Reich completely. And two months later, America joined the war, cutting off all communication with and funding into Vienna. For years, this foreign aid had sustained the community, providing both practical and moral support. Now it came to an abrupt end. As 1941 drew to a close, the IKG had already organized the deportation of some 13,000 members, and the possibility of others getting out had vanished. The IKG's days of rescue had come to an end and now it was ordered to carry out destruction alone. On 20 January 1942, at Wansee, the Germans officially entrusted the "final solution" to the "Jewish problem," to Heydrich's authority, but the genocidal process had already long begun and, in Vienna, the IKG had ineluctably become a part of it.

Chapter Eight

Caught in the Vicious Cycle:
From a Working Jewish Community to a Council of Jewish Elders

Dr. Joseph Loewenherz, head of the IKG, declared in a weekly report to the Germans on
4 February 1941 that his community was prepared to be held responsible for "resettling
Jews selected for transport."[1] The Germans had demanded large-scale deportation of
Viennese Jews in the direction of the General Government, and Loewenherz agreed, not
knowing how dire the situation for those deported would be. Dr. Benjamin Murmelstein,
head of the emigration department, also believed that the transports would not be so bad,
that people would go to a place like Nisko where they would be put to work.[2] Likewise,
families selected for transport trusted the IKG, believed they were being resettled some
place for work, and did not resist deportation. Everyone was fooled. The Jews deported
on the first transport that winter (15 February 1941) met a fate far worse than anything
they imagined. They arrived in Opole Ghetto at 11:00 p.m. on Sunday 16 February 1941
after a "wild ride" in the midst of a snow storm.[3] Located at a railroad crossing, the
small town was divided into two parts -- the larger section occupied by Poles and
Germans, the smaller by Jews. The guards ordered the deportees off the trains and took
them to a synagogue where they would stay until the local Jewish council assigned them
berths in Jewish homes. They arrived with hand luggage only, but in order to retrieve it

---

[1] Doron Rabinovici, *Instanzen der Ohnmacht: Wien 1938-1945: der Weg zum Judenrat* (Frankfurt am Main, Juedischer Verlag, 2000) 229.
[2] USHMM, RG-60.5009, Tape 3158-3190, *Claude Lanzmann Shoah Collection, Interview with Benjamin Murmelstein* (Rome: 1975), see tape 3168, camera rolls #44-45 11:00:04 to 11:22:24.
[3] Letter to Vienna from Artur Czuczka in Opole, Tuesday, 18 February 1941. Czuczka Family Archive, Washington, D.C.. Translation, George Czuczka, private email to the author, 8 March 2007.

they had to pay ten of the forty Zloty they had been given in exchange for Reichsmarks before departure. The local Jews in Opole wore white armbands with a blue Star of David, another surprise for the new arrivals. Authorities soon informed them that they too would have to wear such an armband.[4]

A week after the first transport had left Vienna, Loewenherz received his first cry for help from Opole. "Wir sind verzweifelt (We are confused)," the deportees wrote, explaining that they had only enough food from Vienna to sustain them for another fourteen days.[5] What would they do after that? How would they survive? "The strange thing is that almost all of us still cannot fathom what has happened to us," Artur Czuczka wrote (18 February 1941) in a letter to his relative in Vienna. "To me, it feels like being quartered somewhere in wartime for a spell and then moving on. I am waiting for orders, as it were, as though I were in the army. It feels like we are just visiting but then we realize that we are here for good and cannot get away."[6] The deportees had trusted that the situation for them in Poland could not be much worse than in Vienna. Likewise, the leaders of the IKG encouraged them to go, trusting that the new situation would be manageable. The letters Loewenherz and others received told a different story. Loewenherz turned to Alois Brunner, head of the Zentralstelle, and pleaded for his people to be returned to Vienna; Brunner declared that under no circumstance could the Opole deportees return.

---

[4] Letter to Vienna from Artur Czuczka in Opole, Tuesday, 18 February 1941. Czuczka Family Archive, Washington, D.C.. See also, *Survivors of the Shoah Visual History Foundation,* testimonies of Elizabeth Guttmann, Regine Tuter, Herbert Kaufmann and Maximillian Kaufmann.
[5] Quoted in Rabinovici, *Instanzen der Ohnmacht:* 232.
[6] Letter to Vienna from Artur Czuczka in Opole, Tuesday, 18 February 1941. Czuczka Family Archive, Washington, D.C..

A new level of fear and distrust entered the community after word reached home from the first transports to Opole. It escalated in the summer of 1941 when two hundred people escaped from Opole, Modliborzyce, and other ghettos in the General Government.[7] The returnees brought news of the terror that reigned in the east. In addition to the letters and the rumors they generated, these reports spread quickly, driving some people to hide underground[8] or to flee over the green border to Hungary.[9] Most people, however, tried not to think about what they had heard, and chose not to believe what they considered rumors. As one IKG employee, Martha Donath, recalled, "We didn't know where the people were sent, but always heard Poland and heard that letters came back."[10] The return mail signified that the deportees were alive, and this helped to calm fears. But those first cries for help marked a warning sign of the genocide that lay ahead. Confronted with this new information, the pattern of cooperation between the Germans, the IKG, and its members reached a potential turning point.

The deportations stopped in spring. Between April and September 1941, Jews continued to emigrate from Vienna and no deportation trains rolled.[11] The emigration, while minimal (the IKG recorded that 19 persons emigrated to Europe, 2 to USA, and 13 to South and Central America in the month of April; 17 persons emigrated to Europe, 153 to USA, 39 to South and Central America, and 1 person to another overseas country in

---

[7] On 13 November 1941 Loewenherz was ordered to deport anyone who returned from the first transports to Opole and about 200 people were sent to Riga and Minsk. See Rabinovici, *Instanzen der Ohnmacht:*237.
[8] Approximately 600 Jews hid as *U-boote* in Vienna. See, C. Gwyn Moser, "Jewish U-Boote in Austria, 1938-1945" in *Simon Wiesenthal Center Annual, Volume 2*. (New York: Kraus International Publications, 1985).
[9] Jonny Moser, *Demographie der jüdischen Bevölkerung Österreichs 1938-1945* (Vienna: DÖW, 1999).
[10] Martha, D., 1997. "Interview by Survivors of the Shoah Visual History Foundation," Australia. Interview Code 34975.
[11] The Germans had the problem of 240,000 people from annexed Poland that they were trying to move to the General Government in addition to the 60,000 Viennese Jews. See Rabinovici, *Instanzen der Ohnmacht:* 83.233.

the month of May),[12] kept hope alive in the IKG and among community members that the rescue of Vienna's Jews was still possible.

The reprieve was deceptive. It did not signify that the Germans intended to ease their policies or scale back their persecution of European Jews. Rather, it was during this lull in the deportations (April- September 1941) that the Nazi administration imposed further restrictions on Jews as they moved towards their ultimate annihilation policy. For example, on 21 May 1941 -- after the first transports had gone, but before the star decree -- Brunner told Loewenherz that all Jews remaining in Vienna had to be concentrated.[13] People had to give up their apartments (particularly those with a bathroom) and move into *Judenhäuser* or collective Jewish housing.[14] Elliot Sauerquell, who was fifteen years old at the time, remembered that his family was given exactly twenty-four hours to evacuate their apartment and find a new place to live. "Then we lived in this horrible little room in the second district, without gas, without light, without other things, and with grandmother."[15] While the Germans never created a closed Jewish ghetto in Vienna, the community was deeply affected. Almost 90 percent of the Jewish population was transferred to collective homes in three neighboring districts of the city (the second, ninth, and twentieth) before the IKG was ordered to launch mass transports to ghettos in the east in October 1941.[16] Gathering the Jews in this corner of the city made it easier for

---

[12] USHMM film # 295, IKG- A/W 115, *Tatigkeitsberichte in Tabellenform (Anschlag?) fuer die Zeit vom 01. Jaenner-30. Juni 1941*
[13] According to IKG figures there were 44,000 Jews living in Vienna at this time. The exact count is uncertain, however. Rabinovici and Hilberg estimate this figure at 53,000. Raul Hilberg, *The Destruction of the European Jews: Revised and Definitive Edition, Volume 2.* (New York, Holmes and Meier,1985). For more on this issue see: footnote 112.
[14] See Rabinovici, *Instanzen der Ohnmacht:* 254.
[15] Elliot, W., 1998. "Interview by Survivors of the Shoah Visual History Foundation," New York, NY, USA, March 25. Interview Code 40985, Tapes 1-5.
[16] See Hilberg, *The Destruction of the European Jews*, 457. His figures are based on Rosenkranz, *Vervolgung und Selbstbehauptung, Die Juden in Österreich 1938-1945* (Wien, Munich: Herold, 1978).

the Germans (and the IKG) to monitor and control their movement, and ultimately made the deportation process much quicker.

Around the same time that Guenter ordered Lowenherz to impose the star (September 1941), the latter heard rumors of further deportations. He confronted Eichmann, who declared them false. Brunner confirmed Loewenherz's greatest fear about three weeks later, on the Jewish High Holiday of Yom Kippur. He explained that Hitler wanted to move some of the Jews from Germany, Vienna, and the Protectorate of Bohemia and Moravia to Lodz; the deportations would begin again and he needed the IKG to organize the process. Brunner gave Loewenherz this new order on the afternoon of 30 September 1941, and that night during the religious service in the temple on Seitenstettengasse, community members observed Loewnherz in tears.[17] For some, this was a moment of realization: the rumors they had heard over the past weeks were true. Deportations to Poland would begin again.

Emigration came to an end when the trains began to roll in October 1941.[18] A new phase in the history of Viennese Jewry began: destruction without rescue. When Loewenherz gave his authorities a list of one hundred fifty people with visas to overseas countries whom he expected to be exempt from deportation, he discovered that emigration was no longer possible. Instead, these people would be sent with a transport of some 1,000 Jews to the newly occupied German territory in White Russia (Reichskommiserat Ostland), where the Germans had already killed 12,000 Jews to prepare for the arrival of 50,000 Jews from the Altreich, Ostmark, and Protectorate of

---

[17] Rabinovici, *Instanzen der Ohnmacht:* 234.
[18] Rabinovici claims that 6,000 people emigrated in the first half of 1941, but according to IKG records only 1,500 people left. Rabinovici, *Instanzen der Ohnmacht:*229 and USHMM film # 295, IKG- A/W 115, *Tatigkeitsberichte in Tabellenform (Anschlag?) fuer die Zeit vom 01. Jaenner-30. Juni 1941.*

Bohemia and Moravia.[19] Until this time, Loewenherz, Murmelstein, and the other community leaders had cooperated with the Germans, believing that obedience was the sole option for a fruitful outcome. And so long as emigration was still allowed, they had been correct: their obedience had promoted escape and survival. Suddenly, this was no longer the case.

From October 1941, the Zentralstelle and the IKG no longer worked together to facilitate emigration; German concessions to the Jews ceased and their demands increased.[20] The Nazi plan to solve the "Jewish Problem" through expulsion was not working -- the policy was shifting toward annihilation.[21] The Zentrallstelle placed the IKG in charge of the first step in this process: deportation. Transports holding approximately 1,000 Jews each were to leave Vienna's Aspang Bahnhof as quickly and efficiently as possible (four times per month was standard) to the designated territories, for as long as necessary, until the country was "Judenrein." These deportations were meticulously calculated and organized -- the initial order, the train departure time and destination, and the list of deportees was the work of the Nazi authorities. The rest of the

---

[19] Rabinovici, *Instanzen der Ohnmacht:* 237.

[20] Claude Lanzmann interviewed Benjamin Murmelstein in 1977 for his documentary film *Shoah,* but never incorporated any of the footage. The outtakes were preserved and recently made public by the USHMM and SOSVHF. During the interview, Murmelstein explained to Lanzmann that he managed to help Jews by working with Eichmann: "Eichmann helped him because if the Kultusgemeinde had been declared illegal, it and the money it generated would be removed from his control....Although he [Murmelstein] would be the last person to say a good word about Eichmann, working with him allowed Murmelstein to accomplish certain goals (saving people from deportation or getting them released from camps)." USHMM, RG-60.5009, Tape 3158-3190, *Claude Lanzmann Shoah Collection, Interview with Benjamin Murmelstein* (Rome: 1975), see tape 3162, camera rolls #33-34-- 05:00:05 to 05:22:37.

[21] The failure of the resettlement plans in Nisko and Madagascar, together with the German invasion of the Soviet Union in June 1941, moved Nazi ideology toward total annihilation of European Jewry, initially, carried out by mobile killing squads or Einsatzgruppen. By October 1941, when the Germans ordered the IKG to transport Viennese Jews to the ghettos in the east, a systematic plan for mass murder was not finalized, but Hitler's ambition to "exterminate the Jewish vermin" was clear. The "final solution" to the Jewish problem -- the systematic plan to annihilate European Jewry -- is most commonly dated to the Wansee Conference in January 1942, but the decision was taken earlier, in the summer/fall of 1941. See Yehuda Bauer, *Rethinking the Holocaust* (New Haven: Yale University Press, 2002).

process was assigned to the IKG. The IKG did not understand what they were facilitating; i.e., what the transports meant, where exactly they carried their people, or for how long the Germans intended to make them continue this work. All they knew was that they were instructed, under force, to carry out another order. The adopted system of cooperation, firmly established in 1938, enabled the IKG leaders and members to oblige with this next instruction despite its unknown implications for their future.

The Deportation Process

The Germans compiled the transport lists but still demanded IKG involvement in the process. While Brunner initially offered Benjamin Murmelstein the authority to compose the deportation lists, he refused.[22] Instead, the Zentralstelle selected people for the deportation transports, based on the central card registry in their office which previously had been used for emigration. They kept families together, listing people numerically, the man first, followed by wife and children. After they drew up the lists, they sent them on to the Gestapo, and then to the IKG.[23] IKG employees sorted, copied, and alphabetized the lists in Room #8 at the IKG main offices on Seitenstettengasse, formerly the emigration department.[24] The lists already identified the names, addresses, and ages of these to be deported.[25]

Certain Jews were excluded at first from the lists. Some Jews were "privileged" according to German law: those in mixed marriages (a Jewish man with an Aryan wife

---

[22] USHMM, RG-60.5009, Tape 3158-3190, *Claude Lanzmann Shoah Collection, Interview with Benjamin Murmelstein* (Rome: 1975), see tape 3162, camera rolls #33-34-- 05:00:05 to 05:22:37.

[23] Franz Josef Huber was chief of the Viennese Gestapo and Karl Ebner was underneath him. See Hans Safrian, *Die Eichmann-Maenner* (Wien, Europaverlag, 1992).

[24] Rabinovici, *Instanzen der Ohnmacht*:264.

[25] USHMM, RG-60.5009, Tape 3158-3190, *Claude Lanzmann Shoah Collection, Interview with Benjamin Murmelstein* (Rome: 1975), tape 3168, camera rolls #44-45 11:00:04 to 11:22:24.

with children, a Jewish woman with an Aryan husband with or without children), Jewish

mothers and fathers of a "mischling" son who died in war, veterans of World War I,

former soldiers who were 50 percent disabled, civil servants who received a pension, and

foreign Jews. While certain people held a "privileged" status, others supposedly could be

"protected" by the IKG. At the beginning of 1941, Brunner ordered Loewenherz to

designate these people and deliver this list to the Zentralstelle. He compiled six main

categories of Jews as protected by the IKG: 1) IKG workers and former workers and

those parents, children, and siblings who lived with them; 2) people who had

arrangements to immigrate to South America; 3) people living in the old-age homes; 4)

blind and handicapped persons; 5) forced laborers; and 6) war invalids and decorated war

veterans. [26]

With the first transport, Loewenherz discovered that no one was truly protected.

He had designated certain people to be excluded, but the Zentralstelle included many of

these "privileged" or "protected" people nevertheless. When the IKG received the lists,

the leaders still had an opportunity chance to make changes, but with much difficulty. [27]

The leadership could claim that a particular person's service to the IKG was

irreplaceable, and that therefore he or she needed to be removed from the list. But the

Zentralstelle had to approve each person the IKG deleted and select someone to go in

that person's place. Although the Zentralstelle had replacement names reserved for this

purpose, they liked to threaten the leaders with having to chose themselves. [28] Again, the

---

[26] Rabinovici, *Instanzen der Ohnmacht:* 261; 268; 262.

[27] Murmelstein claims that he could cut people from the lists after they came into his office. USHMM, RG-60.5009, Tape 3158-3190, *Claude Lanzmann Shoah Collection, Interview with Benjamin Murmelstein* (Rome: 1975), tape 3170, camera rolls #48-49 13:00:04 to 13:22:47.

[28] Rabinovici quotes from testimony of Wilhelm Bienenfeld, a former Gestapo agent, who attested that Loewenherz never picked the replacements. See Rabinovici, *Instanzen der Ohnmacht:* 264. Murmelstein's testimony supports this. He said he called Brunner for more names to be added. USHMM, RG-60.5009,

leaders were trapped in a no-win situation: while they could try to protect some, it was at the cost of others. Loewenherz and Murmelstein simply could not protect everybody.

The Germans did not need the IKG to compile the deportation lists because they had all the information to do so themselves. In addition to the Central Card Index, they had the names and most recent addresses of all Jews living in Vienna as of 1940 because anyone who wanted to receive a food rations card needed to provide the IKG with this basic information.[29] Still, after the Germans handed over the lists, they needed the IKG to organize and carry out the deportation process in a calm and efficient manner. Initially written summons were sent; the Zentralstelle mailed pre-printed postcards to people's homes, telling them when and where to report. Meanwhile, the IKG encouraged people to obey the "resettlement" order when they received it; they warned that if they did not show up as directed (and it was not due to a medical problem that they could prove with a certificate), they would be picked up forcibly. People interpreted these notifications differently and their emotional responses varied, but the majority obeyed this demand without a second thought.

Max Weiss, twenty-one years old, volunteered to accompany his parents when they were ordered to leave their apartment and report to the local school for transfer to Poland in mid-October 1941. He experienced the whole notification and transfer process as "quite normal," whereas thirteen-year-old Walter Feiden, who was also called for resettlement with his family that month, recalled that "everyone always dreaded those notices!" A letter from fifty-six-year-old Marie Kupler to her brother Emil Secher in the

Tape 3158-3190, *Claude Lanzmann Shoah Collection, Interview with Benjamin Murmelstein* (Rome: 1975), tape 3168, camera rolls #44-45 11:00:04 to 11:22:24.
[29] Rabinovici, *Instanzen der Ohnmacht:* 339.

United States (15 October 1941) revealed a similar sentiment: "My dearest loved ones! Mother is doing much better.... But we also had other tsores. It's that P. Action again. You can imagine our anxiety and fear every morning when we await the mail -- and what a sigh of relief when it doesn't bring us that dreaded order.... We shall continue to hope that we will be spared. A large number of our friends and acquaintances have already been affected."[30] These three Jewish victims perceived the situation differently, but still followed orders which led them to await the same unknown fate.[31]

The victims had vanishingly few alternatives, but a small minority chose to disobey nevertheless. Some did not show up for resettlement, and avoided transport by hiding underground. In reaction, the Germans imposed an even harsher regime to punish the rest of the community and enforce deportation. The Zentralstelle appointed some five hundred Jews to the role of *Aushebern* in October 1941.[32] These Jews were responsible for collecting people from their apartments and delivering them to the collection centers. Seven months later (March 1942) they organized a special unit of Jews disguised as non-Jews, known as the *Sonderdienst* or "JUPO," whose job it was to seek out and turn in any Jews attempting to avoid deportation.[33] Alois Brunner, head of the

---

[30] Pierre Secher, *Left behind in Nazi Vienna: letters of a Jewish family caught in the Holocaust, 1939-1941* (Jefferson: McFarland & Co, 2004), 292.

[31] Both Walter Feiden and Max Weiss were deported with their parents in October 1941 to Lodz. Marie Kupler's exact deportation date is unlisted. See *Documentation Center of the Austrian Resistance (DÖW):*DOEW-Project Registration by Name: The Austrian Victims of the Holocaust, 2001. (Database available online: *http: //www. doew.at*).

[32] Jonny Moser, *Demographie der jüdischen Bevölkerung Österreichs 1938-1945*, 45. See order from Zentralstelle to Leib Leo Abraham Israel Strauss (7 October 1941).

[33] Murmelstein states in his testimony that the JUPO "had nothing to do with the Kultusgemeinde" and that these people were really brutal and he once arranged for a group of them to be deported to the east. See, USHMM, RG-60.5009, Tape 3158-3190, *Claude Lanzmann Shoah Collection, Interview with Benjamin Murmelstein (Rome: 1975)*, see tape 3168, camera rolls #44-45 13:11:17. Moser and Rabinovici confirm that the Zentralstelle was in charge. See Rabinovici, *Instanzen der Ohnmacht*, 287 and Moser, "Die Anhalte- und Sammellager fur österreichischen Juden" in *Dokumentationsarchivs des österreichischen Widerstandes (ed.), Jahrbuch 1992*, 75. To the contrary, Hilberg states that the IKG had to organize a

Zentralstelle, appointed former administrators of the emigration department of the IKG to carry out this new detail: Robert Prochnik, Willy Stern, Leo Balaban, Wilhelm Reisz, Kurt Mezei.[34]

Loewenherz, for his part, encouraged these men to cooperate with all new orders and warned that if they did not they would face the most severe consequences. These ordinary people, who had helped with the emigration of thousands, now carried the title "Aushebern" and had the terrible job of picking up the people designated for deportation -- using force if necessary -- and delivering them to the collection points. Typically, they entered an apartment, most often in the night, "station themselves at the door, while an SS man and the chief of the Jewish Commando would seat themselves at a table to inquire about family members and to make sure of property declarations. The SS man might then depart, leaving the Jewish raiders with the victims, allowing them to help with the packing but admonishing them to prevent escapes."[35] Under the direct leadership of Murmelstein, these men reported to Room #8 at the IKG, the same room where emigration efforts originated, and where now deportation lists were sorted, alphabetized, and cataloged. In order for the process to run smoothly, Loewenherz ordered his "Ausheber" to be as polite and respectful as possible when they entered a Jewish home to take the people away, and he ordered his community members to cooperate when it was their turn to be "resettled."

JUPO or Ausheberdienst to assist the Gestapo in the roundups. See Hilberg, *The Destruction of the European Jews.*
[34] Rabinovici, *Instanzen der Ohnmacht:* 341.
[35] Gabriele Anderl, *Orte der Täter, Der NS-Terror in den "Arisierten" Wiener Rothschild-Palais.* (Wien: Band 15 der Schriftenreihe des Instituts zur Erforschung der Geschichte der Gewerkschaften und Arbeiterkammern, 2005), 40.

Holocaust historians Hilberg, Rabinovici, and Moser have pointed to the *Aushebung* or round-ups as a particularly brutal aspect of the deportation process. [36] According to survivor testimonies, this was not necessarily the case. While almost all survivors recalled receipt of the evacuation notice, few, if any, mentioned a forcible transfer from their homes to the Sammellager or train station-- either by Nazis or by other Jews. Freddy Schreiber and his parents, Lotte and Jakob, received a notice in the mail in October 1942 to report from their home on Judengasse 7 just blocks away across the Donau Canal to the school on Kleine Sperlgasse. Freddy recalled that they reported as they were told, and he did not reflect upon the situation as a particularly daunting phase of the deportation process.[37] Walter Hacker described the experience similarly -- his family received a notice to show up at the train station and they simply followed the order; he did not mention arrest or forcible transfer.[38] Elliot Sauerquell's experience differed from that of the other men. After dismissal from his forced-labor detail in January 1942, he was picked up in the street without papers, arrested, brought to the Zentralstelle, put on a list for deportation to the east, and transferred to the school on Kleine Sperlgasse to wait.[39] Still, he made no mention of brutal round-ups. Survivor testimonies suggest that the resettlement notification loomed large, but the transfer itself did not surface as central to the deportation process.

---

[36] Hilberg, *The Destruction of the European Jews,* 458; Herbert Rosenkranz, *Verfolgung und Selbstbehauptung. Die Juden in Österreich 1938-1945* (Wien, Munich: Herold, 1978) 285, 299. For an in-depth account of how the round-ups took place, also see Rabinovici, *Instanzen der Ohnmacht:* 286.

[37] Fred, S., 1994. "Interview by Survivors of the Shoah Visual History Foundation," Los Angeles, CA, USA, December 15. Interview Code 00383, Tapes 1-5.

[38] Walter, H., 1995. "Interview by Survivors of the Shoah Visual History Foundation," Los Angeles, CA, USA, May 23. Interview Code 02787, Tapes 1-4.

[39] Elliot, W., 1998. "Interview by Survivors of the Shoah Visual History Foundation," New York, NY, USA, March 25. Interview Code 40985, Tapes 1-5.

Waiting in the Sammellagern for anywhere from hours to weeks was a scaring

experience. For many, this was where the horror of the deportation process began.

Vienna's first Sammellager, established directly after Anschluss, was outside the city

center, on Karajangasse, a quiet street in the twentieth district. The Germans transformed

the high school on that street into a holding camp for Jews and political prisoners

designated for transport to Dachau (although the prisoners held inside did not know it at

the time). The Sammellager on Karajangasse served its purpose in 1938 and then returned

to its normal operation.[40] Some three years later (February 1941), in response to an order

by Hitler for the mass deportation of 10,000 Jews to ghettos in the Lublin district of

Poland, the Germans ordered the IKG to establish more of these collection stations in the

second district, where most Jews resided. Between February 1941 and August 1942,

Kleine Sperlgasse 2a and Castellezgasse 35 operated as Sammellagern,[41] and in

September 1942, two new locations, Malzgasse 7 (the "Krugerheim") and the adjoining

building on Miesbachgasse 8, took over the function.[42] Originally referred to as

"collection camps" (Sammellager), over time these places were designated as "transfer

camps" (Umsiedlungslager) and "deportation camps" (Abwanderungslager).[43]

The Sammellager was the place to which people designated for deportation were

to report prior to the departure of the train transport. The schools converted into

---

[40] *Gedenkstätte Karajangasse. Die verlorene Insel. Als Schulen zu Gefängnisssen wurden. Pressemappe zur Eröffnung der ständigen Ausstellung am 5. Mai 1999.* Documentation Center of the Austrian Resistance, DÖW - Library #42338.

[41] The school on Castellezgasse ceased to be a Sammellager in September 1942 when the Zentralstelle moved to that building. See Moser, "Die Anhalte- und Sammellager für österreichischen Juden," 75.

[42] DÖW claims that Sperlgasse and Castellezgasse began operation in October 1941, but Moser claims February 1941, which is more accurate because these sites were essential to the first deportations and mentioned in testimonies from Survivors of the Shoah Visual History Foundation. See Moser, "Die Anhalte- und Sammellager für österreichischen Juden," 75 and Documentation Center of the Austrian Resistance (DÖW) (*http://www. doew.at*).

[43] Moser, "Die Anhalte- und Sammellager für österreichischen Juden," 75.

collection centers were relatively small and, to maximize space, there were no tables, chairs, or beds.[44] Held inside these buildings, a perpetual group of between two and three thousand people sat on the floor.[45] Kurt Klein, who worked in the soup kitchen at the Kleine Sperlgasse Sammellager, recalled how the authorities ran these collection centers: "They waited until they accumulated enough people to ship them off."[46] Having arrived with their hand luggage and nothing more, the people just sat and waited -- for an indeterminate amount of time -- for further instruction.[47] Four to five SS men from the Zentralstelle supervised them,[48] and Jewish guards were appointed to ensure that no one escaped. The Germans threatened Loewenherz that two Jewish guards would be deported in the place of every person missing from the premises.[49]

The IKG tried to keep conditions as civilized as possible in the collection stations, but it was practically impossible considering the great number of people and small size of the quarters. Loewenherz pleaded with Brunner for a bar of soap for each deportee and for meals while in the Sammellagern: tea or coffee for breakfast, soup and cheese for the evening.[50] Initially, these concessions were granted. The soup kitchens continued to feed and clothe people in the Sammellager, and supplied them with wash products. Before every transport, those brought to the Abwanderungslager were allowed to bathe. This was very important, because most people lived in apartments that did not have bathing

---

[44] Hilberg, *The Destruction of the European Jews*, 459; see also Herbert Rosenkranz, *Vervolgung und Selbstbehauptung*, 298,230.

[45] Moser, "Die Anhalte- und Sammellager fur österreichischen Juden," 75.

[46] Curt, K.B., 1994. "Interview by Survivors of the Shoah Visual History Foundation," Los Angeles, CA, USA, December 15. Interview Code 00382, Tapes 1-6.

[47] Elliot,W., 1998. "Interview by Survivors of the Shoah Visual History Foundation," New York, NY, USA, March 25. Interview Code 40985, Tapes 1-5; Hilberg, *The Destruction of the European Jews*, 259; Rosenkranz, *Vervolgung und Selbstbehauptung*, 298, 230.

[48] Moser, "Die Anhalte- und Sammellager fur österreichischen Juden," 75.

[49] Hilberg, *The Destruction of the European Jews*, 459; see also Rosenkranz, *Vervolgung und Selbstbehauptung*, 298, 230.

[50] USHMM film # 294, IKG- A/W 116, *Taetigkeitsbericht fuer das Jahr 1942 (2 Exemplare)* 9, 11; Rabinovici, *Instanzen der Ohnmacht:* 229.

facilities. Initially they bathed on Flossgasse 14, a bathhouse which belonged exclusively to the IKG and later they washed in a bathroom specifically installed in the Sammellager for that purpose.[51]

The IKG's efforts were futile. Inmates endured terribly poor hygienic conditions and awaited an unknown fate. It was too much for many to manage. By the summer of 1942, the IKG hospital began removing persons from the Sammellager who had committed or tried to commit suicide there.[52] Freddy Schreiber recalled that although he was still together with his family, the real horror of the deportation process began when he was sent to the Sammellager: "That is where it really started -- fifteen people to a room."[53]

When a sufficient number of people had been gathered for a transport, the guards dragged the deportees outside in broad daylight and shoved them into open trucks. SS man Josef Weiszl from the Zentralstelle, in charge of overseeing this detail, is remembered as exceptionally cruel. Nineteen-year-old Walter Schwarz, who worked for the IKG, recalled how Weiszl herded people as though they were animals -- hitting them with a club if they did not move fast enough.[54] Crammed together, the deportees traveled the ten- to fifteen-minute ride south from the second district to the train station in the

---

[51] USHMM film # 294, IKG- A/W 116, *Taetigkeitsbericht fuer das Jahr 1942 (2 Exemplare)* 9, 11.

[52] For example: seventy-four-year-old Rebekka R. committed suicide with morphine in the Sammellager on Malzgasse7 in July, fifty-one-year-old Artner Rosa S. attempted suicide with sleeping pills in Sammellager Sperlgasse in August, and seventy-seven-year-old Gustav F. committed suicide with unknown sleeping pills in the Sammellager on Malzgasse 7 in August. USHMM film # 742, IKG- A/W 169, *Uebermittlung der seitens der Spitalsdirektion periodisch erstellten Verzeichnisse der Selbstmoerder unde der nach Selbstmordversuchen ins Spital eingelieferten Personen, sowie der seitens des Friedhofsamtes erstellten Verzeichnisse der zur Bestattung freigegebenen Selbstmoerderleichen an die Gestapo, 10.1941- 03.1945* [slide 0226].

[53] Fred, S., 1994. "Interview by Survivors of the Shoah Visual History Foundation," Los Angeles, CA, USA, December 15. Interview Code 00383, Tapes 1-5.

[54] See testimony of Walter Schwarz in Gabriele Anderl, *Orte der Täter, Der NS-Terror in den "Arisierten" Wiener Rothschild-Palais.* (Wien, Band 15 der Schriftenreihe des Instituts zur Erforschung der Geschichte der Gewerkschaften und Arbeiterkammern, 2005) 40.

third district (Aspang Bahnhof) reserved for this process. According to some witnesses, the public jeered as the trucks passed by.[55] When the deportees arrived at the platform, regular trains with second- and third-class passenger cars awaited them, making it psychologically easier to board. Still, the deportees -- men, women, and children -- were forcibly rushed onto the wagons under the close supervision and direction of SS men Alois Brunner and Ernst Girzik.[56] Loading time began at noon and ran until four o'clock in the afternoon; departure time was in the early evening, seven o'clock.[57] Walter Schwarz recalled that for some of the elderly deportees, the transfer from the Sammellager to the station was simply too much to bear; they died before the train left the station.[58]

Each train carried approximately one thousand prisoners, two of whom had to be doctors. Seven Austrian police guarded the transport, along with a handful of Jews who were ordered to be transport leaders and forced to wear an armband to designate them as such. Of the seven policemen, two carried sub-machine guns and the other five were armed with pistols. As the guards did not anticipate any resistance from the prisoners, these pistols were not even fully loaded -- sixty spaces and only fifty bullets.[59]

Once the wheels began to roll, the journey could last anywhere from two to five days. For example, Charlotte Hirschbein, Berta O., and 992 other Jews left Vienna at

---

[55] See: Henry, W.,1998. "Interview by Survivors of the Shoah Visual History Foundation," New York, NY, USA, June 17. Interview Code 42662, Tapes 1-6; George Berkley, *Vienna and Its Jews: The Tragedy of Success: 1880s-1980s* (Cambridge: Abt Books, 1988), 313; Hilberg, *The Destruction of the European Jews:* 459. This is not confirmed. Other witnesses say that they did not want to disturb the public.
[56] Rabinovici, *Instanzen der Ohnmacht:* 238.
[57] This description is based on the transport to Minsk (6 May 1942) described in Hilberg, *The Destruction of the European Jews:* 467 and the transport to Sobibor (14 June 1942) in Rabinovici, *Instanzen der Ohnmacht:* 238.
[58] See testimony of Walter Schwarz in Gabriele Anderl, *Orte der Täter:*40.
[59] Rabinovici, *Instanzen der Ohnmacht:*238.

7:00 p.m. on Wednesday 6 May 1942 on a transport to Minsk.[60] The train passed through main stations such as Olmutz, Neisse, Warsaw, and Siedlce before it stopped more than two full days later, at 11:00 p.m. in the town of Wolkowysk. There, in the middle of the night, and within just a couple of hours, the guards transferred the deportees to freight cars; at 2:45 a.m., the engines roared again. Twelve hours later, at 2:30 p.m. on 9 May, the train stopped upon order of the security police in Minsk approximately twenty-three miles southwest of its final destination. There, in the small village of Koydanov, formerly a Jewish shtetl, the transport sat for almost thirty-six hours. During this time, eight dead persons were taken off the cars and buried at the railway station. At nine o'clock on the morning of 12 May 1942 the train resumed its course. Just ninety minutes later, it finally arrived in Minsk (10:30 a.m.).[61] After a treacherous five-day journey, Vienna's Jews had reached the "resettlement" site. SS men and local police unloaded them from the freight cars, led them into the woods, and shot them -- one after the next -- into mass graves.[62]

All deportation trains from Vienna between February 1941 and October 1942 left with the aim of transporting Jews to a place from which they would never return. However, not all trains traveled the same path, took the same amount of time, or carried the prisoners to the same fate. The first transports in February, March, and October went

---

[60] Johanna Saper, daughter of Charlotte Hirschbein, email correspondence with author, September 2003. See: Johanna, S., 1996. "Interview by Survivors of the Shoah Visual History Foundation," Miami, FL. Interview Code 12280; *Documentation Center of the Austrian Resistance (DÖW)*:DOEW-Project Registration by Name: The Austrian Victims of the Holocaust, 2001. (*http://www. doew.at*).
[61] Hilberg, *The Destruction of the European Jews,* 467. For more information on the transport of 6 May 1942 see: Arad, Yitzhak, Israel Gutman, and Abraham Margaliot. *Documents On the Holocaust: Selected Sources On the Destruction of the Jews of Germany and Austria, Poland, and the Soviet Union.* (Jerusalem: Ktav Pub. House in association with Yad Vashem [and the] Anti Defamation League, 1981), 409.
[62] Emil and Wilhelmina Eckstein (Paul Slaton), from Reimergasse, Wien 1, to Minsk, Maly Trostinecs 20 May 1942; Leo, Elka, and Mia Gruenberg, from Ferdinandstrasse, Wien 1, to Minsk, Maly Trostinecs on 27 May 1942; Joseph, Hilde, and Vera Grabkowicz from Johanessgasse, Wien 1, to Minsk, Maly Trostinecs on 14 September 1942. For deportation records see: *Documentation Center of the Austrian Resistance (DÖW)*: DOEW-Project Registration by Name: The Austrian Victims of the Holocaust, 2001. (*http://www. doew.at*).

exclusively to ghettos in the General Government of Poland (Wlodowa, Izbica); by November, transports began to head to ghettos in German-occupied White Russia (Reichsgebeit Ostland) as well. The transports ran simultaneously to these two different regions until the institution of a third destination in the summer of 1942, Theresienstadt. In June 1942 trains left Vienna weeks apart for the ghetto of Izbica in the General Government of Poland,[63] the annihilation site Minsk, Maly Trostinecs in the Reichsgebeit Ostland, and to the "model ghetto" of Theresienstadt, in the German Protectorate.[64] Some 45,700 Jews boarded trains to one of these three regions between February 1941 and October 1942.[65] A total of 15,993 went to ghettos in the General Government (4,993 to Lodz), 14,789 to the Reichskommissariat Ostland, and 13,926 to Theresienstadt. In 1942, the number of women deportees (21,551) almost doubled that of men (11,170).[66] The Germans had targeted the men for arrest and deportation first, beginning in 1938, and the IKG had focused on their immediate emigration. Thus, by the time of the mass deportations there were twice as many women than men in the community.

---

[63] The transports did not always go to the intended destination: a train for Izbica on 14 June 1942, went directly to the death camp Sobibor. The train left Vienna at 7:08 p.m. and arrived 2 days later in Lublin at which point 51 able-bodied Jews were taken out (ages 15-50); the rest went to Sobibor where they were gassed upon arrival. Rabinovici, *Instanzen der Ohnmacht:* 238.

[64] Order of the Vienna Schutzpolizei command concerning the provision of a transport detachment for a transport to Theresienstadt, 24 February 1943. For these deportation records, see *Documentation Center of the Austrian Resistance (DÖW)*: (Database available online: *http://www. doew.at*).

[65] Author's calculations, based on deportation figures from Jonny Moser, *Demographie der jüdischen Bevölkerung Österreichs 1938-1945* and USHMM film # 294, IKG- A/W 116, *Taetigkeitsbericht fuer das Jahr 1942 (2 Exemplare).*

[66] USHMM film # 294, IKG- A/W 116, *Taetigkeitsbericht fuer das Jahr 1942 (2 Exemplare).*

Table 12: "Transports from Vienna"

Transport #	Departure date	# of people	Arrival date	Destination
	20 October 1939	912		Nisko
	26 October 1939	672		Nisko
1	15 February 1941	996		Opole
2	19 February 1941	1004		Kielce
3	26 February 1941	1049		Opole
4	5 March 1941	981		Modliborzyce
5	12 March 1941	995-997		Opatów & Lagów
6	15 October 1941	1005/999	16 October 1941	Łódź
7	19 October 1941	1001/1003	20 October 1941	Łódź
8	23 October 1941	991/1000	24 October 1941	Łódź
9	28 October 1941	998/999	29 October 1941	Łódź
10	2 November 1941	998	3 November 1941	Łódź
11	23 November 1941	998	26 November 1941	Kaunas
12	28 November 1941	1001	5 December 1941	Minsk
13	3 December 1941	1001	6 December 1941	Riga
14	11 January 1942	1000	15 January 1942	Riga
15	26 January 1942	1201	31 January 1942	Riga
16	6 February 1942	1003	10 February 1942	Riga
17	9 April 1942	998		Izbica
18	27 April 1942	998	29 April 1942	Włodowa
19	6 May 1942	994/1000	11 May 1942	Minsk
20	12 May 1942	1001	15 May 1942?	Izbica
21	15 May 1942	1006	18 May 1942?	Izbica
22	20 May 1942	986/1000	23/26 May 1942	Minsk
23	27 May 1942	981	1 June 1942	Minsk
24	2 June 1942	999	5/9 June 1942	Minsk
25	5 June 1942	1001	8 June 1942?	Izbica/Sobibór
26	9 June 1942	1006	13/15 June 1942	Minsk
27	14 June 1942	996	17 June 1942	Sobibor
28	20 June 1942	996/1000	21 June 1942	Terezin
29	28 June 1942	983/1000	29 June 1942	Terezin
30	10 July 1942	993/1000	11 July 1942	Terezin
31	14 July 1942	988/1000	15 July 1942	Terezin
32	17 July 1942	995	18 July 1942	Auschwitz
33	22 July 1942	1000/1005	23 July 1942	Terezin
34	28 July 1942	988/1000	29 July 1942	Terezin
35	13 August 1942	1000	14 August 1942	Terezin
36	17 August 1942	1003	21 August 1942	Maly Trostinec
37	20 August 1942	1000	21 August 1942	Terezin
38	27 August 1942	1000	28 August 1942	Terezin
39	31 August 1942	967	2/4 September 1942	Maly Trostinec
40	10 September 1942	1000	11 September 1942	Terezin
41	14 September 1942	992	16/18 September 1942	Maly Trostinec
42	24 September 1942	1300	25 September 1942	Terezin
43	1 October 1942	1290/1299	2 October 1942	Terezin
44	5 October 1942	544/547	9 October 1942	Maly Trostinec
45	8/9 October 1942	1323/1306	9/10 October 1942	Terezin
—	8 December 1942	9		Auschwitz

46a	5 January 1943	100	6 January 1943	Terezín
46b	8 January 1943	100	9 January 1943	Terezín
46c	11 January 1943	100	12 January 1943	Terezín
46d	28 January 1943	9	29 January 1943	Terezín
46e	25 February 1943	70	26 February 1943	Terezín
47	3 March 1943	75	5 March 1943	Auschwitz
46f	30 March 1943	101	1 April 1943	Terezín
47b	31 March 1943	85		Auschwitz
46g	1 April 1943	72	2 April 1943	Terezín
IV/14g Ez	27 April 1943	2	28 April 1943	Terezín
46h	25 May 1943	205/203	27 May 1943	Terezín
46h	16 June 1943	2*	17 June 1943	Terezín
46i	24 June 1943	151/152	26 June 1943	Terezín
	15 July 1943	17	16 July 1943	Terezín
	2 September 1943	20	3 September 1943	Terezín
	9 September 1943	10		Terezín
	15 September 1943	1		Terezín
47c	7 October 1943	21		Auschwitz
	11 November 1943	91	12 November 1943	Terezín
	30 November 1943	46	1 December 1943	Terezín
47d	1 December 1943	25		Auschwitz
	14 December 1943	1		Terezín
	10 January 1944	6**	11 January 1944	Terezín
	19 January 1944	1		Terezín
47e	24 February 1944	41		Auschwitz
	10 March 1944	84	11 March 1944	Terezín
47f	26 April 1944	19		Auschwitz
	28 April 1944	80	29 April 1944	Terezín
	17 May 1944	1**	18 May 1944	Terezín
	18 May 1944	4**	19 May 1944	Terezín
	2 June 1944	1†	3 June 1944	Terezín
	21 June 1944	4*	22 June 1944	Terezín
47g	27 June 1944	22	28 June 1944	Auschwitz
	28 June 1944	18	29 June 1944	Terezín
—	28 June 1944	38	29 June 1944	Auschwitz
	9 July 1944	5**	10 July 1944	Terezín
	23 July 1944	1*	24 July 1944	Terezín
	16 August 1944	16	17 August 1944	Terezín
—	21 August 1944	2		Auschwitz
47h	1 September 1944	29	4 September 1944	Auschwitz
	21 September 1944	2**	22 September 1944	Terezín
—	5 October 1944	100		Auschwitz
	20 November 1944	4	21 November 1944	Terezín
	22 November 1944	1	23 November 1944	Terezín
	1 February 1945	4	2 February 1945	Terezín
	15 February 1945	7††	16 February 1945	Terezín
		1074	8 March 1945	Terezín
	19 March 1945	11	20 March 1945	Terezín

*Vienna and Linz
**Vienna and Graz
†Vienna and Traunkirchen
††Vienna and Salzburg

Source: Alfred Gottwaldt and Diana Schulle, *Die "Judendeportationen" aus dem Deutschen Reich 1941-1945*, (Wiesbaden: Marix Verlag GmbH, 2005); Jonny Moser, *Demographie der jüdischen Bevölkerung Österreichs 1938-1945* (Vienna: DÖW, 1999). Table designed by Dr. Tom Weiss.

While Jews selected for transport sat on trains headed to their new "residence" in the east, others continued their work for the IKG without pause. Some stayed busy organizing the next transports; others were assigned to apartment cleaning -- an aspect of the deportation process the Germans regarded as highly important. They expected that after every transport, the apartments of deported Jews would be cleaned, and that every item left behind would be carefully accounted for. Punctuality was essential for the cleaning cycle to occur effectively, and they assigned Robert Prochnik of the IKG to manage this detail. [67] They expected IKG employees to retrieve the keys from the Sammellager, return to the apartments, and take out the remaining objects together with the assets lists. Cleaners were permitted to keep certain items that could help to sustain the remaining community. Cheap but necessary possessions such as old clothing, simple beds, and inexpensive furniture went to the welfare department of the IKG.[68] The valuable items, went to the Vuguesta (Office for the Disposal of the Property of Jewish Emigrants).[69] These goods were taken to a warehouse in Vienna's nineteenth district, where IKG workers sorted them in preparation for sale. Some items were shipped to Germany. Ernst Neumann recalled moving furniture and goods in this warehouse and described the building, full of looted Jewish goods, as "gigantic... with bookshelves rising to the sky."[70]

While Ernst Neumann and other IKG employees sorted the furniture of deported Jews, Dr. Joseph Grabkowicz received notice in September 1942 for his family to report

---

[67] USHMM film # 294, IKG- A/W 116, *Taetigkeitsbericht fuer das Jahr 1942 (2 Exemplare)*.

[68] Rabinovici, *Instanzen der Ohnmacht: 257.*

[69] For more information on the VUGESTA, which was created on 7 September 1940 and operated until the end of the war, see Robert Holzbauer, "Einziehung volks- und staatsfeindlichen Vermögens im Lande Österreich". Die "VUGESTA" - die "Verwertungsstelle für jüdisches Umzugsgut der Gestapo"in *Spurensuche* 1-2 (Wien, 2000) 38-50.

[70] See testimony of Ernst Neumann, who worked for the Vuguesta in Rabinovici, *Instanzen der Ohnmacht:* 255; 257.

for transfer to the east.[71] Neumann remained employed by the IKG because his function still helped the Germans; Dr. Grabkowicz -- whom the Germans had permitted to continue his dental practice among Jews from 1938 to 1942 -- was no longer needed.[72] By this time, the community had been greatly reduced and his dentistry skills were of little importance. His professional appliances were still valuable, however. On 31 August 1942, the Zentralstelle ordered the seizure of all medical appliances belonging to deported dentists and doctors. Two weeks later, Dr. Grabkowicz's name appeared on a list with fifteen other doctors deported on transport #41, whose homes were to be entered and whose medical equipment was to be handed over to the Gestapo immediately.[73] Two days after he boarded a train to Minsk, Maly Trostinecs with his wife Hilde and their daughter Vera, IKG workers -- perhaps his former colleagues -- received this next instruction (14 September 1942). The protocol from their leader, Robert Prochnik, instructed them to enter the doctor's home on Johannesgasse, in Vienna's first district. It was just one of 110 apartments from which IKG employees were ordered to seize medical apparatuses following the decree of 31 August 1942 and one of 976 apartments across Vienna's twenty-one separate districts cleaned that year. The IKG employees who carried out this final step of the deportation process felt protected. They avoided deportation for as long as their service was necessary to the Germans, and they did not

---

[71] For information on another IKG employee with the VUGUESTA, see Martha, D., 1997. "Interview by Survivors of the Shoah Visual History Foundation," Australia. Interview Code 34975.

[72] Internal IKG document from Loewenherz to the Commissioner of Jewish Doctors, lists the 20 doctors released from practice and deported in September 1942. Initialed by Loewenherz and dated 2 October 1942. Dr. Victor Frankel is also on this list. USHMM microfilm #Alpha T2, *Auswanderungsfrageboegen der Israelitischen Kultusgemeinde Wien (IKG)* [slide 0469]. See alsoUSHMM microfilm #Alpha T3, *Auswanderungsfrageboegen der Israelitischen Kultusgemeinde Wien (IKG), Dr. Josef Grabkowicz,* [slides 1113-1114].

[73] Internal IKG notice from Robert Israel Prochnik to the *Rechnungskontrolle,* dated 16 September 1942. See USHMM film #898, A/W 443, *Wohnungsangelegenheiten, Aushebungen* [slide 0955].

know how long that would be.[74] They continued their work and continued to have hope, but it was only a matter of time before they too received a notice to "resettle" in the east. They were among the last to go.

Daily Life, 1941-1942

People carried on with their daily lives while the deportation process ran in full swing, but life became a continuously greater challenge. Kurt Klein remembered an atmosphere filled with tension and distress: "I don't think I can tell you the fear and the gradual horror that just that type of life can bring," he recalled, "when you are constantly worrying about what is going to happen."[75] After the Wansee Conference in January 1942, well into the deportation process, the Germans imposed additional restrictions on Jews which exacerbated their already inadequate living conditions. Not only did they have to say goodbye to family and friends who were being "resettled," but they had to part with almost all personal possessions.[76] Nazi law decreed that deported Jews' possessions became property of the Reich, but the regime could not wait for all the Jews to be deported. The Gestapo ordered the IKG to carry out "collection drives" (Sammelaktion) and the IKG followed this instruction. Like all measures the Germans forced the IKG to carry out, the collection drives had to be carefully planned and orchestrated. They

---

[74] Peggy Rawitt, daughter of Regina Rawitt, email correspondence with the author, 26 May 2003. See Regina. R., 1995. "Interview by Survivors of the Shoah Visual History Foundation," Brooklyn, NY, USA, March 7. Interview Code 01279, Tapes 1-4.

[75] Curt, K.B., 1994. "Interview by Survivors of the Shoah Visual History Foundation," Los Angeles, CA, USA, December 15. Interview Code 00382, Tape 2, 2:30.

[76] 26 June 1942, Order that "all Jews who are obligated to wear the star, and all persons who live together with them, are forbidden to keep a household pet -- a dog, cat, or a bird. This is to be taken into account immediately." USHMM film # N/A, IKG- A/W 134, 5, *Zirkulare der Amstdirektion und des Amtsvorstands an saemtliche Abteilungen bzw. Alle Angestellten und Mitarbeiter, 1942.*

operated from January through July 1942.[77] The IKG quickly arranged for community

members to deliver the required items to the collection center at Seitenstettengassse 4.

Jews had two to three days to deliver the items which were received between the hours of

8 a.m. and 6 p.m.[78] The IKG informed them that, according to the German order, they

would not receive compensation for their goods. During some collection drives,

however, people received a receipt for their donation -- including name, signature, and

exactly how many pieces were delivered.[79]

Most collection drives required all community members to hand over their

belongings, but some exempted "privileged" and "protected" persons, at least

temporarily. During the clothing drive on 15 June 1942, the Germans ordered the IKG to

collect towels, sheets, hats, ties, and all other fabric or material. This applied to all Jews

within the community, and everyone cooperated: 5,627 heads of household delivered a

total of over 13,869 kg of material.[80] Three days later, when the Germans ordered Jews

to turn in all electrical appliances (ovens, heating pads, hotplates, irons, hair driers,

records and record players), they did not require "privileged" Jews -- foreigners,

mischlinge, and Jews in mixed marriages -- to follow this order. They also made certain

exceptions: items being used in the hospital or children's home, or by authorized doctors

---

[77] On 10 January 1942 Jews had to deliver furs, skis, and wool items. USHMM film # 294, IKG- A/W 116, *Taetigkeitsbericht fuer das Jahr 1942 (2 Exemplare)*, 13.

[78] USHMM film # N/A, IKG- A/W 134, 5, *Zirkulare der Amstdirektion und des Amtsvorstands an saemtliche Abteilungen bzw. Alle Angestellten und Mitarbeiter, 1942.*

[79] There is no clear reason for these differing practices. USHMM film # N/A, IKG- A/W 134, 5, *Zirkulare der Amstdirektion und des Amtsvorstands an saemtliche Abteilungen bzw. Alle Angestellten und Mitarbeiter, 1942.*

[80] For further details of this clothing drive, see USHMM film # 294, IKG- A/W 116, *Taetigkeitsbericht fuer das Jahr 1942 (2 Exemplare).* See also USHMM film # N/A, IKG- A/W 134, 5, *Zirkulare der Amstdirektion und des Amtsvorstands an saemtliche Abteilungen bzw. Alle Angestellten und Mitarbeiter, 1942.* A similar decree passed on 10 July 1942 ordered all Jews to deliver fur items. The IKG received 138 rare furs and 2,798 other furs and fur items. USHMM film # 294, IKG- A/W 116, *Taetigkeitsbericht fuer das Jahr 1942 (2 Exemplare); Judisches Nachtrichtenblatt* on 31 July 1942.

and dentists, could remain if needed by "protected" Jews. [81] Again, when it came time to

surrender previously registered items such as bicycles, typewriters, calculators, copy

machines, photo film, magnifying devices, photo/light meters, binoculars, spyglasses, and

theater glasses on 30 June 1942, "privileged" Jews received a pass [82] and IKG workers

were permitted to keep certain office appliances essential to the functioning of the

community -- typewriters, mimeographs, and paper supplies. These IKG employees and

other protected Jews, such as authorized doctors, could request to continue using an item

needed for work purposes. By writing to the Advisory Office for Assets Concerns in the

IKG, Seitenstettengasse 4, Door 11, physicians, for example, could request to keep their

bicycles for the purpose of house visits. [83]

The collection drives served as a final means to rob Jews of their last possessions

before deporting them to the east. Everyone in the community forced to follow these

demands suffered. The privileged and protected persons whom the Germans permitted to

keep certain items, doctors like Dr. Grabkowicz, were spared only temporarily. They

would be robbed after deportation. The Germans had expropriated the property of Jews

since they entered Vienna, but this final call to hand over remaining possessions was a

grievous blow. For some people, clothing, bedding, and other simple household items

---

[81] During this Sammelaktion, 394 Jewish households delivered 855 pieces. For further details see:
USHMM film # 294, IKG- A/W 116, *Taetigkeitsbericht fuer das Jahr 1942 (2 Exemplare)*; USHMM film
N/A, IKG- A/W 134, 5, *Zirkulare der Amstdirektion und des Amtsvorstands an saemtliche Abteilungen
bzw. Alle Angestellten und Mitarbeiter, 1942.*

[82] According to the decree of 13 December 1941, Jews were required to register these items with the state.
See Martin Dean, *Robbing the Jews: the Confiscation of Jewish Property in the Holocaust, 1933-1945*
(Cambridge: Cambridge University Press, 2008). A total of 1,105 pieces were delivered. For further details
of this collection drive see: USHMM film # 294, IKG- A/W 116, *Taetigkeitsbericht fuer das Jahr 1942 (2
Exemplare)*; USHMM film # N/A, IKG- A/W 134, 5, *Zirkulare der Amstdirektion und des Amtsvorstands
an saemtliche Abteilungen bzw. Alle Angestellten und Mitarbeiter, 1942.*

[83] USHMM film # N/A, IKG- A/W 134, 5, *Zirkulare der Amstdirektion und des Amtsvorstands an
saemtliche Abteilungen bzw. Alle Angestellten und Mitarbeiter, 1942.*

carried deep meaning; these tangible objects reflected the past, the family members who had gone before them, the loved ones who gave them hope to carry on.[84]

The Germans ordered the IKG to run the deportations and to systematize depradation. So too did they require the assistance of the IKG as they clamped down on Jewish life, micromanaging people's daily activities. While they never established a sealed ghetto in Vienna, the Nazis' fist clenched tighter and tighter around the Jews. The concentration of Vienna's Jews started in May 1941 as they forced Jews into collective apartments in the second, ninth, and twentieth district. At that time Jews could still move about the city without necessarily being recognized, but not for long. In September 1941 the Germans ordered them to mark their clothing with a Star of David, and some seven months later (April 1942) the Jewish paper announced: "By order of the authorities... All persons ... must attach a Jewish star to the outside of the doorway to their home."[85]

As with all German orders, the IKG immediately prepared to implement this next decree. Loewenherz sent a memorandum on 9 April 1942 explaining that in accordance with the decree from the Reich Security Main Office, and under official order of the Zentralstelle,[86] "the following is to be made known: the Jewish star is to appear on all Jewish homes and institutions."[87] He sent this memo to all offices, divisions, and employees of the IKG, and to organizations under their supervision. The IKG arranged this next detail, and the disbursement of the stars was carried out over the course of five days: Friday 10 April from 8- 6, Saturday 11 April from 8-6, Sunday 12 April from 8-1,

---

[84] See final letters in Secher, *Left behind in Nazi Vienna*, 253-296.
[85] "Verlautbarung" in *Jüdisches Nachtrichtenblatt*, Friday, 3 April 1942.
[86] USHMM film # 294, IKG- A/W 116, *Taetigkeitsbericht fuer das Jahr 1942 (2 Exemplare)*.
[87] USHMM film # N/A, IKG- A/W 134, 5, *Zirkulare der Amstdirektion und des Amtsvorstands an saemtliche Abteilungen bzw. Alle Angestellten und Mitarbeiter, 1942*.

Monday 13 April 3:30-6, and Tuesday 14 April 3:30-8:15. There was a total of 7,430 stars: 6,260 stars provided for distribution, plus an additional 37 sheets with 6 stars on each and 79 sheets with 12 stars on each. Although the first count was not completely accurate -- some of the stars were missing, some people ordered too many, some were torn or damaged, some people had two doors to hang the star on -- from this grand total, some 6,762 were distributed to Jewish households, institutions and organizations throughout Vienna's twenty-five districts. The IKG carried out this order successfully and with efficiency. Community members cooperated and took the new order seriously. In a follow-up report to the Germans, the IKG noted that recipients had complained about the quality and cleanliness of the stars, requesting that more stars be made and placed in the community storage.[88]

Jews remaining in Vienna through the great deportations in April 1942 lived under ghetto-like conditions. Although barbed wire did not physically confine them, and they lived in districts throughout the entire city,[89] they did not move freely, nor were they able to evade German orders. While some individual Jews risked removing the star from their clothing, they could not escape from their lodgings now marked with a star.[90] Of the approximately 6,500 stars distributed,[91] 3,742 went to the second district, where the Jews were concentrated; but the ninth district received 848; the first district, 621; the twentieth, 308; the third, 206; the seventh, 131; the eighth, 103; and the rest of the

---

[88] USHMM film # 898, IKG- A/W 431, *Summarischer Bericht ueber die Ausgabe der Kennzeichen fuer Judenwohnungen, 04.1942.*

[89] According to Raul Hilberg by 1941 Jews lived in one of three districts designated for Jewish residency (2, 19, and 20) but this is inaccurate. Many Jews lived in these three districts, but not all. See Hilberg, *The Destruction of the European Jews,* 457.

[90] See "Warnung," May 1942 in USHMM film # N/A, IKG- A/W 134, 5, *Zirkulare der Amstdirektion und des Amtsvorstands an saemtliche Abteilungen bzw. Alle Angestellten und Mitarbeiter, 1942.*

[91] According to a second IKG report, during 10-11 April, Jewish stars were distributed to 6,350 Jewish heads of household. USHMM film # 294, IKG- A/W 116, *Taetigkeitsbericht fuer das Jahr 1942 (2 Exemplare).*

districts received 100 or fewer. For Jews living in Vienna in 1942, hiding was practically impossible; their clothing was marked, their homes and institutions were marked and, most significantly, their names had been listed in a central registry shared by the IKG and Zentralstelle. There was no way out: hiding did not surface as a viable option to resist Nazi oppression. Thus, without actually building a ghetto, the Germans had managed to create a ghetto-like atmosphere which helped them to achieve the same end: deportation.

Table 13: "The Jewish Star is to appear on All Jewish Homes and Institutions, April 1942

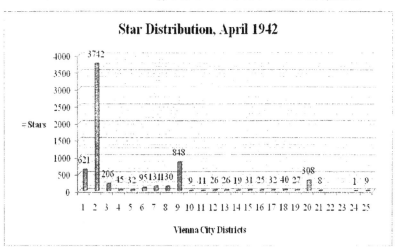

Source: USHMM film # 898, IKG- A/W 431,
Summarischer Bericht ueber die Ausgabe der Kennzeichen fuer Judenwohnungen, 04.1942.

If Jews could not hide, they also could not evade the orders and restrictions the Germans continued to impose upon them. Four years after Anschluss, racial terror pressed down on them more viciously than ever. Jews were given a curfew, forbidden to use certain public transportation,[92] and summoned randomly to forced labor details.[93] Even for IKG workers who were supposed to be protected, the noose tightened. The Germans determined how long they would work (their hours were extended to include Saturdays); how they could travel to and from work (their transportation to the IKG on the tram or by bicycle was permitted, but only for travel between their apartment and place of work); and which equipment they could and could not continue to use in the IKG offices (telephone use was heavily restricted).[94] The Germans even designated the hours when IKG workers could bathe: all department heads -- from the cemetery office, the financial affairs office, the bookkeeping, cashier, research group, the tax office, the central registry office, the newspaper office, the technical office, the doctor's office, the rabbinate, the assets affairs office, the housing office, the correspondence office, the material administration, the welfare office, the personal registry -- had to sign a document stating that they received the order that the IKG bathhouse on Flossgasse 14 in the second district was open to them on Sunday afternoons from 2 p.m. to 6 p.m. -- for a fee of 50 pfennig per person.[95] In the spring of 1942 the Jewish newspaper listed by name and district all parks forbidden to Jews, but by that time they had already accepted the Jewish cemeteries as their new places for outdoor recreation.[96] The community no longer

---

[92] See "Verlautbarung" in *Jüdisches Nachtrichtenblatt*, 4 July 1942. See also, USHMM film # 294, IKG-A/W 116, *Taetigkeitsbericht fuer das Jahr 1942 (2 Exemplare)*.

[93] Gestapo order to IKG regarding forced labor deployments, 28 May 1942. From 31 May to 23 August, on 13 consecutive Sundays, 1,360 Jews were pressed into a wood-collecting action. This was similar to the order for 3,000 Jews to shovel snow in Vienna during Feb and March 1942. For details see: USHMM film # 294, IKG- *A/W 116, Taetigkeitsbericht fuer das Jahr 1942 (2 Exemplare)*. For more on forced labor see: Wolf Gruner, *Jewish Forced Labor Under the Nazis, Economic Needs and Racial Aims 1938-1944* (Cambridge: Cambridge University Press, 2006).

[94] See notice from 14 May 1942 in USHMM film # N/A, IKG- A/W 134, 5, *Zirkulare der Amstdirektion und des Amtsvorstands an saemtliche Abteilungen bzw. Alle Angestellten und Mitarbeiter, 1942.*

[95] Order from 28 August 1942 in USHMM film # N/A, IKG- A/W 134, 5, *Zirkulare der Amstdirektion und des Amtsvorstands an saemtliche Abteilungen bzw. Alle Angestellten und Mitarbeiter, 1942.*

[96] "Verlautbarung" in *Jüdisches Nachtrichtenblatt*, 8 May 1942; USHMM film # 294, IKG- A/W 116, *Taetigkeitsbericht fuer das Jahr 1942 (2 Exemplare)*.

had any freedom to think or act on its own terms; the leaders served as messengers for the Germans, ensuring that their employees did their work, and together they ensured that all others cooperated. They believed that survival depended upon obedience, upon the community's ability to follow German demands efficiently. Again, resistance to authority did not surface as an option.

From the IKG to a Council of Jewish Elders

The last mass transports left Vienna in October 1942. The trains carried many IKG employees and volunteers whose work had both enabled the deportation process and sustained the welfare of the community that remained behind. Two transports left that month for Theresienstadt, carrying approximately 1,500 IKG workers and their dependants, as well as some people previously protected by German law,[97] and "privileged" people, including injured or decorated war veterans and some Jewish partners and mischlinge. Five hundred forty-four persons were deported to Minsk, Maly Trostinecs. Those who went to Theresienstadt instead of Minsk, had a chance of survival; the others faced immediate death.[98] Everyone who had worked for the IKG believed their employment would spare them from deportation, but they were all fooled. "I was supposed to be protected from deportation!" Martha Donath recalled, reliving the moment of shock when she received notice to "resettle" in October 1942. "We [who

---

[97] For more information on the treatment of "privileged" Jews in Vienna see, Rabinovici, *Instanzen der Ohnmacht:* 277. Also see "Special Problem I. Michlinge and Jews in Mixed Marriages," in Hilberg, *The Destruction of the European Jews*, 417-430.

[98] Jews were shot upon arrival at Maly Trostinecs; 30 percent of Vienna's Jews deported to the Theresienstadt ghetto survived, the other 70 percent were sent on to annihilation camps and murdered. Rabinovici, *Instanzen der Ohnmacht:* 238-9.

worked for the IKG] always felt that there was a 'protektion.'"[99] As Martha boarded the

train to Theresienstadt, it is hard to speculate what thoughts went through her head. The

deportation notice had come to her as a surprise. Did she suddenly feel betrayed by the

IKG, and as if her years of service had been in vain? Were her thoughts shared by other

IKG workers on the transport? Or, had some former employees accepted "resettlement"

as imminent, and continued to work for their community despite this understanding? The

last mass transport left the Aspang Banhof for Theresienstadt on 9 October 1942 carrying

Martha Donath and many other IKG workers. It was the largest transport ever to leave

Vienna, carrying 1,306 persons. It brought to an end the vicious cycle of transports of

Jews organized and carried out by other Jews.

As the IKG employees disappeared, so too did their institution. The Zentralstelle

essentially fulfilled its goal of making Vienna "Judenrein" that October. On 23

November 1942 the IKG became the "Council of Jewish Elders in Vienna," operating

with a staff of 334 persons, 254 paid workers and 80 volunteers.[100] The German

authorities permitted the new council to maintain a hospital, children's hospital, an old-

age home, a community kitchen, clothing department, welfare department, cemetery

administration, emergency shelter, technical office, bathhouse, newspaper, and a library

for the 7,989 remaining members. These people, including the IKG workers who now

worked for the new Council of Jewish Elders, were still subject to German demands.[101]

Loewenherz and Murmelstein sent out a memo including six new regulations to their few

---

[99] Martha, D., 1997. "Interview by Survivors of the Shoah Visual History Foundation," Australia. Interview Code 34975.

[100] USHMM film # 294, *IKG- A/W 116, Taetigkeitsbericht fuer das Jahr 1942 (2 Exemplare)* 20: Rosenkranz, *Vervolgung und Selbstbehauptung:* 523.

[101] Among these demands was forced labor. In 1943, the Germans deployed 3,800 persons, 578 of which were full-professing Jews and the rest were in mixed marriages. Wolf Gruner, *Jewish Forced Labor under the Nazis, Economic Needs and Racial Aims 1938-1944* (Cambridge: Cambridge University Press, 2006).

remaining employees. The bulletin addressed the new work hours (which included Saturday and Sunday) and the proper use of heat, desk lamps, and overhead lighting, as well as paper and writing utensils. "All printed matter with the heading *Israelitische Kultusgemeinde Wien* is to be printed over with the division name or the institution stamp .... Stamps that read *Israelitische Kultusgemeinde Wien* are to be turned in to the material administration."[102] The transformation was official. The orders remained the same. Although 90 percent of the community had vanished through emigration or deportation, still the leaders passed down demands and instructed those who remained to obey. The deportation of Jews by other Jews came to an end in 1942, but the pattern of Jewish cooperation with the Germans did not.

Nor did the deportation of Jews terminate completely. In November and December 1942 no further transports left Vienna, but in January 1943 they commenced again, now prepared by the Gestapo, and they continued until the end of the war.[103] The Council of Jewish Elders remained in Vienna at the start of 1943 together with 7,898 "Jewish" persons: 3,839 men and 4,150 women. Within this community there were approximately 3,000 Jews of faith or *Glaubensjuden,* plus another 5,000 *Nichtglaubensjuden* who did not profess the Jewish faith.[104] 5,564 individuals were intermarried, 3,665 living in "privileged" and 1,881 "non-privileged" mixed marriages.[105]

---

[102] See, USHMM film # N/A, IKG- A/W 134, 5, *Zirkulare der Amstdirektion und des Amtsvorstands an saemtliche Abteilungen bzw. Alle Angestellten und Mitarbeiter, 1942.*

[103] The Gestapo controlled the deportation after October 1942. USHMM film # 294, *IKG- A/W 117, Taetigkeitsbericht fuer das Jahr 1943 (2 Exemplare)*

[104] Moser, *Demographie der jüdischen Bevölkerung Österreichs,* 47, 50.

[105] USHMM film # 294, *IKG- A/W 117, Taetigkeitsbericht fuer das Jahr 1943 (2 Exemplare).* Due to the death of the Aryan spouse, these persons would be considered Jews overnight. For a complete description of "privileged" vs. "non-privileged" mixed-marriages, see Hilberg, *The Destruction of the European Jews,* 427.

Another 2,425 persons remained who the Nazis considered Jews: Mischling of the first

degree, also called *Geltungsjuden*.[106]

During the year of 1943, the Gestapo deported 1,216 of these persons from

Vienna to Theresienstadt (1,078) and directly to Auschwitz (139) in small transports of

only 80-150 people.[107] These transports included mischlinge children like Helga Feldner-

Busztin[108] and Kurt Klein[109] and formerly protected IKG workers Henry Wegner[110] and

Lizi Sussmann.[111] They also carried 152 employees from the Council of Jewish Elders,

including Dr. Benjamin Murmelstein.[112] At the beginning of 1944, 3,045 men and 3,214

women remained in Vienna, the majority of which were in mixed-marriages, 1,080 who

were considered full-Jews or *Geltungsjuden* (including the remaining staff of the Council

of Jewish Elders), and 85 foreign Jews. Small transports continued to carry these people

away to Theresienstadt and Auschwitz throughout 1944 and the start of 1945. The final

transport holding 11 persons left Vienna for Theresienstadt on 19 March 1945. When

Soviet troops marched into Austria in April 1945, only 5, 512 persons were registered

with the Council of Jewish Elders: Vienna was essentially "Judenrein."[113]

---

[106] A Geltungsjude or Mischling of the first degree was a person who had two Jewish grandparents.

[107] USHMM film # 294, *IKG- A/W 117, Taetigkeitsbericht fuer das Jahr 1943(2 Exemplare)*.

[108] Helga Feldner-Busztin was deported to Theresienstadt on 25 February 1943.

[109] Kurt and his brother Egon reported to Kleine Sperlgasse Sammellager in January 1942 but, after coming down with jaundice, they were released and transferred to the hospital. Curt, K.B., 1994. "Interview by Survivors of the Shoah Visual History Foundation," Los Angeles, CA, USA, December 15. Interview Code 00382, Tapes 1-6.

[110] Henry Wegner worked for the IKG. Henry, W.,1998. "Interview by Survivors of the Shoah Visual History Foundation," New York, NY, USA, June 17. Interview Code 42662, Tapes 1-6.

[111] The deportation process differed after October 1942. For example, Henry Wegner and Lizi Sussmann describe wearing white tags with their transport numbers when they were deported to Theresienstadt in 1943. Henry, W.,1998. "Interview by Survivors of the Shoah Visual History Foundation," New York, NY, USA, June 17. Interview Code 42662, Tapes 1-6; Liz, M., 1996. "Interview by Survivors of the Shoah Visual History Foundation," New York, NY, USA, March 8. Interview Code 12674, Tapes 1-8.

[112] Murmelstein left Vienna for Theresienstadt in March 1943. USHMM, RG-60.5009, Tape 3158-3190, *Claude Lanzmann Shoah Collection, Interview with Benjamin Murmelstein* (Rome: 1975).

[113] This group of 5,512 was non-representative of the original Jewish population. Those who remained were protected by their marriage to a non-Jewish spouse and many did not profess to the Jewish faith, but were considered Jews by Nazi definition. Moser, *Demographie der jüdischen Bevölkerung Österreichs*, 55.

Illustration 29:
"IKG Population Statistics: Deportations, Deaths, Births: 1 January 1942 - 31 December 1942" [114]

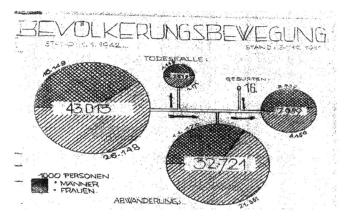

Source: Original IKG Diagram, USHMM film # 294, *IKG- A/W 116, Taetigkeitsbericht fuer das Jahr 1942*

---

[114] IKG reports from May 1938 through January 1944 track the population demographics of the Jewish community of Vienna. Reports are directed to the foreign aid committees from May 1938- July 1941, after which point the reports are written for the German authorities and internal IKG use. The reports up until July 1941 note a continual decrease in the population count due to "auswanderung" or emigration; after January 1942, due to "abwanderung:" a euphemism for deportation. (There is no report for the period between August- December 1941, when 8,000 persons are deported and no further emigration is permitted.). All IKG reports are exceptionally detailed, but the accuracy of the figures is still problematic. Following the deportations to Nisko in October 1939, an IKG report listed the 1,584 deportees as if they had immigrated to Poland (USHMM film #294, IKG- A/W 130 *Report of the Vienna Jewish Community July -October 1939 [2 Exemplare]*). However, following the transport of 5,000 persons in February and March 1941, the IKG report made no mention of the action. The report continued to list emigration figures, but disregarded the 5,000 deportees. Likewise, between October and December 1941, another 8,000 people were deported and the report of January 1942 does not account for the reduction of these people, but remains with the same figure (43,031) as the report of July 1941(44,000). The population figure of 43,013 from 1 January 1942 (shown in the diagram above) therefore, must include a large percentage of *Nichtglaubensjuden*, estimated at 10,000. Total Jews in Vienna as of **September 1939: 66,260** (USHMM film # 294, IKG-A/W 126, *A description of the activity of the Israelitische Kultusgemeinde Wien in the period from May 2ⁿᵈ 1938- December 31ˢᵗ 1939 [2 Exemplare]*; **January 1940: 55,500; May 1940: 50,385** (USHMM film #907, IKG- A/W 2533, *Twelve Questions about Emigration from Vienna, 01.01- 30.04.1940*); **September 1940: 48,465** (USHMM film #295, IKG- A/W 131, *Israelitische Kultusgeminde Vienna. Activity During Twelve Months of War, 01.09.1939-31.08.1940*); **January 1941: 46,200** (USHMM film # 294, IKG- A/W 113, *Bericht in Tabellenform betreffend Auswanderungsangelegenheiten, Bevoelkerungsstand, Fuersorgeangelegenheiten und Umschulung, Jaenner- Dezember 1940*; USHMM film # 295, IKG- A/W 132, *Israelitische Kultusgeminde Vienna. Survey on Nineteenhundredfourty*).Total Jews (including non-professing Jews or *Nichtglaubensjuden*) as of **July 1941: 44,000** (USHMM film # 295, IKG- A/W 115, *Tatigkeitsberichte in Tabellenform [Anschlag?] fuer die Zeit vom 01. Jaenner-30. Juni 1941*; **January 1942: 43,013** (USHMM film # 294, IKG- A/W 116, *Taetigkeitsbericht fuer das Jahr 1942 [2 Exemplare]*); **January 1943: 7,989** (USHMM film # 294, IKG- A/W 116, *Taetigkeitsbericht fuer das Jahr 1942[2 Exemplare]*); **January 1944: 6,259** (USHMM film # 294, IKG- A/W 117, *Taetigkeitsbericht fuer das Jahr 1943 [2 Exemplare]*).

A Vicious Cycle

The Jewish community of 1941, composed predominantly of old people and females (and most particularly elderly women) was a small and dying remnant of a society that had once flourished. The Germans' demands upon the IKG leaders and workers after October 1941 differed from those of the past, as did the process the latter facilitated: deportation. While the Zentralstelle ordered the IKG to organize and manage the transports, sealing the final destruction of the community, they no longer permitted the IKG to rescue others, as they had allowed during the previous three years. Despite this knowledge, neither the IKG leaders nor the rank and file changed their reaction or response to their oppressors; they continued to carry out the Germans' demands with the utmost diligence as they had all along. Transport lists, round-ups, collection centers, and Jewish stars, orders with implications significantly more drastic than those of the past, went unchallenged and were accepted as simply more rules to be obeyed.

The population was disproportionally female and elderly; those remaining were too weak, spiritually and physically, to oppose or resist Nazism at this late date, too unprepared to resist organizing the deportations or to attempt to spare the last Jewish children from an unknown but feared fate.[115] Then too, after years of "success" from their policy of co-operation, the leaders did not believe the risk of resistance was worth its possible repercussions. A vicious cycle of codependency and cooperation took hold in 1938, enabling the deportation of tens of thousands of Jews, by other Jews, in 1941 and 1942. These Jewish-run processes which facilitated the deportations, were only possible after years of cooperation between the Germans and the IKG.

---

[115] Rabinovici shares a similar sentiment about resistance. He mentions that since essentially all young men had emigrated or been deported by October 1941, the remaining population was too weak to resist, even if they had known what lay ahead. Rabinovici, *Instanzen der Ohnmacht*, 339.

Holocaust historian Raul Hilberg analyzed the plight of Vienna's Jews and offered an analysis of their reaction and response during the deportation period "The Jewish community was now expected to do the ultimate: Jews had to seize Jews. It did so, rationalizing that thereby it would assure a more humane procedure."[116] Hilberg's explanation for Jewish cooperation with the Germans at this time deals very superficially with this knotty problem, identifying one way in which the victims became agents of their own destruction: in order to avoid further harm. Historian Doron Rabinovici analyzes this problem in greater depth. Depicting the IKG's struggle during this time, he has offered a key explanation for their reaction and response: "[the IKG] followed the rules, so that at the least, they could save as many Jews as possible. Yet as they followed the rules, they helped the perpetrators to murder as many people as possible."[117] Rabinovici illuminates the codependent relationships between ordinary Jewish people, IKG leaders and workers, and the German authorities, drawing our attention to the trap the Nazis led the Jews into in May 1938, and from which they never escaped: "All those who wanted to eat were registered with the community.... Every [IKG] organization that was [initially] established to provide the healthcare and maintenance of the Jews, [eventually] served its undoing -- expropriation, deportation, and murder -- the machinery of destruction."[118]

What Rabinovici, Hilberg, and other historians have not come to a conclusion on, is how and why leaders and workers remained dedicated to the work of the IKG, even after the Germans ordered them to arrange the deportations and the destruction of their own community. How and why did people continue to follow these orders? As we have

---

[116] Hilberg, *The Destruction of the European Jews*, 458.
[117] Rabinovici, *Instanzen der Ohnmacht*, 277.
[118] Ibid: 222.

seen, by 1941 a pattern of codependency and cooperation had been long established between the Germans and the IKG. With the Anschluss pogrom in 1938, the sudden arrests and transports to Dachau that following spring, and the pogrom of November 9-10, Vienna's Jews quickly learned that resistance to Nazism was not viable solution to their misery. Even at these early stages during the developing genocide, it was clear that attempting to avoid, challenge, or disobey German orders was not only futile, but could have terrible repercussions on the entire community. The only response to Nazi oppression that surfaced as a popular alternative to cooperation was suicide.

The leaders, workers, and community members responded in the most rational way they knew. There are a number of reasons for this. First, it is important to note that everyone existed -- ate, slept, worked, and made all decisions -- in a situation of extreme duress. When filmmaker Claude Lanzmann interviewed Murmelstein decades later and asked him what he thought the Nazis had planned for the Jews, Murmelstein explained that he and his workers did not have time to think about such things, they only had time to act.[119] He clarified that the IKG employees did not have the chance to contemplate their actions; orders became orders, and people did as they were told. There is a ring of authenticity to Murmelsteins observation and, if true, it is likely that the same situation obtained for most (if not nearly all) community members.

If, however, Murmelstein's viewpoint reflects the exception, and others took time to contemplate the situation and how best to respond, it would seem that they had too little information and they certainly did not and could not transform that information into knowledge. People did not fully grasp the danger they were in; they did not believe that

---

[119]USHMM, RG-60.5009, Tape 3158-3190, *Claude Lanzmann Shoah Collection, Interview with Benjamin Murmelstein* (Rome: 1975), see tape 3170.

they were targets for murder. Regardless of what they heard, neither the leadership nor the rank and file truly believed that the Germans aimed at the mass annihilation of European Jewry: this was an incomprehensible idea. For example, when Loewenherz heard rumors of gas chambers and mass murders in the summer of 1941, he approached his Nazi boss and Brunner dismissed his fears, telling him such allegations were false, evil reports.[120] Brunner told Loewenherz precisely what he needed to hear in order to continue his work. And Murmelstein, for his part, did not believe that such rumors *could* be true. While he understood that deportation was a wrenching ordeal he believed that if people were healthy it did not mean automatic death; he thought the final destination of the transports would be something like Nisko.[121] Even when both IKG leaders traveled to Berlin (19 February 1942) to meet with their counterparts from Prague and Berlin and learned that the Germans intended to "evacuate" all Jews from the Altreich, Ostmark, and Protectorate, they still did not believe that mass murders had occurred or would occur. Loewenherz rationalized that this evacuation could not be possible in Vienna because the remaining population consisted of mostly "privileged" or "protected" persons -- or persons not capable of being moved because of old age or illness.[122] He still believed what his German superiors told him.

What about the rest of the people in the community -- IKG workers and ordinary people, the people who were selected for deportation? Did they know where they were going? Or what awaited them when they were told they were being resettled in "the east"? Elliot Sauerquell recalled that "word got around from mouth to mouth that they are

---

[120] Hilberg, *The Destruction of the European Jews*, 459.
[121] USHMM, RG-60.5009, Tape 3158-3190, *Claude Lanzmann Shoah Collection, Interview with Benjamin Murmelstein* (Rome: 1975), tape 3168, camera rolls #44-45 11:00:04 to 11:22:24.
[122] Rabinovici, *Instanzen der Ohnmacht*, 238.

putting them [transports] together to go and work in the east. Gentlemanly you know, they didn't say you are going to go and get killed." People knew that the transports meant to go east for labor, and they believed the lie they were told because no one would have imagined the reality. "We heard transports were going to Lodz and people were even sending postcards from there. So we thought we too were going to a ghetto... not that that was pleasant...but the purpose was labor.... Nobody thought that there will be shooting or killing. Maybe we were naïve, maybe the older ones had an idea -- but who imagines a thing like this?" Elliot Sauerquell left Vienna with his mother Anna on transport #15 on 26 January 1942 to Riga.[123] When he arrived he encountered a much different situation than he, his mother, or the others ever anticipated. "The SS said, 'Ladies and gentlemen...*Meine Damen und Herren*, we have buses. The way to the ghetto is very difficult, so we suggest that you take the buses.' The ones who took the buses didn't see the sun go down anymore," Elliot Sauerquell recalled. "They brought them straight into the woods and shot them."[124]

Sauerquell's recollections speak for his community; people thought they were being transferred east for the purpose of labor. People did not know -- not when they received the evacuation notices, left their homes, waited in the Sammellager, were transferred to the train station, boarded the train, or suffered on the long journey -- they were going to be killed. Despite all rumors, people did not know or *believe* that what lay ahead was certain death.

---

[123] *Documentation Center of the Austrian Resistance (DÖW):*DOEW-Project Registration by Name: The Austrian Victims of the Holocaust, 2001 (*http://www. doew.at*).
[124] Elliot,W., 1998. "Interview by Survivors of the Shoah Visual History Foundation," New York, NY, USA, March 25. Interview Code 40985, Tapes 1-5.

The reaction and response of the leadership, like that of the rank and file, is an important issue for analysis. And the first questions are: What options did they have? Was there an alternative to cooperation? According to Doron Ravinovici, there was none. In Rabinovici's view, all Jews were innocent victims, the leaders included; "the perpetrators left their victims with no way out of their moral dilemma."[125] He claims that neither they, nor any other victim group, could have responded differently under those circumstances, neither then, nor today.[126] Absolving the IKG leaders of the guilt charged against them for their cooperation with the Germans, he shows clearly and accurately how there was no other way they could have responded.[127] I agree with Rabinovici on this point.

Furthermore, I would argue that the question of how and why Loewenherz, Murmelstein, and the other Jewish leaders handled their situation as they did, and if they directed their community in the best possible way, has no clear answer. Supporting the analysis drawn from Auschwitz survivor and Nobel Laureate author Primo Levi, I believe that the actions of the Vienna IKG, like those of Jewish Police or kapos or Sonderkommandos, fall into a grey zone.[128] As Levi explained, every accused collaborator had his own motive, to be scrutinized individually, but the "greatest responsibility lies with the system, the very structure of the totalitarian state.... The

---

[125] Rabinovici, *Instanzen der Ohnmacht:* 340.

[126] Ibid: 426.

[127] For a discussion of IKG cooperation following the war, see "Fragen des Charakters" in Rabinovici, *Instanzen der Ohnmacht:* 354-411. After the war the Czechs charged Dr. Benjamin Murmelstein as a Nazi collaborator. His trial in Leitmeritz lasted almost a year until the prosecutor withdrew charges because Murmelstein was able to disprove all accusations against him. Still, Murmelstein lived on as a controversial figure until his death in 1989. Most allegations were against his activities as one of the Jewish Elders in Theresienstadt, although he was also accused of teaching Eichmann to read Hebrew. See George E. Berkley, *Hitler's Gift: The Story of Theresienstadt* (Boston: Branden Books, 1993). Also, in numerous testimonies in *Survivors of the Shoah Visual History Foundation,* both Viennese émigrés and survivors criticized Dr. Benjamin Murmelstein's character, referring to his last name as Murmel-"schwein" (pig).

[128] See "The Grey Zone" in Primo Levi, *The Drowned and the Saved* (New York: Summit Books, 1988) 36-69.

condition of the offended does not exclude culpability...but I know of no human tribunal to which one could delegate the judgment."

There are two key explanations why victims respond to their perpetrators with obedience: hope and fear. Elliot Sauerquell, for example, lost hope when he exited the train in Riga, but until that time hope helped sustain his daily life, as it did for many others in his community. And hope served as a motivation for continued cooperation by the IKG and everyone in the community. Whether religious, moderate, or secular, most individuals had faith in humanity and believed that the Germans' demands could not get much worse. Despite rumors and outbursts of crime, most Jews living in Vienna still viewed the Nazis as agents of a legitimate state bound to the rule of law. In the case of Josef Loewenherz, Benjamin Murmelstein, and the other IKG leaders who actually corresponded with the Germans, this hope was exceptionally deceiving. They believed they could continue to receive concessions in exchange through cooperation with the Nazis and the continued obedience of their fellow Jews.

In many ways, the results achieved justified that belief. Between 1938 and 1941 cooperation with the Germans had enabled them to provide for the welfare of all community members and to facilitate the emigration of two-thirds of the community. Now, although emigration was no longer an option for the remaining one-third, the leaders believed they could at least protect those Jews who worked for the IKG and those who were privileged. The leaders and employees continued to work for the IKG, hoping and trusting that they would be spared. They did not believe the Germans wanted to deport *all* Jews; they thought *they* would be protected. They had no way of knowing that as soon as their service was not needed, they would be subject to the same fate as the others.[129]

While the community carried on fueled by hope of survival, by 1941 they continued to cooperate because they *lacked* hope. The Jews who remained in Vienna during the year of the great deportations had suffered from utterly reduced physical conditions and severe emotional trauma. They were far too weak, tired, and drained of hope and ambition to collectively resist their situation, and even individual resistance was extremely rare. Fear invaded people's lives, causing them to feel withdrawn -- to see no alternative response to their condition other than to do exactly as told. Plus, one survivor, Max Weiss, recalled reading about Hitler's victories in the newspaper and how this contributed significantly to his lack of morale.[130] IKG leaders and ordinary people feared the repercussions of disobedience more than they feared following orders. Loewenherz, for example, did not need to know or believe rumors about mass murders to understand the danger of sending his people to these places in the east, but he feared jeopardizing the safety of those people who he thought were guaranteed protection, and his own life. Marie Kupler, on the other hand, attempted to make peace with her unknown fate before her deportation. In a letter to her nephew in New York, she described the fear which ate away at her day after day as she waited. "If only there wouldn't be that nagging fear that we shall be sent away; unfortunately that continues...."[131] But she also confronted her inability to alter her situation in any way. Two days later she wrote to her nephew again: "If, God forbid, we shall indeed be forced to leave, do not worry about us and let it

---

[129] Rabinovici, *Instanzen der Ohnmacht: 179-180.*
[130] Max, W., 1996. "Interview by Survivors of the Shoah Visual History Foundation," Staten Island, NJ, USA, February 25. Interview Code 12544, Tapes 1-4.
[131] Letter, 9 November 1941: Secher, *Left behind in Nazi Vienna:* 294.

depress you. We are calm and prepared to face the worst."[132] Not all Jews confronted the

uncertainty of their future with such profound expressions of aplomb as Marie Kupler,

but most shared in her feelings of helplessness, feelings they had been trying to resist for

years.

Final Words

In a report for the German authorities dated 31 December 1942, Loewenherz summarized

his community's work over the previous twelve months, including graphs, charts, and

precise figures. The first subject he addressed carried the subtitle "Abwanderung," a

euphemism for deportation.[133] After he laid out the steps the community had followed to

facilitate this process, he stressed that due to their hard work, dedication, and long hours,

they had fulfilled the task set before them.

> The year 1942 was occupied by the assignment of the
> *Abwanderungstransporte* (deportation transports) organized through the
> Central Office for Jewish Emigration. The duties of the *Israelitische
> Kultusgemeinde Wien* in conjunction with these transports were complex
> and required the strength and endurance of many departments and
> institutions.... This required great efforts from the employees, and was
> made possible through their hectic days -- many times they worked
> through the night....With exception of the month of March ... the
> transports were dispatched rapidly until 9 October 1942, so that in the
> entire time a total of 32,721 Jews left. [134]

---

[132] Final letter, 11 November 1941: Secher, *Left behind in Nazi Vienna*: 296.

[133] The use of the word "abwanderung," literally translated to "exit" or "emigration" is a euphemism for deportation. This is the first time the IKG uses the term "abwanderung;" in all previous reports they use the term "auswanderung" to refer to the emigration.

[134] USHMM film # 294, IKG- A/W 116, *Taetigkeitsbericht fuer das Jahr 1942 (2 Exemplare)*.

When he compiled this report, the vast majority of the people he referred to as "hard workers" had been sent to Theresienstadt and felt betrayed by the IKG leadership. Hard work had not saved them from deportation as they had believed it would. The IKG leadership sent them when they were no longer needed. Likewise, many of those who remained employed by the new Council of Jewish Elders (at the time this report was written) would be deported the following year.

Loewenherz nevertheless continued to focus on rescue. Toward the end of the report, he emphasized the IKG's many accomplishments, reflecting back to the beginning of the Nazi occupation in May 1938 through the IKG's final days in November 1942. He pointed out that the IKG had enabled the emigration of 136,000 Jews from Austria in the years 1938 and 1939. To make this possible, they had raised $4,500,000.00 and established 3,101 retraining courses through which 42,205 men and women learned a new trade. He also took pride in the IKG's social welfare achievements: the community went from one old-age home with 460 beds to 12 homes for 2,563 elderly; 19 soup kitchens feeding 38,500 per day; and a hospital with 450 beds that still managed to treat 90,131 patients as late as 1942. Loewenherz's final words for his report on 1942 read: "In this report which has detailed the IKG's service over the last year until it was shut down, it can be said without question that the IKG worked in the name of public law and in Jewish interest and fulfilled its duty fully and completely."[135]

Loewenherz, an ordinary man forced to lead a community during an extraordinary time -- like all other *Judenrat* leaders -- responded to his situation the only way he knew how. Initially, he set out to construct and enable the rescue of his community. Ultimately, he ordered his community to carry out and seal its own destruction.

---

[135]IKG- A/W 116, *Taetigkeitsbericht fuer das Jahr 1942 (2 Exemplare)*, 24.

Conclusions

As we examine Loewenherz's role -- the responsibilities he had, decisions he made and passed down, and his power and influence over fellow Jews -- we begin to recognize the enormous weight that he and other leaders carried. Did Lowenherz do his best to provide for his people? What about Benjamin Murmelstein and the other IKG leaders who worked side by side with him? Did their involvement in the rescue of 136,000 Jews absolve them of their participation in the subsequent deportation of some 50,000 others, as Rabinovici seems to claim? Or did some leaders abuse their power? And, was there any other way? Or, as Lawrence Langer would put it, did they face "choiceless choices"?[136] In Murmelstein's testimony with Lanzmann, he explained that "his way" was to save as many Jews as he could. He pointed to the head of the Jewish council in the Warsaw ghetto, Adam Czernaikow, who committed suicide, and declared that there was nothing else he or any of the other Judenrat leaders could have done in that situation, except kill themselves.[137] Was his conclusion accurate? Was suicide the only alternative to cooperation?

Some have judged Judenrat leaders -- how much they knew, and whether they responded morally or immorally. But it is essential to remember that they, like the rest of the community, were victims of unprecedented evil, charting unknown territory. In his interview with Lanzmann, Murmelstein observed that he can be condemned but not judged, "that the Judenaelteste should not have survived the war, they are an

---

[136] See: Lawrence Langer, *Art from the Ashes: A Holocaust Anthology* (New York: Oxford University Press, 1995); "The Dilemma of Choice in the Death Camps," *Centerpoint: The Holocaust 4, no. 1* (1980).
[137] USHMM, RG-60.5009, Tape 3158-3190, *Claude Lanzmann Shoah Collection, Interview with Benjamin Murmelstein* (Rome: 1975), see tape 3170.

uncomfortable remnant, like dinosaurs on the Autobahn."[138] Murmelstein's metaphor paints a vivid and accurate picture of the aftermath of this tragedy. These people who tried to help, but as victims themselves got caught up in the enterprise, were not supported after the war, but shunned. I would argue that neither the leaders' nor ordinary Jews' response and reaction to the Nazi net in which they were trapped were morally culpable. I would further argue that the IKG leaders, employees, and ordinary members, continued to cooperate with the Germans, hoping to prolong their situation long enough for intervention to come from the outside. They waited for a miracle: they prayed that someone -- God, a neighbor, even the enemy -- would spare them. [139] This glimmer of hope that encouraged them to follow orders day after day -- until their time came to an end -- should not be confused with passive obedience; they did not go like "lambs to the slaughter." Their efforts to resist the destruction of their community and of their own individual family units, under unprecedented circumstances during the pre-genocidal and genocidal years, paint a new picture of the Viennese Jew, revealing an active and ongoing struggle to carry on.

---

[138] USHMM, RG-60.5009, Tape 3158-3190, *Claude Lanzmann Shoah Collection, Interview with Benjamin Murmelstein* (Rome: 1975), see tape 3174, CR 58, 17:11 23.

[139] It is interesting to note that the role and response of the outside world to the plight of Vienna's Jews has never been given close attention. The bystanders -- those persons, institutions, governments, and countries which might have reacted differently to this humanitarian crisis and changed the course of history, warrant our close scrutiny. They are key actors in the genocidal process who historians have yet to put on trial.

Map 4: "Deportations from Vienna, 1941-45"

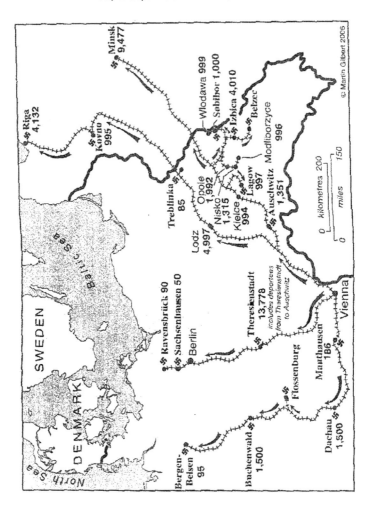

Source: Martin Gilbert, *Atlas of the Holocaust* (London: Orion Publishing Group, 2006).

Epilogue

Going "Home"? The Aftermath of the Holocaust for the Jewish Community of Vienna

The End of Communication

Fifteen-year-old Pierre Secher left Vienna with his forty-year-old mother Johanna and his forty-five-year-old father Emil on 30 October 1939. The IKG had summoned his father to report for "resettlement" just weeks earlier, but due to the stamped visa in his passport and his booked ship tickets to the United States, he was exempted from the transport.[1] Almost eighteen months after the German takeover of Austria, the family managed to secure exit papers and departed together from the Südbahnhof on a train to the port of Trieste, in northern Italy. Pierre remembered a crowded station full of civilian passengers, among them about fifty Jews, including both those who were leaving and those who accompanied them to say goodbye. The parting was "much more serious than an *Auf Wiedersehen* (till we see each other again)," he recalled many years later. "We wondered if we would meet anytime in the near future."[2]

The concern for loved ones left behind on the platform at Vienna's south train station did not subside over time. It intensified. The Secher trio managed to arrive safely in New York just three weeks later. Pierre recalled the balmy November morning when he and his mother first saw the statue of liberty on Ellis Island. He remembered that his father was not with them, but "already at his usual place, in one of the ships public rooms, writing his weekly report to the relatives whom we had left behind only a few weeks ago."[3] Emil Secher's correspondence with his family members in Vienna began while he was still in transit and did not cease until America joined the war and regular mail service came to an end. According to Pierre, it became a habit of

---

[1] The transport was headed to Nisko, Poland.
[2] Pierre H. Secher, *Left Behind in Nazi Vienna* (Jefferson, North Carolina: McFarland and Company, 2004) 9.
[3] Ibid,10.

his father's. He used every available opportunity to send bright, encouraging words about the future to his relatives, beginning with a chronicle of the voyage to America. As time passed, no matter how difficult the pressures of daily life became, Emil always found time to write to the family remaining in Vienna. His goal was to provide them with hope while they waited to exit.

Two years and dozens of optimistic letters later, Emil broke down for the first time and began to reveal deep feelings of frustration, worry, and hopelessness. Despite great efforts, he had still been unable to secure passage for his relatives to come to the United States, as he had promised them he would do before he left, and as they were counting on him to do. Emil was losing hope in his ability to ameliorate their rapidly deteriorating situation and began to fear for their fate in Nazi hands. "I am desperate over my total inability to help you," he wrote to his eighty-year-old mother Fannie, his fifty-seven-year-old sister Marie, his sixty-four-year-old brother-in-law Emil, and his in-laws on 14 October 1941 (by this point they shared a one-room flat). [4] Four days later he lamented further, "Again I've spent another week in anxious suspense, waiting from one day to another for a few lines....What is the cause of your silence now lasting over two weeks?...There were some very alarming reports again in the newspapers in recent days that made our blood run cold....It is getting more and more difficult for me to inspire you, from this distant vantage point, with hope and courage.... My heart is so heavy, so very heavy." [5]

For five weeks Emil heard nothing. He became so tormented in the absence of communication that the letters he wrote took on a whole new tone. Instead of finding the strength to provide a glimmer of sunshine with happy news from abroad, he began to divulge the truth of his daily existence since their abrupt separation years earlier. Despite his escape, he had been unable to step out of the past: "Please do not think for a minute that we can ever be truly

---

[4] Ibid., 338.
[5] Ibid., 338-39.

happy here," he wrote on 17 November 1941.[6] "We are farther away than ever from attaining true happiness. Can all this here give us happiness when we know you are so far from us and engulfed in your great misery? Sometimes we forget, enjoy our presence here but only ... to prepare the way for you.... But that lasts only as long as your letters keep coming and we know that you're healthy and well." Emil's mental outlook deteriorated further without word from his relatives. Still, he continued to write through December 1941. He expressed his grief over their recent disappearance and how it impaired his ability to carry on a "normal" life.

> During the last weeks our anticipation for your news has grown even more. [We are] obsessed by an oppressive anxiety, which literally robs us of sleep in the night from Sunday to Monday... Again no mail ...and we're really driven to despair. Our concern about you dear ones has now reached the stage where we cannot even comfort each other. We're simply no longer able to do anything -- our imagination plays tricks on us and we are subjected to think up the most terrible scenarios....We are completely at our wits end, nerves raw and at the breaking point, choked up with tears, and sobbing aloud whenever we think of you. ...We feel your misery, as well as our own, mixed with shame for not only having left you behind, but also for having been unable to do anything worthwhile for you! We must ask ourselves whether our coming here was really worth it and whether it would not have been better for us to remain with you. We feel it would have been much easier, then, for you but also for us, to share with you in your suffering.[7]

In reply to Emil's final letters, filled with angst, guilt, and sorrow, his sister Marie Kupler penned a note on 11 November 1941 on behalf of the entire trapped family. Emil received her letter a month later, on 10 December 1941, three days after the Japanese attack on Perl Harbor and one day before regular mail communication between Germany and the U.S. ceased. It was

---

[6] Ibid.
[7] Ibid., 238-39, 244, 247- 248.

the last letter he received from the family he had left behind. Acknowledging and addressing his recently expressed concerns, his sister wrote, "My dearest Emil, you continue to blame yourself --for leaving us here all by ourselves. But it is precisely that decision which now enables us to bear our fate more easily, knowing that the most precious people we have in this world have been spared all this....It is still mother's greatest pleasure to think back on those weekly Wednesdays or Thursdays she spent at your home -- that was her greatest joy."[8]

The Germans deported Marie and Emil Kupler and the rest of the family to "the East" over the next years in the course of their plan to make Vienna Juderein.[9] Emil did not know what happened to them, only that they were trapped inside the Nazis' realm. A month earlier, he had written: "There is nothing worse than to live in ignorance of the fate of your loved ones separated from them at a distance of thousands of miles."[10] But such was his reality, and the reality of thousands of other Jews who had reached safe haven in the United States or elsewhere throughout the world, but whose families had remained behind. The final correspondence between Emil and his sister Marie represents the tragedy that thousands of families faced: after the letters stopped, those trapped in Nazi Europe were targeted for murder, and those safely abroad were left in the shadows of this destruction. Emil, like so many others, would have to wait for years as the war dragged on and the postwar chaos cleared before he got information about the fate of his Viennese Jewish family. And even then, answers did not come readily.

The wait proved unbearable for some Jews and drove them to seek alternative methods to reach their family before the war's end. Like Emil Secher, thirty-two-year-old Dr. O. was safe in New

---

[8] Ibid., 296.
[9] Only the eldest family member, Emil's mother Fannie Secher passed a natural death in Vienna. She died of cardiac arrest at the age of eighty-one in the IKG's old-age home/hospital on Malzgasse 7 and was buried in the Jewish cemetery in 29 November 1941. Emil got this information from the IKG death records in May 1946.
[10] Secher, *Left behind in Nazi Vienna*, 246.

York, far from the all too well known dangers of Nazism, when America entered the war. The doctor had escaped from Vienna in early January 1939 after spending close to six months interned in Dachau and Buchenwald. The camp administration had authorized his sudden discharge from Buchenwald and gave him fourteen days to exit German soil: to organize his papers, check in with the Gestapo, and bid farewell to his parents, who had organized his release from the camp, and delayed their own emigration while waiting for his dismissal. Unlike Emil Secher, Dr. O. needed to get out of the country immediately, and he left on his own. But like Emil, he promised the family he left behind that he would enable their escape. Once the doctor reached safety in America, his life was as much about arranging immigration papers for the family he left behind as it was about adapting and assimilating and providing for the new nuclear family that surrounded him.

Dr. O. set out to secure himself financially. It was not long before he passed his medical board exams, moved from Manhattan to a small town in upstate New York, and began a private practice out of his home. On 45 West Main Street, in Caledonia, NY, the doctor settled with his wife, her daughter, and her mother in-law, Jewish refugees from Vienna who had escaped just after Anschluss.[11] By the time America entered the war, Dr. O. had built a family and a new life for himself safely outside the Nazis' realm, but that life was utterly incomplete: he had been unable to secure the escape of his parents from Nazi territory and bring them to the United States. Living with that reality proved too much to bear.

Like Emil Secher, and the thousands of other Viennese Jews who struggled to bring their relatives to safety, Dr. O. anguished over the sudden breach of communication in 1941 and the unknown fate his parents faced. He tried to carry on with daily life, but he was unable to cope. Despite his safety, his financial security, a happy marriage and a newborn son, he applied to the

---

[11] File #08124, *Alte Hilfsfonds*. Austrian State Archives: OstA/AdR/BMF/06/AHF/08124.

United States Army Medical Corps hoping to be sent back to Europe. Like so many Jewish men who had escaped from Nazi Europe, he was volunteering to go back into the storm -- to help defeat the enemy, yes, but mostly for the slim chance to find his family.[12]

To his surprise and great dismay, Dr. O. received a rejection letter from the Headquarters of the Army Service Forces in Washington DC, signed by Lieutenant Colonel, R.G Harrison, on 11 January 1945, three months before the liberation of Austria. "While your desire to be of service is appreciated," the letter read, "favorable action cannot be taken as you have been found to be physically disqualified for general or limited military service." The US army had refused the thirty-two-year-old doctor entry to the medical corps due to "X-ray evidence of pulmonary tuberculosis, undetermined activity."[13] Dr. O. had contracted the TB infection while incarcerated in the German concentration camp over six years prior. Now, this inactive, yet lingering remnant of the torture he experienced in 1938, prevented him from returning to Europe to search for his parents and left him in the same hapless situation as the vast majority Vienna's Jewish émigrés, sitting with their hands tied, waiting for war's end.

The end of the World War 2 brought little hope of reunification for the thousands of broken Viennese Jewish families dispersed around the world. War's end brought more questions and fewer answers about the fate of missing family members. When the Russians liberated Vienna on 12 April 1945, only 5,512 Jews remained.[14] The group was not representative of the original

---

[12] See, for example, testimony of Johanna Saper née Hirschbein, whose brother went back with the US Army to try to locate their mother. Charlotte Hirschbein left on the same transport as Dr. O's mother Berta (6 May 1942 to Minsk). Johanna, S.,1996. See Chapter 8 for a description of this transport. See also, "Interview by Survivors of the Shoah Visual History Foundation," Miami, FL, USA, February 21. Interview Code 12280, Tapes 1-7; Joanna Saper, private email correspondence with the author, 5 September 2003.
[13] Letter of 11 January 1945. File #08124, *Alte Hilfsfonds*. Austrian State Archives: OstA/AdR/BMF/06/AHF/08124.
[14] Jonny Moser, *Demographie der jüdischen Bevölkerung Österreichs 1938-1945* (Vienna: DÖW, 1999).

Jewish body[15] comprised as it was of non-professing Jews, half-Jews or Mischling, Jews in

mixed marriages, and only 619 Jews that had managed to survive in hiding.[16] In addition to this

number, a mere 2,142 of the estimated 67,601 Jews deported from Vienna escaped annihilation

and returned to the city in 1945.[17] Emil Secher, Dr. O., and the 136,000[18] Viennese Jews

scattered around the world, were unlikely to find their missing family.[19]

Still: Vienna's Jews did not give up hope easily. Forty-year-old Erna Fischer née Frenkel,

for example, having just barely escaped from the Nazis' clutches in late 1941 with her five-year-

old son Tom at her side, searched desperately after the war to find her father Max, from whom

she had parted in Vienna in 1939.[20] Erna did not give up hope of reunification for many years.

Her father was not among the survivors who remained in Vienna at the end of the war, nor was

he among those who returned from the camps, but in her mind there was a chance that he was

still alive. On 21 August 1948, after years of persistent searching, Erna placed a final "missing"

notice in the Viennese newspaper, *Wiener Zeitung* that read, "Max Frenkel…deported from

---

[15] For more detailed demographics of the Jewish community during the final years of Nazi rule see, USHMM film # 294, IKG- A/W 117, *Taetigkeitsbericht fuer das Jahr 1943 (2 Exemplare)*.

[16] C. Gwyn Moser, "Jewish U-Boote in Austria, 1938-1945" in *Simon Wiesenthal Center Annual, Volume 2* (New York, Kraus International Publications: 1985). Older studies estimated far fewer persons in hiding (219 persons).

[17] Figures based on George Berkley, *Vienna and Its Jews: The Tragedy of Success: 1880s-1980s* (Cambridge: Abt Books, 1988), 297; Walter B. Mass, *Country Without A Name: Austria under Nazi Rule 1938-1945* (New York: Frederick Ungar Publishing Co., 1979) 47.

[18] The final IKG report lists a total of 136,000 Jews for emigration between 1938-1941, see USHMM film # 294, IKG- A/W 116, *Taetigkeitsbericht fuer das Jahr 1942 (2 Exemplare)*. Jonny Moser's figures are slightly lower, with 130,742. See Jonny Moser, *Demographie der jüdischen Bevölkerung Österreichs 1938-1945* (Vienna: DÖW, 1999) 56.

[19] Author's figures total 55,000 Austrian Jews deported from Vienna. Figure includes Dachau (Buchenwald) deportations in May and November 1938 minus releases (2,000), Nisko deportations in October 1939 (1,584); and all mass deportations between February 1941 and October 1942 (51,000). Jonny Moser puts the figure slightly lower at 48,389 (not including Dachau deportations); Raul Hilberg estimates over 50,000 deportees; USHMM lists approximately 50,000. See Moser, *Demographie der jüdischen Bevölkerung Österreichs 1938-1945*, 56; Hilberg, *The Destruction of the European Jews*, 1220. Author's figure does not include the estimated 15,000 Austrian Jews who escaped Vienna, but were deported from other European countries. See: Berkley, *Vienna and Its Jews*, 297; Mass, *Country Without A Name*, 47.

[20] "Max Frenkel's Fate" in Thomas Fischer Weiss, *I Owe It To…* (Newton: unpublished memoirs, 2002). For more on Max Frenkel see, OstA/AdR/VVst/VA #09999.

Vienna to Minsk on 11 January 1942 and is missing since then..." She hoped to hear something. But no word came in response to her inquiry.[21]

After too many unsuccessful searches, Erna eventually opted to initiate a legal proceeding in Vienna to have her father declared dead. The country of Austria declared him legally dead on 4 April 1949 and Erna finally put her hopes aside.[22] When Erna passed away three years later (1952), she still did not know what had happened to her father. Only decades later did her son Tom first unpack the grim fate of his grandfather, Max Frenkel. Born on 8 June 1876, the sixty-five-year-old former businessman was transferred from his last residence in Vienna's second district Grosse Mohrengasse 40/24 to the Sammellager on Sperlgasse on Thursday, 8 January 1942.[23] After three days in the terrible conditions of this holding camp, he boarded a train at the Aspangbahnhof for Riga.[24] Max Frankel departed on Vienna's fourteenth mass-deportation transport and was never heard from again. Whether he survived the journey and was forced out of the train with some 1,000 other prisoners at the Skirotava station on 15 January 1942, or whether he perished at some point along the way, will never be known. Like so many of Vienna's Jews who were deported and murdered, there was no precise record of his death and there was no grave or site at which his surviving family could mourn.

---

[21] For more information on the search for missing relatives after the war, see "Lists of the Living," in Debórah Dwork and Robert Jan van Pelt, *Flight from the Reich: Refugee Jews, 1933-1946* (New York: W.W. Norton & Co., 2009) 340-359.

[22] Landesgericht für ZRS in Wien (file number 48 T 4380/48). As noted in, "Max Frenkel's Fate" in Weiss, *I Owe It To...*

[23] See Max Frenkel in the following online datatbases: *www.lettertothestars.at/cms, www.doew.at.*

[24] For more on the deportations of Jews from Vienna to Riga see, "Journey into Terror: Story of the Riga Ghetto," in Wolfgang Scheffler and Diana Schulle, *Book of Remembrance: the German, Austrian and Czechoslovakian Jews deported to the Baltic States* (Munich: Saur, 2003).

Final Destruction

In the end, Nazi Germany crumbled before the allies, but the Nazi administration essentially attained its goal of racial purification in many German cities, including Vienna. From a pre-Anschluss population of nearly 200,000 Austrian Jews, the Germans forcibly expelled 130,742 during the pre-genocidal period (1938-1941) and murdered another 65,000[25] in the final solution (1941-1945). Over the course of the Nazi occupation, the Germans and their Austrian allies brought an end to centuries of Jewish life in Vienna: they ripped families apart and separated them permanently.[26] Few families and not one of those we have discussed remained intact by the end of the war. Nor did any individual escape the immediate and permanent consequences of the violent family separation. The deep trauma persisted long after war's end, and for many would prove permanent. The division between those who got out and those who were trapped behind severed family bonds and, ultimately, wiped out the community. After centuries of persecution and peace, Jewish Vienna came to a close. The many Jews who survived could do little more than bear witness to the tragedy. They could not come back to Vienna and reconstruct that which was lost, for it was irreparable. They had left during the mass exodus, dispersed to any country that would offer them a haven, and waited until they were permitted to return home. But at the end of the war, when their families had vanished, they had no "home" to which to return.

The Not so lucky "Lucky-Ones"

Austria had a very high survival rate due to the Germans' early policy of forced emigration, which was designed and implemented in Vienna.[27] Over 120,000 Austrian Jews had already

---

[25] See Yehuda Bauer, *A History of the Holocaust, Revised Edition*. (Danbury: Franklin Watts, 2001).

[26] Email correspondence with George Czuczka, 28 September 2009.

[27] For more on the "Vienna Model," see chapter 3 in David Cesarani, *Becoming Eichmann: Rethinking the Life, Crimes, and Trial of a "Desk Murderer"* (Cambridge: Da Capo Press, 2004). See also, Hans Safrian, "Expediting

escaped the Greater German Reich before the Nazi administration decided upon the final solution to the Jewish question. In this respect, in comparison with other Jewish communities persecuted during the Nazi period, Vienna's Jews appeared in later years to have been the "lucky ones."[28] After the war, Viennese Jewish émigrés realized their great fortune to escape from the Nazi Reich via emigration, and most attributed their escape and survival to luck. Rudi Tausz, deported to Dachau, released from Buchenwald after six months, and on a boat to the United States one month later, noted after the war: "Just plain luck -- that is why I survived....I consider myself simply lucky to be around."[29] Herta Drucker left Vienna at age eleven and fled to Sosúa in the Dominican Republic. She recalled that her immigration was "all luck," that at the time she took a chance, leaving her cushy home.[30] Elisabeth Guttmann agreed: "Pure Luck. That's why I survived," she remarked, reflecting on her immigration to England in 1939.[31] Alois Gottfried, who fled from Vienna to Palestine in 1939, contemplated his escape and the role of luck a bit further: "My life individually is only one of many thousands who survived by sheer luck. People don't realize it, but...who survived Hitler and who didn't was a matter of luck. A combination of lucky circumstances.... I compared it to a ship wreck: who gets in the life boats and who doesn't

---

Expropriation and Expulsion: The impact of the 'Vienna Model' on Anti-Jewish Policies in Nazi-Germany, 1938," *Holocaust and Genocide Studies*, 14:3 (2000).

[28] Approximately 33% of Austria's pre-Anschluss population was murdered in the Holocaust, as compared to Norway 50%, Romania 50%, Belgium 60%, Yugoslavia 60%, Ukraine 60 %, White Russia 65%, Hungary 70%, the Netherlands 75%, Greece 77%, Slovakia 83%, Protectorate 89%, Germany 90% , Baltic Countries 90%, and Poland 90%. See Lucy Dawidowicz, *A Holocaust Reader* (New York: Behrman House, 1976) 381.

[29] Rudolf, T., 1997. "Interview by Survivors of the Shoah Visual History Foundation," Margate, FL, USA, April 9. Interview Code 27990, Tapes 1-3.

[30] Herta Drucker, née Wellisch, private correspondence with the author, *KTA Conference,* Orlando, FL, 2008. For more on emigration to Dominican Republic see, Marion Kaplan, *Between Dignity and Despair: Jewish Life in Nazi Germany* (New York: Oxford University Press, 1998).

[31] Elizabeth, G., 1996. "Interview by Survivors of the Shoah Visual History Foundation," Dobbs Ferry, NY, USA, May 16. Interview Code 15247, Tapes 1-5.

and got stuck on the sinking ship is a matter of luck.... I was lucky and so were all those who survived."[32]

While it is legitimate to remember Vienna's thousands of Jewish émigrés as the "lucky ones," the many ways in which they were also not so lucky, are important, too. Fortuitous circumstance may have helped them to escape, but many did not feel fortunate to have survived, and this became evident particularly after the war. Many Jews felt condemned to live in the shadows of the final solution through which their families were brutally annihilated. Notwithstanding their great fortune to have survived, Vienna's Jews could not rebuild the lives, families, or community that the Germans and their allies had destroyed. Most Jews remained, often reluctantly, in the host countries where they had been accepted in 1938-1939 and tried to carry on. They assimilated to that culture the best they could, but never truly acculturated. Outside of their native Austria, they felt permanently displaced and, as historians Dwork and van Pelt put it, "never quite at home."[33] Some managed to overcome past tribulations; others did not. Years of uncertainty regarding the fate of loved ones provoked various anxieties, as well as feelings of guilt, sorrow, fear, and depression, sending some émigrés into a deep trauma from which they were never able to emerge.

How a person coped with the loss of family after the war depended upon the age, background, and personal experience of the individual at the time of the separation. For some Jews, the family parting had been so confusing, chaotic, or simply traumatic, that after the war it was too difficult to reconstruct any family relationships, even with other surviving family members. For example, Isidor and Berta Helwing sent their son Kurt to England on a Kindertransport in 1938. As a young man Kurt did not understand this separation from his

---

[32] Alois, G., 1996. "Interview by Survivors of the Shoah Visual History Foundation," Los Angeles, CA, USA, February 23. Interview Code 12444, Tapes 1-2.
[33] Dwork and van Pelt, *Flight from the Reich:* 380.

parents, and he did not understand it any better over the many years that followed, when he received no word from them. Kurt could not cope. The separation had been too traumatic. After the war he refused to answer any letters from his surviving cousins who had immigrated elsewhere.[34] Kurt's postwar reaction was not unique; many émigrés cut off ties with the past, trying to look only forward.[35] The separation between Kurt and his parents that began in 1938 and was not solidified until many years later left permanent psychological scars, as it did on thousands of others. And for some persons, for whom the loss became too much to bear and carrying on proved impossible-- suicide became the only solution. Both during and after the war's end, Viennese Jews living abroad chose to end their lives by suicide.[36] This decision symbolized the ongoing and complete destruction of this genocide-torn community. Too many Viennese Jewish émigrés, too many of the "lucky ones" who had managed to escape the clutches of the Nazi final solution, felt not so lucky to be alive.

A Heroic Effort

"The Nazification of Vienna and the Response of the Viennese Jews," has laid bare the destruction of the Jewish community of Vienna. It has identified turning points and marked specific steps along the path to genocide. It has uncovered the roots of the genocide on the streets of Vienna in March 1938 and followed its development, locating moments of indecision and inaction on the part of the United States government and the rest of the free world when they

---

[34] Dr. Lisa Gruenberg, letter to author of 11 February 2007. See also, Gruenberg Family Archive, Weston, Massachusetts.

[35] For example, Ernst Gerstenfeld, released from Dachau, became an atheist once he escaped and settled in America in 1940. He later insisted that his daughter marry a gentile, convert to Protestantism, and not associate with any European-born family relatives. See *Ernst Gerstenfeld Archival Collection*, Letter from Ted Shealy/ 3G, 27 June 2005.

[36] The exact number of suicides by Viennese Jewish émigrés during and after the war's end is unknown. The most common example is Stefan Zweig, who committed suicide on 23 February 1942 near Rio de Janeiro, Brazil. For the postwar period: Gerstenfeld Famly Archive, Arlington, Virgina; Winterstein/Adler Family Archive, Lenox, Massachusetts; Offenberger Family Archive, Beverly Farms, Massachusetts.

may have been able to help the Jews. It has also showed how individual Jews and Jewish philanthropic organizations tried to help Vienna's Jews escape -- how much they did help, and the times when there was nothing they could do. Above all, however, "The Nazification of Vienna and the Response of the Viennese Jews" has illuminated the efforts of ordinary Jews and the IKG to promote the escape, rescue, and survival of Viennese Jewry.

In the end, the history of Vienna's Jews during the Nazi period is as much about the final destruction of a community as it is about recognizing its ongoing struggle to resist that destruction. Henry Wegner worked for the IKG until October 1942, when he was deported to Terezin, from where he was later transferred to Auschwitz. Some fifty years later, when asked why Vienna's Jews did not physically resist German orders, he explained: "It was an impossibility to resist. These people had weapons -- we had nothing. What were we going to do? With our fists kill the Germans?"[37] Wegner was right, armed resistance to Nazism was never a viable possibility for Vienna's Jews, even at the start.

The Nazi attack came so suddenly, and was so unexpectedly brutal, that not only the Jews -- but even foreign reporters and members of the US Consulate -- were shocked and appalled. Beginning with the violent outbursts during the Anschluss pogrom and peaking ten weeks later when the first group of innocent men were randomly arrested and deported to Dachau, the Nazis continuously terrorized Vienna's Jews, encouraging them to cooperate if they wanted to save their lives. The outside world did not see or believe what Vienna's Jews had endured until the Pogrom of 9-10 November 1938. By that time, close to 50,000 Austrian Jews had already emigrated; they had already made great sacrifices and taken a great risk: they had left their families, homes, and lives for the chance to live in safety abroad. They had taken action again

---

[37] See, Henry, W., (date currently unavailable). "Interview by Survivors of the Shoah Visual History Foundation," (location currently unavailable). Interview Code 42662.

the Nazi -plan to destroy their community. No Viennese Jew waited placidly for deportation.[38]

Carrying on with daily life, day after day, was in itself a struggle and an act of resistance.

Vienna's Jews who were deported in 1941 or 1942 spent years trying to escape from Nazi

territory and when that proved impossible, to endure indignities and restrictions. They sought to

persevere in the face of an unknown but predictably ominous fate.

Beginning directly after Anschluss, Vienna's Jews mounted a robust resistance campaign

to the destruction of their community. On a daily basis, ordinary people worked to save

themselves, their families, and community, unifying behind the IKG in what became a grand

effort to promote escape and rescue. Their efforts were noticeable immediately. By October

1938, close to 50,000 individuals had already escaped and the remainder of the community --

male and female, young and old, from different class backgrounds, religious backgrounds, and

profession -- were registered for emigration, ready to support the process, no matter how great

the sacrifice.[39]

Individually, Jews helped one another to escape. Parents put their children on

Kindertransports or sent them off to Palestine, and the IKG supported this difficult decision.

Parents, siblings, and wives determined to get their loved ones out of the concentration camp

when that was still an option in 1938-1939, and the IKG did all they could to financially and

strategically back these efforts. Children and grown adults reluctantly left their parents behind in

Vienna for a chance to start a new life abroad, and the IKG encouraged this action. Moreover,

parents waited in Vienna for their children to get out of the German Reich safely before they

---

[38] Vienna's Jews rarely disobeyed German orders, although some did try to resist humiliation and dehumanization Adults continued to frequent cafés and sneak into theaters, children sneaked into movie theaters (and later removed their star to do this), and one Jews even sat on park bench marked "Only for Aryans," and smiled for a photograph. See Leo Spitzer, *Hotel Bolivia: The Culture of Memory in a Refuge from Nazism* (New York: Hill and Wang, 1998).
[39] USHMM film # 295, IKG- A/W 121, *The Household of the Jewish Community of Vienna for the months of November and December 1938.*

secured their own escape, and some children tried to do the same for their parents. And when Vienna's Jews made it to safety, they did not forget about those left behind, or the sacrifices that family members and friends had made to promote their safety. Children and adults struggled unendlessly from their host countries to bring their parents, siblings, relatives, out of Austria to meet them. And those trapped behind, wrote to their loved ones who had survived, begging them to help, but also telling them not to worry or blame themselves. All parties involved in this crisis committed to carry on. The history of Vienna's Jews during the Nazi period is thus as much of a testament to their resilient character as it is the tragic tale of their ultimate destruction.

Emigration Questionnaire, English Translation

FÜRSORGE-ZENTRALE (Welfare Department)

Jewish Community Vienna

Auswanderungsabteilung (Department of Emigration)

Nr........

QUESTIONNAIRE

(Fill precisely - with ink, if possible with typewriter)

Name... First name ....

Residence.. Exact address...

Date of birth.., Place of birth...

Status (unmarried – married-widowed-divorced)...

Nationality.......................................Resident in Vienna since ....

Prior residence (place and time) ....

....

Profession...

....

....

Professional education...

....

....

Previous job and last occupational status...

....

....

....

Was a new profession learnt? If yes, which? ....

....

....

Training for the new profession ....

....

....

Proficiency in a foreign language...

....

Current economical situation and monthly income...

....

....

Are you able to obtain all the necessary documents for emigration ?...

....

Where do you want to emigrate to?...
....
Which plans do you have for your new residence?..
....
Which (monetary) resources do you dispose of for the emigration?..
....
Which connections do you have abroad, especially in the country you want to emigrate to?

	Fist name and last name	Residence	Exact address	Degree of relationship
a) Relatives				
b) Friends				

References...
....
Do you have a valid passport? ....
Valid from   ....Valid until.............................

Relatives

Degree of relationship	Name	Place of birth	Date of birth	Profession
1)				
2)				
3)				
4)				
5)				
6)				
7)				
8)				
9)				
10)				

Which of the above mentioned relatives shall emigrate now and which shall emigrate later?
....
....
Vienna, ...193.....

....
Signature

"Organized Emigration," *Zionistische Rundschau,* **3 June 1938**

The emigration department of the IKG informs you of the following:

1. To carry out the organized Jewish emigration from German-Austria the following organizations are concerned:

A) for emigration to all lands with the exception of Palestine, the emigration department of the IKG Vienna, Seitenstettengasse 2-4, B) for emigration to Palestine, the Pal-Amt on Marc Aurelstr. 5.

2. For the registration of all persons ready to emigrate, it is necessary to fill out a questionnaire distributed by the emigration department. Questionnaires are available free of charge on the ground floor of the main IKG offices on of Seitenstettengasse 4. The forms should be filled out and returned to the same office.

3. The care of already over 25,000 filed questionnaires can by nature only gradually follow. At this stage a personal office meeting is available only for those people who are already in possession of a visa to some country. In these cases the applicant should bring all required documents and verification. This section of the emigration department is open to the public daily from 9:00 to 1:00.

4. Emigration possibilities to European countries are at this time uncertain. As a general rule, only positions for domestic help are to be considered for emigration to England, Holland, and Sweden – to be discussed by the appropriate advisory office. (Open to the public Monday through Thursday afternoons, 2-6 p.m. on the second floor, Seittenstettengasse 4.)

5. Of the overseas countries, the first to be considered is the United States of America, especially for people who can secure a visa due to relatives or friends willing to sign an "affidavit" on their behalf. Those persons having difficulty obtaining affidavits from their relatives in America, we suggest that you turn to the HIAS, and there are forms to this end sitting in the emigration office.

6. Other overseas countries come only in limited measures and these are mostly available for countrymen and qualified craftsmen. To make use of these possibilities, occupational advice, education and retraining will be carried out through the emigration department of the IKG to train Jewish youth in such occupational crafts. At the same time, language courses will be established. Details will be noted in a timely fashion in an official bulletin.

7. For certain professional groups, like doctors, lawyers, technicians, artists, industrialists, craftsmen, movers, an expert advisor will be at the IKG on certain days to forward interesting information on emigration. The advisory office for doctors is already established. Meeting hours are every Monday and Thursday from 6-8 in the evening on the second floor of the IKG offices, Seittenstettengasse 4.

8. Emigration to German or needless trips to Germany are emphatically cautioned/ advised against.

9. The emigration department will also issue suggestions for emigrants concerning the travel procedure, including the boat and rail tickets, transportation of luggage, etc.

10. For the purpose of processing an organized emigration as in the interest of the emigrant, it is advised to liquidate one's assets, particularly business establishments, as soon as possible. The emigrants should then as soon as possible, sell/liquidate assets that they will not take with them, as soon as it is finally clear that within a distinct amount of time they will be leaving. As far as the conditions for transferring cash or goods to the land of immigration, this will be released in an order according to the law and you will be informed.

Assets Declaration Form, English Translation

Before filling out the Assets Declaration Form the following instructions are to be read through with precision!

Take Notice!

1. Who has to fill out an Assets Declaration Form? Everyone who is applicable, including spouse and children.
2. When must the Assets Declaration Form be submitted? Up until 30 June 1938. Whoever is responsible to fill out a form and does not do so correctly and honestly **will face severe punishment (monetary fines, arrest, seizure of assets).**
3. How should the Assets Declaration Form be filled out? Fill out all applicable questions and cross out those statements that do not apply.
4. If doubt should arise over the exact worth of a particular asset and if it should be registered or not in the Assets Declaration Form, be sure to register it anyway.

Declaration of Jewish Assets
According to Decree of 27 April 1938

Name (last, first).. ..... Occupation..

Address..

Information on the Person

I was born on ....

I am a Jew (according to the 5th paragraph of the first order of the Reich Citizens Law of 14 November 1935, Reich Law 1, page 1333) and of German Nationality/............................. ... . Nationality? I have no Nationality.

Since I am a ....Jew of German Nationality)........a Jew without Nationality) I have evaluated and declared in the following Assets Declaration Form my total domestic and foreign assets.

Since I am a Jew of Foreign Nationality I have evaluated and declared in the following Assets Declaration Form my total domestic assets.

I am married to..born...

My spouse belongs to the following race: Jewish/ Non-Jewish ---- and belongs to the ....
religious community.

Information on the Assets

1. Land and Forestry...Total Amount in RM:.............
2. Real-Estate..... ....Total Amount in RM:.............
3. Business and Enterprise..Total Amount in RM:.............
4. Other Assets, Capital...Total Amount in RM:.............
5. Liabilities and Encumbrances......... ....Total Amount in RM:.............
6. Additional Notifications..

I hereby testify that the above information is filled out to the best of my knowledge and that I have declared all of my assets in this form.

Signature:... .... Place and Date:................................ 1938

List of Jewish Families and Individuals (alphabetical)

Jewish Families and Individuals
Abrahams, Valerie
Adler, Dr. Ernst
Adler, Fritz
Adler, Selig
Adler-Forscher, Trude
Aflen, Marion
Altmann, Maria
Andersmann, Arthur
Apfelgruen, Klara and Osias
Artz, Heinrich
Austerlitz, Walter
Bandler, Hans
Bauer, Franz
Benedikt, Lucie
Bentwich, Norman
Berger, Dr. Paul
Berju-Kohn, Edith
Berl, Leopold
Birnstein, Dr. Max
Blaustein, Simel
Bleichfeld, Simon, Fritz
Brod, Josef, Emil
Buchwalter, Siegfried
Czuczka, Artur, Charlotte, Fritz, George
Deutsch, brothers Leo, Karl, Alexander
Deutsch, Karl
Deutsch, Walter, Rosa, Edmund
Engel, Emil
Feiden, Walter, Moses, Emilie
Feldner-Busztin, Helga
Fellner, Elisabeth
Fritz, Ludmilla
Fuchs, Lilli, Karl
Fuchs, Melanie
Gerstenfeld, Ernst
Gitter, Lena
Glaser, Otto
Goetzl, Otto
Goldrei, Irene

Gottfried, Alois
Gottfried, Dr. Oskar
Grabkowicz, Dr. Hans, Dr. Joseph, Hilde, Vera, Alix
Gruenberg, Leo, Elka, Harry, Uri, Mia
Grunwald, Karl
Hacker, Walter
Hasten, Efraim, Betty, Jacques
Heilpern, Otto
Helving, Isidor, Berta, Kurt
Herlinger, Fritz, Leopold
Herz, Oskar, Helen, Suzanne, Elenor
Hirschbein, Charlotte, Johanna
Hochsinger, Dr. Flora
Jasssem, Gerta, Lotte
Jekel, David, Klara, Margit, Ella
Jekel, Samuel, Blima, Julius, Berthold
Jung, Franz
Kammerman, Natalie
Katz, Anne
Kaufmann, Herbert, Maximilliane
Kaufmann, Josefine
Klaar, George
Klein, Kurt
Kluger, Ruth
Klugmann, Raoul, Edith
Knie, Walter
Korn, Wilhelm
Kupler, Marie
Kutner, Trude
Langer, Lawrence
Lencz, Erwin, Erika
Linder, Otto
Loomer, Harry
Lowenherz, Dr. Joseph
Malkin, Elisabeth
Malkin, Lizbeth
Mandel, Melanie, Enoch, Ernesto
Mandelstam, Lucy
Mass, Leopoldine, Ernst
Mayer, Emil
Milch, Dr. Michael Albert, Emma, Regina, Kitty
Mintz, Gabrielle
Monias, Wilhelm

Murmelstein, Dr. Benjamin
Neumann, Ernst
Offenberger, Berta, Dr. Fritz
Oppenheim, Marta
Pick, Rudi
Pischler, Josef, Helene
Popper, Paula
Reinhard, Max
Saurquell, Elliot, Anna
Schatzberg, Paul
Schreiber, Jakob, Lotte, Freddy
Schwarz, Walter
Spainermann, Greta
Spitzer, Fritzi
Spitzer, Leo
Sptizer, Hugo, Erika
Stein, Charles
Steiner, Charlotte, Liesl
Steiner, Richard
Sussmann, Liz
Tausky, Alfred
Tausz, Albert, Sidonie, Rudi, Julie
Ultmann, Sandor, Ida, Heinrich
Verstandig, Emil
Vulkan, Leopold, Mathilde, Edith, Gertrude
Wegner, Henry
Weiss, Edward
Weiss, Max
Wellwarth, Erwin, Marta, George
Wengraf, Ernst
Winter, Regina
Ziegler, Betty
Zipper, Herbert

BIBLIOGRAPHY

PRIMARY SOURCES

Archives of the Jewish Community Vienna (IKG)
House Lists (1942)
Transport Lists (May 1942)
Death Books (May-July 1942)

Austrian State Archives (OstA), Archive of the Republic (AdR), Division of Finance (BMF/06)
Assets Transfer Agency: (VVst -Vermögensverkehrsstelle)
Assets Declaration Form: (VA-Vermogensanmeldungen)
Real-Estate: (Lg, Liegenschaft), Trade: (Ha- Handel), Statistik: (St -Statistik)
    OstA/AdR/06/VVst/VA # 0872, Leopold Berl
    OstA/AdR/06/VVst/VA # 16802, Leopold Herlinger
    OstA/AdR/06/VVst/VA # 2770, 2771, Albert Tausz; Sidonie Tausz
    OstA/AdR/06/VVst/VA # 5889, Mathilde Vulkan
    OstA/AdR/06/VVst/VA # 33074, Ha #951, Leopold Vulkan
Restitution Files
    AHF (Alte Hilfsfonds)
    NHF (Neue Hilfsfonds)
Lehmann's Wohnbuch: Viennese Phonebooks 1930-1943

Austrian State Archives (OstA), Staatsarchiv
Divorce/ Death/ Inheritance/ Restitution records
OstA/Bezirksgericht Innere Stadt/Verlassenschaftsabhandlung/ 1-31
OstA/M. Abteilung 119/ VEAV/ MBA 3-31

Documentation Center of the Austrian Resistance (DÖW)
Deportation Lists: *Project Registration by Name: The Austrian Victims of the Holocaust, 2001. (http://www. doew.at)*
File, 2536. Report by the Central Office for Jewish Emigration, October 18, 1939

Gedenkstaette Buchenwald Archiv
Datenbank: Haeftlingsnummernkartei
Enlassungscheine

Thueringisches Hauptstaatsarchiv
Geldkartei

NARA, US-State Dept. Records, RG 59/M1209/Reel 7, 863.4016/172. Dispatch No.166, "Action Taken Against Jews in Austria," Vienna, 25 March 1938.

NARA, US-State Dept. Records, RG 59/M1209/Reel 7, 863.4016/172. "Seizure of Jewish Property and Persecution of Jews in Austria," in dispatch No.166, "Action Taken Against Jews in Austria," Vienna, 25 March 1938, Gardner Richardson, Commercial Attaché.

NARA, US-State Dept. Records, RG 59/M1209/Reel 7: 863.4016/174. Dispatch No.202, "Situation of Jews in Austria," Vienna, 15 April 1938. (John C. Wiley, American Consul General to Mr. Messersmith, Secretary of State).

NARA, US-State Dept. Records, RG 59/M1209/Reel 7: 863.4016/174. Enclosure No. 1 to dispatch No.202, "Translation of Anonymous Letter received by the Consulate General," Vienna, 6 April 1938.

NARA, US-State Dept. Records, RG 59/M1209/Reel 7: 863.4016/175. Enclosure No. 1 to dispatch No.206, "Statement by Harry P. Loomer," Vienna, 19 April 1938.

NARA, US-State Dept. Records, RG 59/M1209/Reel 7: 863.4016/177. Report No.217, "Intensified Persecution of the Jews in Austria," Vienna, 4 May 1938 (John C. Wiley, American Consul General to Secretary of State Mr. Messersmith).

NARA, US-State Dept. Records, RG 59/M1209/Reel 7: 863.4016/177. Enclosure No. 4 to dispatch No.217, "Statement by Treasury Representative Wallenfels," Vienna, 4 May 1938.

NARA, US-State Dept. Records, RG 59/M1209/Reel 7, 863.00/1674, Report # V-4527, "Political Issues and Problems. Latest Developments in Austria," Vienna, 12 March 1938, Lowell M. Riley, US-military attaché.

NARA, US-State Dept. Records, RG 59/M1209/Reel 7: 863.00/1654. "A Petition to the President of the United States: For Affirmative Announcement of the Application of the Diplomatic Policy of Non-Recognition with Respect to the Forced Annexation of Austria by Germany, from Joint American Committee for Protection of Minorities," 30 March 1938: 1-6.

NARA, US-State Dept. Records: RG 59/M1209/Reel 7: 863.00/1672. Report No. 15 - 798, 14 March 1938.

United States Holocaust Memorial Museum (USHMM)

USHMM, RG-60.5009, Tape 3158-3190, *Claude Lanzmann Shoah Collection, Interview with Benjamin Murmelstein* (Rome: 1975), tape 3168, camera rolls #44-45 11:00:04 to 11:22:24.

USHMM: Archives, Acc. # 2000.32. *Harriet Postman letters, 1939-1941*, Crane, Evelyn P., donor.

USHMM: International Tracing Service Digital Collection, Individual Documents Male Buchenwald, Effektenkarte.

USHMM: CAHJP, IKG Archiv, Aktenverzeichnis 2.Teil -B, A/W, XXV.Auswanderung, H. Fragebogenausgabe, (2337) 2590, 1-274 *Über die Auswanderungwilligen angelegte Akten (Von den Parteien ausgefüllte Emigrationsfragebögen,alph.; mit Bearbeitungsvermerken und diversen Unterlagen)....1938- (1940).*

USHMM film #Alpha T2, *Auswanderungsfrageboegen der Israelitischen Kultusgemeinde Wien (IKG)*, Alfred Tausky., # 32406.

USHMM film #Alpha T3, *Auswanderungsfrageboegen der Israelitischen Kultusgemeinde Wien (IKG)*, Hans Grabkowicz, #12,630.

USHMM film #Alpha F3, *Auswanderungsfrageboegen der Israelitischen Kultusgemeinde Wien (IKG)*, Elisabeth Feller, # 42110/15701.

USHMM film #Alpha C7, *Auswanderungsfrageboegen der Israelitischen Kultusgemeinde Wien (IKG)*, Fritz Czuczka, # 21,297.

USHMM film #Alpha S7, *Auswanderungsfrageboegen der Israelitischen Kultusgemeinde Wien (IKG)*, Hugo Sommer, # 437/11982.

USHMM film #Alpha J1, *Auswanderungsfrageboegen der Israelitischen Kultusgemeinde Wien (IKG)*, David Jekel, # 24196.

USHMM film #Alpha J1, *Auswanderungsfrageboegen der Israelitischen Kultusgemeinde Wien (IKG)*, Samuel Jekel, # 33401.

USHMM film #Alpha G7, *Auswanderungsfrageboegen der Israelitischen Kultusgemeinde Wien (IKG)*, Oskar Gottfried, # 36537.

USHMM film #Alpha H7, *Auswanderungsfrageboegen der Israelitischen Kultusgemeinde Wien (IKG)*, Oskar Herz, # 28729.

USHMM film #Alpha G4, *Auswanderungsfrageboegen der Israelitischen Kultusgemeinde Wien (IKG)*, Otto Glaser, #24866.

USHMM film #Alpha G8, *Auswanderungsfrageboegen der Israelitischen Kultusgemeinde Wien (IKG)*, Otto Goetzl, # 35145.

USHMM film #Alpha L7, *Auswanderungsfrageboegen der Israelitischen Kultusgemeinde Wien (IKG)*, Otto Linder, # 42838/23409.

USHMM film #Alpha K5, *Auswanderungsfrageboegen der Israelitischen Kultusgemeinde Wien (IKG)*, Walter Knie, # 9324/25882.

USHMM film #Alpha V5, *Auswanderungsfrageboegen der Israelitischen Kultusgemeinde Wien (IKG)*, Heinrich Verstandig, #13404.

USHMM film #Alpha U1, *Auswanderungsfrageboegen der Israelitischen Kultusgemeinde Wien (IKG)*, Sandor Ultmann, # 1,458.

USHMM film #Alpha A5, *Auswanderungsfrageboegen der Israelitischen Kultusgemeinde Wien (IKG)*, Walter Austerlitz, # 1894.

USHMM film #Alpha G10, *Auswanderungsfrageboegen der Israelitischen Kultusgemeinde Wien (IKG)*, Simon Grossman, # 14864/18663.

USHMM: CAHJP, IKG Archiv, Aktenverzeichnis 2.Teil -B, A/W, XXV.Auswanderung, H. Fragebogenausgabe, (2336) 2589,1-120 ,*Von den Parteien ausgefüllte Emigrationsfragebögen der Auswandergungsabteilung, Nr. 1-56319 (ohne Bearbeitungsvermerke; vereinselt mit Beilagen)...1940.*

USHMM film #4, *Auswanderungsfrageboegen der Israelitischen Kultusgemeinde Wien (IKG) (Numerisch geordnet):* Heinrich Akselrad, file #1893.

USHMM film#7, *Auswanderungsfrageboegen der Israelitischen Kultusgemeinde Wien (IKG) (Numerisch geordnet):* Irma (Spitzer) Austerlitz, file #3510.

USHMM microfilm #10, *Auswanderungsfrageboegen der Israelitischen Kultusgemeinde Wien (IKG) (Numerisch geordnet):* Erwin Wellwarth-Velwart, file #5,871.

USHMM microfilm#31, *Auswanderungsfrageboegen der Israelitischen Kultusgemeinde Wien (IKG) (Numerisch geordnet):* Karl Deutsch, file #19,940 .

USHMM microfilm #31, *Auswanderungsfrageboegen der Israelitischen Kultusgemeinde Wien (IKG) (Numerisch geordnet):* Josef Brod, file #19,882.

USHMM film#74, IKG-A/W 2589,120, *Auswanderungsfrageboegen der Israelitischen Kultusgemeinde Wien (IKG) (Numerisch geordnet)*: Robert Waldner, file #54,927.

USHMM: CAHJP, IKG Archiv, Aktenverzeichnis 2.Teil -B: XXV.Auswanderung:

USHMM film #295, IKG- A/W 113, *Bericht in Tabellenform betreffend Auswanderungsangelegenheiten, Bevoelkerungsstand, Fuersorgeangelegenheiten und Umschulung, Janner-December 1940.*

USHMM film # 295, IKG- A/W 115, *Tatigkeitsberichte in Tabellenform (Anschlag?) fuer die Zeit vom 01. Jaenner-30. Juni 1941.*

USHMM film # 294, IKG- A/W 116, *Taetigkeitsbericht fuer das Jahr 1942 (2 Exemplare).*

USHMM film # 294, IKG- A/W 117, *Taetigkeitsbericht fuer das Jahr 1943 (2 Exemplare).*

USHMM film # 294, IKG- A/W 119, *Auswanderung, Umschichtung, Fuersorge 02.05.1938-31.07.1939 (Bericht, deutsch, englisch, franzoesisch).*

USHMM film # 295, IKG- A/W 121, *The Household of the Jewish Community of Vienna for the months of November and December 1938.*

USHMM film #295, IKG-A/W 122, *Financial and Statsitical Report of the Jewish Community of Vienna, December 1939(2 Exemplare).*

USHMM film # 295, IKG- A/W 125, *Report of the Vienna Jewish Community, May-June 1939.*

USHMM film # 294, IKG-A/W 126, *Report of the Vienna Jewish Community. A description of the activity of the Israelitische Kultusgemeinde Wien in the period from May 2nd 1938- December 31st 1939 (2 Exemplare).*

USHMM film #295, IKG- A/W 131, *Israelitische Kultusgeminde Vienna. Activity During Twelve Months of War, 01.09.1939-31.08.1940.*

USHMM film #295, IKG- -A/W 132, *Israelistische Kultusgeminde Vienna. Survey on Nineteenhundredforty.*

USHMM film # 295, IKG- A/W 134, 5, *Zirkulare der Amstdirektion und des Amtsvorstands an saemtliche Abteilungen bzw. Alle Angestellten und Mitarbeiter, 1942.*

USHMM film #295, IKG-A/W 142, *Report of the Vienna Jewish Community, March-April1939(2 Exemplare).*

USHMM film #907, IKG- A/W 2533, *Twelve Questions about emigration from Vienna, 01.01. - 30.04.1940.*

USHMM film # 907, IKG-A/W 2532, *Statistische Berichte der Auswanderungsabteilung ueber die Auswanderungsbewegung (gegliedert nach den die Emigranten aufnehmenden Ziellaendern).*

USHMM film # 1264, IKG- A/W 2492, 3, Auswanderung, Abfertigung, *Propositions for the Emigration to SanDomingo, March 1940.*

USHMM film # 1264, IKG- A/W 2686, Auswanderung, Abfertigung, *San Domingo "C" (Listen der Transportteilnehmer).*

USHMM film # 1264, IKG- A/W 2954, Auswanderung, Abfertigung, *Emigration nach den USA, Amerkanisches Konsulat Wien 1938-1940.*

USHMM film #U52, IKG- A/W 2591, *Berichte ueber die Organisation und die Taetigkeit der Auswanderungsberatungsstelle.*

USHMM film #UZ/2, IKG-A/W 2623, *A. Schmerler, The action for change of profession of the Emigration Department of the Jewish Headquarters in Vienna and its success during the year 1938*

USHMM: CAHJP, IKG Archiv, Aktenverzeichnis 2.Teil -B: Various:

USHMM Film # 281, IKG- A/W 442. *XIII.Akten und Schriftstuecke, C.Thematisch geordnete Akten und Schriftstuecke, 2. Beschlagnahmen (Schadensmeldung).*

USHMM film # 281, IKG-A/W 442, *Beschlagnahmungen (Schadensmeldungen) 11.1938* Letter from Theodor Rechnitzer to the IKG, 3 December 1938.

USHMM film #288, IKG- A/W 466, 1-2, *Ausgabe von Judenkennzichen. 09.1941-10.1941.*

USHMM film #742, IKG- A/W 300, *Besprechung des Amtsdirektors mit Vereinsvertretern betreffend die Aufloesung bzw. die weiteren Aktivitaeten von Vereinen. 11.05.1938.*

USHMM film # 898, IKG- A/W 431, *Summarischer Bericht ueber die Ausgabe der Kennzeichen fuer Judenwohnungen, 04.1942.*

USHMM film #T1, IKG- A/W2612, XXIV. Aerzteberagtung, *Verpflichtungserklaerungen zugelassener Aerzte, auch Spitalsaerzte.*

USHMM film #T1, IKG-A/W2612, XXIV. Aerzteberagtung, *Verzeichnis der juedischen Krankenbehnadler und Zahnbehandler nach dem Stand vom 08.02.1940, (8.12.41).*

USHMM film # V10, IKG- A/W 2697, 6, *Bemuehungen, die Auswanderung von in Abwanderungstransporte eingeteilten Personen und deren Angehoerigen in die Wege zu leiten, 1. Transport (Opole ue/Pulawy).*

USHMM Film #V10, IKG-A/W 2696, *Deutsche Staatsbuerger: Abgelegte Akte, Enthaftet - Gestorben von A-Z, Josef Pichler.*

USHMM film # VZ48, IKG-A/W 2687, *Report from the Reichsvertretung der Juden in Deutschland to the German Jewish Aid Committee, 29 January 1939.*

USHMM film # VZ48, IKG-A/W 2689, 2, *Ansuchen um Aufnahme in das Transitlager Richborough (Alphabetisch), A-B, 1939: Walter Austerlitz, 29 January 1939.*

USHMM film # VZ48, IKG-A/W 2689, 2, *Ansuchen um Aufnahme in das Transitlager Richborough (Alphabetisch), B, 1939: Paul Berger.*

USHMM film # VZ48, IKG-A/W 2689, 2, *Ansuchen um Aufnahme in das Transitlager Richborough (Alphabetisch), A-B, 1939: Dr. Ernst Adler, 15 May 1939; Edwin Bibring, 17 October 1938.*

Private Interviews/ Family Archives

Alix G. Kowler, letter to the author, August 2003. Tucson, Arizona

Charles Stein, private interview with author, May 2005. Washington, D.C.

Elli Caroll, private interview with author, December 2006. Washington, D.C.

George Czuzcka, private interview with author, May 2007. Washington, D.C.

Gertrude Silberstern, phone interview with author, May 2007. Washington, D.C.

Jacques Hasten, private interview with author, May 2004. Newton, Massachusetts

Lucy Benedikt, private interview with the author, October 2008. Orlando, Florida

Czuzcka Family Archive, Washington, D.C.
(Courtesy of George Czuzcka)
Fritz Czuzcka: Manuscript, BMS GER91(45), Houghton Library, Harvard
University

Gerstenfeld Family Archive, Arlington, Virginia
(This collection was made possible by Ted Shealy, the survivor's grandson)

Gruenberg Family Archive, Weston, Massachusetts
(This collection was made possible by Dr. Lisa Gruenberg, the survivor's daughter)
Gruenberg family letters 1938-1941
Harry Gruenberg's unpublished memoirs
Letters from Simel Blaustein

Lencz Family Archive, Sharon, Massachusetts
(This collection was made possible by Larry Lencz, the survivor's son)

Offenberger Family Archive, Beverly Farms, Massachusetts

Weiss Family Archive, Newton, Massachusetts
(This collection was made possible by Tom Weiss)
Weiss, Thomas Fischer. *I Owe It To* (Newton: unpublished memoirs, 2002).

Survivors of the Shoah Visual History Foundation Archive, (SOSVHF)
(Shoah Foundation Institute, University of Southern California)
Video-recorded Survivor Testimony and Oral Histories (1,457 born in Vienna)

Alix , K., 1997. "Interview by Survivors of the Shoah Visual History Foundation,"
Lenox, MA, USA, October 16. Interview Code 34544, Tapes 1-5.

Alois, G., 1996. "Interview by Survivors of the Shoah Visual History Foundation," Los
Angeles, CA, USA, February 23. Interview Code 12444, Tapes 1-2.

Betty, D., 1995. "Interview by Survivors of the Shoah Visual History Foundation," Del Rey, CA, USA, August 7. Interview Code 05289, Tapes 1-4.

Charles, D., 1997. "Interview by Survivors of the Shoah Visual History Foundation," Hasting-on-Hudson, NY, USA, February 5. Interview Code 25520, Tapes 1-4.

Curt, K.B., 1994. "Interview by Survivors of the Shoah Visual History Foundation," Los Angeles, CA, USA, December 15. Interview Code 00382, Tapes 1-6.

Edith, B., 1997. "Interview by Survivors of the Shoah Visual History Foundation," Vineland, NJ, USA, July 22. Interview Code 43759, Tapes 1-4.

Edward, W., 1996. "Interview by Survivors of the Shoah Visual History Foundation," Chicago, IL, USA, April 21. Interview Code 14235, Tapes 1-3.

Elizabeth, G., 1996. "Interview by Survivors of the Shoah Visual History Foundation," Dobbs Ferry, NY, USA, May 16. Interview Code 15247, Tapes 1-5.

Elliot, W., 1998. "Interview by Survivors of the Shoah Visual History Foundation," New York, NY, USA, March 25. Interview Code 40985, Tapes 1-5.

Erica, B., 1996. "Interview by Survivors of the Shoah Visual History Foundation," Upminster, Essex, UK, October 15. Interview Code 20825, Tapes 1-6.

Erna, G., 1995. "Interview by Survivors of the Shoah Visual History Foundation," Miami Beach, FL, USA, May 16. Interview Code 02588, Tapes 1-4.

Eugenie, C., 1996. "Interview by Survivors of the Shoah Visual History Foundation," Deerfield Beach, FL, USA, October 3. Interview Code 20484, Tapes 1-3.

Fanny H., 1997. "Interview by Survivors of the Shoah Visual History Foundation," New York, NY, USA, March 30. Interview Code 27142, Tapes 1-4.

Frank, B., 1996. "Interview by Survivors of the Shoah Visual History Foundation," Los Angeles, CA, USA, March 14. Interview Code 13282.

Frank, D., 1995. "Interview by Survivors of the Shoah Visual History Foundation," Los Angeles, CA, USA, April 27. Interview Code 02123, Tapes 1-4.

Fred, H., 1995. "Interview by Survivors of the Shoah Visual History Foundation," Bronx, NY, USA, October 26. Interview Code 08022, Tapes 1-4.

Fred, S., 1994. "Interview by Survivors of the Shoah Visual History Foundation," Los Angeles, CA, USA, December 15. Interview Code 00383, Tapes 1-5.

Fritzi, S., 1998. ""Interview by Survivors of the Shoah Visual History Foundation," Lugarno, NSW, AU, December 13. Interview Code 49107, Tapes 1-5.

Gerda K., 1996. "Interview by Survivors of the Shoah Visual History Foundation," Toronto, ON, Canada, May 31. Interview Code 15910, Tapes 1-4.

Gerta J., (date currently unavailable). "Interview by Survivors of the Shoah Visual History Foundation," (location currently unavailable). Interview Code 12715.

Gertrude, S., 1998. "Interview by Survivors of the Shoah Visual History Foundation," Cranbury, NJ, USA, May 28. Interview Code 42400, Tapes 1-7.

Greta, L., 1997. "Interview by Survivors of the Shoah Visual History Foundation," Vienna, AU, March 11. Interview Code 27903, Tapes 1-3.

Greta, S., 1995. "Interview by Survivors of the Shoah Visual History Foundation," New York, NY, USA, May 8. Interview Code 02424, Tapes 1-3.

Hans, B., 1995. "Interview by Survivors of the Shoah Visual History Foundation," Turramurra, NSW, AU, August 9. Interview Code 04421, Tapes 1-5.

Helen, H., 1995. "Interview by Survivors of the Shoah Visual History Foundation," Newbury Park, CA, USA, February 21. Interview Code 00903, Tapes 1-2.

Helga, F.B.,1998. "Interview by Survivors of the Shoah Visual History Foundation," Vienna, AT, December 20. Interview Code 48947, Tapes 1-4.

Herbert K., (date currently unavailable). "Interview by Survivors of the Shoah Visual History Foundation," (location currently unavailable). Interview Code 01867.

Henry, W.,1998. "Interview by Survivors of the Shoah Visual History Foundation," New York, NY, USA, June 17. Interview Code 42662, Tapes 1-6.

Herbert, Z., 1995. "Interview by Survivors of the Shoah Visual History Foundation," Los Angeles, CA, USA. Interview Code 00833, Tapes 1-5.

Irene, G., 1997. "Interview by Survivors of the Shoah Visual History Foundation," London, England, UK, July 10. Interview Code 31296, Tapes 1-5.

Irene, S., 1997. "Interview by Survivors of the Shoah Visual History Foundation," London, England, UK, July10. Interview Code 31296, Tapes 1-4.

Johanna, S., 1996. "Interview by Survivors of the Shoah Visual History Foundation," Miami, FL, USA, February 21. Interview Code 12280, Tapes 1-7.

Joseph, B., 1996. "Interview by Survivors of the Shoah Visual History Foundation," Encinitas, CA, USA, March 15. Interview Code 13315, Tapes 1-4

Karl, G., 1997. "Interview by Survivors of the Shoah Visual History Foundation," New York, NY, USA, March 16. Interview Code 27992, Tapes 1-8.

Lena, G., 1997. "Interview by Survivors of the Shoah Visual History Foundation," Washington, D.C., USA, January 29. Interview Code 25357, Tapes 1-5.

Leo, D., 1997. "Interview by Survivors of the Shoah Visual History Foundation," San Francisco, CA, USA, May 17. Interview Code 29174, Tapes 1-5.

Liz, M., 1996. "Interview by Survivors of the Shoah Visual History Foundation," New York, NY, USA, March 8. Interview Code 12674, Tapes 1-8.

Lisbeth, M., 1995. "Interview by Survivors of the Shoah Visual History Foundation," Tenafly, NJ, USA, December 6. Interview Code 09668, Tapes 1-4.

Maria, A. 1996. "Interview by Survivors of the Shoah Visual History Foundation," Los Angeles, CA, USA, March 31. Interview Code 13821, Tapes 1-3.

Marion, A., (date currently unavailable). "Interview by Survivors of the Shoah Visual History Foundation," (location currently unavailable). Interview Code 42176.

Martha, D., 1997. "Interview by Survivors of the Shoah Visual History Foundation," Hawthorn, VIC, AU. Interview Code 34975, Tapes 1-4.

Maximillian K., (date currently unavailable). "Interview by Survivors of the Shoah Visual History Foundation," (location currently unavailable). Interview Code 07225.

Max, W., 1996. "Interview by Survivors of the Shoah Visual History Foundation," Staten Island, NJ, USA, February 25. Interview Code 12544, Tapes 1-4.

Natalie, P. 1997. "Interview by Survivors of the Shoah Visual History Foundation," Kew, VIC, AU, June 20. Interview Code 32803, Tapes 1-3.

Otto, L., 1997. "Interview by Survivors of the Shoah Visual History Foundation," Valley Stream, NY, USA, February 27. Interview Code 26151,Tapes 1-6 .

Raoul, K., 1996. "Interview by Survivors of the Shoah Visual History Foundation," Great Neck, NY, USA, April 23. Interview Code 14413, Tapes 1-3.

Regine, C., 1995. "Interview by Survivors of the Shoah Visual History Foundation," Los Angeles, CA, USA, January 10. Interview Code 00751, Tapes 1-3.

Regina. R., 1995. "Interview by Survivors of the Shoah Visual History Foundation," Brooklyn, NY, USA, March 7. Interview Code 01279, Tapes 1-4.

Rudolf, T., 1997. "Interview by Survivors of the Shoah Visual History Foundation," Margate, FL, USA, April 9. Interview Code 27990, Tapes 1-3.

Sandor, U., 1997. "Interview by Survivors of the Shoah Visual History Foundation," Bondi, AU, July 20. Interview Code 04144, Tapes 1-4.

Siegfried, B., 1996. "Interview by Survivors of the Shoah Visual History Foundation," Baltimore, MD, USA, October 18. Interview Code 21190, Tapes 1-7.

Stefan, S., 1996. "Interview by Survivors of the Shoah Visual History Foundation," Washington, D.C., USA, September 10. Interview Code 20268, Tapes 1-5.

Trude, A., 1996. "Interview by Survivors of the Shoah Visual History Foundation," West Los Angeles, CA, USA, January 10. Interview Code 10786, Tapes 1-3.

Trude K., 1995."Interview by Survivors of the Shoah Visual History Foundation," Denver, CO, USA. Interview Code 06321, Tape 1.

Valerie, A., 1995. "Interview by Survivors of the Shoah Visual History Foundation," Santa Barbara, CA, USA, November 3. Interview Code 08291, Tapes 1-4.

Walter, A., 1995. "Interview by Survivors of the Shoah Visual History Foundation," Glenview, IL, USA, May 31. Interview Code 02907-0, Tapes 1-6.

Walter, B. F., 1997. "Interview by Survivors of the Shoah Visual History Foundation," Jackson Heights, NY, USA, April 10. Interview Code 27974, Tapes 1-7.

Walter, D., 1995. "Interview by Survivors of the Shoah Visual History Foundation," White Plains, NY, USA, September 15. Interview Code 06673-3, Tapes 1-6.

Walter, H., 1995. "Interview by Survivors of the Shoah Visual History Foundation," Los Angeles, CA, USA, May 23. Interview Code 02787, Tapes 1-4.

Walter, K., 1997. "Interview by Survivors of the Shoah Visual History Foundation," Allentown, PA, USA, November 19. Interview Code 35772, Tapes 1-4.

Wilhelm K , 1996. "Interview by Survivors of the Shoah Visual History Foundation," East St.Kilda, VIC, AU, August 28. Interview Code 19014, Tapes 1-8.

Newspapers
Austrian Newspaper Collections:
Neue Freie Presse (Feb – April 1938)
Zionistische Rundschau (May 1938- November 1938)
Jüdisches Nachtrichtenblatt (1940-1943)

US Newspapers and Journals
New York Times (March 1931- April 1938)
The Nation (1938)
The New Republic (1938)
Boston Herald (2000)

SECONDARY SOURCES

Anderl, Gabriele. *Orte der Täter, Der NS-Terror in den "Arisierten" Wiener Rothschild-Palais* (Wien: Band 15 der Schriftenreihe des Instituts zur Erforschung der Geschichte der Gewerkschaften und Arbeiterkammern, 2005).

Arad, Yitzhak, Israel Gutman, and Abraham Margaliot. *Documents On the Holocaust: Selected Sources On the Destruction of the Jews of Germany and Austria, Poland, and the Soviet Union* (Jerusalem: Ktav Pub. House in association with Yad Vashem [and the] Anti Defamation League, 1981).

Arendt, Hannah. *Eichmann in Jerusalem: A Report on the Banality of Evil* (New York: Penguin Books, 1994).

Bailer-Galanda, B. *Die Entstehung der Rückstellungs- und Entschädigungsgesetzgebung: die Republik Österreich und das in der NS-Zeit entzogene Vermögen* (Wien: Oldenbourg, 2003).

Bajohr, Frank. *Aryanization in Hamburg* (New York: Berghahn Books, 2002).

Bankier, David. *The Germans and the Final Solution: Public Opinion Under Nazism* (Oxford: B. Blackwell, 1992).

Bartov, Omer. *The Eastern Front, 1941-1945: German Troops and the Barbarisation of Warfare* (New York: St. Martin's Press, 1986).

Bauer, Yehuda. *A History of the Holocaust.* Rev. ed. (New York: Franklin Watts, 2001).

———. *Rethinking the Holocaust* (New Haven: Yale University Press, 2001).

———. *Jews for Sale?: Nazi-Jewish Negotiations, 1933-1945* (New Haven: Yale University Press, 1994).

Beller, Steven. *A Concise History of Austria* (Cambridge: Cambridge University Press, 2006).

———. *Vienna and the Jews, 1867-1938: a Cultural History* (Cambridge: Cambridge University Press, 1989).

Bentwich, Norman. "The Destruction of the Jewish Community in Austria1938-1942," in Josef Frankel ed., *The Jews of Austria: Essays on their Life, History and Destruction* (London: Valentine Mitchell, 1967).

———. *They Found Refuge: An account of British Jewry's work for victims of Nazi oppression* (London: Cresset Press, 1956)

Berkley, George E. *Hitler's Gift: The Story of Theresienstadt* (Boston: Branden Books, 1993).

———. *Vienna and Its Jews: The Tragedy of Success: 1880s-1980s* (Cambridge: Abt Books, 1988).

Black, Edwin. *The Transfer Agreement: the Untold Story of the Secret Agreement Between the Third Reich and Jewish Palestine* (New York: Macmillan, 1984).

Botz, Gerhard. *Nationalsozialismus in Wien. Machtübernahme, Herrschaftssicherung, Radikalisierung 1938/39 (Wien: Mandelbaum Verlag, 2008).*

————. *Wohnungspolitik und Judendeportation in Wien 1938 bis 1945 zur Funktion des Antisemitismus als Ersatz nationalsozialistisches Sozialpolitik* (Wien: Geyer Verlag, 1975).

————. *Wien, Vom "anschluss" Zum Krieg: Nationalsozialistische Machtübernahme U. Polit.-soziale Umgestaltung Am Beispiel D. Stadt Wien 1938/39* (Wien: Jugend & Volk, 1978).

Breitman, Richard. *American Refugee Policy and European Jewry 1933-1945* (Indiana, Indiana University Press, 1987).

Bretholz, Leo, and Michael Olesker. *Leap Into Darkness: Seven Years On the Run In Wartime Europe* (Baltimore: Woodholme House Publishers, 1999).

Brezina, Corona. *The Treaty of Versailles, 1919: A Primary Source Examination of the Treaty that Ended World War I* (New York: Rosen Publishing Group, 2006).

Brook-Shepherd, Gordon. *The Anschluss* (Philadelphia; New York: J.P. Lippencott Company, 1963).

Browning, Christopher. *Initiating the Final Solution: The Fateful Months of September-October 1941* (Washington, D.C.: United States Holocaust Memorial Museum, Center for Advanced Holocaust Studies, 2003).

Bukey, Evan. *Hitler's Austria: Popular Sentiment in the Nazi Era 1938-1945* (Chapel Hill: The University of North Carolina Press, 2000).

Cesarani, David. *Becoming Eichmann: Rethinking the Life, Crimes, and Trial of a "Desk Murderer"* (Cambridge: Da Capo Press, 2004).

Clare, George. *Last Waltz in Vienna: The Rise and Destruction of a Family: 1842-1942* (New York: Holt Rinehart and Winston,1982).

Cummins, Paul. *Dachau Song: The Twentieth Century Odyssey of Herbert Zipper* (New York: Peter Lang Publishing, Inc., 1992).

Dawes, Frank Victor. *Not In Front of the Servants: Domestic Service In England 1850-1939* (London:Wayland Publishers, 1973).

Dawidowicz, Lucy. *A Holocaust Reader* (New York: Behrman House, 1976).

——. *The War against the Jews, 1933-1945.* 10th ed. (New York: Bantam Books, 1986).

Dean, Martin. *Robbing the Jews: the Confiscation of Jewish Property In the Holocaust, 1933-1945* (Cambridge: Cambridge University Press, 2008).

——. *Robbery & Restitution: the Conflict Over Jewish Property In Europe* (New York: Berghahn Books, 2007).

——. *Collaboration In the Holocaust: Crimes of the Local Police In Belorussia and Ukraine, 1941-44* (New York: St. Martin's Press, 1999).

Dwork, Debórah. *Children with a Star: Jewish Youth in Nazi Europe* (New Haven: Yale University Press, 1991).

Dwork, Debórah and Robert Jan van Pelt. *Flight from the Reich: Refugee Jews, 1933-1946* (New York: W.W. Norton & Co., 2009).

——. *Holocaust: A History* (New York: WW Norton and Company, 2002).

Edmondson, E. C. *The Heimwehr and Austrian Politics: 1918-1936* (Athens: University of Georgia Press, 1978).

Feikes, Renate. *"emigration Wiener Jüdischer Ärzte Ab 1938 In Die Usa, Speziell Nach New York"* (Wien: Universität Wien, 1999).

Feingold, Henry L. *Bearing Witness: How America and Its Jews Responded to the Holocaust* (New York: Syracuse University Press, 1995).

Ferris, Paul. *Dr. Freud: a Life* (London: Sinclair-Stevenson, 1997).

Frankel, Josef, Ed. *The Jews of Austria: Essays on their Life, History and Destruction* (London: Valentine Mitchell, 1967).

Friedenreich, Harriet. *Jewish Politics in Vienna, 1918-1938* (Bloomington, Indiana University Press, 1991).

Friedlander, Saul. *Nazi Germany and the Jews: Volume 1: The Years of Persecution 1933-1939.* (New York: Harper Collins, 1997).

Frier, Recha. *Let the Children Come: The Early Story of Youth Aliyah* (London: Weidenfeld and Nicolson, 1961).

Fuchs, Gertrude. *Die Vermoegensverkehrstelle als Arisierungsbehoerde juedischer Betriebe* (Vienna: Master's Thesis- University of Vienna, 1990).

Gedye, G.E.R. *Fallen Bastions: The Central European Tragedy* (London: Victor Gollancz Ltd, 1939).

Gilbert, Martin. *Atlas of the Holocaust* (London: Orion Publishing Group, 2006).

Golabek, Mona. *The Children of Willesden Lane: Beyond the Kindertransport: a Memoir of Music, Love, and Survival* (New York, N.Y.: Warner Books, 2002).

Gottlieb, Amy Zahl. *Men of Vision: Anglo-Jewry's Aid to Victims of the Nazi Regime, 1933-1945.* (London: Weidenfeld & Nicolson, 1998).

Greenberg, Marian G. *There is Hope for Your Children: Youth Aliyah, Henrietta Szold and Hadassah* (N.p.: Haddassah, the Women's Zionist Organization of America, 1986).

Gruner, Wolf. *Jewish Forced Labor Under the Nazis, Economic Needs and Racial Aims 1938-1944* (Cambridge: Cambridge University Press, 2006).

Hackett, David A. *The Buchenwald Report* (Boulder: Westview Press, 1995).

Hamann, Brigitte. *Hitler's Vienna: A Dictator's Apprenticeship* (New York: Oxford University Press, 1999).

Heppner, Ernest G. *Shanghai Refuge: a Memoir of the World War II Jewish Ghetto* (Lincoln: University of Nebraska Press, 1993).

Herbert, Ulrich, Ed. *National Socialist Extermination Policies: Contemporary German Perspectives and Controversies* (Oxford: Berghahn Books, 2000).

Hilberg, Raul. *The Destruction of the European Jews: Revised and Definitive Edition, Volume 2.* (New York, Holmes and Meier,1985).

Hochstadt, Steve, and Gerda Neu-Sokol. *Shanghai Geschichten: Die Jüdische Flucht Nach China* 1. Aufl. (Teetz: Hentrich & Hentrich, 2007).

Hofmann, Paul. *The Viennese : Splendor, Twilight, and Exile.* (New York: Anchor Press, 1988).

Horn, Pamela. *The Rise and Fall of the Victorian Servant* (New York: St. Martin's Press, 1975).

Jászi, O.*The Dissolution of the Habsburg Monarchy* (Chicago: University of Chicago Press, 1961).

Jenks, Jeremiah Whipple, W. Jett Lauck, and Rufus Daniel Smith. *The Immigration Problem: a Study of American Immigration Conditions and Needs* 5th ed., rev. and enl. (New York: Funk & Wagnalls Co., 1922).

Johnston, William M. *Vienna, Vienna: The Golden Age 1815-1914* (Milan, Italy: Arnoldo Mondadori Editore, 1981).

Kaplan, Marion. *Between Dignity and Despair: Jewish Life in Nazi Germany* (New York: Oxford University Press, 1998).

Kapp, Yvonne, and Margaret Mynatt. *British Policy and the Refugees, 1933-1941* (London: Frank Cass, 1997).

Keyserlingk, Robert H. *Austria in World War II: An Anglo-American Dilemma* (Kingston; Montreal: McGill-Queen's University Press, 1988).

Kluger, Ruth. *Still Alive, A Holocaust Girlhood Remembered* (New York: The Feminist Press at the City University of New York, 2001).

Kurzweil, Edith. *Nazi Laws and Jewish Lives: Letters from Vienna* (Edison: Transaction Publishers, 2004).

Langer, Lawrence L. *Art from the Ashes: A Holocaust Anthology* (New York: Oxford University Press, 1995).

Levi, Primo. *The Drowned and the Saved* (New York: Summit Books, 1988).

Levin, Alexandra, Ed. *Henrietta Szold and Youth Aliyah: Family Letters, 1934-1944* (New York: Herzl Press, 1986).

Lockhart, R.H. Bruce. *Guns or Butter. War Countries and Peace Countries of Europe Revisited* (London: Putnam, 1938).

London, Louise. *Whitehall and the Jews, 1933-1948: British Immigration Policy, Jewish Refugees, and the Holocaust* (New York: Cambridge University Press, 2000).

Lowenthal, Marvin. *Henrietta Szold: Life and Letters* (New York: Viking, 1942).

Maas, Walter. *Country Without a Name: Austria Under Nazi Rule, 1938-1945* (New York, F. Ungar Publishing, 1979).

Macmillan, Margaret. *Paris 1919: Six Months That Changed The World* (New York: Random House, 2003).

Malkin, Peter and Harry Stein. *Eichmann in My Hands* (New York: Warner Books, 1990).

Mayer, Emil and Emil Rosser. *Viennese Types [Wiener Typen]: Photographs c.1910 by Dr. Emil Mayer* (Blind River Editions, 1st Edition, 2000).

Mendes-Flohr, P. R. *German Jews: A Dual Identity* (New Haven: Yale University Press, 1999).

Meyer, Beate. "The Restructuring of a Jewish Gemeinde into the 'Prototype' of the Judenrat" in *Yad Vashem Studies, XXX* (Jerusalem: 2002).

Michman, Dan. *Holocaust Historiography: A Jewish Perspective, Conceptualizations, Terminology, Approaches and Fundamental Issues* (London, Vallentine Mitchell: 2003).

Mikolas Teich and Roy Porter, eds. *The National Question in Europe in Historical Context* (Cambridge: Cambridge University Press, 1993).

Moser, Gwyn C. "Jewish U-Boote in Austria, 1938-1945" in *Simon Wiesenthal Center Annual, Volume 2.* (New York, Kraus International Publications: 1985).

Moser, Jonny. *Demographie der jüdischen Bevölkerung Österreichs 1938-1945* (Vienna: DÖW, 1999).

——. "Die Anhalte- und Sammellager fur österreichischen Juden" in *Dokumentationsarchivs des österreichischen Widerstandes (ed.), Jahrbuch 1992* (Wien, DÖW- Bibliothek, 1992).

——. "Österreich," in Wolfgang Benz, ed., *Dimension des Völkermords, Die Zahl der jüdischen Opfer des Nationalsozialismus* (München: Oldenbourg Verlag, 1991).

——."Die Verfolgung der Juden," in Wolfgang Neugebauer, ed., *Widerstand und Verfolgung in Wien 1934-1945, Eine Dokumentation,1938-1945, Band 3* (Vienna: Oesterreichischer Bundesverlag fuer Unterricht, Wissenschaft, und Kunst, 1975).

Mosse,Werner Eugen, and Julius Carlebach. *Second Chance: Two Centuries of German-speaking Jews In the United Kingdom* (Tübingen: J.C.B. Mohr [Paul Siebeck], 1991).

Neugebauer, Wolfgang. *Rede (geschichtlicher Ruckblick) anlässlich der Enthüllung einer Gedenktafel am Hause 1020, Leopoldsgasse 13/Malzgasse 7 (Sammellager während der NS-Zeit). Beigebunden: Gesammelte Unterlagen für diese Rede)* (Wien, DÖW- Bibliothek, 2000).

Ofer, Dalia and Hannah Weiner. *Dead-End Journey: The Tragic Story of the Kladovo-Sabac Group* (New York and London: University Press of America, Inc., 1996).

Ofer, Dalia. *Escaping the Holocaust, Illegal Immigration to the Land of Israel 1939-1944* (New York: Oxford University Press, 1990).

Palmer, A. W. *Twilight of the Habsburgs: The Life and Times of Emperor Francis Joseph* (New York: Grove Press, 1995).

Pauley, Bruce. *From Prejudice to Persecution: A History of Austrian Anti-Semitism* (Chapel Hill & London: The University of North Carolina Press, 1992).

Perloff, Marjorie. *The Vienna Paradox: a Memoir* (New York: New Directions Books, 2004).

Pick, Hella. *Guilty Victim: Austria from the Holocaust to Haider* (London: I.B. Tauris, 2000).

——. *Simon Wiesenthal: a Life In Search of Justice* (Boston: Northeastern University Press, 1996).

Pollack, Sir Frederick. *The League of Nations* (London: The Lawbook Exchange, Ltd., 2003).

Rabinovici, Doron. *Instanzen der Ohnmacht: Wien 1938-1945: der Weg zum Judenrat* (Frankfurt am Main, Juedischer Verlag, 2000).

——. "Die Wiener Judenraete unter der NS-Herrschaft," Vortrag am 14. Februar 2002 in Ebensee, in *Eine Zeitschrift des Zeitgeschichte Museums under der KZ-Gedenkstaette Ebensee* (Ebensee, Austria) 2002:20.

Luža, Radomír. *Österreich Und Die Grossdeutsche Idee In Der Ns-zeit* (Wien: H. Böhlaus Nachf., 1977).

——. *Austro-German Relations in the Anschluss Era* (Princeton: Princeton University Press, 1975).

Rathkolb, Oliver. *Die Paradoxe Republik : Österreich 1945 Bis 2005* (Wien: Zsolnay, 2005).

Rechter, David. *The Jews of Vienna and the First World* (London: Littman Library of Jewish Civilization, 2001).

Rosenkranz, Herbert. *Verfolgung und Selbstbehauptung. Die Juden in Österreich 1938-1945* (Wien, Munich: Herold: 1978).

Ross, James R. *Escape to Shanghai: a Jewish Community In China* (New York: Free Press, 1994).

Rosseau, Jean-Jacques. *The Social Contract* (England: Penguin Books, 1968).

Rozenblit, Marsha. *Reconstructing a National Identity: The Jews of Habsburg Austria during World War I* (Oxford: Oxford University Press, 2001).

——. *The Jews of Vienna: Assimilation and Identity.1867-1938* (Albany: State University of New York Press, 1983).

Rozenkranz, Herbert. "The Anschluss and the Tragedy of Austrian Jewry 1938-1945," in Josef Frankel ed., *The Jews of Austria: Essays on their Life, History and Destruction* (London: Valentine Mitchell,1967).

Rubin, Evelyn Pike. *Ghetto Shanghai* (New York: Shengold, 1993).

Safrian, Hans. *Eichmann's Men* (Cambridge: Cambridge University Press, 2010).

Schatzberg, Paul. *Plunder in 1938: Aryanization of Jewish Assets in Vienna, Austria and Causal Connections* (Philadelphia, St. Joseph's University: The 33rd Annual Scholars' Conference on the Holocaust and the Churches, 2003).

Scheffler, Wolfgang and Diana Schulle. *Book of Remembrance; the German, Austrian and Czechoslovakian Jews deported to the Baltic States* (Munich: Saur, 2003).

Schneider, Gertrude. *Exile and Destruction: The Fate of the Austrian Jews, 1938-1945* (Westport: Praeger, 1995).

Scholem, Gershon. *Major Trends in Jewish Mysticism* (Jerusalem: Schoken Publishing House, Ltd., 1941).

Schorske, Carl. *Fin-de-siècle Vienna: Politics and Culture* (New York: Vintage Books, 1981).

Schuschnigg, Kurt. *Austrian Requiem: Chancellor of Austria and Prisoner of Hitler* (New York: G.P. Putnam's Sons, 1946).

Secher, Pierre H. *Left Behind in Nazi Vienna: Letters of a Jewish family caught in the Holocaust, 1939-1941* (Jefferson: McFarland & Co, 2004).

Simmons, Erica. *Haddassah and the Zionist Project* (Lanham: Rowman and Littlefield, 2006).

Spiel, Hilda. *Vienna's Golden Autumn, 1866-1938* (New York: Weidenfeld & Nicolson, 1987).

Spitzer, Leo. *Hotel Bolivia: The Culture of Memory in a Refuge from Nazism* (New York: Hill and Wang,1998).

Steinberg, J. and P. Sichrovsky. *Born Guilty:Children of Nazi Families* (New York: Basic Books, 1988).

Tausig, Franziska. *Shanghai Passage: Emigration ins Ghetto*. 2. Aufl. (Wien: Milena, 2007).

Taylor, A. J. P. *The Habsburg Monarchy, 1809-1918; A History of the Austrian Empire and Austria-Hungary* (London: H. Hamilton, 1948).

Tec, Nechama. *Resilience and Courage: Women, and Men, and the Holocaust* (New Haven: Yale University Press, 2003).

Tyner, James A. *War, Violence, and Population; Making the Body Count* (New York, Guilford Press: 2009).

Vansant, J. *Reclaiming Heimat: Trauma and Mourning in Memoirs by Jewish Austrian Reémigrés* (Detroit: Wayne State University Press, 2001).

Von Frentz, Christian R. *A Lesson Forgotten: Minority Protection under the League of Nations The Case of the German Minority in Poland, 1920-1934* (Hamburg: Arbeiten zur Geschichte Osteuropas, 1999).

Waller, James. *Becoming Evil: How Ordinary People Commit Genocide and Mass Killing* (Oxford: Oxford University Press, 2002).

Walzer, Tina and Stephan Templ. *Unser Wien--Arisierung auf österreichisch* (Berlin: Aufbau Verlag, 2001).

Weinzierl, Erika. *Zu wenig Gerecht: Österreicher und Judenverfolgung, 1938-1945,* 3rd ed. (Graz: Verlag Styria, 1986).

Wellwarth, George E. *Leben mit österreichischer Literatur: Begegnung mit aus Österreich stammenden amerikanishen Germanisten 1938/1988: Elf Erinnerungen* (Wien: Dokumentationsstelle fuer neue österreichische Literatur, 1990).

Wistrich, Robert. *The Jews of Vienna in the age of Franz Joseph* (Oxford: Oxford University Press, 1989).

Witek, H. and Hans Safrian. *Und Keiner War Dabei: Dokumente des alltaeglichen Antisemitismus in Wien 1938* (Wien: Picus, 1988).

Wyman, David. *The Abandonment of the Jews: America and the Holocaust, 1941-1945* (New York: New Press,1998).

Young, James E. *The Texture of Memory: Holocaust Memorials and Meaning* (New Haven: Yale University Press, 1993).

Zucker, Bat-Ami. *In Search of Refuge: Jews and US Consuls In Nazi Germany, 1933-1941* (Portland: Vallentine Mitchell, 2001).